THIS BUSINESS OF RADIO PROGRAMMING

CLAUDE AND BARBARA HALL

A COMPREHENSIVE LOOK AT MODERN PROGRAMMING TECHNIQUES USED THROUGHOUT THE RADIO WORLD.

THIS BUSINESS OF RADIO PROGRAMMING

INTRODUCTION BY JACK G. THAYER, PRESIDENT, NBC RADIO

A BILLBOARD BOOK

Copyright © 1977 by Billboard Publications, Inc.

First published 1977 in New York by Billboard Publications, Inc.,
1515 Broadway, New York, N.Y. 10036

Manufactured in U.S.A.

Library of Congress Cataloging in Publication Data
Hall, Claude.
    This business of radio programming.
    Includes index.
    1. Radio programs. 2. Radio broadcasting—United
States. I. Hall, Barbara, 1937-joint author.
II. Title.
PN1991.75.H3   791.44'3   77-1994
ISBN 0-8230-7760-8

First Printing, 1977

To Jeff and Evalee Hall on behalf of their son.

To the late Francis Schwartz on behalf of her daughter, Barbara L. Hall.

Acknowledgments

There is no way in the world I could thank the 35,437 disk jockeys, the 4,728 program directors, and the 5,321 general managers who made valuable contributions to this book. It was from them that I learned radio programming, as well as from hundreds of other people in the record business and allied industries.

Special thanks goes to Eileen Herskovitz, a radio wife of expert knowledge, who helped type many of the interviews presented here.

Claude Hall
Radio-TV Editor;
Member, Executive Editorial Board,
Billboard Magazine
Director, International Radio
Programming Forum

Contents

Introduction

Welcome to the Land of the Giants!

Gathered here in one place, you'll meet face-to-face the innovators of today's radio, the programming Giants of the AM and FM bands. Claude Hall, the radio-TV editor of *Billboard* is your guide and his knowledge, experience, and ear for quality assures you a fascinating series of visits with the superstars of sound.

As Babe Ruth is to baseball, as Ben Hogan is to golf, as Vince Lombardi is to football, as Muhammad Ali is to boxing—these men of radio combine the qualities of imagination, persistence, dedication, aspiration, perspiration, and motivation to add color and excitement for an unseen audience reflected only in a rating book.

And it all began a short few years ago, in the 1950s, with men like Todd Storz, Gordon McLendon, and the Bartells. And from the Top 40 lists came the ideas supplied by the Bill Stewarts, the Bill Drakes, the Ron Jacobs, the George Wilsons. There were dreamers who added service to sound—Elmo Ellis, Rick Sklar, Val Linder, and Bob Hyland. There were those who added sparkle to the great communicator—Paul Drew, George Burns, Dick Drury, Kent Burkhart, Scott Burton, Bob Pittman, John Rook, Mike Joseph, Chuck Blore, and the list goes on and on. Each of these giants knew the odds, but accepted the challenge. They knew that the bio-computer between their ears could receive two million impressions a second, and that each year was divided into 31,536,000 seconds—31 million opportunities to try something new, without any guaranteed result—because in radio your EFFORT is its own reward.

These are the men who put the *PRO* in promotion. And in these interviews Claude Hall shows the growth and the nuances of modern techniques that increase the quarterhour maintenance or put impact on the cume. He shows the quantum leap from the early "write-in-and-win" or "luck house number" contest to the Million Dollar Giveaway/78 Cars In 78 Hours/A Trip Around The World/The American Revolution Bicentennial—and the thousand and one new promotions that are counter-programmed by stations in every city coast to coast.

These are the men who ponder over lists—local and national. They call the stores, the one-stops, the jukebox distributors. They listen to the promo-men with stories of "breaking in Pittsburgh" or "it's 98 in *Billboard* with a bullet!" They listen constantly—to their own station, to the competition, to airchecks, to auditions—always with an ear for the next big hit or for the deejay sound that may be the next Don Imus or Robert W. Morgan. These are the men who give support to a talent when he's down or bring him down when he's too high. They are counsellor, friend, critic, boss. They share the good news and take the blame for the bad. They are there when you need them with a "hit" in their hand—the newest discovery from an LP released in '73. They work around the clock for the honor of saying, "We're Number One!!"

I know these giants are something special. I've worked with them, for them, against them. I admired them, envied them, despised them. They've made me happy, proud, angry, ashamed. They play to win, today, tomorrow, and forever!

The fun is about to start. Prepare yourself for a journey in excitement. Your guide, Claude Hall, beckons you to *experience* the magic of the radio GIANTS.

On Your Side,
Jack G. Thayer

PART I
PROGRAMMING

1 This business of programming

Radio programming was once considered somewhat of a thankless task at a radio station (usually dumped on the disk jockey with the most years, or months, at the station), but is now becoming increasingly accepted as a science in addition to being a highly professionalized craft.

Without question, the goal of any commercial radio station should be to make a profit. The station must also operate on behalf of the public and radio stations are only granted the temporary "privilege" of using a frequency by the Federal Communications Commission. However, unless a radio station meets its bottom line it cannot be of benefit to anyone, because the bottom line shows whether or not a radio station is profitable. In fulfilling their bottom line goal, radio station owners and managers have been discovering that the insight and ability of the program director is equal to, if not more important than the skill of the general sales manager. There is no doubt that without an audience—which good programming creates—there can be no bottom line.

Thus, at many radio stations today the program director may not command a salary comparable to a general sales manager, but he certainly occupies an equal position of importance, and his salary level is constantly increasing. In some stations, the position of the program director is above that of the general sales manager and rightly so. Unless the program director does his job well, there will be nothing for the general sales manager and his account executives to sell. When it comes to skills—later we'll discuss skills and qualifications of everyone on a radio station staff—the program director is the most important man at the station. And he must know everything that a disk jockey knows and have at least half (if not more than) the knowledge of the general manager. In addition, he must be a mixture of engineer, news director, music director, research specialist, psychologist, production specialist, educator, politician, public benefactor, promotion and public relations expert, lawyer, musician (in order to help produce the jingles for his station as well as make the final decision on what records to play on the air), mathematician, and sometimes a salesman as well.

And it also helps if a program director has nerves of steel, guts wired to exist on black coffee and french fries for days on end, plus a wife who likes to spend her evenings alone (and this type of woman is hard to find, reinforced by the fact that the divorce rate among radio people is extremely higher than the general population). The program director should also have 15 years of experience in radio, be only 25 years old, have a liberal arts degree from college, and also know business and finance. The program director literally has to be a superman.

The program director shoulders vast responsibilities in a radio station today—in many ways more than the general manager himself, except that the general manager must be responsible for the program director. One of the major responsibilities of the program director is to coordinate everything that is broadcast over the air. He may also create the concept that emerges as the station's format, or he could use someone else's concept. But it is the program director's job to execute that concept, regardless of who devised it. This means that the program director is not only responsible for the music that is played over the station, but is also accountable for jingle identification package, PSAs (public service announcements), news, and promotions. In addition he is the administrator of all personnel that contribute anything to that air sound, including the selection and control of air personalities.

Another duty of the program director is the approval of all commercials, including those not created by the station—to rearrange their broadcast order, if necessary, to achieve less of a tuneout factor. A tuneout factor is an element that causes a listener to stop listening. Finally, the program director must fulfill all government regulations pertaining to radio today. This is one aspect of radio that deserves a book unto itself, but governmental edicts and observations are pouring out so fast from the Federal Communications Commission that even the working program director cannot keep up with them. In fact, most major radio operations have either a staff attorney or a legal representative in Washington (at no small cost) to keep them apprised of new and proposed regulations. The key criterion that allows a program director to succeed, if he has the talent, the knowledge, and the experience, is the autonomy needed to do his job. More radio stations than the world has known have been ruined because of interference in programming by either a manager who just doesn't "like that record" or a sales manager who insists on adding "one more commercial" per hour.

The Death of Radio

The evolution of the job of radio program director coincides—though it took several years to really mature—fairly close to the history of modern radio.

In the early 1950s, everyone knew that radio was a dying medium. Nearly anyone who had a smattering of talent deserted radio for the new medium of television. Many people who owned radio stations quickly sold them and got into television, because everyone thought that no one would listen to Fibber McGee and Molly on radio when they could see them on television. Who wanted to listen to Red Skelton when they could actually see him playing the Mean Little Kid? Perhaps one of the major problems of television today is that it took radio's has-beens and kept them without generating much fresh blood. On the other hand, radio from the middle 50s to the present, was made up of devotees who lived, ate, breathed, and slept radio. Aside from radio, they didn't like much, unless you include women and drinking. A perfect case in point is that of Jack McCoy who when taking over as program director of KCBQ in San Diego a few years ago, moved a cot into his office in order to save time commuting until the station's programming reached his standards.

Of course, the disk jockeys of those early days grew into legends, constantly adding to their own myths with zany promotions on and off the air. But what regenerated radio day by day was a myriad of young kids who listened to these legends—Alan Freed, Bill Randle, Dick Biondi, Howard Miller, Tom Clay, Frank Ward, Arnie Ginsberg, Hy Lit, Joe Niagara, Peter Potter, Al Jarvis, William B. Williams—and had dreams of becoming a disk jockey and then one day fulfilled their dreams.

For quite a few years, you could buy almost any radio station in the United States at bottom dollar. However, the death of radio was somewhat exaggerated in the early 50s primarily because a few good radio men refused to roll over and play dead. People such as Todd Storz and Gordon McLendon are today considered the fathers of Top 40 radio and therefore the fathers of modern programming concepts. Speaking before the Chicago Federated Advertising Club, in March 1966, Gordon McLendon said: "To many, the end of radio seemed near that summer of 1954. Throughout the nation radio lay apparently dying in the wake of television's first apparently irresistible onslaught.

"I have often been reminded of the almost perfect parallel in the war— the Russian winter of 1942. Crack Nazi panzer divisions had pushed to the endless marshes only 50 miles away from Moscow itself and there at Smolensk, military experts gave the Russians two days to live. But then in the blinding snow and the high winds over the marshes, the German attack inexplicably stalled. After six months, even Nazi Field Marshall Wilhelm Keitel confessed himself baffled at the lack of success of the German progress. After six months Russia still lived and so analogous has been the situation of radio, which stubbornly refused to die.

"Finally, it rose to become the healthiest corpse in history.

"Well, the old world has turned over many times.

"But I remember that summer of 1954 when I whiled away a soft summer afternoon with an old friend named Todd Storz. It was June in Kansas City and we were young. The afternoon was one of brilliant sunshine and for both Todd and I it seemed impossible on that faraway summer afternoon that the future could offer anything other than bright and unlimited promise.

"Todd and I always had fun together because we were both desperately in love with radio. Both of us were wildly imaginative, terribly young, terribly certain of everything. We sat down together on the wooden steps that warm summer afternoon—in shirt sleeves and with the wooden steps baking underneath us—and talked about the common love affair we shared with radio.

"Because many summers have come and gone since then, much of what the two young boys discussed has slipped away, but I can still recall Todd's face as he mopped his brow on his sleeve and said: 'You know, Gordon, I have the feeling that there are literally scores of radio formats still waiting to be found.' "

In that same speech McLendon said: "There is really no end to the new formats that are possible for radio because by the time all of the new ones have been tried, all of the old ones will be new again. Radio, as a medium, seems to be totally self-regenerating."

Gordon McLendon is not only one of the fathers of Top 40, but he also gave birth to the beautiful music format at KABL in San Francisco and experimented with an all-classified advertising format in Los Angeles, in addition to the world's first all-news format in Los Angeles with XETRA beaming from Mexico. He also put one of the major pirate radio ships on the air in Europe—thus affecting radio programming throughout the United Kingdom. McLendon always considered radio the eighth "and perhaps the greatest" wonder of the world and the "most enveloping means of communication in the universe."

There were other people who played significant roles in bringing about modern radio, specifically two men, Bill Stewart and Chuck Blore. Stewart worked at different times for both Todd Storz and Gordon McLendon and, was with Storz in an Omaha bar when one of them, or both, conceived what is today known as Top 40.

The Birth of Format Radio

In reality, there were radio stations prior to the Omaha bar incident that were playing

40 or 50 records over and over, rotating them consecutively. Moreover, during the 1950s more than one radio station was hooked up to a jukebox device for the records—the disk jockey's talking time was limited from the second the needle lifted on one record until it plunked down on another. What Storz and Stewart came up with, because of those few hours in a bar, was a rotation pattern for records. This concept was based on the fact that people wanted to hear some songs, even among the so-called best sellers, more than others. Today, the science of programming has progressed far beyond its past, and we'll discuss that later.

Stewart was the first program director to install a known rotation pattern, as well as a closed music list (prior to his closed music list, air personalities played whatever version of a song that appealed to them and there were literally half a dozen versions of any great song). Today, as few as 4 and as many as 12 to 17 records are kept in high rotation, depending on the radio station. And, this high rotation concept is the foundation of all viable formats, including the more successful (at least in audience ratings) progressive rock stations. Even Gordon McLendon paid tribute to Bill Stewart for putting polish on the programming of KLIF in Dallas, which became one of the most historic Top 40 stations in the world.

McLendon, fondly remembered as the Old Scotchman in his on-the-air recreations of baseball games (for years, people thought he was broadcasting the games live, and even after they discovered he wasn't they preferred his version to the live baseball broadcasts that sprang up in competition; McLendon's recreations were carried on radio stations coast to coast), was a pioneer of Top 40 more than just in the format itself. He was a master craftsman of promotion, but his major contribution to Top 40 and radio in general was in news programming. He realized early that radio could capture an immediacy in news that television, at that time, could not compete with. He also realized the power of radio in covering local news. Speaking before the Georgia Association of Broadcasters, In August 1957, McLendon stated: "We localize a great many of our news stories. We have a list of 250 top citizens in each of our cities and we're expanding this list all the time. We subdivide the list into the top leaders in oil, banking, industry, society, business, education, etc. We use this list to get their names and voices on the air just as often as possible. For instance, when a story arrives concerning a development on the cotton market, we'll immediately call a top local cotton leader, record his comments, and localize the story around him."

McLendon felt that even the smallest radio station could do the same type of news coverage. In those days, television was virtually locked into a studio, but McLendon's news cars flooded Dallas. If you wanted to find out what was happening before tomorrow, you had to listen to McLendon's KLIF.

McLendon also made other contributions to radio. His disciples—the people who worked for him at one time or another and carried forth Top 40 concepts throughout the United States and the world—include some of the best men in radio: Chuck Blore, Kent Burkhart, Don Keyes, Art Holt. Not even Todd Storz contributed so much to the careers of so many people in the radio industry as far as owners, managers, programmers, and air personalities. At the Todd Storz Disk Jockey Convention in Miami in 1959, keynote speaker Gordon McLendon addressed the crowd with: "Hello, ex-employees."

One of the men who made a very unique contribution to early Top 40 and has ever since sparked the imaginations of others is Chuck Blore. Blore, president of Chuck Blore/Don Richman, Los Angeles, runs a radio-TV production firm that deals in commercials from mini-dramas to intro records. For instance, it was Chuck Blore who did the hamburger commercial with Little Rodney Allen Rippy that not only sold a

few more hamburgers but launched the kid to national fame. Considered a genius by
his peers and probably the most imitated man in the world, Blore worked for a time at
KELP in El Paso, Texas, when it was owned by Gordon McLendon. Perhaps it was at
this time that Blore learned many of his basic Top 40 techniques from the Old Scotchman. But later he added an equally important contribution of his own to radio—showmanship. Blore, with a magic touch, promoted his radio stations like P.T. Barnum had
promoted the Greatest Show on Earth. In fact, his promotions were so effective that
he caused FCC rulings against them or, at least they were a principle factor in the
rulings.

Blore, of course, did more; he believed that radio should be exciting, dramatic,
and entertaining. He coached his disk jockeys, and he inspired them.

The Drake Format

Overall there weren't many other inroads made in programming, especially in Top 40,
until the advent of Bill Drake, a Georgia boy whose real name was Phil Yarbough.
Although several of the people who worked for Drake had very high IQ's (such as Ron
Jacobs), Drake was and still is a great thinker; he has the unique ability to figure things
out. Positive proof that IQ, which is mostly an educative factor, isn't all it's cracked up
to be when it comes to radio. Maybe radio is something that can't be taught as much as
learned—meaning that it must be emotionally absorbed by listeners who, in turn, use
that emotion as a creative base which can lead to programming applications. Constantly, program directors speak of a gut feeling about a particular aspect of radio programming. They can't say it any other way, because they're reacting instinctively to something that is a combination of reason and emotion.

Even today, Bill Drake enjoys puzzling over a particular aspect of programming.
As in the cases of many dedicated radio men, Drake's personal life has suffered somewhat, to which his ex-wives can testify. Once, when asked what hobbies he had, Drake
couldn't think of any, he simply lives radio. In his days as programming consultant for
RKO General (now known as RKO Radio), he could cause a program director to
quiver in fearful anticipation that he might or might not like a particular thing on the
radio station that day. One program director commented, after being in his presence,
"When he asks what happened that day, you don't ever say: 'Nothing.' "

Bill Drake has probably been radio's greatest scientist and is also the creative
father of countless topnotch program directors of today, several of whom are considered to be geniuses in programming su h as Ron Jacobs. Among the people who've
worked under Drake are Paul Drew Ron   obs, Tom Rounds, Robert W. Morgan,
Don Steele, Bill Wade Ted Atkins, Sebastian Stone, Bill Watson, Bernie Torres, and
Gary McDowell.

Bill Drake was primarily responsible for eliminating the clutter in Top 40 radio.
Later these concepts spread to other formats such as soul radio, country music radio,
middle-of-the-road (MOR) radio, and progressive rock (which took that theory one
step further with album-oriented rock format, AOR). Though Drake did not conceive
the so-called Q-format, without his earlier concepts, the Q-format would probably
have never developed. Drake never liked the pure progressive format and so he changed
WOR-FM (now WXLO) in New York—the birth station of the format—to an oldies/rock
station. But his concepts weaved their way into almost every other existent format. In
fact, the term "Drake Syndrome" became a popular term in regard to disk jockeys
who said little on the air except the time, the temperature, and the title of the next

record. They didn't even say their own name too often, at least not on the stations he consulted, because Drake recorded the promos for their shows himself. Promos are promotions for the station, disk jockey or station event.

The clutter that Bill Drake helped to banish almost totally from the air included disk jockey verbosity, redundant ID (identification) jingles, dead air (silence on the air), and overcommercialization. Drake was also extremely careful in his selection of new records; he considered them potential tuneout factors and would only introduce a new record between two that were familiar. He called this introduction technique "sandwiching."

Drake also refined a lot of other concepts such as finishing the news (he considered the news a potential, if not outright, tuneout factor, as well as most commercials) as fast as possible with a tune—usually one that everyone knew such as "Up, Up and Away" by the Fifth Dimension. He often refused to play a record, even though it might be a big hit, because he felt that the radio listening audience he wanted to reach wasn't the people who were buying that particular record. He also put the damper on many bubblegum records, including some by the Monkees. By doing so, he was really one of the first programmers to actually use music, i.e. a specific record, as a tool for appealing to a target demographic audience. Needless to say, Bill Drake's theories proved highly successful at KHJ in Los Angeles, which he consulted, and where Ron Jacobs programmed during its Boss Radio days. Together, they took a dog of a radio station in the market and worried it into the No. 1 position in audience and radio history. Drake eventually took over the programming on a consultant basis, covering most of the RKO Radio stations coast to coast before he parted with the chain.

Of course, there are a few other program directors and programming consultants who have contributed to the state of the art. Mike Joseph, the first full-time programming consultant (for years unemployed program directors would call themselves programming consultants and this practice still goes on somewhat), may have been the first to play oldies as a programming tool. Joseph was probably the first to do in-depth studies on a given market. His forte was finding out what people were listening to radio at a particular time period and then catering to each audience with the programming.

For years, Joseph was also thought to be the first programmer to use a tight playlist (records played), but that was dispelled recently by Gordon McLendon who confessed that when he first changed KLIF in Dallas to a Top 40 format, his playlist was only 25 singles. Earlier, Bill Stewart had decreased a playlist used at a New Orleans Top 40 station to 12 records, but that was only a promotional stunt to gain attention. However, Stewart soon returned to a much higher list (in those days, the usual playlist of a Top 40 station ran as high as 55 records, the term Top 40 referred to the number of records that could ordinarily be played in a deejay's show).

Though Mike Joseph may have done many original things in radio, oddly enough his influence on other program directors has only been slight, perhaps because he was never eager to talk about his philosophies. Thus, there is very little connection between the research techniques of Mike Joseph and the methodologies that sprang up with a newer generation of programmers including Buzz Bennett, Mark Driscoll, Jack McCoy, Todd Wallace, Al Casey, Gerry Peterson, John Gehron, and others. True, many of these younger program directors and other people such as Lee Abrams and Charlie Van Dyke worked or studied with some of the leading program directors of the day. However, much of their programming philosophies and research theories were their own ideas. What the younger program directors have accomplished is an ultra-refinement of all aspects of radio programming. Sebastian Stone, when he programmed WOR-FM (now WXLO) in New York, would set his alarm for a strange hour of the night in order to wake up and listen to his radio station to make sure the disk jockeys were following format. Obviously, the enormous dedication of these younger program directors—many of whom are still in their 20s or early 30s—has played an important role in the development of programming as a science.

It should be noted that there is another group of programmers who consider radio programming an art form rather than a science. George Wilson, when he was national program director of Bartell Broadcasters before he was its president, once flew to Miami, heard WMYQ (now billed as 96X under different call letters) and revamped the whole playlist because he instinctively felt that the music was all wrong. He may have made this judgment based on personal taste or experience, since he programmed more No. 1 Top 40 stations in his career than any man in the world, but there certainly wasn't any science associated with his changes. Bill Young at KILT in Houston probably programs more from a gut feeling rather than statistics. J. J. Jordan when in radio, Les Garland at WRKO in Boston, and Michael Spears at KFRC in San Francisco are men who most likely use a combination of instinct and research, guided by the experience of their national program director Paul Drew of RKO Radio, with headquarters in Los Angeles.

Although George Wilson often programmed by gut feeling, many of the people who worked for him at one time or another were deeply into research, including Jack McCoy. Wilson freely admitted that half of the time he didn't understand (he wasn't alone) what McCoy was saying "but it works." McCoy came up with theories such as "recycling listeners" and later started a firm with Doug Herman, a computer expert, to sell audience information to radio stations. While he was program director of KCBQ, (a Bartell Broadcasters station in San Diego), he created the promotion "The Last Contest" that was syndicated coast to coast and literally blew opposing stations off the dial in ratings.

2 The disk jockey in radio

Unfortunately, the development of programming, as either a science or art form, has met many obstacles over the years. First, the press has seldom been kind to the image of the disk jockey because, after all, radio competes with newspapers for the advertising dollar. And as a rule, the result has been that when a disk jockey does something wrong, it makes banner headlines; when he does something beneficial, he's lucky to get page 49 and two lines of copy. Top 40 disk jockeys, perhaps because they were a little wilder in accordance with the music they played (remember when Elvis Presley was shown on *The Ed Sullivan Show* on television from the waist up?) were especially vulnerable. On one occasion a disk jockey got caught with some pills coming across the border of Mexico and made headlines in most Texas newspapers. The same man, visiting a crippled children's home to entertain, warranted no print at all.

In reality, no industry devotes as much personal time and service to the community and public projects as the people in radio. This devotion is not just because they've got a good heart, but also because these activities look impressive at license renewal time (when the radio station must submit a massive document to the Federal Communications Commission as evidence that it deserves to keep its right to broadcast a few years longer). However, a lot of air personalities and radio station personnel are sincerely involved in public service above and beyond the duties of their job. Gary Owens, afternoon drive (3-7 PM when people drive home from work) personality at KMPC in Los Angeles, devotes a considerable portion of his time to charity projects. WABC in New York has an air personality on tap almost any hour of the day for any worthwhile event in the area.

Being personally involved, usually at the expense of many hours of private time, in community service is just one of the things that's expected of a radio man in addition to his hours on the air or laboring over a tape deck in a production studio. Fortunately, most radio men enjoy doing things to help people, whether its bicycling 600 miles as three San Antonio radio men did a few years ago for charity, or just participating in a Leukemia Radiothon (with 40 other stations, WMAL in Washington became involved in a network hookup to raise funds in 1976 and collected over $70,000 in donations from listeners. Think about it, in only 22 hours this radio station raised $70,000 aided by friends like Ethel Kennedy, Brig Owens, Joe Theismann of the Redskins, and the various WMAL air personalities. Bill Mayhugh broadcast for all of the 22 hours. There were other fund raising events—radio stations in New York raised over $57,000, Philadelphia $55,000, and Los Angeles $38,000.

Concerning the WMAL effort, WMAL general manager Charles Macatee said: "This once again reinforces my belief in the power of radio and confirms my conviction that we broadcast to one of the most generous audiences in the country."

What he didn't say was that WMAL has enormous power and potential to accomplish good in its community and that it performs for public welfare as well as entertainment. Yet, the press image of the disk jockey and the radio station has always been a little dim. And this reflects not only upon the disk jockey, but the program director and the entire radio industry as well.

However, that image is improving—slowly.

Payola

Radio is still a constant target, as is the entire music industry. For example, the Grand Jury payola investigations in New Jersey were somewhat of a political boondoggle for publicity, and the biggest conglomeration of fishing expeditions ever held. The only things gained were some newspaper headlines for some self-seeking politicians and some attention drawn away from the political skulduggeries of Watergate. And true, a few were found guilty but, what was unusual was that one company found guilty, Brunswick Records, hadn't had a decent hit worthy of the charges of payola. Obviously, payola hadn't succeeded.

Most recent payola has been in the soul music format where, quite frankly, white owners have been underpaying black disk jockeys for years and purposely turning their heads to payola. Unfortunately, in radio, the guilt of the few reflects on the mass. A doctor can overcharge you, a garage mechanic can "fix" a brake that really didn't need repairing, a plumber can bill you for $100 for unstopping a drain, but a disk jockey or program director can't even accept a bottle of diet soda if it has anything to do with playing a record on the air. The law is that it's a federal crime for any radio or television station to accept or agree to accept money, services, or anything of value for broadcasting any material without disclosing acceptance or agreement to accept. This includes people producing shows aired on the station, even though they do not officially work for the station.

Back in August 1973, the Recording Industry Association of America adopted a program of its members—all belonging to the recording industry—that stated:

Recording companies and their employees shall not:

1. Engage in payola practices of any kind, as defined and prohibited in the federal payola statutes.

2. Ask for or receive kickbacks from artists, producers, or others.

3. Provide illegal drugs to any person, or cause them to be provided.

4. Attempt to influence in any illegal or unethical manner trade media chart ratings or reviews.

Later, the program stated that recording companies shall require employees who maintain contact with broadcasting stations and personnel to sign "no-payola" affidavits. The program, printed in *Billboard* magazine, also stated: "Our association has continuously demonstrated its concern over the problem of drug abuse. The RIAA was among the first industry groups to volunteer and contribute its expertise, creativity, and facilities to the government back in 1969 to help in the fight against drug abuse. Similarly, many individual companies, artists, and writers have volunteered their time and talents to create and record anti-drug abuse songs.

"We have long shared the national concern with the drug abuse problem. However, drugs are a problem of the total society, and it is unfair and unrealistic for anyone to attempt to seek a scapegoat for the drug problem in either the manufacturers of recordings, or the creators of recordings, or the performers."

Now, in spite of the Grand Jury investigations and everything else, payola hasn't been abolished in radio. Radio playlists are extremely tight, yet, the corresponding need to get a record on those playlists, especially in the larger market, is huge. As long as this situation exists, record companies are literally forced to use every means possible to invade the tight playlist barrier. In some ways, this leads to payola. In other ways, it leads to psychological warfare whereby the men and women who cater to the egos of program directors, music directors, and even general managers and owners, are hired by record companies to do their thing. There's nothing immoral about this, in fact, it is seldom planned. It's a Darwinian plausibility. As the science of radio programming has grown, so has the art of record promotion and the skill of the record promotion person.

At the current time, there's a promotion executive in Nashville who is a personal friend of at least four Top 40 program directors. He specializes in country music artists going pop—this is, selling in the pop market outside of just ordinary country sales, and he is quite successful. Yet, there is nothing wrong on either his part or on the part of the program directors, who just might take a chance on a country artist on their playlist, and when the particular trial record makes it and starts selling pop, they're pleased and this refortifies their faith in "old whatishisname" from Nashville. The truth is, the relationship between the radio station's program or music director and the promotion executive is a nebulous one and we'll explore it more in detail later.

Concerning payola, it ended on a mass scale in 1959 as a result of the disk jockey convention in Miami sponsored by Todd Storz and attended by at least 2,000 people—the majority of whom were owners and managers, not disk jockeys, who have quietly and effectively disappeared from any role call. You can't find any records of the event today. That meeting resulted in the press headlines: (again, please remember the antagonism that always existed, and still does, between the printed word and the spoken word) "Babes, Booze, and Bribes." Bill Stewart, then working for Todd Storz, helped organize the convention. He recalled having a couple of drinks the night before the convention with a reporter. Stewart claimed the reporter had been assigned to do a hatchet job on the convention. In any case, the resultant press and investigations hindered the development of radio programming for years.

Payola hasn't been abolished in radio—there's little way even federal investigators can dampen the loan of a credit card for a night out on the town. But payola is an extremely ineffective tool for promoting records in radio, and considering the total picture of the industry, it has relatively small usage for two major reasons:

First, most program directors are more concerned with playing records. Money can't influence them to play what might be a stiff and a tuneout factor plus the demeaning aspects affecting their professional pride as a good program director would be unbearable to most.

Second, most record promotion executives are so skilled in their craft, as presenters of valid programming information and as psychological motivators (often unknown to themselves), that payola would be demeaning to their professionalism.

Now, it should be affirmed that prior to the investigations stemming from the 1959 Miami convention, there were many record companies and disk jockeys involved in payola, and it wasn't considered a crime (except in regard to possible income tax evasion). Several record companies quickly signed consent decrees not admitting anything, but stating that they wouldn't do again whatever it was they might or might not have done. And the matter, at that level, was finished.

In fact, Alan Freed was indicted in March 1965 by a Federal Grand Jury on charges of evading $37,920 in income taxes for 1957 through 1959, all stemming from payola, according to Robert J. McGuire, Assistant U. S. Attorney. Freed had been hit for payola activities in 1962 under New York State's commercial bribery law. He received a six month suspended sentence and a $300 fine after pleading guilty. At that time, the former WINS disk jockey, known for inventing the term "rock and roll," was living in Palm Springs, Calif. After WINS in New York, Freed worked for a while at KDAY in Los Angeles, but his career had effectively been wiped out by the payola investigations along with the careers of several others, including Peter Tripp and Mel Leeds. While countless others had also been involved, they bore the brunt of the attack but it more or less finished them as far as ever being on the air or programming a radio station again.

In September 1972, at a radio programming meeting in Los Angeles, William B. Ray, chief of the Complaints and Compliance Division of the FCC, warned broadcasters of payola investigations, but also stated that payola was the "actions of a relatively small number of persons in your industry." He also called on everyone to provide information freely. "It is certainly not in your interest to let the finger of suspicion be pointed at every radio station, disk jockey, program or music director, record promotion man or record company."

According to section 508, added to the Federal Communications Act in 1960, any radio station employee accepting "money, service, or other valuable consideration" for broadcasting must disclose it to the station licensee. The person offering the bribe is also required by law to inform the licensee. Failure to do so can bring a fine of up to $10,000 and one year in jail. At the same time, Section 317 of the Communications Act was amended to require on-the-air announcements of all payments for broadcast material. The FCC is empowered to find evidence of payola violations and turn it over to the Justice Department for criminal prosecution.

About the biggest crime of this nature in recent years has to be called drugola—the gift of drugs to certain program directors—not for playing a record as much as just to win their goodwill. Though this whole syndrome has faded sharply, at the closest estimate only a handful of program directors may have been guilty even when drugola was in full swing, and the efforts of other program directors at radio stations coast to coast more than offset any public damage. In fact, Rick Sklar, then programmer of WABC in New York and now vice president of programming for all ABC-owned AM stations, launched a massive anti-drug abuse campaign providing advice and consolation to listeners confidentially over the phone and then editing their comments and broadcasting (anonymously) their drug plights over the air as a warning to other listeners. Other radio stations also became involved in anti-drug abuse campaigns and were largely instrumental in dampening the cult syndrome about use of hard drugs affecting youth across the nation.

As for disk jockeys and payola—very few disk jockeys today are involved in the selection of new records for broadcast—the old days of "Babes, Booze, and Bribes" have long been over for the disk jockey and are extremely trivial in regard to overall radio. And in spite of generally bad press, radio continues to survive and improve, and many people feel it is the most effective medium in the world for achieving public good.

Salaries

Another obstacle that has hindered the development of radio as a programming science has been management. For every Gordon McLendon and George Wilson who believe in programming, there's four dozen to a hundred managers who have little liking for their craft, little respect for the music they play (a lot don't even like to listen to their own station), and by default, little respect for the people that work under them. Though things are changing as more program directors move into management, such as Charlie Murdock at WLW in Cincinnati (who started as a disk jockey); Ted Atkins at WTAE in Pittsburgh; Gary Stevens (never a program director, but once a major Top 40 jock at WMCA in New York); Norman Wain, now president of his own radio operations; Dan Clayton, now general manager of WBBF in Rochester, N.Y.; and David Moorhead, general manager of KMET, Los Angeles.

In addition, there have been several general managers who took an active interest in programming—Bob Klieve of KLIV in San Jose, Calif., who helped the development of Top 40 radio in Spain; George Duncan, now president of Metromedia; Stan Kaplan, general manager of WAYS in Charlotte, N.C.; and Les Smith, head of Kaye-Smith Enterprises. There were others who abounded throughout radio not only in the United States, but worldwide—people such as Kevin O'Donohue at 2SM in Sydney, Australia; Luis Brunini, head of Radio Globo in Brazil with headquarters in Rio de Janeiro; David Gapes at Radio Hauraki in Auckland, New Zealand (which started out as a pirate station and succeeded so well the government had to ask it to become a legalized land-based station).

For a long time, however, with only few exceptions, owners and managers considered program directors and air personalities cannon fodder. Gary McDowell, who worked with Bill Drake under the name of Gary Mack and later programmed such stations as WNEW in New York and WGST in Atlanta, once commented that you could always tell the size of the city a disk jockey was working in by the size of the U-Haul Trailer on the back of his car. The job security of either the program director or the disk jockey was, and still is, uncertain to say the least. Disk jockeys have been fired for wearing the wrong tie to work or not wearing a tie at all. Program directors have been fired for trying to program a radio station right, in spite of the contrary wishes of the general manager. Both program director and disk jockey are usually fired for bad ratings at the radio station, which is the most ridiculous reason of all for losing a job, as you'll realize yourself when we get into the topic of ratings later on.

One general manager of a Top 40 station used to bug not only the disk jockey lounge, but also the phone calls. One particular disk jockey recalled being summoned into the general manager's office and was forced to listen to his wife's phone call to him earlier in the day. Ordinarily, that wouldn't have gotten him fired except that during the conversation he referred to the general manager as "that old bastard."

You can also get fired for trying to join a union. Ken Mezger said that he'd gotten fired from a major market radio station for signing a petition requesting union representation. "The next morning as I walked through the door of the station, I was fired. He immediately gave me a quick excuse that I hadn't been doing too well on the air lately and he claimed that I had been looking for a job."

It wasn't much of a job; his salary at the radio station in the Washington market, was only $140 weekly "and an average of one record hop per week which provided an additional $75 to $100."

Record hops have been the mainstay of the disk jockey for many years, going back to the heyday of the record hop when Jerry Blavat (who called himself "The Geator With the Heator" though no one ever translated that into English), Hy Lit, Joe Niagara, and perhaps Georgie Woods were literally kings of the record hop. On one occasion (and perhaps more than once) Blavat did four hops in one night, flying from one site to another by chartered helicopter. Niagara and Lit often had 1,000 kids dancing live to spinning records. Of course, they often had recording artists drop by to sing live and for a time, recording companies used this avenue to expose new acts (until the FCC once asked several radio stations to reply that there was no connection between the hops and the radio station's playlist). There was no connection, but it cost more than a dozen radio stations rather high legal fees in Washington just to answer letters of inquiry from the FCC. The result was that a lot of radio stations did away with record hops by air personalities.

Today, for the most part, the record hop is a matter of ancient history. The disco craze has somewhat replaced the departed record hop except that it costs a lot more money to attend, because drinking is an additional expense. The major income of many present day air personalities comes, not from their radio jobs, but from doing voice-overs on commercials and later we'll get into the modus operandi of that.

Bill Mercer, a black disk jockey who used the air name Rosko, earned only $52,000 in his final days as an air personality on WNEW-FM in New York, a progressive rock station. But he made perhaps $150,000 doing radio and TV spots. His voice is distinctive, and you've probably heard him. Today, Scott Muni and Gary Owens are two voices (not necessarily names) that you would recognize. Owens, the man who put his hand up to his ear on TV's *Laugh In,* may earn up to $150,000 in commercials per year. Casey Kasem, who does the announcing on the weekly syndicated *American Top 40* radio show produced by Watermark, easily has the same earnings. Muni, in 1976, could be heard on TV in advertisements for Rolaids, for toothpaste, and Lite Beer, in addition to radio spots for LPs. Not bad earnings for a disk jockey who was told that he couldn't make New York radio because of his voice (which then and now sounds like a gravel truck in reverse; we'll later discuss how important a voice is in radio).

At WABC in New York, air personalities are not allowed to earn outside money except from outside business investments (nonconflicting) and doing voice-overs for commercials. Program directors have seldom had the leeway to earn extra money unless they also were on the radio. One country music program director in Evansville, Ind., eventually left radio to join the grocery business, and Jim Embry earned about $20,000 from radio and things such as announcing at the local stock car racetrack on Sundays. Selling cans of chili and loaves of bread was much easier than radio and only required five or six days a week rather than six or seven. In Shreveport, La., one program director named Larry Ryan remained at KEEL for more than 10 years. Why? For one thing, he excelled in programming the radio station. Also, management allowed Ryan and the disk jockeys to earn extra money from local production on commercials. The result was that Ryan seldom lost a disk jockey except to a major market position for a rather extraordinary salary. He only left KEEL recently to become a general manager at another station.

Program directors and air personalities are drastically underpaid, believes Scott Shannon, ex-program director, who is currently national director of record promotion for Casablanca Records. It should be noted that even in the record industry jobs change rather rapidly, but people rarely leave the industry as did Jim Embry, MOR program director Dale Andrews, or MOR program director Jon Holiday (Andrews did quite well at WCBM in Baltimore and Holiday created a landmark station at KMBZ in Kansas City).

Program directors "mean too much to a radio station," Shannon said. "And I predict that if radio management doesn't adjust or begin to realize that the program director is a very talented and valuable individual to a radio station, the radio industry will start losing more good program directors."

Scott Shannon denied leaving radio for money alone; he said his aim was "always in the direction" of the record industry. He thought that being national promotion director for a record label and program director of a radio station were similar. Part of the job of a promotion director is "to motivate the people you work with—and instill pride. Being a program director is like being a national promotion direction—you're dealing with people, dealing with motivation, dealing with winning."

As for salaries, program directors are being drastically "underpaid as a rule," said Shannon. "You can't imagine how many good program directors are knocking their brains out for less than $15,000 a year—a hell of a lot less than the manager or the sales manager; that's a sad state. This is not true of every station, but, unfortunately, it's the rule rather than the exception."

Shannon went on to say, "Management must realize that they have to take care of their program directors. Don't they realize that it seriously hurts a station to have a successful program director leave for greener pastures? It often means that some of the air staff leaves also. And consistency is one of the most important factors of a good radio station. Pay those program directors more and radio stations will never have that kind of problem."

Shannon programmed WMAK in Nashville, then became national program director of the Mooney chain. He then joined WQXI in Atlanta as program director in late 1974, working under Gerald Blum, general manager. He joined Casablanca Records in early 1976.

Slowly, the pay of the program director has been moving up. Many of the RKO Radio program directors were quite well paid in 1976—somewhere around $35,000 as a rule, which was above average. The highest paid program director was receiving somewhere around $50,000. In a recent radio survey, it was found that the average program director in a small market radio station was receiving about $14,000 to $14,522 with a few people earning around $18,000. (You can easily see that some general managers in small markets knew which side of the bread their butter was on and paid their program directors commensurate with the earnings of the radio stations.) In medium markets, the program director earned $18,913 to $22,000 in general, and many of these program directors were also on the air, thus the extra salary. In major markets, the average salary was $26,666.66 to $29,000; several program directors earned around $35,000 or more, pulling this average up. In general, the salaries of disk jockeys were: major market—$23,000 to $25,000; medium market—$11,467 to $13,000; small market—$174.40 average per week.

In some radio stations, even the figures of $350,000 (which is reportedly what John Gambling earns at WOR in New York for doing the morning show) might be considered appropriate. And both Gary Owens at KMPC in Los Angeles and William B. Williams at WNEW—AM in New York are earning well over $120,000 per year (we won't divulge their real salaries—or their total earnings, which are considerably more). Dick Whittinghill, who does the morning show at KMPC in Los Angeles, also earns enough to pay his green fees at any golf club he wants to swing at. And there are many more disk jockeys around the country who do quite well, in some cases, better than many program directors. Aku Head, a disk jockey who couldn't really score in the United States, is a hero in Hawaii and probably earns more than any other air personality in the world in a good year—even more than John Gambling in New York.

But salaries are nebulous; it's all a matter of how much you can keep. One disk jockey, earning more than $125,000 a year in New York, had to get himself a chauffeured limousine, an apartment on Sutton Place, and a home out in Connecticut. The result was that he ended up with nothing more than a bunch of lawyers telling him how good he was and how much money he owed. The wise disk jockey banks his money and rides the high times the same way he rides the mediocre ones.

In many markets, the program director or the disk jockey receives "hidden" salaries, i.e., a tradeout on an apartment, a car, gasoline, or even hamburgers at a particular restaurant. This is not necessarily bad. Economically, it means that the radio station can save money by inducing potential low-dollar clients to trade out services for air time. Though domestic airlines do not trade out air travel, international airlines do trade, thus radio stations are sometimes able to offer a trip to Japan or London, all expenses paid (meaning that the hotel chain was also traded out in Tokyo or London) as a prize for a contest on the air.

And there are barter companies—(the William B. Tanner Co. in Memphis is by far the largest) who'll trade a radio station anything from a credit card with limited expenses to a new car for a given amount of air time (usually, they offer much less than what the air time is worth on the local market, if the station were able to sell it). Bartering is one of the facts of life of modern radio, and something the program director and the air personality should understand. In Huntsville, Ala., the disk jockey might get a luxurious apartment free, in addition to tradeouts at a local clothing store, the loan of a car, or get free meals occasionally at a restaurant. Even in Los Angeles, a general sales manager of a major station might spend one day a month setting up tradeouts for the staff, especially for the management level.

Capitol Cities Broadcasting in 1976 passed an edict that there would be no more tradeouts. One program director, in Los Angeles, had been trading out air time for free albums (most major market radio stations get free singles and albums for promotional considerations), he ended up having to pay Wallich's Music City cash for albums. There was nothing wrong with this, he could have called the record companies and received the same albums free.

Record Problems

The problem of free albums and singles for radio stations is slowly moving into a crisis. On one hand, you have the record company faction that claims radio stations should pay for the privilege of programming material. On the other side, the radio stations claim that without radio exposure the recording companies would never have any hits to sell.

Radio stations in England are forced to program a percentage of live music. In Australia, Canada, and England, not only are radio stations restricted in needle time (amount of local product they must play), but they also have to pay a copyright fee to the record companies and the record artist for playing their records. In the United States, fees are paid only to the writer of the song and the publisher of the song. Those fees also have to be paid in other countries in addition to programming fees.

For several years, there has been a strong movement in the United States to require radio stations to pay fees for airing the song to the artist and the record company—as well as fees for the writer and the publisher of the song. Whether these extra fees will come to pass or not is debatable. Many broadcasters have always been allergic to payments to ASCAP, BMI, and SESAC in the United States for copyright protection on songs. And they are putting up a strong battle against extra payments for broadcasting records. It is especially exasperating to see a record sell a million-plus copies after a radio station has paid to get a copy. Then the record artist ends up with several hundreds of thousands of dollars while the little station in Lubbock,

Texas, ends up having to pay for the next single they want to play. What the program director and the general manager of that Lubbock station do not realize is that their broadcast exposure accounted for only 200 sales of a single at most. The profit margin on that single may have been 12 cents, but it cost more than that to ship it into the market, because it's outside normal distribution patterns. Thus, the record company might lose anywhere from two to ten cents per single sold in a given market.

Naturally, the record company is more interested in a healthy bottom line and doesn't care to service a radio station with free records in a losing marketing area. That's why special marketing divisions have sprung up at most major record companies and that's why you'll see service diminishing for free promotional records to radio stations. One record company internal survey showed that only 150 radio stations actually were worthwhile to service free records to. These were the stations that influenced record sales in regard to singles. And there might be another 150 stations, mostly FM, that influence album sales, but even they have faded back in power. The total statistic is that less than .08 percent of the nation's radio stations actually influence record sales.

The key is that some of the stations are just thermometers for record sales, above and beyond their ability to spur sales of that particular record. When a record gets substantial feedback on that station, the record industry realizes it might have a hit on its hands. A case in point is WLOF in Orlando, Fla.; when Bill Vermillion was programming the station, it was considered a record breakout station, and it has never been the same since he left. If a program director wishes to take the viewpoint that he's helping record companies choose hits, he may be worth sending free singles to; if not, it's fair that he should pay for the music his station plays on the air. Of course, this does not meet with the philosophies of the general manager and/or the owner of a radio station, who usually can't understand why record companies want to charge radio stations for records. The cry is that there wouldn't be any hit record without the important exposure of radio, and to a very large extent, this is true. There have been very few records that became hits without early radio airplay.

The Record Saved Radio

The record played an extremely important role in the rebirth of radio after television gave it a sharp setback in the early 1950s. The record, as we know it today, was invented in 1887 by Emile Berliner, a native of Germany who emigrated to the United States in 1870. On April 14, 1877, Berliner filed a patent for the battery-operated loose-contact microphone, (used also in the telephone). Aside from the disk record (Thomas Edison had invented a cylinder phonograph), Berliner invented a disk player and coined the word *gramophone,* in addition to the system for mass production of records from metal stampers. Later, he established one of the first record companies in the world—Deutsche Grammophon Gesellschaft mbH (Polydor). It should be noted that the U.S. Supreme Court in 1897 swept aside patent interferences and declared Berliner the sole inventor of the microphone. And although Thomas Edison sued Emile Berliner in 1900 for phonograph patent infringement, the court ruled that the gramophone and disk were diametrically opposed to the cylinder. But Berliner was financially ruined and Eldridge Johnson acquired Berliner Gramophone Co. and renamed the firm the Victor Talking Machine Co., later to become RCA Records. And in 1902, Enrico Caruso agreed to make a disk record, paving the way for other major artists to also record on them.

For our purposes, modern radio programming did not really get into high gear until the advent of the 45 rpm single, a development out of RCA Records (the album came out of Columbia Records and later it was the viability of album sales that fostered the growth of FM radio via the progressive rock format).

True, the old 78 rpm had done well for radio since Martin Block at WNEW-AM in New York spun his way into legend as perhaps the world's first major disk jockey (the West Coast always refuted this, claiming they had the first record spinner in Al Jarvis with *Make Believe Ballroom*). In any case, the 78 rpm disk was neither easy to program nor was it easy to buy, as far as handling is concerned.

Billboard magazine, in the Jan. 14, 1950 issue, reported that "I Can Dream, Can't I?" by the Andrew Sisters was the No. 1 record most played by disk jockeys. And in Hazard, Ky., a WKIC disk jockey named Jerry Leighton told *Billboard* that in order to stop phone requests he played nine different versions of "Mule Train"—the biggest version was by Frankie Laine on Mercury Records. In those days, the cover record was widely in existence—any time someone came up with a hit, everyone else would rush into a recording studio to do their version. But the record wasn't that popular in comparison to what it is today. In fact, a survey of Girl Scouts in 1950 revealed that only 67 percent of junior high school girls had record players. And that year disk jockeys weren't any big deal either—truthfully, they weren't really disk jockeys, just announcers. Early in 1950, the American Federation of Radio Artists (television wasn't part of the name then) signed a contract with WMCA in New York which gave the station announcers a hike in salary to $121 a week.

But at the same time something was beginning to happen in records. Ben Parsons, a disk jockey at WRBL in Columbus, Ga., noted that he thought he was the only "disk spinner" to use 45 rpm singles in the entire South. His show was called *Dancing Party* on the station, and he mentioned that Victor and Capitol 45s had been used. And disk jockeys were rather casual in style. Hugh Cherry in those days was still at WKDA in Nashville, and he reported that he also broadcast news about country music sidemen and composers on his country music show.

An interesting story was printed in the Jan. 28, 1950 *Billboard* about RCA Records launching a heavy promotion campaign on the 45 rpm single; the report stated that sales were strong on both the 45 rpm and the 78 rpm singles.

And in 1950 something extremely important happened that affected the future of radio—the Jan. 7 issue of *Billboard* reported that NBC had slated the *Fibber McGee and Molly Show* as the first top radio show to take TV tests. "If successful, an early entry into video is foreseen for the veteran comedy show."

You could see the handwriting on the wall at the headquarters of the National Association of Broadcasters when WNEW in New York resigned. In fact, the previous year the NAB lost 88 AM stations and 137 FM stations, while gaining 33 TV stations. In 1950, the NAB had only 1,152 AM, 497 FM, and 37 TV stations.

All this time, Bill Randle was flying daily from Detroit to WERE in Cleveland to do an afternoon disk jockey show. Others, such as Harry (Mushmouth) O'Connor, at KMAC in San Antonio, were beginning to experiment with live shows.

In November 1950, Seeburg, one of the major manufacturers of jukeboxes, announced that it was going the 45 rpm singles route exclusively. The fate of the 78 rpm disk was sealed, though record dealers continued to report to *Billboard* that customers were confused about the different record speeds. Pamela Parandes of Rosenblatt Electric Co. in Hartford, Conn., claimed that "many people think 45 rpm records play for 45 minutes." During this period, Zenith Radio, a Chicago record distributor for MGM Records (to illustrate how trivial record sales were, dealers also sold everything from pianos to guitars and perhaps refrigerators) decided that buying commercial time was the best way to promote a record. After a year of buying time on the Howard Miller Show on WIND, sales for MGM products had increased 30 percent. It was announced that Miller had no previous experience as a deejay, and he was doing two half-hour shows six days a week.

Overall, radio wasn't doing too badly; according to the NAB, radio's gross for 1949 (compared to 1948) was up 4.5 percent to the area of $435,279,000. Of course, the damage (or fear of damage) from television was yet to come. In Dallas, Gordon McLendon, after studying what Todd Storz was doing, started using a top 25-record playlist (updated daily) in the early part of 1953. McLendon realized that television was killing radio. He had been denied rights to broadcast baseball in 1952 as The Old Scotchman (he was upstaging live broadcasts with his recreations of games and he had the second largest network in the nation) so he was forced into doing something new in programming.

"I thought that the only way that radio was going to stay around was through concentration on music and news and nothing else but," said McLendon, "Television was already usurping the major sports events."

As radio dwindled in programs, it developed as a medium for programming of music. And while programming developed, the disk jockey began to ascend—not so much in salary, but for the most part, in local prominence, (as witnessed by the fact that ratings reached as high as a 70-plus share of the market). The disk jockey gained importance with the record industry for breaking in new hits that reached sales never before dreamed of, and his total earnings increased through record hops, personal appearances, and payola. In his autobiography, as yet unpublished, Detroit air personality Tom Clay recalls visiting a boat show with a record man; when he remarked that a certain boat really looked good, the record man bought it for him on the spot.

Among the few famous radio personalities who weren't involved in some kind of outside dealings about the music they played was Clark Race (then with KDKA in Pittsburgh and years ago earning as much as $45,000 in salary). This is not an accusation against all of the other disk jockeys. In cities such as Boston, Washington, and Philadelphia disk jockeys were paid low wages. Even in the 1970s, one Washington, D.C. Top 40 station paid only $150 a week; the general manager of the station collected weekly fees from a local nightclub where his jocks did emcee work, took a cut, and then divided the rest among the deejays in lieu of paying them a decent salary. This sort of thing still goes on—in Alabama, one disk jockey is partially paid with a luxury apartment and a car, both of which are traded out for advertising time by the radio station. There's nothing essentially wrong with this, though it is a pity that air personalities aren't given better salaries; if so, the entire industry would gain more respect nationally and in the local marketplace.

3 A people medium

L. David Moorhead worked his way up through the ranks, starting as an air personality back in the crazy heyday of Top 40 radio. He has worked in several radio positions ranging from Tucson to New York where he worked on the corporate level of CBS; he is now general manager and vice president of KMET, an FM progressive station in Los Angeles. Today, as in the past, Moorhead has associated himself with outstanding personnel—as friend, employee, or employer.

"Every time a radio station achieves a modicum of success, the world begins beating a path to its door (or frequency) in the hopes of discovering the magic formula that creates the better mousetrap." Moorhead continued, "A radio station, however, is only people—just as listeners are people."

Then why does management apparently have a driving compulsion to reduce everything to a simplistic formula which reduces the human element to a bare minimum, or even eliminates it entirely?

"Basically, because it is the line of least resistance. Machines, in many ways, are easier to handle than people," Moorhead said. "The worst a machine is going to do is break down. People break down, break up, and foul up." And, Moorhead wondered, isn't it better that way?

"Every time a station or format is copied, it is just that—a copy, a carbon without the warmth and color of the original—essentially without the human element.

"The magic formula, from my experience, is like Einstein's theory of relativity—very few can grasp the whole thing because it appears to be different, depending on your view."

Thus, Moorhead states, to a person in programming, good ratings and audience reaction are the major goal. To the sales person, gross revenue is the objective; to the business office and bookkeeper, collection of gross revenue is the end; to the general manager, the owners, and the stockholders, the ultimate radio station is the right combination of the above—to achieve the largest audience which will generate the most collectible dollars.

"Some radio stations would rather be No. 3, 4, or 5 in a market because in that ratings position, they can actually generate top billing—more than the No. 1 station." The success of a radio station, Moorhead said, is solely dependent upon the right combination of people properly playing their roles.

"When you think of the great radio stations where you have worked—if you're a professional radio man—I'll bet dollars to donuts that you remember people, not the cart machines, transmitter or console. My own memories of my days as a program director are of people who made the station click. To me, Tucson is still Phil Richardson, Frank Kalil, Mikel Hunter, Ray Tenpenny, Dotty Smith, Jerry Stowe—the people who built KTKT into a 1960s legend.

"Milwaukee is Jack Lee, Raleigh Abrams, George Wilson, Robert L. Collins, Dick Casper, and Ralph Barnes—some of whom are still making a contribution to radio in that market."

Each successful station brings to mind the people who made it happen, and it is usually a good balance between sales, programming, and operations, Moorhead said.

"There are others in my memory, either short-term successes or failures, who had one thing in common: They ran like railroads—they followed schedules, treated the staff like porters, and gave their listeners all the care, consideration, and attention railroads notoriously have reserved for passengers. Which is not too strange, considering that when our industry's original regulations were set forth they were patterned after the Railroad Act which stated that the railroads would operate for the public interest, convenience, and necessity. It has been attributed to the late Senator Burton Wheeler that when guidelines were formulated, those words from the Railroad Act made sense, as applied to the fledgling broadcast industry. The original legislators' interpretation, however, was that programs would be interesting; stations would be convenient to find on the dial; and *necessity* scanned well."

But, like their brothers in the railroad industry, too many broadcasters deduced that the answer was to pack the passengers in and haul the freight. Then the airlines came along, they pampered the passengers, put the freight in perspective, and gave Harry Nilsson 10 years worth of song material.

"Draw your own analysis," Moorhead said. "The quickest way for me to judge the *people strength* of a radio station is to find its public service programs. A good *people* station usually fulfills both interpretations of public interest. They fill a community need and they hold interest. Nowhere in the Communications Act is it dictated that public affairs programs must be boring. It's just traditional. Show me a radio station whose public service programs are interesting and, even more important, entertaining, and I'll show you a radio station peopled with the likes of Phil Richardson, Shadoe Stevens, Billy Bass, Howard Bloom, George Duncan, Jack Thayer, Mel Karmazin, or Tom Donahue.

"One of the disasters of our business occurs when, in quest of the Holy Grail of success, an individual is transplanted from a successful team where the magic formula is working to a hostile environment where the jocks talk only to the program director—the program director speaks only to the general manager and the sales manager speaks to everyone—and the general manager speaks only to God. Everyone sits around waiting for something to happen as they individually do their own thing, without coordination or communication. And when the Good Ship Formula Format hits the rocks, each sits isolated on the beach wondering what went wrong . . .

"And then calls friends looking for a job."

Chain of Command

In the programming department of a radio station, the disk jockey reports to the program director, as does the music director (who is often one of the disk jockeys, especially in smaller cities). Sometimes the program director will report to the operations manager, at other times, the operations manager reports to the program director. Usually, the program director does the work of the operations director and the latter job doesn't exist at all in title. In any case, either man would report to the general manager, as does the general sales manager. In many stations, the program director is also the music director and also does a show on the air each day.

Incidentally, the on-air program director exists in all sizes of markets. For example, Larry Ryan, general manager of KBCL (former program director of KEEL) in Shreveport, La., does a daily radio show, and Charlie Van Dyke, program director of KHJ Los Angeles, does a daily radio show. But at WIOD in Miami, both Jim Gallant, former program director and Al Anderson, the operations manager, did a Sunday morning show for kicks on the station but otherwise confined their creative instincts to staff operations. In some markets, even the general manager and/or owner will also do a radio show. It's all a matter of economics. In Colorado, using the name of Pappy Dave Stone (David Pinkston), the owner of KPIK has been a legend for many years on the air. It is believed that he may have started the first totally country music format station.

Some program directors like to be on the air, some don't. The philosophy of those who're on the air is that they're able to keep in closer touch with what's happening via audience feedback, and they can strongly relate to the role of the disk jockey. On the other hand, those program directors who aren't on the air claim that they're better able to control the disk jockeys—the disk jockeys aren't able to compare their own work with that of their boss. During a strike at WABC several years ago, executives stepped into the gap and went on the air while the disk jockeys walked in the picket line on the streets of New York City. Dutifully, then program director Rick Sklar tested himself as a possible substitute deejay and turned himself down as not being as well qualified for the job as other people around him. The result was that people such as public relations executive Marty Grove and an engineer went on the air. History will record that ratings went up with these amateurs doing their thing. Would you believe that the engineer—calling himself Bernie the K in honor of Murray (the K) Kaufman—wasn't all that bad?

But there's more to being a disk jockey than just going on the air and rattling off a few adverbs and adjectives for an hour or so each day. Harvey Glascock, when he was vice president and general manager of WNEW-AM-FM in New York and sort of a spearhead in the entire Metromedia Radio chain, once referred to his air personalities as "super salesmen." He was referring to Gene Klavan, William B. Williams, Jim Lowe, and Ted Brown, among others. To a great extent, this is true. Among the criteria each year in the annual awards competition for the International Radio Programming Forum (these awards honor all aspects of radio programming, including the disk jockey) is the ability of the disk jockey to sell not only the music that he plays, but also the live commercials, the live PSAs, the call letters of the station, the other air personalities that he might cross-promote, and himself.

But the disk jockey is much more than a salesman, he must also be a craftsman. And learning that craft has been traditionally an on-the-job aspect of radio. Eddie (Jimmy Rabbitt) Payne, Charlie Tuna, Michael Spears, Art Roberts, Charlie Van Dyke, and Steve Lundy are a vast number of today's successful air personalities who got their start in small market radio where a program director (such as Bill Young) took patience and time to teach them the basics of operating a console, handling a mike, cueing a record or triggering a cart machine. Years ago, Young programmed a small station in Tyler, Tex., and while there he contributed immensely to the careers of several disk jockeys. Today Young programs KILT in Houston.

Radio Education

To a certain extent, the growth of automation has hurt the number of disk jockey jobs available in radio. But, perhaps the radio field needed a shakedown anyway; this might dampen the dollared enthusiasm of the so-called broadcasting schools that abound coast to coast. As these schools will be able to place less and less of their "students" into radio, they'll be able to bilk fewer people. It's not that all of the schools are fly-by-night ripoff operations. The Don Martin School in Los Angeles has maintained a healthy reputation over the years, with some excellent instructors ranging from Jack Brown of American Forces Radio and Television Services to Russ Barnett, who programmed KMPC in Los Angeles for several years.

But the honest truth is that most of the so-called broadcasting schools in cities ranging from New York to Los Angeles accept students who cannot possibly qualify even in small market radio, and then charge outlandish fees and promise jobs that can't possibly exist. One school has been charging students $1,550 for a 12-week semester and enrolls about 100 people each time. This means that approximately 400 students per year leave that school bound for a supposed radio career. The number of such broadcasting schools varies month by month, but have run as high as 25. Let's assume that only 5,000 students are being cranked out each year by these so-called schools. To that, add the students of some 500 universities entering the professional field each year. At the lowest possible estimate, there are 10,000 new people trying to enter radio each year. Even if you calculate that 25 percent of these people are extremely qualified and already have some experience from their local hometown radio, you still have to consider that there are probably only 4,400 AM and 3,400 FM stations. In addition, many FM stations still simulcast some AM programming and about 17 percent are automated. There can't possibly be more than 1,000 disk jockey jobs available in a year, because there just aren't 40,000 disk jockey jobs in the entire United States. There are other jobs in radio—in news, traffic, production, sales, and engineering.

But, as automation grows, the jobs will be diminishing somewhat. And even though the FCC has been forcing AM and FM (those stations with the same ownership in a market) to separate programming more and more, the trend has been to further automation and not to create more jobs. It should be noted at this point that a college degree doesn't mean much for the man or woman beginning a radio career. A well-rounded education pays off later, but universities haven't been able to fulfill the total needs of the radio business world in a very long time. In turn, the so-called broadcasting schools have been able to harp to prospective students that college professors haven't kept up with radio while the broadcasting schools have hired professionals as instructors. It's a turntable ratrace with no real solutions—though several universities are shaping up their radio education programs.

Recently at the annual meeting of the Wisconsin Broadcasters Association, it was stated that: "college students today are not being taught the right things about broadcasting in the courses they study at the university level." Jay Patrick Walsh, director of radio services at the University of Wisconsin at Oshkosh, questioned the statement, and at the same time agreed in principle. "There is a problem for those of us involved in the academics of teaching something as changeable as broadcasting and mass communications. There are a lack of updated, viable text books. We are trying to teach today's ideas with the backup of antiquity." For a new course in Radio Production Techniques, Walsh said there was no text available to fit his needs.

Walsh, who worked many years in commercial radio, is fortunate to have been involved in one of the most progressive and demanding crafts in the world on a professional level. He felt that even if new textbooks were written, they would be almost outdated by publication. And "it seems to be the sad fact that while broadcasters are critical of the system as it now exists, they prefer to take a 'Pontius Pilate' approach to the whole thing; just wash their hands, turn their back, and continue to bitch."

Walsh, once a production manager for a leading medium market rock station, called on the professional world to "help in putting together academic programs that will be beneficial to the student of the electronic medium as well as to the broadcaster—we all have to work together."

In truth, a lot of universities are making vast strides towards improving the radio curriculum. Rick Sklar (vice president of operations for ABC's radio stations and a program director who built WABC in New York to the most-listened to radio station in the United States) was appointed professor of communications arts at St. John's University. In this case, the students go to Sklar, they meet in downtown New York once a week and not only are able to partake of Sklar's extremely valid experience, but also that of other professionals invited to speak as guest lecturers.

Perhaps a better situation has developed at the University of Cincinnati where Dr. William M. Randle Jr., head of the division of broadcasting, has been incorporating professionals into the staff. Randle is the same Bill Randle of disk jockey fame who previously worked at WERE in Cleveland; at one time he was probably only second to Alan Freed as the most important Top 40 air personality in the nation. Randle believes that "the sophisticated, everyday working professional in a good market with competition and constant input would have to know more at a given time than most people teaching in a university environment. However, having been in both areas of expertise for many years with fair to middling success in both, I think it only fair to say that most professional radio people do not have the total background and multiple skills that are standard with contemporary broadcasting education professionals.

"Besides, more and more universities that are seriously involved in contemporary broadcasting education are using top of the line active professionals as adjunct professors or lecturers to supplement standard hardware and academic curriculum. I am constantly recruiting and utilizing area and national professionals for workshops, seminars, etc."

Randle suggests that the university situation could be improved if professionals would take a year to teach at a university on a graduate level to "refresh and broaden themselves and also cross-fertilize the university community while they are in residence."

It is true that stronger alliances need to be established between the professional world of radio and the academic world of radio education. While some universities are proceeding toward modern radio education, radio is advancing toward its own form of *Future Shock* in on-the-job training that is just as valuable even after a university degree is won. The wise university student spends a great deal of time at the local radio station and tries to pick up as much of the basics as possible.

Getting Radio Experience

Gregory B. Straubinger gives a very good example of the launching of a career: "I have just graduated with a B.S. in radio-TV—I've worked nights, weekends, summers, right through my four years in various Top 40 stations in upper New York and Pennsylvania, including WENE in Endicott, N.Y., and WHFM in Rochester, where I'm still on weekends after a year." Straubinger wrote that letter in May 1975; he added that he was "ready to go and willing to learn."

If Straubinger's career follows the usual steps, he'll end up working under the *nom de aero* (air name) of Robert W. Steele, Johnny Dark (Johnny Dollar was a popular name for years, but has faded somewhat) or Grey in the Morning or something equally innocuous such as Coyote McCloud, Johnny Rabbitt or Charlie Tuna. The early days won't be easy. For one thing, even though he has a college degree, he'll be vastly underpaid—about the same as a 19 year old whose dad got him a job at the station because he's the biggest advertiser in town—and he'll have to start out in small market radio unless he's extremely good and extremely lucky.

Tom Keenze, manager of KWPR in Claremore, Okla., feels that a small town radio station should be prepared to be a training ground for fledgling disk jockeys. He realizes that disk jockeys who start in such stations will not stay long because they will want to become better. For that reason, and because stations like KWPR are paying about the same as they paid 10 years ago and they will probably pay that amount in the future (it's a matter of budget). At small town stations disk jockeys work a five-hour shift on the air and sometimes double as salesmen and engineers. Keenze said that he would like to provide his disk jockeys with three-hour shifts, but the budget doesn't allow for that large a staff. So, the staff is mostly made up of younger men—ages 17 to 19—who are either local students or trying to break into radio for the first time. There are advantages, of course. Small market radio gives Keenze a chance to try out some programming theories without worry about ratings.

"If listeners don't like something, in a small town, they'll tell you," Keenze said.

The same thing applies to the fledgling disk jockey. And small market radio can give you a wide range of experience that may later prove valuable. Disk Jockeys at KXOJ, Sapulpa, Okla., work six-hour shifts and read their own news.

There are many elements that a disk jockey must handle on the air, whether the market is small or large. These include:

1. Records—on disk or cartridge (seldom on reel);

2. Commercials—these may be on disk, cartridge, or reel-to-reel tape;

3. Station ID (identification) jingles;

4. Call letters—weaving them in live as much as possible (one station owner did a test with a medium market property and found that audiences didn't realize they were listening to his station—when disk jockeys announced the call letters more frequently, the ratings doubled);

5. PSAs (public service announcements)—these may be live, on tape or disk, or sometimes produced on cartridge;

6. Promotions—these may be live, on tape, or produced on cartridge;

7. Contests—either produced or live;

8. Weather and time reports;

9. News—live or via network feed (some stations have a separate news staff to handle the news; however, in many stations the news director will also do a regular daily show or a weekend show);

10. Sports—some stations get deeply into sports, especially high school and local college activities and the disk jockey may also be called upon to do play-by-play announcing or report on sports along with the news;

11. Last, but not least, entertain—this entertainment might range from just introducing the records on the air (and more about live production techniques will be discussed later) to doing humorous material—this varies from one-liner gags to real humor;

12. Providing information about various things—from a lost dog in a small town to a

rock concert schedule in a major city (Pat Patterson, morning air personality at WKIX in Raleigh, N.C., until moving to KULF in Houston, told luncheon menus at local schools and you'd be surprised how many people tuned in every morning just to hear what their children were going to have for lunch that day);

13. Cross-promoting the other disk jockeys on the station;

14. Generating a certain atmosphere (this can range from a feeling of excitement on a high intensity Top 40 station to a "good ole boy" friendly feeling on a country music station. It all depends on the particular kind of sound that the program director is trying to create for the station);

15. And talking with listeners on the air (some stations put listeners on the air, usually with a seven-second delay, others do not).

Of course, disk jockeys have many other duties. At some stations they probably operate their own boards. Many stations—from KMPC in Los Angeles to WABC in New York—have engineers who handle certain chores for the disk jockey and help him in his job. The WABC setup is rather interesting, the disk jockey and engineer sit in the same room opposite each other; the theory is that they can communicate better and achieve better harmony.

Jose M. Llombart, an engineer from CKLW in Detroit, offered this personal viewpoint about being an engineer and comments about his relationship not only to programming but to the disk jockeys he works with: "One of the most underrated performers in rock radio today is the board engineer, also known as a transcription operator. Generally, broadcast people are not aware of the professional excellence and devotion that these men bring to their jobs. An operator actually runs the show, is responsible for all mistakes, controls operation of the on-air board, rides voice and music levels, knows the format and must have a good sense of timing.

"The operators at the Rock of the Motor City give all they have, which will be borne out by any air personality who ever practiced his craft here. Announcers rely on their operators for smooth segues, suggestions for lines, and encouragement, as well as criticism. CKLW operators are an integral part of the Big Eight sound. Every good operator feels that 'it takes two' to make a good show, and a good rapport between the two major ingredients on the air is necessary to insure that the show will cook. CKLW's strong ratings position in Detroit is undisputed and each operator is proud to be a member of the winning team. The Big Eight engineers are marked by their youth and gung ho attitude; two factors which combine to make CKLW one of the most popular contemporary stations in North America. Most of the air personalities working at the Big Eight never experienced sharing a show with an engineer prior to arriving here. Now, all of the Big Eight disk jockeys swear by the setup and enjoy the teamwork utilized in producing a highly rated show."

There are some disk jockeys who prefer to engineer their own show. Tom Clay, one of the great one-on-one on-the-air communicators of all time and well-known in the Detroit area as a disk jockey, was extremely good at live on-air production—talking over the intro of a record and off the outro, weaving back and forth between two records spinning at the same time on two turntables (always on the right word or the right musical note), or producing a live special. Not even the best engineer can read a disk jockey's mind and it would have taken that kind of mentalist to keep up with Clay. He believes that he and Frank Ward (one of the great rock disk jockeys of Buffalo) were the first to use modern production techniques with records—talking over the intro and off the outro.

Dave Dexter Jr., formerly an executive with Capitol Records and now a staff member of *Billboard* magazine, said that Al Jarvis was the first disk jockey. Until Jarvis, various announcers played records on radio, usually in the same solemn tones with which they read the poetry broadcast on the same station. "Al Jarvis had migrated to Los Angeles from Canada." He'd been a bank teller, but in Los Angeles he talked his way into a job as announcer at KFWB. According to Dexter, Jarvis liked music and he enjoyed records. He made $15 a week and from the beginning, he talked about records. "Here's a swell new orchestra from England," he might ad lib. "It has a big sound like Paul Whiteman and the leader is Jack Hylton. The song is a big success in Germany and we think it will soon be up on the *Lucky Strike Hit Parade* now that they've put English words to it. Let me know what you think of Jack Hylton's brand new Victor recording of 'Just a Gigolo.' "

Dexter said that Jarvis got his information about song and artists from *Billboard, Metronome,* and *Variety.* And as the mail flowed into KFWB, he learned that none of the other guys at the station read the trades. "I told them I acquired all those facts about musicians and songs up in Canada," he said. By the time other announcers on the station began to copy him, he had started a program called *Make Believe Ballroom* that ran five and six hours a day and sponsors were waiting in line.

A young man who worked as a library assistant and gopher at KFWB quit and moved to New York, where he eventually started his own version of *Make Believe Ballroom* on WNEW. Dexter said, "The late Martin Block was to become a far more publicized and wealthier radio personality, but Jarvis never became bitter. 'He was a bright guy who had talent and determination', Jarvis said." Jarvis and others like Ira Cook and Peter Potter were to become famous on the West Coast, but Block was to become the king of disk jockeys. Block felt that a disk jockey was honor bound to serve his listeners by playing the new releases from leading record companies as well as some of the smaller labels. He also felt that the listener should be told something about the record before it was played in order to learn something about the record artist and the songwriter. "If the platter is a good one," Block said in a 1942 *Billboard,* "the most effective type of direct marketing has just taken place. And sales are sure to reflect the airing of the disk."

Thus, the disk jockey was born.

Since that time the disk jockey has evolved and, considering the attitude Block had, perhaps it was for the best. We may fondly look back on Arnie "Woo Woo" Ginsberg of Boston and his cowbells and train whistles, Gary Stevens and his Woolybooger, and the disk jockey with his suitcase of wild tracks, but that type of disk jockey has little place in today's radio. Inadvertently, Stevens proved this at WMCA in New York in its Top 40 days under program director Ruth Meyer. Stevens saw the handwriting on the wall, to use an appropriate cliche, and resigned, but was still on the air for a month or more. Since he was leaving the station, ostensibly to market TV shows in Europe (which he did for a couple of years before returning to the United States to become a very successful general manager for the Doubleday radio chain, first at KRIZ in Phoenix, then KDWB in Minneapolis), Stevens cut back on all of the labors involved with doing wild tracks. He was as surprised as anyone when the next ratings came out and showed he'd increased in audience without the Woolybooger!

Bill Drake's theories on the disk jockey had begun to shape a new destiny for the jock on the air. Wild tracks and cowbells and Woolyboogers were considered clutter by Bill Drake. And the so-called "time and temp" jock was arriving and was to reshape radio, though Bill Drake hadn't thought of taking the disk jockey into that limbo himself (his own disk jockeys included such zany machine-gun people as the Real Don Steele and the witty Robert W. Morgan, among others, on stations such as KHJ in Los Angeles).

What's expected of a disk jockey

Each individual radio station dictates what is expected of their disk jockeys. Just as the characteristics of people differ, radio stations take on atmospheres. Some disk jockeys are lucky enough to become involved with a radio station where their own personality seems to mesh with that of the radio station, e.g., Mike Reineri—the morning man at WIOD in Miami; Dan Ingram—the afternoon man at WABC in New York; Dick Haynes—the morning man at KLAC in Los Angeles; and Salty O'Brine—the 30-year morning man at WPRO in Providence, R.I. At most radio stations a disk jockey will work during his business life, though he'll have to make adjustments to the demands of the radio station. At most radio stations, the atmosphere is determined or guided by the program director. At some stations, such as WSB in Atlanta, the total motif of the station, which is quite dignified and sophisticated, is largely due to general manager Elmo Ellis whose personal charisma characterizes that of the radio station. Harvey Glascock, when he was general manager of WNEW-AM in New York, gave the station a certain dramatic flair that was literally an outgrowth of his own personality. Pat O'Day, when he managed KJR in Seattle, gave the station its character, guided that character, and contributed to it.

On the other hand, when KRIZ in Phoenix was a giant power, program director Pat McMahon virtually *was* the radio station. As proof, when new owners took over, the general manager who was hired for the station terminated McMahon (it didn't matter that the radio station was No. 1 in the market, the new general manager wanted his own man in that position). The result was that the radio station dropped in ratings and even to this day has never regained that previous command of the market, though it does well now.

In any case, if a disk jockey doesn't already have an extremely good working knowledge of the radio station—its image in the market (or the image that the general manager and/or program director is trying to create), the disk jockey's duties and what's expected of him both on and off the air—then he should have a personal talk with the program director and get everything straight before taking the job. Actually, the wise program director briefs the disk jockey prior to hiring him. Once he is hired by the radio station, the disk jockey has a greater responsibility to his job than the ordinary person who works in a bank or in a factory, because of the unique obligations a radio station has toward the public. Owners own or lease the property where the studio is, the transmitter site, and the equipment; the broadcast frequency itself belongs to the public and is governed by the Federal Communications Commission. The broadcaster has a license to broadcast and must constantly renew that license at the end of a given period (presently, the period is three years, although broadcasters are striving to gain a five-year license agreement). The responsibility of the license is not only the owner's, but also descends via the chain of command to the actions of the disk jockey. In February 1974, the FCC notified WBAP in Fort Worth that it was liable for a $4,000 fine because of failure to log disk jockey promotional plugs as commercials.

At the time, the FCC took the opportunity to warn all stations that the broadcast of ad-libs that promoted a show or dance in which a disk jockey had an interest is commercial matter and must be logged as such. Also, time given to playing the records of artists who are scheduled to appear at a disk jockey-promoted event is also considered commercial matter. The FCC reported in its 1973 field investigation that on several occasions WBAP all-night disk jockey Bill Mack had promoted his personal appearances at nightclubs and that disk jockey Don Thomson promoted his paid personal appearance at a western wear outlet. The station did not include all the plugs as commercial time on the log. This whole area is somewhat nebulous. In some cases, the FCC considers the entire program produced by a record label which features that label's product as a commercial—though it may be a very entertaining show.

What's really messy about the entire stiutation is that sometimes the rules are not clearly defined. Whatever rules and regulations the program director outlines for the staff, the disk jockey is obligated to follow. These may be FCC or station taboos. If the station has a format, the disk jockey owes it to the station and to his own professionalism to follow that format precisely. If every record is slated, there is no excuse for not playing a given record, and there can be no excuse for adding a record not slated. If (as at most stations) the disk jockey is allowed to create his own show from a list of records or from several lists of different records, he must follow the programming guidelines set down by the program director.

It would also be practical for the disk jockey to keep the program director informed of any unusual activities that happened during his shift. If something seriously goes wrong during an on-air shift, the disk jockey should immediately telephone the program director regardless of the time. One of the major responsibilities of the program director is to be aware of what's going out over the air—music, news, disk jockey patter—everything; its not exactly an 8 AM-5 PM responsibility. It would be senseless to telephone the program director at 3 AM just because a record is scratched and you can't find the backup copy or because a cart fouled. Talk to the program director; he'll let you know what kind of trouble necessitates a phone call.

At WABC in New York, emergency instructions are posted on the wall of the control room—right at the top: Call the program director. If the power fails, the disk jockey should switch to an auxiliary generator and get the station back on the air; then call the program director. During the legendary power blackout that hit New England and New York several years ago, Lee Gray was doing a radio show at WTRY in Troy, N.Y. When the electricity went kaput, he had the foresight to climb into the remote unit and go back on the air with reduced-power equipment—the station was off the air only moments. At WMCA in New York, then a Top 40 station, the auxiliary generator kicked on automatically. The evening disk jockey immediately went to emergency status and broadcast news with the help of the station's staff; for the moment, hit records were forgotten. Ironically, the news station in town, WINS, went to music. When power failed in Manhattan a standby transmitter went on in New Jersey, and there was a music tape slotted that hit the air until WINS engineers could get things straightened out.

If emergency instructions aren't posted or explained to you, it's your professional obligation to find out what the procedures should be—regardless of the market size—because emergencies happen everywhere. When a flood hit a little east Texas town, the station quickly got permission (it was a daytime operation) from the FCC and went on the air full-time until the emergency was over. That 'above and beyond the call of duty' broadcasting earned the station an award at the International Radio Programming Forum, as well as the sincere appreciation of every citizen in its town.

Not every program director is a polished and experienced craftsman—the program director may have been promoted only last week from the ranks of the disk jockey. Anyway, even a program director with 20 years' experience doesn't profess to know everything about radio (he might, but that's his mistake because even the great program directors have to learn new procedures every day in order to keep up). Although no one can fault you for not doing so, it's your professional duty to assist whenever and wherever possible. If you have a suggestion for improving the format or even the image of the station in the marketplace, then tell the program director. The wise program director, experienced or not, will set up procedures to accept your input, not suggestion boxes, but disk jockey and/or staff parties where people can let their hair down (excuse the cliche) and participate in the total radio station. This "rapport party" should include all members of the staff, including sales. In many cases, one or more of the sales account executives are former disk jockeys or program directors. For instance, at KCBQ in San Diego, one of the first morning disk jockeys on the station was Harry Martin. He was known as Happy Hare and became one of San Diego's most successful and popular personalities of all time (his ratings on the morning show rose from 3 to 40 in one year!). Can you imagine having all that professional disk jockey experience at your beck and call, both as a disk jockey and as a program director? You would be missing an opportunity to perfect your craft as a professional disk jockey, if you did not take advantage of the occasion to seek the advice of the old pros.

True, a healthy ego is what sustains you as a disk jockey. It's what keeps you going despite bad ratings, and lets you philosophically accept the times you have good ratings; it's what makes you do a good show right after the program director has ripped apart your entire morning's work (when you had thought you'd done great); it's what keeps you going even though the general sales manager just passed you in the hallway and said that you'd lost the local supermarket account for him forever because you'd played their commercial next to the carwash ad or loused up on that tag line. But the good disk jockey doesn't survive on ego. At best, he accepts it within himself as the factor that keeps him going in a very crazy business. A disk jockey should enjoy being egotistical as does Larry Lujack, who takes everything (including himself) with a grain of salt, and shrugs a bad day—as well as most good days—off with determination to do even better tomorrow.

What really makes a good disk jockey is craftsmanship. Although this has not always been the case, the disk jockey of today is a professional craftsman of even greater skill than the silversmith who deals only in metal, the banker who deals only in money, or the magician who deals only in sleight of hand. The disk jockey—and we should be proud of that term—has to maneuver both tangible and intangible objects. Besides cueing up records, spots, IDs, PSAs, and cross plugs of other disk jockeys, the disk jockey must deal with influencing people's minds. This comes about in the patter between records (if he's allowed to talk); the way he or she blends the music; and the manner in which he creates the entire show (which may consist of elements from news to music, humor to documentary, and jingles to the PSAs). The disk jockey must consider all of the elements as his working tools. So, if you can pick something up (however minor) from one of the persons at your station, or any station you may listen to, do it. And this brings up a very valuable asset in our business.

The disk jockey in a major market is usually, though not always, doing something right. The copycat syndrome is a crime or a sin, whichever. But the stealing syndrome is all right, as long as it's tailored to fit you. By that, I mean that even Einstein did not "invent" $E=MC^2$. What he did was synthesize all known data on the subject up to that time and put it all together. Mike Joseph used to claim that he was the first to "invent" a programming technique. He might have done a few things first, but it was Bill Drake who synthesized everything and as a result became one of the greatest program directors of today's time.

So, when you happen to be rambling through the next town, if you aren't DXing (listening up and down the dial), then you'd better get into selling shoes or real estate. That disk jockey in Albuquerque, Denver or Dirt, Neb., may have found a unique way of coming out of a produced spot or the news. He or she may have a new gag line about that old Rolling Stones or Tony Bennett record which you think is a little stagnant (this is an illustration that even a tired record to you might be made interesting with the proper intro). Fortunately, the disk jockey has several crutches to lean upon that can help make his show interesting, though not entirely, because anything used to excess may become boring. This includes the disk jockey who doesn't talk but plays music and the disk jockey who doesn't play music but only talks. A disk jockey's talent often lies in the blending process.

The crutches may include a lot of things. For example, one-liner bits of information about the records or artists taken from a publication such as *Kaleidoscope,* the back of album jackets, or publicity handouts from record companies. In addition, one can glean information from trade publications such as *Billboard, Record World, Cashbox* or record news publications including the *Bill Gavin Report* or *Radio and Records.* In the consumer field, publications such as *Rolling Stone, Gig, Cream, Crawdaddy, Music City News,* and others can help. And there are various regional publications that provide news. One should not have to wait for newspapers and/or magazines such as *Time,* or *Readers Digest*—you have to be faster and more aware of your specific audience.

Another crutch (although it's unfair to call them that because they are information services that help the disk jockey entertain—as opposed to just playing records) is the humor services. In Los Angeles, Ed Hider operates a humor service called Hype Ink, and he also does fill-in disk jockey work on such stations as KFI. His entire radio career is funny, as opposed to being a gag.

Ed Hider started in the Binghamton, N.Y. area and remarks:

"This being my hometown and my second job in radio, my father persuaded several of his business friends to sign up for my morning show as sponsors. Six months later, I was called into the front office and was given two pieces of advice as I was being fired. One, stick to a small market station and, two, you aren't cut out to do a comedy show on radio. Five years later, I was doing a morning comedy show on WINS in New York. Who said management has no insight?

"I was also told that if I would not ask my father's business friends to cancel, the station would send me a check, once a week, for the next three months. The result? I left. The sponsors didn't. And that ended the brief saga of the local boy trying to make good in his hometown. And just think: A few short ratings periods ago I was told: 'You're going to be here as long as I am, kid.' "

Hider writes continuous humor for disk jockeys, on a subscription basis. He also has books of running gags available. In his personal career, he notes: "The early 60s found me working mornings on a top rock station." He is afraid to identify it for fear of retribution. After all, "the owner is now there in that big Hooper in the sky, but his legend lives on. I should have sensed something when I reported for work the first morning at 5:30 AM and saw someone else sitting behind the console. It was the old jock who hadn't been told he was being replaced. So I had to break the sad news to him."

Hider is a good example of the trials and tribulations that can happen to a disk jockey in his career. Can you imagine having to tell another guy he's fired and you're replacing him? If Hider is funny today, it's because he *had* to laugh—it beats the hell out of crying. By the way, Hider once found out that he'd been fired from a weekend gig in Los Angeles when he noticed that his name was missing from the weekly work sheet on the bulletin board. In both these situations, a program director was hiding in a closet rather than doing his job. We'll talk more about that later.

Hider's experiences were not totally unique (I know of another market where the same thing was done), but he reported: "The owner had a cute way of connecting all of the telephones in the station to a speaker in his office so he could monitor all outgoing and incoming calls. Once, he overheard a conversation between a Chicago station and one of his jocks (would you believe Larry Lujack, who later went to WLS?) whom the Chicago station wanted to hire. A second call was to follow for a decision. When the phone call came into the station, the owner himself answered the phone as the jock, and rudely turned the job down, saying he had a change of heart and was very happy where he was. The owner also had the ingenious idea to give us all 'station names', so that when we left the audience wouldn't know the difference because the shows still had the same sound.

"Often, he would place ads in the trade papers for, 'A top jock for top pay at the station at the tippity top of the old pop crop.' " He would be flooded with air-checks from all over the country.

"My job was to go through all the tapes and copy down any contest ideas, one-liners, station promotion ideas, and even cut out bits of their jingles we could safely use by splicing in our own call letters at the end. Then, I was to erase all the tapes left over and use them for our own production purposes. This practice not only kept the station well supplied with tapes, but with 'original' ideas for at least six months before he placed another ad.

"One day, when he took me aside and said: 'You're going to be here as long as I am', I asked for a raise, which he promptly turned down, explaining, 'Sure, you're No. 1 now, but you could drop in the next book!' How could anyone argue with such brilliant logic? It was at that moment that I decided to move on and landed a job at WINS in New York City.

"When I gave my notice at that radio station, the owner refused to give me a release, which WINS required. I finally had to track down the owner, through a series of expensive lawyers, to finally get the release. When the new morning disk jockey came to replace me, he was told by the owner: 'I got Hider that job in the Big Apple and if you play your cards right, I'll do the same for you'."

Later in San Francisco a station was sold and the new manager put his arms around Hider and whispered: "I like you ... I like your attitude ... I like your work ... as far as I'm concerned ... (here it comes) ... you're going to be here as long as I am."

Since he had learned, obviously at radio manager's school, that the quickest way to show the home office you were making money was to let the high-priced help go. "I was fired. While I was on the air. During my show!

"While a record was playing, he called me out into the hallway to ask me something and, suddenly, out of nowhere a strange little guy with earphones growing out of his head ran into the studio, sat in my chair, and finished my show without even a word about where I'd gone."

However, by this time, Ed Hider had become a little more wise to the ways of radio. "The strange thing about this firing was that I only had a month to go on my contract. Being a little upset and putting my creative mind to work, vengeance was all I wanted. I persuaded five teenage girls to sign a letter saying the manager had made a pass at them, which, of course, he hadn't. Then, four engineers, who also had been recently fired, signed papers stating the manager had falsified station contests, which, again, he hadn't. I promptly visited my favorite friendly neighborhood lawyer, we promptly documented these facts and sent a threatening letter to the station.

"Needless to say, it did the trick. I was called in the next day and not only hired back, but at a raise in salary. The first week back on the job, the manager broke into my locker trying to find something incriminating against me to offset the charges I'd made. But, to no avail.

"When the remaining 30 days expired on my contract, I was fired again and I promptly sent him another letter. Again, I was summoned into his office and he made me an offer I could refuse. He wanted me to set up in business—with his money—producing all of the commercials for the station. He said he couldn't put me back on the air because it was . . . 'out of his hands at this point'."

But Hider never intended to follow through on the infractions. "My ego had been bent out of shape and I just wanted to do something about it," Hider said. "Six months later, I moved to Los Angeles and not only left my heart, but a paranoid manager, in San Francisco."

Other Entertainment Sources

Probably, Bob Orben does better than any other comedy service. However, one disk jockey named Tom Adams, who once worked at WIOD in Miami on the afternoon show, began typing up the one-line stuff he was using on the air and selling it as The Electric Weenie. It took a while for Tom Adams to make it, but eventually he was earning two or three times his WIOD salary with the Electric Weenie. One of the first things he did was move to Hawaii and recently did a morning show on an MOR station there, more or less just for fun. His earnings from The Electric Weenie are unbelievable. Other gag services abound, including The Fruitbowl, by Jay Trachtman in California.

It's not unprofessional to use humor sources, according to Gary Owens, who does the afternoon show on KMPC in Los Angeles. Owens is perhaps one of the funniest men on the air. "Ninety-nine percent of The Gary Owens Show is from the brain of Gary Owens," he said. "The other one percent may come from a variety of sources: (I'm an antiquarian book collector and have over 7,000 volumes); listeners; newspapers; friends; magazines; threatening letters; or gags from guys in the business trying to make a buck with a joke service." Owens believes that the beginner in radio should subscribe to every gag service possible.

Owens said, "When I was with Don Burden, Gordon McLendon, John Box, Crowell-Collier, and Winnie Ruth Judd, all the jocks were whizzing through their Orben books and tying the jokes in cleverly to the commercials or the events of the day. Even though I've been a comedy writer since I was in high school, there is no reason why you can't also use an additive to ease your daily strain. But I believe that one should never take a gag, per se. Instead, rewrite it in your own manner, reshaping it with your individual nuances or shtick. If you want to bring yourself into that category of performer who takes in mucho loot instead of scale, you must be an individual on the air."

In 1962, when a strike at KFWB in Los Angeles left several disk jockeys out of work, they got together to form Humor-Esq, a disk jockey gag service. Besides Gary Owens, the others included Joe Smith, now chairman of Elektra/Asylum Records (Joe Smith was a well-known Boston disk jockey several years ago); Bill Ballance, a disk jockey who launched the "feminine forum" type of show that was imitated coast to coast (Ballance is currently doing a talk show in Los Angeles); and writer Bob Arbogast.

When David Moorhead was a disk jockey, he had a personal collection of one-liners on index cards and filed alphabetically by topics. He was never without an instant quip on about every subject until a burglar hit his U-Haul trailer and stole his two most important items—his custom-tailored tux and his joke file. He offered an enormous reward for the joke file, but it never showed up.

Another important source of information is the chart data on records. Joel Whitburn, who operates a firm called Record Research in Milwaukee, publishes several booklets that cross-reference information from the *Billboard* magazine charts; these booklets are even more important to the program director in programming oldies. Personal research by a disk jockey can prove invaluable. The disk jockey who doesn't take every opportunity to learn about his market (the public) may soon not have a market to work in. Dan Daniel, when he was on WMCA during its Top 40 years, used to keep pretty close tabs on Manhattan. For instance, he might notice that Con Edison, the electric company, was digging again on Fifth Avenue and comment about it on the air, then tie it into a record.

Getting out into the public is valuable for the disk jockey. One disk jockey, who always manages to work major markets and does quite well in ratings, asks people he meets to listen to him on the air. And why not? If he meets 10 new people a week and actually persuades four of them to listen to him, and one of them turns up in ARB diary in a survey—the disk jockey might amply improve his audience ratings. Mentioning people on the air (listeners and potential listeners) is always good and the smaller the market, the greater the benefits. This is especially true in markets too small to have regular audience ratings of any kind—markets where the stations have to depend on community rapport for sales. The wise disk jockey keeps posted on news, especially local news, by reading local newspapers, magazines, watching television, and talking with people.

One very important asset is knowing the artists and the music you play. Attend concerts and nightclub performances. If you're in a good music area, then get to know local artists—Elvis Presley was big around Memphis and Shreveport, La., a long time before he became a national and international star; and Rusty Weir, bound for national success, has been performing around Austin, Tex., for a time along with several other outstanding artists. Just about every area of the country has local music people and any one of these people could leap to stardom at any time. Murray the K always capitalized on his early association with the Beatles on the air. George Klein, of WHBQ Memphis, is a friend of Elvis Presley; that kind of close rapport with music doesn't exactly hurt. Paul Drew, head of programming for the RKO Radio chain, has made use of his personal association with people like Paul McCartney and Elton John to obtain personal interviews and specials for his radio stations.

Obligations to Management

Very few disk jockeys are able to spend their entire business career on the air. Unless you're William B. Williams or Gene Klavan at WNEW-AM in New York or a similar legend in radio, you'd better plan an evolution in your career. Some of the legends of radio include John Gambling and his father, the late John Gambling Sr., who have been doing the morning show at WOR in New York for generations of listeners; Carl De Suze, who has been with WBZ in Boston more than 35 years; Gordon Hinkley, who has spent more than a quarter of a century at WTMJ in Milwaukee; Walter (Salty) Brine who has been at WPRO in Providence, R.I., throughout several changes in format, and program directors, and though nearing 60 years old, he's still king of the market; Barney Keep, who has been at KEX in Portland, Ore., about 32 years, gets up every morning at 4 AM in order to reach the station about 5:30 AM to hit the air at 6 AM; Wally Phillips, who has been with WGN in Chicago more than 20 years, garners more than a quarter of the city's listeners daily (which is usually all sold out in advertising); Dick Whittinghill, the morning man at KMPC in Los Angeles, has been with the MOR format station around 27 years and claims that he enjoys doing a morning show because it pays "more money and I can get away early for golf!"; and Howard Viken, who has been at WCCO in Minneapolis over 25 years, easily gains more than half of the radio audience and gets most of his material from newspapers, magazines, and music trade publications.

Perhaps one of the reasons these men have been legends—and remain so—is that they enjoy radio. Viken said that he enjoys informing listeners, entertaining them, and "being a close personal friend with each one in a kind of one-to-one relationship. The pay is good and being a local celebrity isn't all bad, though it does have its responsibilities." The only things that irritate him are reporting about the south St. Paul markets, "I don't know what the hell I'm reading"; and selling a product "that I don't believe lives up to its claims. But I enjoy my work so much that I actually don't have any real irritating aspects. And that must be why I've kept my good health and friendliness and a good number of listeners for quite a few years." He likes doing a morning show because "I am sharpest then; my listener is the most receptive because he is refreshed; and the audience is the largest we have all day. And it's the best time of our day, especially during the summer months when my wife cooks a great breakfast."

There are other legends and near legends in radio. Bob Van Camp is retired now from WSB in Atlanta. Robert E. Lee Harwick has been with KVI in Seattle about 17 years, and he's fairly young (only around 45) in comparison to Viken and some of the others. But Harwick is well established in the market and the list of his audience-involved expolits range from guiding a group to the top of Mt. Kilimanjaro to leading another group to push for tax reform in the state capitol.

Aside from being a public service, audience involvement is one of the key factors in becoming a legend or if not a legend, then at least a name in the market. However, the disk jockey should plan his career so that it evolves from being on the air to management. Thus, not only are client calls with a sales account executive important, but also educational. Incidentally, throughout his career, client calls may be part of a disk jockey's obligation to the general manager and sales manager—up to the largest market, such as New York. Not only is it impressive for a client to meet a disk jockey, but it's another aspect of getting out into the public—whether it's over lunch or at a cocktail party.

This is why lifestyle plays an important role in the career of a disk jockey. For a long time, long hair and beards were in and still are, if you wish to assume that kind of professional look, but long hair and beards can be neat especially if you're going to be out on an occasional client call. And it's all right to dress funky if you wish, but neatness is not a crime. If you're on a country station, there's nothing wrong with boots and Stetson, and on an MOR station, a suit and tie might be more appropriate. Naturally, there are no rules about lifestyles for disk jockeys, but some radio stations have standards that you may have to follow. The only guideline might be that you should have respect for your craft and that you should dress and act accordingly. A sports jacket or suit and tie might actually be more appropriate for a client call, depending either on the city and the station. And it would be advisable for the sales account executive to give you enough notice so that you won't be wearing blue jeans and a Rolling Stones teeshirt the particular day he needs you for a client call.

Client calls will help the disk jockey become adapted to a future career in sales, if he plans to head in that direction when his on-air days fade away. And you should be aware that the chances of being on the air as long as Whittinghill and Viken are pretty rare. The practical disk jockey builds up career alternatives. Some radio men have stepped sideways into the record industry (it is, in many ways, parallel to the radio industry). These include Joe Smith, who gave up being a disk jockey to become a record promotion man at Warner Bros. Records; Bob Sherwood, now involved in record promotion for Columbia Records, headquarters in New York; LeBaron Taylor, probably one of the greatest soul disk jockeys of all time who is now an executive with Columbia Records; and others such as Scott Shannon, Dutch Holland, Woody Roberts, Eddie Wright, Buddy Blake, Biff Collie, Joe Sullivan, and the late George Brewer. Wright once programmed WABQ in Cleveland; he became a personal artist manager and owns his own public relations firm in Los Angeles. Sullivan programmed WMAK in Nashville, then left to promote concerts and today manages the Charlie Daniels Band. Jonathan Fricke and Ron Elz went into record promotion, but are now back in radio.

However, radio men usually make careers in radio itself. Johnny Borders in Fort Worth and Terrell (Mitch Michaels) Methney are now in sales and management. Methney was once national program director of the Southern radio chain and programmed WMCA in New York in its last days as a music station (it is now two-way talk). Borders was a successful disk jockey in rock radio in Fort Worth as well as a program director. Ex-disk jockeys now in programming include Paul Drew, vice president of programming for RKO Radio; George Williams, national program director of Southern; Al Casey, Al Brady, Scotty Brink, Chuck Dunaway, and thousands of others. Very few program directors were not, at one time, disk jockeys. There is always the exception, such as Rick Sklar of ABC.

The next step could be into management. At one time, most radio station general managers came directly from the sales department. For a while, program directors were moving into sales in order to gain the experience to move into management when the opportunity came. And this is still a good idea. However, today many program directors and ex-disk jockeys are stepping directly into management roles, such as Woody Roberts at KTSA in San Antonio; Charlie Murdock, who manages one of the great stations—WLW in Cincinnati; David Moorhead stepped into management at WMMS, a Cleveland FM station, after being an operations manager and disk jockey at KMET in Los Angeles. Others include Jim Hilliard, general manager of WIBC in Indianapolis; Burt Sherwood, general manager of WMEE in Fort Wayne, Ind.; Norman Wain, now president of his own station in Dallas; and Don

Nelson, general manager of WIRE in Indianapolis and part owner in other radio operations.

Some radio men eventually end up in related radio fields. Bill Randle, one of the greatest Top 40 disk jockeys of all time, is now head of broadcasting for the University of Cincinnati. Todd Wallace, once program director of KLIF in Dallas, now operates an audience research firm called Radio Index in Phoenix. Jack McCoy, who once programmed KCBQ in San Diego, now has a firm called DPS that analyzes ARB ratings. Sebastian Stone operates a firm with Willis Duff in San Francisco that does research projects for radio stations; both are ex-program directors. Duff was head of a small broadcasting chain before teaming up with Stone in Entertainment Response Analysts.

As a disk jockey, you have obligations to other disk jockeys on the staff—expecially on the air. This ranges from cross plugs to promotion of your fellow disk jockeys, or working swing if the station doesn't have a part-time personality handy. It goes without saying that a certain amount of respect is due each person on your staff both on and off the air—if not for the individual, then for his craft which is the same as yours, and for the station which pays your salary. You also have an obligation to protect the radio station from problems with the FCC, by protecting its image both on the air and off the air. For example, you are required not only to notify a person on a phone call that he or she is on the air, but you must also obtain their permission before you put their call on the air.

Victims have complained to the FCC that embarrassing phone conversations have been broadcast without notice. The FCC warns that disk jockeys must have a beeper tone on any two-way phone call broadcast or it should be taped, and the caller must be notified up front. A 1966 public notice from the FCC about "Contests and Promotions Which Adversely Affect the Public Interest" and a public notice following that warn about prohibited practices—these include alarming the public about imaginary dangers, infringing on the right of privacy, and causing annoyance or embarrassment to innocent parties. For your information, many so-called phone calls aren't real. One disk jockey who quickly rose to fame from a Sacramento, Calif. radio station, actually recorded his calls in the station's studios with the program director or professional actor as the fall guy. And why not? These calls are intended to be entertainment bits, and a professionally produced entertainment bit stands up better than an impromptu thing.

Maintaining Your Professionalism

The one thing that you owe a radio station is respect. And you also owe it to your own professionalism to avoid signing off the job on the air. Because of bad incidents in the past, many program directors notify a disk jockey that he's been terminated after he ends his shift. Over the years, disk jockeys have gone on the air after being fired or after deciding to quit and did a number. This sort of stunt is uncalled for. It's certainly not conducive to a prosperous career, because word spreads among program directors and general managers. If a disk jockey has built a very strong reputation in a market, it might be wise to say goodbye in some manner when he leaves the radio station. Though he should leave it up to the program director whether he does say goodbye or not. Some radio stations have even held going away parties to wish the departing disk jockey good luck and that is good public relations. However, sometimes because of format, the program director might want to smooth over the abruptness of a disk jockey leaving and not mention anything at all on the air. With many of today's Top

40 or Q-format stations, the exchange of one disk jockey for another is hardly noticed.

In the case of WCFL in Chicago, when the rock format was dropped in favor of beautiful music, many of the disk jockeys signed off on the air, and to their credit, the majority did it with class. If you've been fired, it's probably best that you leave the air and the station as quickly as possible—not only for the station's benefit, but for your own. If a station has given you notice and you're still on the air, then you owe it to the radio industry to do a professional show until you segue into the news or a record for the last time on that frequency. For one thing, radio is a very small industry. The program director who decides you may not fit the sound he's trying to create, could one day be handling production on a station where you're the No. 1 disk jockey. There's a constant fluctuation in radio jobs. Jack Thayer was dropped from KLAC, then a talk station in Los Angeles, and four years later rose to become president of radio for NBC. George Wilson, fired many times, rose to become president of Bartell Broadcasters. Chuck Knapp, fired at WRKO in Boston because he couldn't adapt to the new Drake-style format, was hired the next day at WIXY in Cleveland with an increase in salary. Pat Patterson, when he departed WLW in Cincinnati, became program director of WKIX in Raleigh, N.C., in addition to being the station's morning man. Patterson literally owned the market—even the governor and the mayor call to go on the air with him. Incidentally, he makes more money today than he ever did on WLW and more than anyone else at that station other than the owner/manager.

Sometimes, a disk jockey in one city who is extremely successful can't do well in another city. Rege Cordic, a star in Pittsburgh, never amounted to much in Los Angeles. Most of the time a disk jockey can expect to work several cities in his career, and as his career progresses he should strive to work in larger cities.

Pat Whitley, a veteran program director now with WMEX in Boston, had this to say when he was programming WNBC in New York, "How do you get from there to here?"

1. Develop your own style, always remaining an individual, and never attempt to become a carbon copy of anyone else;

2. Do not get caught up in just one aspect of broadcasting. It is a multi-faceted field. It is important that you become involved with other departments in your radio station, such as sales. Get out and meet your sponsors and understand their needs. Remember, besides ratings points, there will always be a bottom line;

3. Get involved in your community. Communicate with your audience on a one-to-one basis without the aid of a microphone. Look them in the eye and you will be able to better understand the many lifestyles you're speaking to daily. Never attempt to relate to an audience by only being humorous. That's only one aspect of being a personality. It's important to your development that you let the audience know you are one of them and you are just as concerned about the needs of the community as they are. This kind of disk jockey not only builds an audience, he becomes a public necessity;

4. Be prepared to learn just as much from failure as success, and be mentally prepared for both to come rapidly;

5. Never leave a radio station without being certain you deserve and would receive a good reference rating from management;

6. If you are successful in both ascertainment and accompaniment of Steps 1 through 5, you will then achieve a prerequisite for a major league broadcaster—self-confidence.

"Finally, bear in mind the most exciting, challenging and sometimes discouraging years of your career are yet to come. Wear them well, and broadcasting will reward you well. And never forget steps 1 to 6—if you want to travel to the top."

Local press is important. This comes in more than one manner; if your station has a promotion and publicity director, (even if he's also a disk jockey), it's his job to try to gain stories in local newspapers and magazines. Usually, these are easy to obtain; sometimes the disk jockey can get the publicity himself. Gary Owens at KMPC recommends that the disk jockey write and submit articles, reviews, etc., to local and regional publications. When J. J. Stone was a disk jockey at KFH in Wichita, he was able to get press in the *Wichita Beacon.* He once discovered a guy named Mickey Briggs who, of all things, played his mouth. The natural thing to do is call up the local paper and ask if they're interested. Stone broadcast a brief interview and a performance with Briggs playing "Popcorn" and the resultant picture in the *Beacon* was a bonus. Tom Campbell, both in Ohio and in San Francisco, managed to write a local newspaper column on music artists. In just about every city in the nation, the local newspaper is willing to accept a free weekly column from a music expert, meaning you.

Some events warrant coverage because they're a benefit event. For instance, KIOI in San Francisco broadcast the Snack Concert one Sunday in March 1975, about 10 hours of live music ranging from Bob Dylan to the Grateful Dead, organized by Bill Graham to raise funds for athletic and cultural projects in local schools. That kind of public involvement is extremely valuable not only for building a radio station's image, but also a disk jockey's image and usually results in free press. In addition, there are several trade publications—*Billboard, Broadcasting, The Gavin Report, Cashbox, Radio & Records, Record World*—that have columns about disk jockeys, program directors, and managers. You can usually get a couple of lines about yourself and your station in these columns. All it takes is a postcard, letter, or phone call. In any case, you should be striving to build up a rapport with someone at each of these publications.

5 Getting another job

If you're a daydreamer, you probably think you're good and that you'll receive gigantic ratings, then the world will hear about you, and a New York program director will fly to listen to you and immediately hire you for the major markets.

Well, in truth, this sometimes does happen. Miracles aren't uncommon in radio—miracles of all kinds. Just out of curiosity, Bobby Cruz sent an aircheck to Rick Sklar, vice president of program development, and Sklar thought he sounded a little like WABC's Dan Ingram (even sounding a little bit like Ingram is a desirable thing in the radio world). The result is that Cruz is now doing the all-night show on WABC in New York, a pretty large step up from Miami. When Bobby Rich, program director of KFMB-FM (they call it B-100) in San Diego, wanted to build a new staff as the station went to a live rock format, he flew back into Oklahoma and Texas and listened to many radio stations seeking potential San Diego disk jockeys—and he got them.

But the disk jockey who waits for the world to discover him may have to wait an awfully long time. The best advice would be to constantly improve yourself; this will help you keep your present job. Since you may not be able to judge your own flaws, get a friend to critique your aircheck, and you can return the favor. If you're lucky enough to have a friend who has already worked his way up to a larger market, perhaps he'll critique your aircheck. Sometimes, you can build up a rapport with a program director in a major or medium market and he'll give you advice.

All of the disk jockeys who applied for an opening in late 1975 at WLW in Cincinnati got lucky. Mike O'Shea, who was then program director, commented: "I have never listened to so many airchecks in my life. At last count, we had received 516 with about a dozen a day still coming in. Thanks to a four-day Thanksgiving weekend, I've had a chance to review all of them.

"What amazes me is the consistently high quality of these young broadcasters that are applying. I'm very encouraged at the talent and hard-core enthusiasm so many of these presentations gave. I've got over 50 finalists to choose from. Of these 50, over half of them could work any shift on this station. The most encouraging thing about it is that nearly all of them are in their mid to low 20s and have four to five years of experience in markets like Moline; Huntington, W. Va.; Spartanburg, S.C.; and Jacksonville, Fla. And they're ready for Cincinnati, Dallas, or even New York."

O'Shea, who left WLW to climb higher in management with WFTL in Fort Lauderdale, Fla., commented that every disk jockey wants "to do their own thing and express themselves in their own manner" on their show. "But a developing talent needs direction and critiquing in what I call their formative years—when they get four to five years of experience; after five years they've mastered the mechanical and methodical end of broadcasting and it's time to start polishing and perfecting the talent end of the business. It is then that they need the direction from their program

52

director or manager."

O'Shea answered all of the letters and tapes sent in. "I remember only too well when I was jockin' and would send out a tape into oblivion." But most program directors probably wouldn't have taken the trouble; after all, they're probably working from 10 to 16 hours a day and often on weekends, and they simply don't have time (and probably don't even have a secretary) to help though they'd like to. A disk jockey can critique himself, if he's a real student of the business. Record an aircheck and put it on the shelf two to four weeks before listening; you'll be amazed at the little things you'll notice which can stand improving or smoothing out.

Another method of keeping a job is to become ingrained in the community by spearheading charity causes and becoming known in the advertising community, so that if management even wanted to hire another disk jockey they would have to think twice about it. A case in point is that when Gerry Peterson took over programming at KCBQ in San Diego he let most of the disk jockeys go and hired men who he felt would fit the format better. He did not replace Shotgun Kelly, since Kelly was chairman of at least one major local charity event, plus he was involved in countless civic projects.

However, let's assume that you have made vast improvements in your work, your ratings are pretty good, and your image off air is decent. You feel it's time to move on to a larger market and to a better program director who'll be able to teach you more. Assuming that you have been constantly making airchecks, one of the last three or four should be pretty good. Sharpen it up with some editing and splicing, but not too much. Remember that getting the new job is only one facet—you have to be good enough to keep it. True, you could go into a studio and produce a damned good aircheck. One Miami disk jockey did this and got a New York job; but as soon as the contract ran out, so did his New York job and he had trouble getting back on the air in Miami. It's much better to build a career at your own pace than to get a job on false pretenses. There are many stories about disk jockeys rising rapidly to the top—and just as rapidly down because they hadn't paid enough dues. If you don't have an aircheck taken off the air and you're forced to produce one, by all means tell the program director at the station where you're applying for a job. If he has any qualms about your produced aircheck, but likes other aspects of your work, at least he'll give you a chance to do an audition at his station.

Usually, an aircheck can be made on a cassette; the cassette player has become a daily working tool of the program director. However, the traditional aircheck is on a little three-inch reel—music and news is chopped down and mostly edited out. The aircheck should include an intro and outro on several records, live commercials, and anything else that you may do during your show ranging from news to weather. The aircheck should be in a new box and on a new tape. An aircheck done on frayed tape or in a tape box that previously contained a PSA from some church group, may not bother all program directors. However, it might bother the program director who's offering the job (at $22,000 a year) that you wanted very badly.

Airchecks are not cheap. Throughout your career it's going to be a burdensome expense and usually frustrating because the station seldom sends them back. Postage will also put a dent in your pocketbook. You can help cut down on such expenses by:

1. Selecting the markets and stations you would like to work, and directing your attention to only those choices;

2. Sending out airchecks to only those radio stations that are looking for disk jockeys

(listings of job openings can be found in various trade publications and often in state radio association publications).

After a good clean aircheck, one of the most important aspects of seeking a job is the resume. You'd be surprised how many people in radio don't know how to do a resume. First, it should be concise, brief (no more than a page to a page and a half) and very readable. (See sample on opposite page.) The most important aspects of the resume are your job experiences, skills and qualifications, and references (you don't have to have many, but it's advisable to have a general manager, a program director or two, and a fellow disk jockey, plus one or two non-radio references such as a local banker, the editor of a radio trade publication, the president of your state radio association or someone similar. Always ask permission to use someone as a reference.

Incidentally, if you've built a valid and strong rapport with station management where you work, the possibility is strong that when it's time for you to move onward and upward, they'll help.

Programming is a science with Gene Nelson, station manager and program director of WLCS in Baton Rouge, La. He conducts work sessions with the disk jockeys to help them improve their on-air work. This is done in several ways; one method is to aircheck the disk jockey on a random basis, unknown to the disk jockey. Nelson goes over these airchecks with the disk jockey, not in a cruel way, but as constructively as possible. He also obtains airchecks of successful disk jockeys in larger markets and plays them for the disk jockeys at WLCS. In one week the staff listened to disk jockeys from WQAM in Miami, WIXY in Cleveland, KILT in Houston, and CKLW in Detroit.

"I have every deejay listen to these tapes. How else is a guy going to improve unless he listens to people supposedly better?"

The alumni of Nelson's workshop sessions includes disk jockeys such as Ron Lundy of WABC, New York, Bob Raleigh Gaines, and Skip Boussard.

"We're a medium market station, but the goddamndest medium market you ever heard!" Nelson said.

It's true that you will meet a few crazy people in radio—at the management level as elsewhere, but Gene Nelson has no animosity when a disk jockey leaves for a larger market. After all, the guy who leaves takes a part of Nelson with him.

Don Nelson (no relation) is general manager of WIRE in Indianapolis; he called in his play-by-play sports announcer the other day and told him: "I know you're ready for a larger market and a better paying job. You're good. Why don't you look around—see if you can find a job." But Don Nelson wanted the guy, if he hadn't found a better position in a given time, to agree to another year in Indianapolis. This kind of frankness between the on-air talent and management is the kind of atmosphere that should be fostered by management. In the case of Don Nelson, if a disk jockey or other staff member levels with him, he'll help the guy look. There are many reasons for a disk jockey or program director wanting to change jobs. These may range from wanting to be close to relatives, liking a particular city, or having a local sideline business (Deano Day, a country disk jockey at WDEE in Detroit, owns a local country music nightclub that is doing quite well financially; if he were to move to another city, it could mean a loss in total earnings).

There have been cases of managers firing a disk jockey just because he was looking to move onward. Unfortunately, it's one of the handicaps of the business. But, if you're working at your career in a serious, constructive manner, you wouldn't be at a radio station where such a manager is in control. If a manager or program director can

SAMPLE RESUME

Scotty Rocque
2800 Moraga Dr.
Los Angeles, CA 90024

213-476-3953

SEEKING:	Late afternoon or evening show on a medium market country music FM station. Fringe benefits important. Salary open.
EXPERIENCE:	1973-present—3-7 PM personality and production director, KLAC, Los Angeles.
	1969-1973—7-midnight personality and music director, KLIF, Dallas.
	1968-1969—weekend personality, WRCP, Philadelphia.
SPECIAL SKILLS:	Production; strong knowledge of country music with personal collection dating back to rare Jimmie Rodgers records; audience research.
CREDITS:	Wrote, produced, hosted award-winning documentary called "Up With Country"; 1970 winner Best Public Service Documentary, International Radio Programming Forum. This was later rebroadcast on 42 major radio stations throughout southwest.
	Speaker, annual Country Music Seminar, Nashville, 1968.
	Speaker, annual convention, "Radio '75," Sydney, Australia.
	Hosted weekly country music syndicated radio show, three hours, produced by Target Syndications, Los Angeles, called "Country Starlight." It was featured for 1973-74 on 21 radio stations coast to coast.
SOCIAL:	Advisory Committee, music industry benefit dinner, City Of Hope, for 1973 and 1974 representing radio.
	Member, International Radio and Television Society, Country Music Association, Friends of John Edwards Memorial Foundation at UCLA, others.
	Contributed to activities on anti-drug abuse projects both in public and ultra-public, on air and in various local committees.
EDUCATION:	University of Texas, Austin, B. J.
	UCLA courses in Spanish, music, economics
PERSONAL:	Married, father of three boys, age 43, born in Brady, Tex.; veteran, U.S. Army; wife Barbara is a professional writer of NBC-TV network programs such as *The Dr. Joyce Brothers Show* and magazine articles in *Family Circle*, etc.

check your references when you apply for a job, you have every right to check out the station, the manager, and the program director. Call another disk jockey in the same market; if you know of a trade publication that is close to the scene, then call the radio-TV editor. Generally, word spreads about messy stations.

There was one general manager at a major market Top 40 station who developed a bad reputation in radio. He kept this reputation from the owners, but not from the firm that eventually bought the station who wondered why he'd never been able to keep a good jock for any length of time, even if he could hire one. The truth is he was seldom able to lure a talented serious disk jockey to the station. When a disk jockey would leave the station, this manager always found a few bad words to say about him. The same goes for his ex-program directors, and as you might have expected, he had many.

If you get a valid stigma on your record it's not the end, but it is difficult to overcome. One disk jockey had problems in Akron but ended up in a larger market because he leveled with the management at that station and they believed him. One disk jockey had the bad mouth put on him four stations before that kept him from getting a New York job, but he ended up in Connecticut and has done well. Disk jockeys, especially in Top 40 or country music radio (sometimes r&b radio, too) were sometimes a little wild. Perhaps they didn't understand the industry or the industry didn't understand them. Who knows?

The real idiotic troublemaker has no place in radio—we hope! A few years ago, a medium market program director wrote this note: "I just had to write and let you know about a terrible disease going around in the broadcast industry. It's called: The___ ___. To begin with, the guy is a basket case! I hired him because I needed a strong talk factor at the time and he was that. Unfortunately, he was impossible to direct. We are a very total personality-oriented/entertainment-oriented radio station, but his was probably the most obnoxious personality I've ever run across. Nevertheless, I tried with him, tolerated him, and watched as he attempted to set up two of the other guys on my staff, apparently because he didn't like them. He'd even hide oldies to make it appear as if others were ripping them off. And lie? I couldn't believe it! If there was a hurricane going on, he'd look you right in the eye and tell you it was a beautiful and sunny day! So, after all this (and I was especially surprised to witness his total lack of professionalism in things like being on time to work—I mean, 12 years or 15 years or 20 years or however long he has been in the business!) the crowning blow came when I was driving home one Saturday. I heard him talk for 20 minutes without playing one single record. *Twenty minutes!*

"So, I got home and called him. 'Tighten up a little, okay?', 'Okay, no problem.' Fifteen minutes later, I got a call from my general manager who had gotten a call from our newest salesman (who didn't know what in the hell radio was all about anyway). He'd received a call from___ ___ who had stated that he quit.

"I called___ ___back. 'I hear you quit?' 'Right.' 'You going to give me two weeks?' 'No, today's the last day.' A weekend goes by. No word from this supposed disk jockey."

The program director made other arrangements for Monday night, but on Monday, the disk jockey was in the office of the general manager asking for his job back. After a couple of meetings, the disk jockey realized he was not going to be allowed back on the air.

"But that's not where it ended," stated the now battered program director. "He went to as many of our sponsors as he could find and really put the bad mouth on me—everything from sexual deviation to hard drug use, to me being wanted on a manslaughter charge in Ohio. He sent threatening letters to people, and those who wouldn't help him get revenge, he went after. He wrote an anonymous letter to a general manager saying that two of the station's disk jockeys were dope fiends.

"It got to the point that he was actually calling random numbers in the phone book and telling people all these stories, the prime one of which was that I had been fired and he didn't quit. He even took that story to the Atlanta owner of this station."

Fortunately, that kind of person, a minority, has been fading from radio. And that's all for the good. Radio is too much in the public ear to tolerate foul-ups. One person can shatter the careers of many, simply because the press is not too friendly, and the disk jockey may often be the most closely watched figure in the community among people of impressionable age-groups—from 12-34 and especially 12-15. If you do something good, you're heroic; if you do something bad, you're abominable—there is seldom a mid-point. Hero or villian, the choice is often yours.

This is why you, personally, have an obligation to your listeners, in addition to your program director, manager and owner, and fellow staff members. You must never bore them. You must never fail to keep them totally informed, musically and otherwise. And you must never violate their trust.

Voice Styles

Aside from your personal appointment on the air and off, there are many craftsmanship skills that must be developed from basic training in order to give you proper background so that you can use your talent to its fullest potential. One of these skills is the voice itself. The voice is a tool. If you've got to give it a parallel, think of it as the chisel a sculptor uses to create a work of art. Every inflection over the oral chords of a master means something. The disk jockey with a well-trained voice can entertain you, charm you, warp your thinking (even on trivial matters), convince you to buy a lawn mower you don't need (but not when you live on the 23rd floor of an apartment building—no listener is really that dumb), sell you a new car (Detroit believed for years, quite profitably to stockholders, that everyone had to have a new car every year because this year's model had a longer fin—remember those years when you were assured that Cadillac, Plymouth, and other cars were more stable with fins in spite of the fact that all cars were stable, with or without fins, at the former speed limit of 65 m.p.h.? Though cars with or without fins have been stable at 100 miles an hour).

The voice is more important in radio than in television, where a pretty face and a good public relations staff might pave your way to the presidency of the United States. Or a poor tape deck might lead the way out of the presidency (it should be noted that very few radio men would have made the mistake Nixon made; at least they would have had the foresight to throw those productions into the erase bin).

There are many types of voice styles that you may develop. Some of the better disk jockeys develop more than one voice. Dick Haynes has invented a character who does the time on his show on KLAC, Los Angeles. Gary Owens admits to being able to do a few voices. The old man or old woman voice is not difficult to do for an experienced disk jockey. Joey Reynolds was able to do more than two dozen voices. However, at one time, Reynolds also held the record for losing a vast number of major market radio jobs. Eddie Payne, better known on the air as Jimmy Rabbitt, was known for losing more jobs in a major market, namely Los Angeles, where he lost jobs on such call letters as KLAC, KMET, KHJ, KABC-FM, KRLA, KROQ, KLOS, KBBQ, and KGBS-FM. And you could probably credit another call letter or two to the fantastic Rabbitt. In between some of those call letters he had to break broncos for a living. If he'd been able to do voices, he might have had less job problems. The same could be said of Dale Andrews, once program director of WCBM in Baltimore, who always kept his license to drive such things as bulldozers and trucks—he needed it on occasion.

Among the voice styles that you should master a speaking knowledge of are:

1. Smooth, polished;

2. Machine-gun, wild, zany;

3. Hip, extremely knowledgeable about music and record acts especially for kids on an evening show;

4. Sexy, being slightly risque;

5. Smart aleck (also for kids; this doesn't always work too well, though some disk jockeys have risen to fame doing so, e.g. Larry Lujack); it can appeal to youth as well as adults;

6. Insulting (this is a form of being smart aleck and has worked well for disk jockeys such as Don Imus and Robert W. Morgan—on occasion, though Morgan never overused the style);

7. Informative (not about records but about local activities ranging from traffic to weather);

8. Friendly (especially important in a country music format);

9. Wooing (a technique used quite effectively by some midday disk jockeys, but which you try to charm housewives and other nonworking females—the majority of listeners who are available to radio at that particular time);

10. Sophisticated (used much too often by classical and jazz disk jockeys who often think they're above a mass audience and talk to just a few ultrasophisticated listeners and gain them and not much else);

11. Humorous (who can explain humor?);

12. Time and temp (the disk jockey who gives the name of the artist, the record, time of day and sometimes the weather, all briefly);

13. The announcer (the man who tells you the station you're listening to and perhaps his name).

Style doesn't mean as much as that undefinable quality to communicate. It's called many things, but what it essentially means is the ability to get people to listen to you, and then being consistent so that the audience wants to tune in again and again. It's a better magic than Houdini ever performed.

Victor Ives, program director of KSFO in San Francisco began his radio career while in high school working as a go-fer at a San Francisco station. He has worked at stations in Tucson, Ariz.; Portland, Ore.; and Bakersfield, Calif., and said that he is still thrilled by radio's "most unique potential, its ability to provoke an emotional or intellectual response from its listeners . . . listeners are exchanging energies with the broadcaster. When radio causes the listeners to cope with broadcast material either because it's so funny, so beautiful, so ludicrous, so profound, so informative, or so interesting it's performing its greatest magic . . . frankly, I'm proud to say I'm in show business!" He remembered the kind of radio magic "as great as when millions conjured up mental images of Jack Benny's vault, Amos and Andy's taxi, or vividly pictured in the mind's eye fictional characters like the Shadow or Ma Perkins!"

He felt that this same entertainment power was today generated by MOR radio stations and MOR personalities. "Today's great personalities have a credibility with their audiences as great as Arthur Godfrey had with his listeners."

He pointed to the Simmons Study (compiled for Golden West Broadcasters stations) that "confirmed the superior listener recall of MOR personality radio."

Rock disk jockeys, after going through a period when they let the music do the talking, are returning to the trend of being entertainers at many Top 40 stations. J.J.

Jordan, once program director of WRKO in Boston, said when he was programming KISN in Portland, Ore., "Man, we need some 'fun' put back into radio. We are running a tight, more music format here, but everytime a jock of mine opens the mike, he generates excitement! I want my listeners to really listen and get off on the excitement that comes across the air."

Increasing Vocal Believability for Live and Produced Commercials

One of the prime methods of making outside money as a disk jockey is doing voice-overs for commercials. In a city like New York, a disk jockey can easily double his/her on-air salary by doing commercials. Some of the great voices haven't done a radio show in years, but probably are the most often heard voices in the world—Norman Rose, Allan Swift. Swift is a voice man, capable of imitating anybody or anything.

In Los Angeles, the great names in commercials would certainly have to include Gary Owens, Johnny Dark, and Casey Kasem. The money from voice work other than radio can be phenomenal. Gary Owens used the money he got from the *Roger Ramjet* cartoon television series to buy a home. In a good year, it's quite possible for a good voice man to earn an extra $100,000, or much more.

Casey Kasem, as host of the weekly *American Top 40* three-hour radio program produced by Watermark Inc., is heard on several hundred radio stations in the United States, as well as in Australia, New Zealand, and Japan. If you watch the kiddie shows on Saturday morning television, you'll see his name for half a dozen voices of cartoon characters. He has personally voiced more than 200 radio and television commercials and is so well-known for his ability to voice commercials that he often lectures on the topic at universities. Kasem offers the following guidelines for improving the voice and making it more effective; the suggestions can be applied to live spots as well as produced spots, and even to just announcing records on a program.

People ask, "How can I sound more natural, believable and sincere in delivering a commercial?"—and they usually want a one-line answer. I'd have to say: "Stop being an announcer." But it really involves more than that. I came out of radio acting in Detroit on shows like *The Lone Ranger* where you had to sound believable. First, you learn to use a mike the way a violinist does his instrument. Control your voice; let the mike do the exaggerating for you. It makes a slight rise in volume sound bigger than it is. When you underplay, it picks up every little nuance you breathe. Get closer and let your voice drop and come out easily, your voice sounds bigger; further away, it sounds thinner.

To sound natural, place someone 10-12 feet from you and read the copy so that the person cannot hear what you're saying. If he does, you're not talking, you're announcing.

Use your body physically, too. Sometimes the mike has to be a lady's ear or a child's face. If a line calls for a smile, smile. When doing kids' parts, I stood on one leg like an ostrich to get a precarious feeling; kids are like that, sort of off-balance—you never know which direction they'll head next. Sometimes when I do a very gentle commercial (like a public service spot about forest fires), my hands look like I'm praying. I let my body do what it has to do to create a mood.

When I started as a deejay it was the scream and rant era of early rock 'n' roll. The old deejays sounded like evangelists. If I was a shouter, it was typical of the music of the day. People never tire of an honest, danceable beat, and it's hard to stay cool with that kind of music. Instinctively you want to groove with it. Other deejays did funny stuff and chatter, but I opened up playing hits back-to-back to give the listener more music. Often, between records, I'd have up to three or four local spots. You can't do three or four minutes sounding like an announcer, so I integrated my personality with the commercials. I learned to hook people, get 'em interested in my story, deliver the payoff, then hook 'em again. It taught me about a deejay's one-to-one relationship with his listener.

The national commercials came "canned, and they were 'Big-Voiced', hard sell Madison Avenue (C. 1945). People bought it because there was nothing else; radio and TV were both relatively new. But most local spots were done live. The copy came from the station and wasn't always that good (but you can make even bad copy sound better by the way you read it). It was necessary and fun to make up your own commercials from fact sheets. Adlibbing spots forced you to maintain the one-to-one relationship and not switch personalities when you went to the commercial.

All of us wonder about imitating someone else when we start out. The trap lies in *mimicking* someone's style; it's not believable. Each of us has a different style. If you mimic anyone in anything, make it their attitude. Eventually you get out of this and start doing yourself. A lot of deejays are afraid of changes suggested by the manager or program director. Fortunately, it happened to me at a period in my life when I didn't feel I knew it all (I still don't). I had been hired out to the West Coast with some other deejays as a wild-tracker. In a three-hour show, I'd use as many as 100 canned voices. "The Little Girl Without a Name," an imaginary character, used any female voice I had on hand. I tried not to waste words or go off on tangents but say interesting things relevant to the commercials, music, promos, etc. It often took me two to eight hours to write this show.

One day the manager told me not to do that kind of show any more, despite the fact that I was rated No. 1 in San Francisco. He wanted me to talk to people about the artists and their music, as they used to do in the 1940s. That night I hadn't the slightest idea what I was going to say, but I accepted the challenge with a positive approach. I had been doing low-keyed numbers in the final half-hour of the show, so elements of the real me were already familiar to the listeners as well as the wild stuff in front.

As luck would have it, I found a copy of *Who's Who in Music, 1962* in the big scrap barrel wedged in the studio door the next day. Those statistics saved me. That day I began the teaser biography format which became today's *American Top 40* show. Not one word of explanation to the audience, but they accepted it. Remember: As much as you may love what you're doing, don't think the audience necessarily loves it as much as you. If you have to head in a new direction, make up your mind to do it better than anyone else ever has. If I hadn't accepted the change but had stuck to my old image, it would have limited my appeal and I wouldn't be where I am today.

With most commercials pretaped now, you don't have as much opportunity for creativity. So take advantage of the public service spot; pretend it's the only one you have on the air. If your warning can prevent someone from, say, becoming an alcoholic or having a fatal accident, you've done more than entertain; you may have saved someone's life. There are still some local spots that are done live. If you adlib them from your own fact sheet, use what I call *handles*—words the listener can grab onto with his five senses (tree, red, soft, hot, square). Think like an actor—find vivid words in the copy with which to paint visual images for more impact.

There are 25 ways to read any line; often it's just a difference in attitude. Take Union Oil's, "Put a man with spirit on your side—the Spirit of '76!" Try saying it like a father to son, bank pres to employee, angry, sexy, tongue-in-cheek, and so on. Or Gillette's deodorant (protects, won't sting): "Soft 'N Dry—it does, and it doesn't."

Deal with the thought behind the line and bracket important words and phrases. Softening a key word makes it stand out, as does laying back with it or raising your voice level. For a natural, actor-like quality, DON'T clear your throat before speaking; you'll sound less like an announcer. Leaving the garbage (saliva) in makes a young voice sound older and has a boy-next-door or man-on-the-street effect. This is a handy tip if you're doing voice-over commercials on the side—but on your own show, it doesn't pay to switch personalities. Instead, adopt the attitude that fits.

The most important thing you can bring to a spot is attitude. Maybe the listener doesn't buy all that you're saying, but he can appreciate your talking to him like an adult and being as sincere as you can. If a commercial sounds a bit impossible and you don't believe it yourself, react normally as anyone else would—not cynically, but with an inquisitive or curious tone. This strengthens the audience's belief in you, lets you sell the product better for the 95 out of 100 reputable sponsors who don't make incredible claims, and allows management to proudly maintain its air talent's credibility. If you still have doubts, check it out; a simple call to the Better Business Bureau is a good place to start.

Don't be afraid to help people. Treat a commercial as something you're introducing to someone that might help him, the way a grocer points out a new product to a housewife. When you find yourself selling something you really like, give it your best. However, don't feel that after reading a 60-second (or 30 to 10 second) spot, you have to add 15 seconds of your own to it. This is cheating the sponsor, the station, the listeners, and yourself. It only means you weren't good enough the first time you read it, or that the copy should be rewritten.

If you get a spot for, say, a restaurant you haven't tried personally, you can still personalize it with your tone. In effect your voice says, "I haven't tried it yet, but here's what they say they've got" and "It's my job to tell you about it and your prerogative to test it." Overdoing believability in your delivery can be risky, especially using first person ("I think it's great and I want you to buy it"). Don't say "I" when you really mean "they" unless you've bought or used the product, talked with the company, or the like. Don't say "I" as if you were part owner of the product but only as a broadcaster who has an obligation to give the client his money's worth. Your audience knows you're informing, not selling direct from the store.

It helps for on-the-air talent to meet the clients. Air talent is often tremendously isolated from other parts of the business, and even a simple call from sponsor to disk jockey is the best thing a salesman could arrange. When a disk jockey speaks to an agency man or station salesman, he can ask for more of the human interest side and go after things the copy might not contain. It helps add that personal touch to his tone. The brass is on his side, wanting him to be great, so he shouldn't be afraid to suggest constructive ideas for improving spots.

It's the station's responsibility to assess material and keep false advertising off the air. Even so, there are times when you feel like drawing the line. In a smaller station, if I thought that what I was required to say would dupe the public, I'd either refuse or have someone else do it. You have a moral and ethical obligation as a broadcaster and to yourself to keep the airwaves free of lies. Sometimes it's the style, not the content, that irritates. In the old days, canned spots were loud and phoney sounding. Some managers still feel you can yell something at the public enough and they'll eventually buy it—but others feel it hurts the station and turns listeners off. If you've emceed a dance or concert, you know an unruly crowd ignores loud announcements, figuring they're unimportant, but quiets down to catch what it thinks might be confindential information delivered in low-keyed intimacy.

If you find yourself sounding "read-y" after doing the same spot several times, you can bounce back by remembering that you're telling a story with a beginning, middle, and summation. And you're telling it to a friend who'll let you open up, be slightly dramatic, laugh at a joke, choke up if it's serious or tender, whatever you want. Disk jockeys who hold back are usually thinking about thousands of strangers hearing them without accepting their words. Remember your one-to-one relationship with that good friend out there. Treat no spot as insignificant. If you earn extra with voice-overs you never know which job may result in landing you a national account.

The disk jockey's job, then and now, is to inform, entertain, and sell the product. But we've come a long way in humanizing this job since the early days of Top 40. There's just no substitute for someone talking to you, giving you information, and you believing what he's saying.

6 What general managers think of disk jockeys

The least understood person in radio is the disk jockey, and the person who least wants to understand him—or even know him—is sometimes the general manager. For too many years the disk jockey has been the cannon fodder of radio. If he didn't achieve high ratings, though it may have been the fault of the format, the program director, lack of promotion, or even the general manager, he was fired on the spot and usually given notice when he reported for work.

On one occasion, a disk jockey called from WIFE in Indianapolis when Don Burden was the boss there. He'd been terminated but given two weeks' salary (which is a rarity at many stations), in addition to a credit card number so he could make phone calls seeking a new job and have the calls billed to the station. He wasn't mad at the station for firing him. He felt that he was better than they thought, and that he could have done better if given more time. But the management of the station had treated him exceptionally well.

"I've no complaints," he said.

Actually, the disk jockey had been treated with exceptional courtesy in comparison to most disk jockeys in radio today.

One general manager of a Top 40 swinging door station used to fire disk jockeys on merely a whim. One day, he fired the entire disk jockey staff. The program director had to go on the air, filling in for everybody! While a record would be playing on the air, the program director would be on the telephone desperately trying to hire another staff.

The station paid terrible salaries; you could earn extra, the manager always pointed out, by guest appearances as an emcee at a local nightclub. And that was true. You could earn up to $350 a week. But you never knew the money from the walk-on appearances went to the general manager and he divided it as he was fit; anyway, you weren't going to be at the station long and so whatever money you scraped up had better be put in the bank as you looked for another job. And that was going to take a while. Because this general manager's sales pitch when he hired new disk jockeys was that he was giving them the opportunity to work in a major market. That wasn't necessarily the situation, since that particular radio station wasn't a credit on a resume. But young and unsuspecting disk jockeys didn't learn that until later. That general manager isn't a typical one but if you're planning to be a disk jockey all of your life you'll still meet his type now and again. Consider it part of your basic training.

Frankly, most general managers are pretty decent sorts. They've got problems far beyond the simple problems of the disk jockeys who are responsible for only getting ratings and doing a professional job on and off the air. He must guide the program director in various facets (the general manager should, in most cases, keep hands off the programming) of a radio station. Some of these areas include following the dictates of governmental regulations, achieving a satisfying community involvement, (this can be neither the total responsibility of the program director, the general manager, nor even a community involvement director, if the station is fortunate enough to afford a large staff). The direct responsibility lies with the owner of the license. He may and usually must, especially in multiple ownership situations, rely on the general manager. But the general manager has other obligations. This is one of the aspects of radio that the general manager may—and should—assign to his program director, and at most radio stations in the United States, the program director is primarily involved in all community activities.

Thus, some community duties eventually get assigned to the disk jockey. This means that he'll be assigned to attend a Rotary Club function, to be the spokesman for a charity event, to visit a high school and present a rose bouquet to a beauty queen, or to do a live remote from a local business establishment (this often makes money for the station, but it's also a method of community relations).

Understanding the General Manager

The general manager has bottom line responsibilities. If the station doesn't make a profit, he's going to find it difficult to meet the payroll. Radio is extremely unusual in that it can make money—in extremely large amounts—but the financial results are slow.

Let's assume that the station is starting out from rock bottom, but decently funded so that basic salaries and operating expenses are met (improvement in all capital equipment, hypothetically, must await a satisfactory profit level). Aside from the capital investment in the radio station itself (radio licenses are extremely costly today, not including the equipment or the property that may be involved) there are also operating expenses.

KJOI, an FM radio station in Los Angeles, was recently purchased for almost $4,000,000. A good AM signal in Los Angeles would go for more than $10,000,000. A decent FM would go for above $1,000,000. Even a lousy AM signal can get a figure that Sam Bass would never have dared don a mask to obtain. Again, there are only so many radio signals and even a bad signal has no excuse for not making money—one way or another! Don't hold that against radio, television is worse. If you turn a television station on the air, in spite of the fact you don't know how to program it and you play old movies and 20-year-old *I Love Lucy* programs, it makes money.

If radio has been called "a license to steal" then television is a crime. And this crime is not just network television, but the independent television stations in market after market. Instead of trying to create, they are willing to take the creations of others, regardless of how poor the material is or whether it suits the prime viewing audience.

That's why syndication in television does so well, and why you can see specials devoted to garter snakes, the Alaskan Fox, or the rare goose of South Africa. And you see not just two minutes (which might be appropriate) but a half-hour of snake, fox, goose. If you're lucky you might only get the 42nd showing of *Casablanca* with Humphrey Bogart on a local independent television station. And that's about the best you can expect from television, unless you love basketball and football—which are covered more extensively than television covered Watergate.

Television has not developed in programming as far as radio. This is because most of the people who were drafted into television in the early days were the establishment of radio and, since they remained at that level, they haven't done anything more to perfect the artform. It's sad to reflect that as far as ancient radio goes, one looks back on Orson Welles' *The War of the Worlds* and not much else. In any 10 seconds of radio today, in more than 1,000 cities, there's a lone disk jockey at a radio station who is creating a gem of a concept, putting the same kind of energy as Welles devoted to *War of the Worlds*, and is then tossing it away before or after a record.

Unfortunately, because of the nature of his job, the general manager doesn't understand creativity in most instances. To a general manager a disk jockey is something like a new sock. Some socks cost more, some less; some wear well, some itch. Some stand out so well that everyone in the market remarks about them and looks at them. The general manager is happy that he bought these new socks, even though he may not like them. It's unfortunate, but that's the way several general managers view radio.

However, there are two other kinds of general managers. The first type is a veteran of sales who is suddenly enlightened by the idea that there is more to radio than just selling time and being active in the community; in other words you have to have something on the air worth selling! By and large, this type of general manager can be highly successful and a good man to work for and with. He will usually—once he realizes the value of good programming—either do his own research into programming science or hire a qualified program director and turn full responsibilities over to that man.

Harvey Glascock, who now owns WSTU in Stuart, Fla., came out of a sales background but learned programming. He managed WNEW-AM in New York during its glory days when it was absolutely the most important radio station in the city. George Duncan, now president of Metromedia Radio, had most of his background in sales until he asked for the managership of WNEW-FM, then floundering around with an all-girl staff. Since 1958, he'd been involved in sales at Metromedia. But something new in music was happening—progressive rock. And Duncan immediately got immersed in the music, learned all he could about it and eventually turned WNEW-FM into the flagship progressive format station and the biggest money-making FM station in the world.

Many other sales-oriented managers are also quite knowledgeable in programming. To mention a few: John Winnaman, vice president and general manager of KLOS in Los Angeles (who is also extremely versed in audience ratings); James Gabbert, owner of KIOI in San Francisco (though he once worked as a disk jockey on a tiny Latin music station in his youth, and learned programming by the seat of his pants); Paul Cassidy, vice president and general manager of KGBS in Los Angeles; Tim Sullivan, vice president and general manager of KHJ in Los Angeles; Kevin O'Donohue, general manager of radio station 2SM in Sydney, Australia; Jay West, owner of KZEL in Eugene, Ore.; Gene Milner, owner of WSHE in Ft. Lauderdale, Fla.; Harold Krelstein, head of Plough Broadcasting, Memphis; Egmont Sonderling, head of Sonderling Broadcasting, Miami; and Russ Wittberger, general manager of KCBQ in San Diego. One of the legends of radio—Gordon McLendon—learned programming from the ground up along with owning and operating radio stations ranging from KLIF in Dallas to KABL in San Francisco. Dan McKinnon, owner of KSON in San Francisco, not only became involved in programming when he switched his station to country music several years ago, but also became extremely involved in all country music—even to the extent of buying a guitar and learning to play it.

The second kind of general manager—and this kind is becoming more prevalent in radio—has a programming background. For example, Don Nelson and Dwight Case were disk jockeys in their early days. Today, Nelson is vice president and general manager of WIRE in Indianapolis as well as part owner in other radio stations. Case is president of RKO Radio with headquarters in Los Angeles.

Other radio men who came out of the programming side of radio (though several gained sales experience somewhere in their careers) include: George Wilson, president of Bartell Broadcasters, New York; L. David Moorhead, vice president and general manager, KMET, Los Angeles; Dick Carr, vice president and general manager of WGST, Atlanta; Pat O'Day, who now owns a radio station in Hawaii but rose from disk jockey to manager of KJR in Seattle several years ago; Dan Clayton, vice president and general manager of WBBF in Rochester, N.Y.; Bill Ward, vice president and general manager of KLAC (country format) in Los Angeles and who once worked as a rock jock; Ted Atkins, vice president and general manager of WTAE in Pittsburgh who programmed such stations as KIMN in Denver, WOL (soul format) in Washington, KHJ in Los Angeles, and KFRC in San Francisco; Charlie Murdock, now president and general manager of WLW in Cincinnati; Bob Bennett, general manager of WBMJ in San Juan, Puerto Rico; and Jim Hilliard, executive vice president of Fairbanks radio chain, general manager of WIBC and WNAP in Indianapolis, and former programmer of WFIL in Philadelphia, a Top 40 station.

These types of general managers are usually quite demanding to work for—from the standpoint of either a disk jockey or a program director. But they're also greatly encouraging to work for since they've done it all. Norman Wain, now president of his own fledgling radio chain, was once a disk jockey at WHK in Cleveland. Years later, when he and Joe Zingale and Bobby Weiss returned to Cleveland as co-owners of WIXY, naturally they not only knew the market but knew what to expect and demand from disk jockeys, program directors, and sales account executives.

If you're a disk jockey, don't bother to tell Frank Ward, owner of WXRY in Columbia, S.C., about the duties of a disk jockey; he was a legend in early rock days in Buffalo, N.Y. And Burt Sherwood, now a general manager, was also a rock jock in the early days. Same with Gary Stevens, general manager of KDWB in Minneapolis. They paid their dues, and they know what it's all about and what to demand from a disk jockey on any of their stations.

As a rule, these men really value a good jock because of their own past experience and/or a good program director. And because of them, and others like them, the importance of a disk jockey has been slowly improving the past few years. The disk jockey is becoming more respected for his craft—Gary Owens warrants an office of his own within the studios of KMPC, Los Angeles, which has a television set, a bar (Gary doesn't drink as a rule). That, of course, is the pinnacle. But even a small studio disk jockey deserves respect for his job and often can obtain it by working for it on and off the air, and by respecting the manager who is, in his way, a skilled craftsman of a different caliber.

Radio Finances

As mentioned earlier, a general manager's obligations are immense, not only because the radio station is a great financial investment, but he has an obligation to meet the bottom line. Though not all general managers are responsible for such a worldly radio empire as Luis Brunini, director superintendent of Radio Globo in Brazil, or E. Fontan, director general of Sociedad Espanola de Radiodifusion in Spain, they are literally captains of their ship, and whether the ship is large or small, it sails on a vast ocean. The problems of operating a radio station such as KAAY in Little Rock, Ark., have much in common with the problems of operating a KHJ in Los Angeles, though the amount of money involved may be different. Except for the possibility of union hassles, the same governmental regulations and *modus operandi* applies.

From the viewpoint of the general manager, radio is a business; it must therefore be operated as any other business. In other words, it must make a profit, but that may take a while. Getting back to the assumption that a radio station is starting out from rock bottom, there are enormous expenses that must be met. These range from salaries of staff members; the cost of getting a flight of advertisements on the air; the expense accounts of the sales executive to entertain the potential timebuyer; the production of the spot (if it is a local account); the costs of processing and logging; etc. There's also upkeep of equipment, both in the studio and at the transmitter; general and administrative expenses; cost of legal aid; and some radio stations have to pay for records. And there are BMI, ASCAP, Sesac, and National Association of Broadcasters fees.

It's no wonder that the general manager tries to cut back on disk jockey overhead; to him that might appear to be the only area in which there is some financial leeway. Unfortunately, this is a misconception.

The radio industry adjusted well to a recent combination of poor economic conditions and audience fragmentation, believes Bruce Johnson, a veteran radio man now president of Starr. But he adds that radio, in general, still has a lot of fat that could be trimmed—"probably as high as 15 percent of the people working at radio stations today are superfluous." Oddly enough, one of his secrets for success (he did a good job as president of RKO Radio before joining SRO) is in hiring good people. "In any turnaround situation, the toughest job is in getting people to come work with you . . . to have faith in you." In 1969 he was general manager of classical-formated KFAC in Los Angeles, which had been losing money. The station "had a terrible image. Then I hired John Wolfe from KPOL and, though I wasn't able to keep him long, he was what I needed to get other people interested in working for me; it broke the dike.

"People are everything, when it comes to radio," said Johnson. "I had the same people problem when I took over as general manager of KLAC in Los Angeles. The station wasn't doing well—it wasn't really a country music station. But I hired Bill Ward as program director and Dick Haynes, Larry Scott, and Sammy Jackson came along with him and KLAC started to happen."

When he went to RKO, he had another hiring problem. "RKO had the image of chewing people up. At first, even some of the people who'd worked with me before weren't willing to join the chain. But, after a while people were standing in line wanting to work for the RKO operation and it's now a hell of a place to work. Getting people to believe in what you're doing, though, is a major difficulty any time you do something new."

Before going to Starr, Johnson was president of radio for the Sterling Recreation Organization. And he felt that small market and large market radio has a lot in common.

Running a radio station in Longview, Wash., is no different from operating a radio station in New York. The same rules apply. "In fact, if more radio stations in New York used the same techniques of business used by radio stations in the Longviews of the world, they would be making more money. The problem is that many people still think that a radio station in a major market has to have a staff of thousands. Well, you might need a larger staff than a small market station, because you have more of a physical area to cover.

"But a station with a large staff really ought to reconsider. The more people you have, the more mistakes are bound to multiply . . . a lot of people make work for other people to do. I learned early in business that if you give someone a job that takes two hours to do and don't give him or her more work to do, the two-hour job quickly becomes an eight-hour job.

"If you look at the expenses of radio as reported by the FCC for 1974, you'll note that profits in radio were down 23 percent as compared with 1973. It was from rising costs. The answer is: Less people. I'd rather have one good person to do two jobs and pay him more than two mediocre people doing the same jobs for less. I'm not suggesting either that radio stations all automate. Because, in many situations automation can't do the job. We automated an SRO station in Seattle, but not to lower the overhead. We automated in order to increase the efficiency of production . . . to make the station sound better."

Johnson feels that radio became complacent with success between 1967 and 1971. "No one was watching the store.

"When things got tight, few radio men knew what to do about it." Johnson continued, "However, slowly, people realized they had to change their methods of operation . . . they began to learn, bit by bit. We learned how to improve our methods of doing business and the bottom lines in 1974 and 1975 for radio were pretty good."

Again, assuming that a typical radio station is decently funded and can ride out the dead period before successful and saleable audience ratings appear, the disk jockey's role is doubly important. Salaries will be at bottom; funds to promote the disk jockeys and the radio station will be in short supply in comparison to the other radio stations in town. It's not an enviable place to be. The disk jockey, as well as the program director, the general manager and the rest of the staff, must exist with the challenge of the job foremost in their minds. And there are many, many instances in radio where the challenger, in spite of a limited budget, knocked off the big station in the market.

Maintaining Staff Morale

The big problem is staff morale. CHUM in Toronto, Can., programmed by J. Robert Wood, conducted a survey in 1974 among managers of Canadian radio stations about staff morale. Roch Demers, president of CKAC in Montreal, said he maintained staff morale "by frequent personal contact and genuine interest in the problems, concerns, and aspirations of all staffers."

Jim Sward, vice president and general manager of CKGM in Montreal, said: "I try to be as honest as possible with them, I care for them as people, I share their enthusiastic love of radio, I try to be as approachable as possible."

Bob Macdonald, general manager of CKOC in Hamilton, said, "I hire them and then I trust them. And I take a personal interest in every person and in what I trust them to do. They are left on their own to fulfill their responsibilities. I set attainable goals and constantly chat with people at their place of work about what can be achieved a step at a time. I need people and I'm not afraid to say so. I need them to give me fulfillment and satisfaction from my job. And I foreshadow, if I can, disappointments and successes so people have a sense of being guided. Beyond that, high morale is generated by the staff itself."

But a disk jockey owes it to his own career and to the success of the radio station to understand the responsibilities weighing upon the shoulders of the general manager.

Demers stated in the survey that "salary increases are tied to ratings for on-air personnel and to productivity for sales, administrative, and technical personnel. The timing varies; on-air people have their salaries adjusted after every rating and all others once a year." Sward said, "I establish a maximum amount per function in the station that I can afford and try to help each person attain that amount by perfecting their particular functions."

It should be noted that the amount of salary any radio station can afford to pay for any particular job, whether it's on or off the air, depends on how well that radio station is meeting its bottom line, and how much of a profit the station is making (the investors certainly deserve a return on their capital). The disk jockey certainly plays a role in achieving this bottom line, but he must *perform* and make his contribution before he can expect to participate in the rewards.

At a 1975 meeting of station managers and program directors within the Nationwide Communications chain in Gatlinsburg, Tenn., John Piccirillo, general manager of WLEE in Richmond, Va., commented: "We are facing a recession, but it is a recession of the mind, a recession of attitudes. We have psyched ourselves into negativism."

Clark Pollock, a vice president of Nationwide Communications, commented at that same meeting: "Communications courses will graduate more than 12,000 people this year. But only 1,500 will be absorbed by our industry. Sixty percent of the graduates will not find employment in broadcasting. These statistics mean that we will have our choice of the best . . . and we need to look for the best."

Pollock continued, "In an uncertain economy, we need to make plans—short-range and long-range, contingency, financial, and job plans. We have to continue to encourage profit consciousness among all our people. As the economy fluctuates, we need to have the people and the plans ready to cut our reaction time. Managers should make plans for the staffing and the operations needed to minimize losses and maximize the opportunities."

As you can see, the general manager has his job cut out for him, and it's a tough job. Both the disk jockey and the program director should try to involve themselves in all aspects of a radio station. The more you know about all operations in a radio station—sales, news, production, management—the better you'll be able to do your own job and the more opportunities will be open to you for advancement if and when the time comes.

7 Personal comments from some disk jockeys

Jack Armstrong, when he was a disk jockey at KTLK in Denver (he's currently at WIFE in Indianapolis, but jobs are always subject to change), said that for 10 years— now more than 16 years—he'd had a "very close relationship with the announcing end of contemporary radio. I've joked with hundreds of jocks, endured engineers, pleaded with promotions, suffered with salaries, sweet-talked secretaries, manhandled maintenance men, and have been nervous with news neurotics. I've announced, mispronounced, been denounced, and otherwise suffered through my end of the radio bargain and, for all this, I still have one unfulfilled, driving ambition, which is to work for a radio station that is run like the million dollar investment it is supposed to be.

"I can truthfully say that to my knowledge there is no other business in the world worth as much as radio—and as mismanaged," Armstrong said. "In this day when radio stations are worth the premium dollars, you find top 10 market stations not only running on a shoe string but also sounding like it!

"I realize that many station owners are merely speculating with the public's property (i.e. air wave frequencies) in hopes of making a short or long-range killing that would rival any brainstorm of any great millionaire, but do they realize that they are playing with the future and livelihood of the thousands of employees who count on them for tomorrow? Do they also realize that maintaining a radio station that appears to lose revenue every year for tax purposes is not only a waste of frequency, but also a waste of the dreams and hopes of those who sweat and worry over this purposeful deception? Hell, no! They don't think about this because somewhere along the line they decided that God or somebody chose them to be millionaires and everybody else is just unworthy.

"Sometimes, you find a truthfully sincere owner who really is interested in entertainment and the public. But, as luck would have it, he usually hires an old crony, who isn't so much dedicated as he is irresponsible, ignorant, or just plain lazy. This good friend of the owner is often the general manager and holds life and death over all subordinates."

Needless to say, Armstong wasn't happy at that point in his career about some general managers. However, over the past six years, there have been rapid changes in general managers as well as program directors and disk jockeys. Armstrong, who'd already worked at stations such as WAYS in Charlotte, N.C., WIXY in Cleveland, WMEX in Boston, WKYC in Cleveland, CHUM in Toronto, and WPOP in Hartford, Conn. (it was a Top 40 station in those days) later offered this advice to other disk jockeys when he worked at WKBW in Buffalo, N.Y.: The job of a "successful Top 40 disk jockey centers around many intangibles, certainly most of these elusive ingredients fall under the vague heading of entertainment. What may be entertainment to you may be mere boredom to me and certainly vice versa. What may mean turn on to you may mean tune out to someone who is a year older or a year younger or even someone your age who simply doesn't recognize your programming genius.

"All in all, entertainment is the very key for any successful disk jockey, no matter what format or music he is working. For that matter, entertainment is the life blood of any radio station for, obviously, people turn on the radio most of the time to be entertained. In my opinion, entertainment in rock radio centers around the word music. I feel that any Top 40 disk jockey who is or wants to be successful should keep an eye on his priorities. As far as I'm concerned, music is first; but I feel just as strongly that the jock is second. A very strong second."

Armstrong believes that a good disk jockey can make the difference in ratings between two or three music-oriented rock stations in the same market.

"Better than that, a good entertaining jock is the one thing your competitor can't imitate. I mean, aren't we all playing about the same music, stealing the same promotions, and generally lacking that dynamic innovative spirit that captured the imaginations of our audiences just a few years back?" Armstrong continued, "Then, there is just one answer: An entertaining disk jockey who is an experience to listen to, or at least interesting in and around his home base of music."

Armstrong claims that entertainment is anything but the very basics of any disk jockey's delivery, i.e. the station's call letters, the name of the disk jockey, the time and temperature, the public service commitments.

"These aforementioned must always exist. They are a permanent part of any program. And that doesn't mean they can't be entertaining, but it does mean that saying your name correctly or with a big deep voice isn't the public's idea of entertainment. Certainly, articulation, pronunciation, and diction are personal accomplishments and the foundation of our trade; but I'm afraid that the public expects us to be versed in these areas and thus finds little interest in our delivery of promised goods."

He recommends that an aspiring disk jockey or a disk jockey who wants to improve himself should "chop down an aircheck and see how much is added besides the basics. Better yet, see if the basics themselves aren't entertaining in some form or another."

Armstong's brand of entertainment centers around humor and speed. "I believe that if you are going to be entertaining you must be quick, so as not to distract from your base of music. Now, you can get a bit carried away with this super-quick philosophy and stop thinking about the quality of your material and start thinking about time. Herein lies, what I consider to be, the main fault of much-more music, strictly formated radio stations. They strangle the entertainment out of the disk jockey presentations by their strict, inflexible, mechanical regulations.

"The main ingredient of an entertainment presentation is preparation. I think that preparation can be broken down into two categories. First, mental preparation. Under this heading would come thoughts about humor and/or bits that will be a show before the show is fact. Thinking ahead about the opening of your show and what you are going to do during the show. It is my belief, for instance, that the first 15 minutes of anyone's show are the most important. In these first few minutes, a jock sets the mood for the rest of his program. If he blows that first 15 minutes, then he has to play catch up ball for the rest of his performance."

The second most important facet about being on the air, according to Armstrong, is "the mental makeup of any jock. I think jocks are, as most performers, mentally insecure. They need public and professional recognition. We need to build ego trips in order to drum up confidence in what we are trying to do on the air. Take away any jock's ego and you may have destroyed the very foundation of his ability to attract and hold an audience."

Armstrong said that he personally likes to work for people "who will compliment as well as criticize. A program director who will talk to his men like they are working with him will have a more together staff. The master-slave relationship is a lousy way to make a guy want to help the station be successful.

"To my thinking, the only thing the public recognizes in rock radio is the music and the man who plays the music. So, with that in mind, I find it hard to believe that a disk jockey is often treated like something the union is forcing the station to employ."

He said that he has found in his years in radio that sales managers, station owners, and general managers treat disk jockeys like animals and pay them on the same scale.

"Then, when they listen to the station and it sounds like a wake, full of uninteresting things and total redundancy, they have merely reconfirmed their own beliefs that the sales executives are the only people at the station that count," said Armstrong. "Anyone who believes that it's the salespeople who make a radio station are talking to the wrong end of the horse. A radio station is selling a product and the product must be good or no one will buy it. The product is music and the successful Top 40 disk jockey ... and a major part of the disk jockey's ability to deliver the goods is his knowledge that he is an important part of obtaining and retaining an audience to make the station a winner."

Armstrong said that if a general manager wants to make a disk jockey try harder, "then give him a half-dollar or a dollar for every spot that runs in his show. You'd be surprised what inducement money can give a man. The thing to realize is that he has goals and ambitions just like the station manager and the owner or anyone else, and it only makes sense that you've got to help him attain them."

He added that when a station manager helps a disk jockey reach his goals and become a success, then the manager becomes a success because he is then delivering an air product that is saleable. While he personally wants guidance from a program director, he thinks "it very ill-advised for a program director to chew out or browbeat air talent just before the man is going on the air. A disk jockey should be trying to build a mental mood just before he goes on the air. If he is forced to defend himself or is totally humiliated seconds before he has to deliver, then how can he be productive?

"In my way of thinking, there is only one time to add direction or to critique a disk jockey performance—that is just after the disk jockey finishes his show. This would hold true even for the all-night jock. The thing I wish program directors would realize is that memos can also have a devastating effect on a disk jockey. I think that program directors should talk to their announcers first and then follow that conversation up with something written."

A good show is often more than just a good disk jockey on the air. Armstrong believes that many disk jockeys have ideas of their own about promotions and bits for their shows.

"I think that a program director is obligated to let a disk jockey insert things into his show that give it character. Sometimes, these bits may distract from the total sound of the station and, in such cases, this should be explained to the disk jockey and then abridged or even refused ... the point here is that a successful rock disk jockey should be able to develop his own style and often *style* is the profitable by-product of imagination and innovation. Also, this can add to the disk jockey's feelings of importance by allowing him to add to the effect of the station."

Another aspect of preparation for Jack Armstrong is all physical. "It is my belief that, as fast-paced as rock radio is, one should try to do as much in advance as possible so as to leave room for thought and concentration at critical moments when on the air.

One such critical moment is at changeover. When you are coming on duty, there is a great deal of confusion going on: Papers lying all about, the other announcer gathering up his golden oldies, signing off the log, spilling his cold coffee down your back, cueing up your lead out record on 33 1/3 rpm when it's a 45 rpm single, the newsperson kibitzing hither and yon or leaving his lighted cigar in your chair, and, to top it off, Sally Secretary, the office ugly, waltzes in and asks if you've got change of a dime. Then, the phone rings and you've got to answer it to see if it's that sweet divorcee calling you back again but, no, it's the finance company wanting to know what happened to the last car payment. And then you look up on the wall to see a sign that says: 'If you value your job, you'll plug the contest hard'. Hell, you haven't had time to read today's memos and underline all the hidden meanings. So you don't even know about the contest. Then, you look at the mail and see a letter from Judy Topheavy and you've just got to read that one. Right now.

"Folks, what we have here is a failure to communicate."

The only sensible way to get ready for a radio show, according to Jack Armstrong, is to arrive at the station at least an hour before the show. He looks at his mail and reads his memos.

"And I have at least an hour to stop the bleeding after I cut my wrist if there's anything offensive in the memos. The next thing on the agenda is to pull my golden oldies, trying to remember when I played them last and trying to pull the oldies that fit today's nighttime audience (while we are talking about oldies, it might be good to mention music mood, if the current survey is a lot of slow ballads, then you really can't play very many slow oldies. Golden oldies can add to the mood, either up or down, at a special time when you need it)."

In regard to preparation, after pulling out the oldies needed for the show, the disk jockey should fill out in advance the music format sheets, Armstrong said. "By that, I mean put in your name, date, and hour. I would then go about specifics, such as how to open your show, the exact bits which are going to be used and where and when you are going to use them. If you do voices, then test them to see if they are all there today, and if you can get into character in order to use them effectively. By the way, your voice is something that needs preparation also. Read a spot or two aloud before you go on the air.

"Doing production just before you go on the air is another way to get your voice, mouth, and mind in gear. But, for crying out loud, don't try to cut a spot with just 10 minutes until you go on the air. That's a good way to get strung out and really nervous. I find that chewing gum loosens my mouths and tongue muscles so as to minimize stuttering and fumbling when I'm talking at higher speeds. In fact, I often will talk with a little piece of gum in my mouth. Now, I can hear you saying, 'No wonder I can't understand him'. But, I find that a piece of gum gives my tongue muscles more control and has the added benefit of controlling salivation. Say, while you are loosening up, why not check and see if you have any new live copy in your forthcoming show.

"The next bit of preparation involves going into the studio . . . that, in itself, is therapy. But it is dangerous therapy. Bull shooting with the jock on duty is fine . . . up to a point. But distractions like that can not only ruin the end of his show, but also cause you to forget your opening and the things you've planned. I cannot emphasize enough the concentration necessary to start a show off properly."

Personally, Armstrong likes to work in a perfectly neat environment with every-thing in its place. "If you are in a hurry and can't find what you need, then you tax your adlib ability beyond the entertainment point and into the 'I'm lost' area. In other words, get it together and keep it together.

"First, clear out the studio. Who needs question-and-answer period or show'n'tell while you're trying to entertain a couple of hundred thousand people? This is espe-cially true of the all important first 15 minutes. The phone? The deadly phone? Stay away from it . . . I cannot begin to tell you why it is bad for a jock to answer the phone while he is doing his trick. All I can say is that there are two types of people who call radio stations: Those who are going crazy and those who have already arrived.

"If you doubt what I'm saying, may I suggest you answer the phones one day and check out the dummies who are trying to ruin your show. I believe that jocks should never answer the phone unless he is doing on-air bits with the audience."

As far as cueing records goes and setting up tapes, Armstrong feels that the disk jockey should cue the next record as soon as he finishes introducing the last one. This way, he can always go to music if everything else fails.

"After cueing the next record, then set up the carts in the exact order in which they are going to be played, including the lead out jingle to music. Try to shuffle the jingles to match the intro mood of the next record. It may also be wise to avoid over-working any one jingle. If there are engineers, the same advice for advanced set prepa-ration holds true. The announcer should remember that he is thinking for two guys and that the engineer may not be overly interested in whether the jock falls on his boom-boom or not. So, the engineer should be given the record first and then the exact order of all spots and jingles to follow. I do not suggest that the engineer be allowed to segue anything, as past experience has proven them to be a bit loose when left to run wild.

"After the engineer is given the setup, repeat it so as not to leave doubt in any-one's mind over what is happening next. Now that the next set is ready, there is about two minutes left to think about the all important entertainment contribution and look over any live copy coming up. This portion should be considerably easier after the advance preparation. If there is any extra time, it should be spent thinking about what record is going to be played after the one already cued. It is important that a mood is being maintained and, at the same time, that the same type of artist is not being played back-to-back. For instance, two Guess Who type of groups back-to-back or two types of Diana Ross singers. Not only is the artist separation important, but also the hard rock from the hard rock, the soul from the soul—these separations need constant attention. The format should be a great help, but make sure to keep playing the big records over and over, no matter how tired you, personally, are of hearing them.

"Jingles, in my opinion, should be used in one place—after the last spot and before the next record. This idea is to associate the radio station and the disk jockey with music and not those nasty old commercials."

As for commercials—though his theory is argued against by many program direc-tors today—Jack Armstrong felt that grouping of commercial spots was the best way to give a radio station an overall sound of "much, more music. By spot grouping, I mean come out of news with at least three records and then cluster no more than two minutes worth of spots together. I feel that records played in threes hold the most value, and any more or less than three in a row only sounds confusing. Two in a row, for instance, has the flavor of being less than a lot of music. Six in a row, on the other hand, should be saved for special occasions or otherwise the audience may learn to live without commercialization and we all know that can't be if we want to keep a job.

"Lastly, remember who you are trying to reach and keep tossing bits to that audience. You must be careful not to scare away everyone else while trying to appeal to any special group or age demographic. But then again you can figure on a lot of housewives 9 AM-noon, Monday through Friday, October through June 1."

Jack Armstrong is a gunner-type of disk jockey. Like Bruce (Cousin Brucie) Morrow, who was on WABC in the evening years ago, Armstrong chatters at the rate of a machine gun. And that style of disk jockeying is often copied. It should be noted that not every station wants such a disk jockey. At one point in his career, John (Jack Armstrong) Larsh spent six months fishing on the rivers and lakes of Arkansas near his home while waiting for radio to go through a time and temperature syndrome. Later, while at WPOP in Hartford, he actually answered a job advertisement for a "Jack Armstrong type" disk jockey to get a job at KTLK in Denver. His argument for the job was that they could have the "real thing" at the same price.

Later, after 13-Q in Pittsburgh folded upon him—it eventually happens to all disk jockeys unless they are especially gifted—he was without work several months until going to WIFE in Indianapolis.

Radio Wives

As rough as the life of a disk jockey or program director is—especially during the career-building days—there's someone who usually suffers more—the radio wife. She must be of a hardy breed, willing to hang around radio stations about half of her life, willing to learn or be interested in radio, and most importantly, be in love with the person.

Radio has been likened to a disease; men and women afflicted with it need an enormous amount of compassion and understanding from their spouses. To a great extent, this compassion and understanding has been lacking over the years. The evidence is obvious—the divorce rate among disk jockeys and program directors is much higher than that of the general populace. Radio life is just too unstable for most spouses, and in most cases women do not want to play second fiddle to a radio station.

Charlie Tuna claims that his wife knows jingles and how to use them.

Bonnie Campbell is probably one of the best production females in the world, as some of the men who remember her will tell you. But, as wife of Tom Campbell, her whole life is devoted to his career. She is one of the few people who worked for Todd Storz both before and during the Miami convention that set radio and disk jockeys back 10 years or more because of the adverse publicity. She knows radio, and what makes it tick.

The same can be said of Gunner Bennett, who operates as comptroller of WBMJ in San Juan, Puerto Rico, but also handles the finances of the consulting and construction firm of Hope, Bennett, Blackburn. She is extremely knowledgeable about all aspects of radio—from programming to management.

Patti Roberts, wife of Brian Roberts, is another woman who knows radio. She'll often answer a question before her husband, a disk jockey who has worked stations such as KYA in San Francisco and KCBQ in San Diego.

Judith Moorhead was in advertising before she met her husband L. David Moorhead of KMET in Los Angeles. Judy Burns, wife of George Burns of Burns Media Consultants, Los Angeles, probably knows as much about radio as most program directors. The truth is that many radio station managers, if they can't find George Burns at home will ask Judy and be satisfied with her reply about a problem.

You can't call Sis Kaplan a radio wife—she's the daughter of Atlass, who was a radio legend in Chicago. But she's married to Stan Kaplan and between them they constitute the greatest combination in radio today.

You'll find a countless number of radio wives in the industry. They might be working as secretaries while their husbands fortify their careers. And occasionally, the times may not be good. Yet, these women pitch in financially when bad times demand, they emotionally support their husbands, and are even willing to talk the merits of PAMS vs. TM jingles. Enough praises couldn't be sung about them.

Disk jockeys are a strange breed, as has been mentioned before. It takes not only a great wife, but a great program director and a great general manager to work with them. Joey Reynolds is a good example. Can you imagine a disk jockey calling the major of Hartford, Conn., (when he was on WDRC) a dumb old broad? Charlie Parker, vice president of programming for the station, explained to Joey that he could not, under any circumstances, call the woman mayor a dumb old broad. But the very next night, Reynolds, true to form, called her a dumb old broad. The next day, he wouldn't even let Parker (one of the nicest guys in the industry) take the trouble to fire him. They talked of other things and then Joey Reynolds walked out of the station with a smile, for the last time.

Of course, the "compassionate" spouse may not necessarily be a woman. Women are quickly moving into all aspects of radio, including programming. Rochelle Staab, for example, rose to become national program director of Bartell Broadcasters, then moved on to become program director of KIIS in Los Angeles.

There are also a number of women disk jockeys—for example, Mary Turner who currently does the late evening show on KMET in Los Angeles, a progressive station. Progressive radio has recently become part of the mainstream of radio, shedding its earlier image of being underground radio. Mary Turner is not the usual hippie-type of disk jockey—she has acquired an enormous amount of radio experience. In college she worked at WIUR, a carrier-current station at Indiana University in Bloomington, Ind. At first, she wanted to be a television director and after graduation she worked in the traffic department of KNEW-TV, San Francisco.

Mary Turner comments, "But in San Francisco, I started listening to KSAN. It blew my mind, having come from Indiana, with its radio. For the first time, I realized that a radio station could be an integral part of a person's life."

Then came stints with KSFX and KSAN, both in San Francisco. She started out as promotion director at KSAN, worked her way up to being an engineer, then became a sales account executive.

"On Sunday nights, I was engineering a talk show on KSAN by Chan (Travis T. Hip) Laughlin. The guy who followed Chan at 1 AM didn't show up a lot. Chan would say: 'You've got a license; I'm going home' and leave. After filling in a couple of times, I realized what I wanted to do—be an air personality."

At KSFX, she was doing a weekend show when the general manager of the station, John Turpin, heard her and asked her to go full-time. In 1972, she joined KMET in Los Angeles. Even though she works for a progressive station, thematic music concepts—the staple of progressive radio—often take a backseat on her show to just good radio programming.

"When you're not following a hot clock, your own taste in music becomes evident," she said. "But that's not what people want to hear. So, while I think about what I'm going to do on the show before I go on the air, I like to program spontaneously, keeping in mind the music that people really want to hear."

Ms. Turner usually has three or four songs picked out prior to going on the air. However, after those records, the show is generally created on the spot from approximately 5,000 albums on hand in the control room. Usually, she sticks to a blend of cuts from best selling albums, mixing in a lot of established older progressive album cuts. The music director of KMET makes a list of the albums and cuts that she thinks merit the attention of the air personalities; these are listened to by the air staff who in turn vote on the cuts. Thus, air personalities play cuts that have a favorable consensus from the entire staff.

More Comments from Disk Jockeys–Past and Present

One of the most popular air personalities in Las Vegas is Red McIlvaine, a morning man who has been in the market for years. On his KORK 6-10 AM radio show, he only manages to play seven or eight records in heavy traffic time. There is less music played in the morning "because people, it appears, want to be heavily informed. They want to be talked to and they want to hear a human voice. Lately the audience has a desire to get involved in things that are really on the lighter side—little put-ons. They want to hear the news at the top of the hour, but they don't want to be bogged down with it all. They know it's depressing."

Between records, McIlvaine sometimes talks on the phone with listeners. "If you come up with the right subject, you get people that just go crazy getting involved. A few years back, you'd be able to mention Vietnam and the phones would light up with calls. For a while, you could mention Watergate and people would call. They won't call about those things any more. They don't care about the heavy subjects. But if you say: 'How do you make a chocolate pie without using any chocolate?' you get 25,000 phone calls. If you do a quiz, people will call right away. Not for the prize, but because of the competition."

Some air personalities may be more famous—and several may be making more money—but few will every become the legend that Wolfman Jack is. He's a living, breathing personification of the word *personality* on radio, via a syndicated show, and various television appearances. Besides that, he's had about half a dozen songs written and recorded about him.

"I play contemporary rock on my show . . . I do vignettes . . . it's strictly a personality show," said Bob (Wolfman Jack) Smith. "And I look for the soul records that can go pop. If I like a new record, I'll go on it immediately. And I like records that I can sing along with . . . I like the records with a good middle part where I can beat on a book, scream, or use the Wolfman 'Herbie' howl."

Smith, who started on WNJR in Newark, N.J., as a $15-a-week go-fer, launched the Wolfman identity in 1959 when he was a disk jockey on XERF in Villa Acuna, Mexico (one of the giant-powered radio stations beaming into the United States) as an outgrowth of his love for horror movies. What he plays on his show is what he listens to at home.

"B.B. King, Ray Charles—all of the blues greats—this is what I like to listen to. What I started with years ago on XERF is really my kind of music. I can get behind country music and even Barbra Streisand, but blues is my stuff." Wolfman uses a playlist on his syndicated radio show, "but I do the show as the mood flows. If I feel like rock, I rock. For 15 minutes. Or I may do half an hour of oldies and talk poetry in between. I do a thing, you know? I can sometimes take an album and look at the linernotes and find a word that may give me a clue to do a rap on."

One of the great MOR air personalities in radio is Wally Phillips, morning man at

WGN in Chicago. He keeps a thread of subtle humor flowing through his show, but tries to have each show make a point; in other words, he tries to find a reason for playing a certain record. On a cold morning, he'll throw out a quip as he goes into Andy Williams' "Summer Wine." Over the years, like Dick Haynes at KLAC in Los Angeles, Phillips uses a "voice" sidekick to say many of his quips. He also does a lot of phone work while on the air and has stock questions to open up conversations. He believes the phone work lends spontaneity to his show. Of course, most of this is self-generated—he maintains a vast file of phone number of important people.

Jay Lawrence, afternoon personality at KLAC in Los Angeles, is a former rock jock who still had a contract with the station when it switched from MOR to country music and grew to like the atmosphere of working at a country music station.

"Country music has certainly done more for me than I've done for it," Lawrence said. He'd only been at the station two weeks when it went country. "I listened to KBBQ, then a country station, and KFOX in Long Beach to find out what I was going to be doing and I got really rattled. I was worried that I wouldn't be able to relate . . . but everyone I talked to just said for me to be an entertainer who just happens to play country music."

In the past, Lawrence liked to do a stream of consciousness type of show—"start on a thought and talk it through, just communicate on how I feel about things. I *think* funny. And you can do more of that sort of thing on a morning show. But in the afternoon people want a different kind of program. It was difficult to adjust to that aspect. But with general manager Bill Ward's help—insistence might be a better word for it—I've managed. The ratings have done well. And the auto racing image of the station, an image that management handed me, has done a lot for me."

KLAC broadcasts auto racing events and accents auto racing news on the air. Lawrence was assigned the task of building up a personal relationship with racing drivers and now calls many of them friends. He'd never been all that involved in racing before; it's a perfect example of a *created* rapport that has broadened the appeal of the station and given the air personality—Lawrence—a wider scope than just being a disk jockey. As for the music itself, Lawrence now has a decent working knowledge of country music and sounds professional on the air.

"Because I know music balancing. Whether you're talking about country music or whatever, I'm using the same techniques that I would for MOR music—soft, hard, female, male, ballads. I treat the records just like any other kind of music, rather than as country music. And perhaps it's a plus factor that I don't have much background in country because then I have no preconceived notions about the artists or the songs; a man more familiar with country music might shy away from a given artist because of not liking him personally."

Lawrence now knows quite a few country music artists. When he ran into Del Reeves once in England, Reeves exclaimed: "Oh, Lord, at last a country face."

Lawrence started in radio at WJPS in Evansville, Ind.; he then worked at WIRL in Peoria, Ill., and advanced to become program director there. His rock career includes a year at KLIF in Dallas doing a 7-10 PM rock show and a 10-midnight thing called *Romance* that blended sound effects of a party being held in a plush penthouse cocktail lounge. "You know, you could hear people stepping out of an elevator into the lounge and there was the soft sounds of glasses clinking, people talking. Irv Harrigan had been doing the show. Then Jack Sharp, the program director, wanted me to do it. That night, I did everything I'd always wanted to do. The 'elevator' got stuck, waiters broke glasses—everything went wrong for two hours. Sharp called the next day and said I'd just have to do my regular rock show 7-midnight from then on."

There are many trials and tribulations that a disk jockey goes through during his career and Jimmy Rabbitt suffered through, and perhaps, *inflicted* them from time to time.

"I was working in San Diego when the station, KCBQ, went to a 30-record playlist. And I went into a depression and wouldn't come out of my house. And George Wilson, who was then just the national program director for Bartell, kept calling and I didn't want to work. I love George, but I didn't want to work on that kind of radio. However, I did go back to work at KCBQ and he put me on afternoon drive and he wanted me to be Don Steele. I did it for one day and you should hear it! I tried to be UP so hard. You know, ye-ye-yeh! And I just couldn't do it.

"So, I went to him and said: 'Nothing's happening' and I went home. And I'm sitting there wondering what in hell I was going to do. I called Charlie Van Dyke first. He was in San Francisco then. He said: 'Nothing here.' I hang up the phone and it rings and it's Doug Cox, who was then programming KRLA in Los Angeles. The great program director in the sky was ready. He said: 'Come on up'. I said: 'Yes, sir, Mr. Cox.' It was January—rainy season in Los Angeles. And I ain't got no tires on my old Cadillac. I came to Los Angeles slipping and sliding. And got the gig." Rabbitt continues, "And what was really funny—well, this may not be funny in a humorous way—was that while I was at the station getting the job and shaking hands and all of the glad-ragging, the other Rabbitt was out in the lobby waiting to talk to Doug Cox about the job. But in the earlier days, I didn't know there was such a Rabbitt. I didn't steal his name. I was a Rabbitt because of a lot of things, you know? But to have him waiting out in the lobby really brought me down a lot—caused me to go have several drinks at the Sheraton bar."

Johnny Rabbitt was one of several Rabbitts at KXOK in St. Louis. When he left to join KRIZ in Phoenix, he took the name with him. In both cities, he created fantastic numbers with his zany and unusual approach to rock music. Today, he does commercials and teaches a commercial (and acting) workshop in Los Angeles.

Jimmy Rabbitt has always wanted to sing. "I became a disk jockey because nobody would play my records. More or less." But he also claims that you can't be a major air personality until you've paid your dues on stations in such markets as Corpus Christi, Tex., or Bakersfield, Calif.

Asked if he thought radio had done well by him, he shook his head. "If I'd been smart, it could have done well by me. But I haven't been *smart*, you know? Because I've always had a belief—it changes a little year by year—but when I came to Los Angeles I thought I was going to revolutionize radio in the city. To my thinking, in a way I have. I think I've loosened it up a whole lot. That's not ego talking. Because when I got to Los Angeles there weren't any long-haired disk jockeys on the air."

It has not been an easy life for Jimmy Rabbitt. Between jobs in Los Angeles, he had to break horses for a living. "But that's okay, because I knew I could do a good job on the radio if someone would only hire me. If I hadn't known that I could be successful, I wouldn't have tried. And I wouldn't have been successful . . . I don't think anyone can teach you radio, though. Not all of the ingredients. Where else can you have a situation like this: You go to work one day after just having fought with your old lady; you get a traffic ticket on the way to work; somebody bangs into the back of your car; wham-wham-wham, things happen to you. Then you get to the station and the general manager tells you that you lost an account last night because you fouled up a spot. And you have to go on the air and *entertain* the people. But you have to go on the air and go: 'Hey!' It drives me crazy sometimes. Some days, I come in and I'm happy and I'm ready. Those are good days. But whether I have good days or bad days, I can always sound the same on the air. That's the job."

Rabbitt genuinely likes being a disk jockey. "When I called in sick, I was really sick. Because I liked to go down to the station." As for an engineer, he said he needed one more for his ego than anything else. "Because I'm a performer. And I need an audience. If I don't see a reaction, I think I've failed. The mistake that many beginning disk jockeys make on the air is talking to a whole bunch of people instead of just to one person. When I'm on the air, I'm talking to just one person. That may sound weird, but that's it."

Rabbitt was fired from several Los Angeles radio stations and one particular time he was fired after only three days on the air at KHJ. "Robert W. Morgan, one of the disk jockeys then on KHJ, called me up when I was working at KBBQ and asked how I'd feel about working at KHJ. I said: 'I ain't making any money here'. He said to meet him in the bar at the Sheraton Hotel at 6 o'clock. Real IBMish. So, I met him and we talked. He asked if I wanted to work there and I said: 'For that kind of money? Are you kidding?'

"He said that they were going to add albums to their programming and that I would be perfect for nights. Which I would have been. So, I went on the air at KHJ. It was all-night practice. I was pretty good; I still have a tape of the show. A good practice tape; I had to talk over records and everything. The second night, I was mediocre. The second night was good enough anyway that program director Ted Atkins called us all down to Nickadell's in the afternoon for a party. Not a big party; but you know they all drank a lot, man. Like me. I love to drink. Let all them dope heads do whatever they want to do; I want to drink.

"Everybody got drunk. So did I. And I had to go on the air at 6 PM. Me and my newlywed (we later got divorced) marched down the aisle toward the radio station gate singing "Bombed in the Big Time" and we got there and I did a good show. I have a tape of it, so I know it was a good show. But it wasn't what they wanted, man.

"Remember a movie out then? A chick was looking into a mirror and there was the reflection of a guy. She was in bronze pants. She's saying that she is what she wants to be or something; I saw that as I went into the station on a billboard. So, on the air I start talking about Don Steele and his bronze panties. And I had this little toy. You turned a crank and it played: 'Here comes Peter Cottontail, hoppin' down the bunny trail—tink, tink, tink.'

"And the memo the next day said: He brought his own logo!"

"Ted Atkins cried. That's no lie. He cried: 'What did you do to my radio station?' Now, that's funny. But here's the sad part. When I got the call the next morning to come down to the station, I was thinking that I had done so well that they were going to give me some kind of raise or something. Because I did do a good show. The engineer told me that he'd never seen anyone ride the Bill Drake format and get away with what I got away with. I didn't break format at all. But I added to it. Stuck things in.

"And I walk into Nickadell's for the second time and Ted Atkins is sitting there. And there are tears running down his cheeks. He says: 'What did you do to my radio station?' Bill Watson came in and sat down. Watson used to be one of my No. 1 fans, I thought. But all of a sudden he ain't saying anything . . . just sits there. Finally, he says: 'We don't want another Robert W. Morgan at night.' I'll never forget that line, man . . . me, a Robert W. Morgan?"

Rabbitt was suspended. "They couldn't fire me because Bill Drake had hired me. And he was in Hawaii at the moment."

Later, of course, he was fired, but the only time "I got hurt real bad" from being fired was at KLAC, the country music station. "Because I am a country music disk jockey, make no mistake about it. I know more about country music than any two country music program directors you can name. When I got fired from there, I thought I was doing my best. And I still think that if I were to choose my best aircheck, it would be one from my KLAC days."

Rabbitt worked for ten (plus) stations in Los Angeles. He got his start in radio as a go-fer for Dick Susman at WMAL in Washington. After the Marines, he went to Tyler, Tex., his home and sold shoes. His first real radio stint was on KGKB in Tyler. He also worked at KLIF in Dallas for Gordon McLendon.

"When I came to KLIF, McLendon had cars turned over on the freeway with signs on them: I Just Flipped For Jimmy Rabbitt. Stations don't do that anymore. My first night on the air at KLIF was McLendon's election night. He was in there with me the whole night. And you don't think it was a job to make McLendon laugh? I felt like a million dollars when he laughed at one of my lines. The lines would probably be real dumb now, but he laughed then."

Pat Patterson worked several larger markets before he settled down in Raleigh, N.C., as morning personality and program director of WKIX. Patterson, who weaves in corny humor that he writes mostly himself, feels that the choice of oldies plays an important role in attracting target demographics for a morning show. "It's a mistake to think Little Richard for a morning audience is any less irritating than he was 15 years ago."

The programming rules aren't as strict on a morning show in Top 40 radio as they are for other parts of the day. Patterson prepares his show and continues to type up copy at a typewriter on a table beside him while a record spins.

"Music is secondary to attracting teens and young adults on a morning show. They'll go along with you, depending on what's between the record, Oldies (WKIX plays an oldie every third record in the morning) are a method of holding adults." He keeps close check of records played because "it only takes about twice during a week for a listener to become convinced you're playing the same records all the time." Patterson recently shifted from WKIX to KULF in Houston.

Don Day, program director and air personality at WBAP in Ft. Worth, has some basic *don'ts* for the country music air personality: Don't daydream, don't dwell and don't play personal favorites. Also, for a country disk jockey it's vital to "get out and meet people and have fun." Day also has some *do's:* When you talk, have something to say prepared in advance that is short and sweet; put a smile on what you say with a very intimate approach stressing personal contact.

Larry Scott, a veteran air personality and country music program director, now at KFDI in Wichita, said that before he goes on the air, he generally has a program laid out in his mind. "For each program, I try to feature a particular artist or a particular sound. I may want to feature a western swing sound, or fiddle sound, or guitar sound." Often, his show is spontaneous. One night when he was doing the all-night show at KLAC in Los Angeles he played "Orange Blossom Special" and "before I was through I had played 18 versions of it."

But the all-night program of a country music station can allow that kind of freedom not available during the day on the same station. He claims that many country music stations of today are "opportunists ... they have little interest in true country product ... they don't have to play a lot of the junk that is being released under the guise of country music. If I were a manager, I wouldn't hire a disk jockey that wasn't a true country music fan. You might have to teach him radio, But I'd much rather teach him something about radio than country music."

Lee "Baby" Simms is another unique personality that has worked several radio stations in the United States and a variety of formats.

"When I'm on the air, I have a degree of theatricality to what I do, due to the fact that I personally like to entertain. I never thought, solely, that the music was what the people wanted to listen to if there was also something really heavy happening. You've got to play the right music, no matter what you do or you lose, but I think presenting the right music the right way is the key. And my presentation comes in the form of high entertainment and involves the people. That's the art in radio. Being a disk jockey is really an intangible thing, as far as the satisfaction to me. You do it and it's gone. It lasts just a moment, unless you tape it and I don't tape much . . . and it's never the same anyway because radio is an instant, right-now thing. Spontaneity."

Simms stated that he doesn't do any physical preparation for his show . . . "I prepare mentally." Simms started in radio in 1961 at WTMA in Charleston, S.C., which was then programmed by George Wilson. "George taught me how to get people to listen to me; he taught me how to relate to them; and he taught me entertainment."

Simms was fired constantly—"I was always getting fired." At WLOF in Orlando, Fla., early in his career, he was fired after a week. "I was doing the morning show and I said: 'If you would like a five dollar bill, send me your name and address with a return envelope.' George Wilson had told me that someone had done it in 1957 and it had been a giant success as a promotion. I wasn't aware that I'd be misleading the audience and get complaints from the FCC. I was just doing something that had been heavy in the past—stealing an idea, which is legitimate.

"The trick is that you don't send them a five dollar bill, you send them a *bill* for five dollars—'you owe me five dollars.' The general manager of the station then was Howard Kester and he heard me do my thing that morning and he was very excited about it, real happy. He thought it was funny." Simms continued, "But the next day here comes, like, three or four thousand letters from people in Orlando who wanted a five dollar bill. Howard took a look at the volume of mail and flashed that if we sent these people a bill for five dollars they'd really be upset. And so he fired me for that."

Asked if it were difficult to be a disk jockey, Simms said that the "physical aspects are not difficult. It's just the mental things I go through. I never think the audience doesn't dig me. I always look at that aspect in a positive manner . . . it's always been hard for me to think of things to say on the air that I think are good enough. The flow, the spontaneity isn't difficult." Regarding how long he intends to be a disk jockey (he's in his early 30s), he replied that he doesn't know. "This is just what I do. It's the only thing I know how to do."

The Magnificent Montague (that's his legal name) prefers to call himself a "leisure time executive." And he is—he has been involved in record production, music publishing, and you can hear him playing congo drums on some fine albums by the Romeros and the Packers. For years, he was also the voice in the black community for products ranging from a local bread to Southern Select Beer; he even went into supermarkets and little mom'n'pop shops to install displays. His start in radio was inauspicious to say the least, since he can't even remember which station he worked for. He thinks it might have been WHAT in Philadelphia in 1952 when he worked as a salesman for Raymon Bruce, whom he believes might have been the first black air personality.

"He had a program called *The Snap Club*. I sold time to retail shops and got out and hustled, emceed live shows, was a manager of some record artists, things like that. Really hustled to make a living."

He thinks that he worked on some 80 stations in about 50 cities and was fired at least 10 times. "The dates and places are all screwed up. For years, I never lived in any one city more than six months. I was the original rebel and I had to move around the country because I was always getting fired for moving my mouth—trying to bring in unions, things like that . . . that's why I've always considered myself a leisure time executive rather than a disk jockey."

But it was as a disk jockey that he helped put together the original National Association of Radio Announcers, now known as the National Association of Television and Radio Announcers.

"The independent record companies flew several of us into Chicago for a meeting. We set up the organization to improve the condition of the black disk jockey. For years, the black jock was prevented from joining any union . . . the typical salary was only $80-$100 a week."

He recalled being on the air at WAAF in Chicago against Howard Miller in 1955-57 and "getting only $125 a week as a draw against what I could hustle in sales. Miller was getting thousands more."

Montague became "The Great Montague" while working in Houston at KCOM, but became famous doing a show on KTLW in the area. "You could hear the KTLW signal all through Louisiana and southern Texas. I was selling time then, too, and at one point also did recreations of baseball games like Gordon McLendon was doing on his network from KLIF in Dallas. Even then, I was hustling, doing shows at Club Ebony in Houston . . . always a hustler."

Along the way, he got involved in record production. His first hit was "Up on the Mountain" by the Magnificents on VeeJay Records. Once, in Chicago he opened a record store and WVON later fired him, saying it was a conflict of interest. He realized early that "spinning records can't be your only life. I think all young black disk jockeys should realize how a Montague developed—my bottom line has always been the dollar. America owes me nothing. I take what I want with my own abilities."

Today, Montague operates a gallery in Los Angeles; he is the world's greatest collector of books, paintings, letters, artifacts, and other items dealing with the black culture in America. But, as an air personality, Montague had few peers in any format. Among his bywords that have become national cliches are:

1. Have mercy, baby;
2. Keep the faith;
3. Can I get a witness;
4. Burn, baby, burn.

"Burn, baby, burn" was Monty's term for a record on the air that he liked; it became a rallying cry for a black social revolution in Watts, Los Angeles, in 1965. Marvin Gaye had a hit record with "Can I Get a Witness." "Keep the faith" became the *modus operandi* of Adam Clayton Powell.

"It was always a pleasure with me," Montague said, "to hypnotize an audience—to psychologically relax people. I'm like a preacher, anointed with the powers of persuasion." He said he was "motivated by the unknown spirit of success. I could wake up at 4 AM and immediately do a show . . . I can hear the first four bars of a tune and know the direction of the song and how to work in and out of it . . . I don't play a record; I play *Montague*. The record is just the tool—I am the star. I add to the record, I merchandise it." He adds, "After all, the vehicle is no better than the driver."

Some disk jockeys who definitely *are* personalities have rough times in radio. Writing from WGR in Buffalo, N.Y., in 1975, Ron (Shane) Gibson commented that he'd just celebrated 11 years in radio. "It's been a hell of a road to haul freight on, considering that half-decade of years when I could not even get a job up the ladder because of what used to be called the Drake-Chenault syndrome (the so-called time'n'temp jock). But I kept on writing and rocking and reaching and touching and refusing to let any jock ever beat me and the few accomplishments I have made I am proud of." He'd just become No. 1 in his target demographics at his third station in Buffalo.

"One day, I'll get a chance to come back home to where I started—Magic Town ... Los Angeles. And when that day comes, you can kiss your old names goodbye, 'cause it's minds that I take on high and I do that with any format that allows me to paint. But I hope the kids coming up in radio will have a little less dues to pay for their careers as personalities. Remember those grand old days when a disk jockey only got fired because he got beat in the ratings? We got started, a few of us, in the personality era of radio and suddenly found out that nobody wanted personality any more, except the people."

Some disk jockeys obtain a vague kind of fame. Harry Chapin, Elektra Records artist, based his hit song "W-O-L-D" on Jim Conners, then a disk jockey at WYSL in Buffalo. Other jocks continue to labor, hoping for the bigger market, the better station. In March 1975, Tom (Chucker Morgan) Watson wrote from U-100 in Minneapolis: "As you know, when my program director job fell through at WQXI in Atlanta, I went to CHUM in Toronto on a 90-day contract. Program director J. Robert Wood thought the afternoon drive jock was leaving, so he made room for me for 90 days, but the guy decided not to leave, so they let me stay until I found a job I wanted. Wood is one of the greatest program directors any jock could work for—he knows what he wants and how to motivate you. I was treated like a professional from the first day until my last. CHUM and J. Robert Wood make radio worth working in!" Watson is now back working in Canada under another name.

Sig Sakowicz is a phenomenon because he has become almost as important and famous as the big name entertainers he interviews on his show. After years in Chicago, Sakowicz now has radio and television shows in Las Vegas. Observing Sakowicz as objectively as possible, you would say that his two major fortes are his interviews and his personal promotion of himself.

"I think that, in radio, you should have a genuine interest in what you're doing—not be in radio just for the money. Maybe, on the other hand, some disk jockeys have been sharper than I ... I did the free benefits and they did the commercials for radio and television where you got paid. I'm no different than any star—and I don't consider myself a star, because stars don't usually have the capacity to promote themselves. They have to hire a press agent. I just save myself the expense. If I'm blowing my own horn, well, so do they."

But personal promotion is a necessity. "The personality has a great responsibility. To the radio station and to the station's sponsors. The responsibility is to keep up a good image. And one of the primary ways to do this is by being active in the community.

"Too many disk jockeys look at themselves in the mirror too much. And they won't do anything for charity unless they get paid for it. Of course, an air personality—especially someone who's known—can get charitied to death.

"But some so-called personalities go into a hospital once a year—at Christmas—just to get their picture in the local paper. I do that same sort of thing 52 times a year ... and not for money. It's a form of public service." Sakowicz continues, "And you have a responsibility to the listener never to con them. They must have believability in you."

Sakowicz never rests. He has made several trips to Europe and to Vietnam during

U.S. occupation days to entertain American soldiers. The first trip to Vietnam in 1966, he was deeply involved in his other forte—interviews. "And there was a group of soldiers from the southern part of Illinois. After getting back to Chicago, I notified each and every family of those soldiers and then drove down state in a blinding snowstorm to a military armory where I showed movies and slides to the families who'd gathered."

Funds for the entire project came out of his own pocket. It wasn't charity, he insisted. "That's like helping your neighbors. And I loved doing it—those people bawling and thanking me, well . . . ."

To illustrate that good turns pay off sometimes, local TV and radio stations gave the event full coverage, as did the newspapers.

Prior to moving to Las Vegas in November 1972, Sakowicz spent 16 years on WGN in Chicago. "When I moved to Las Vegas, I had to burn 1,100 plaques and certificates; they constituted 35 years of charity projects."

Because he was never "staff" at WGN and only on the air a couple of hours a week under a unique free-lance arrangement with Ward Quall, the general manager—and essentially responsible for the success of his show—Sakowicz may have been forced to be promotional minded. It was his special knack at interviews that helped him establish an identity of his own and become successful in spite of his limited hours on the air. But his interviews were largely combined with his personal promotion of himself. Not that he was doing everything *as a promotion* . . . it just worked out that way. First, "I've always felt that out of sight, out of mind." And it's not only just self-promotion; "I think that an interviewer needs a geniune interest in what he's doing and the people he's interviewing . . . he should become a part of what they do."

Many of the people who came into Chicago to appear on his show, Sakowicz would normally have heard from only once a year; they didn't have public relations people working for them either. To keep up with them more personally, he started corresponding with each and every one. He remembered their birthdays and would send them a card. He kept in touch with them throughout the year.

"I kept up with them all of the time. And friends would keep me posted. For instance, when Paul Williams got married, a friend who was at the wedding called me about it and I had the information on my next show."

Sakowicz has easily accomplished more than 50,000 interviews in his career and more than 40,000 are on tape and catalogued for easy reference. Many air personalities who do interviews make the mistake "of interviewing themselves," Sakowicz said. Or often the disk jockey doing the interview is not listening to the person being interviewed. "He's thinking about some chick or the party he's going to that evening." The good interviewer follows certain guidelines:

1. First, research the interview even if you know the person being interviewed. You will have more empathy with the interviewee if you do the research yourself rather than let an assistant or someone else do it;

2. Have the music ready—old and new, in order to make a comparison;

3. Have outside opinions from various people—people whose opinions will be respected; what a great chance to work in local people on a national figure to give the show great local impact;

4. Have a genuine interest in the person being interviewed.

"Because I generally know the person I'm interviewing so well, my own interviews are usually more conversational, and I can sometimes get something good because they trust me."

Sakowicz tries to pick up the next question from the answer just given in order to provide a natural flow to the interview. He sees as many live performances of record artists as possible in order to talk about the music or work of the artist more honestly.

Jack Carney is a radio veteran. "Broadcasting is the whole ball game for me. It's what I love. It's my psychiatrist, confessor, and mistress all rolled into one.

"The first years in the business, when you pay your dues, it's rough. You are the lowest rung on the social ladder. When you arrive in East Armpit, Nev., to work at the radio station, you may think you can walk up to a store and say: 'I'm a new disk jockey here and I would like to open a charge account.' Well, they're not going to open a charge account for you because for the last 20 years there has been a new disk jockey hitting the city every month . . . and they've all been drunks or worse.

"So, when you're getting started and working one-horse towns, the guy who's employed at the bank and making only $200 a month is socially acceptable, but you're not. Your're a leper. Decent people won't even let you date their daughters. You've got to be prepared for that type of thing. A man has to be totally committed to broadcasting to be in it . . . as I am. The only reason that I haven't quit radio on 4,000 different occasions is that I had no alternative." Carney has worked KMOX in St. Louis, WABC in New York, WIL in St. Louis, and other stations.

Radio men of today sometimes forget past disk jockeys and so much could be learned from the experience of someone like Art Linkletter, who while in college was hired by KGB, San Diego, as a part-time announcer in 1933 and was paid $60 a month. After he went to a 60-hour week, the station paid him $125 a month, "but since I was putting myself through college selling my blood, $125 was a lot of money to me," he said in an interview with disk jockey-comedy writer Ed Hider.

"Then, in 1935 I became radio director of the San Diego Exposition and later held the same position at the San Francisco World's Fair in 1937. I did everything from introducing the governor to emceeing cow-milking contests."

Linkletter continued, "Then, I was one of the first in the country to do man-on-the-street interviews, all this while I was at KGB. I soon became program director and my salary zoomed to $175 a month. Soon afterward, I moved to San Francisco and was heard on seven different radio stations. It was a lot of work, but that was 1939. I was doing 21 different programs a week and was earning over $75,000 a year. By the way, these were all programs that I produced, wrote, starred in, and sold. I did an early morning show on KGO called Date at Eight. At 11 AM, I did a disk jockey show on KSFO. At 1 PM, I did a man-on-the-street show from Market Street and on Sunday night, I would do an interview show from the lobby of the St. Francis Hotel called Who's Dancing Tonight? sponsored by Albert S. Samuels' House of Lucky Wedding Rings—the most popular show in San Francisco at that time. Meredith Wilson was the music director of a radio station in San Francisco about that time, and Ralph Edwards was a young radio personality in Oakland."

As a disk jockey, one of his most memorable experiences was something every disk jockey would like to have.

"Since KGB was basically a network station at the time, we only had the late hours to play records, which I handled. The station was on top of a garage behind the Pickwick Hotel in San Diego. The announcer booth window faced the back of the hotel where a lot of sailors brought their girls. For some reason, they always forgot to pull down the blinds and I as an impressionable young announcer would be deeply engrossed in the scenic view. Often, it would be difficult to break away and go back on the air."

Among his highlights, Linkletter mentioned that he was "most impressed with Franklin D. Roosevelt. He was a remarkable speaker who was able to go in and out of written material like no one I've ever seen."

Ed McMahon started his radio career at WLLH in Lowell, Mass., a 250-watt station, "but we had another transmitter just 11 miles away in Lawrence, so we really boomed out with 350 watts. Since I had studied electrical engineering at Boston College, prior to radio, I knew enough about the equipment so that I could go out and do my own remotes. I'd record an hour show, on an acetate disk, then go to Lawrence and set up the remote equipment. When we were ready in Lawrence, I'd cut into the program already on and do a 15-minute band remote . . . things such as: 'And now, while Dick Stabile is off in the service of his country, the lovely Gracie Barry, with baton in hand, takes the musical spotlight and asks the question, Who?' That's the way we did band remotes in those days.

"My shift started at 6 PM and often went until 2 in the morning. I did the news and sports, mainly special features that came off the wire, then, at 10 PM, with the playing of Benny Goodman's 'Let's Dance,' which was my theme, I began my disk jockey show."

Claiming that he worked about a 48-hour week, McMahon figures that he earned about 20 cents an hour before deductions, but "it wasn't as bad as all that because I worked days as a surveyor making about $55 a week. Listen, I loved radio and there were a lot of guys who paid plenty to get a radio job, so at $10 a week I thought I was pretty lucky."

Then, he went into military service and did an all-night show for a military station in Korea.

"One of my idols, when I was still at WLLH, was Paul Douglas, who was a night-time disk jockey on WCAU in Philadelphia. I used to listen to him all the way in Massachusetts. As you know, he later went on to become one of Hollywood's top motion picture actors. I really modeled myself after Paul Douglas. In fact, one of my big dreams was to work at WCAU like he did. Later on, I did a night show at WCAU.

"Anyway, other guys I really admired on radio were guys like Henry Morgan, William B. Williams, and Ted Brown, a guy named Ed Hurst, who was very big at the time; Dick Clark, of course, and one of my biggest rivals on Philadelphia radio was Ernie Kovaks." McMahon added, "Someone else that I admired a lot was Jack Pyle, who always spoke with a one-to-one approach. When he talked it was like he was talking just to you. That impressed me tremendously and stuck with me."

At the end of World War II, NBC held what they called Welcome Home Auditions for all of the guys who used to work in radio before they went into service.

"You'd go to NBC and they'd give you an audition, make a disk out of it, and send it around to all of their affiliates. Out of that audition I got two job offers—one in Montgomery, Ala., and another in Springfield, Mass. The manager at the station in Springfield was the same man who first hired me at WLLH years ago. I turned down both jobs and decided to go to college and get my degree."

McMahon said that Jay Jackson, then an important announcer in New York, was a big help to him in his early career. "He really guided me, told me what to do in New York, who to see, introduced me to agents, managers, etc. One girl, in particular, he introduced me to was with an advertising agency and she sent me to an audition for Cheer Soap and out of 180 of the top announcers in New York, I was chosen as spokesman."

McMahon, of course, rose to national and international fame with Johnny

Carson's *Tonight Show* on NBC-TV network.

"Dick Clark was my next door neighbor in Philadelphia and he was the subject of a *Person to Person* show that Edward R. Murrow did. The crew came to Dick's apartment after the show was over and then we all went to a club, which was part of the apartment complex we lived in. I was sitting with Dick and a man named Chuck Reeves, who produced Dick's nighttime television show from New York. They talked me into going onstage and introducing everyone—put on a show. When it was over, Reeves told me he was very impressed and would keep me in mind. Now, you know how many times you hear that in this business?"

"But he did better than that. Reeves had an office next door to Johnny Carson's office. He did *Who Do You Trust?* and the announcer, Bill Nimmel, had to give up his job with Johnny and they were frantically looking for a replacement. Reeves heard about it and tried to get me on the phone, but it was the exact day I moved and my phone had been disconnected. He called Dick Clark and asked him to find me, but when Dick went next door, he only found an empty apartment. He looked in the phone book and, even though I was unlisted, my daughter had a phone. He got in touch with her, she got in touch with me, I got in touch with New York, flew that afternoon to New York and got the job. If Dick hadn't been persistent, I would never have gotten the job."

It's impossible, of course, to continue feeding you quotes and comments from disk jockeys because those alone could fill a book. And maybe such a book is needed. But, for the moment, it's up to you to do your own research in the area of the disk jockey or air personality (they mean the same thing, though the duties of the latter might be considered more extensive).

Steve Allen does many things. Andy Williams once said: "He's the only man I know who's listed on every yellow page of the telephone book." Steve Allen commented: "Who's Andy Williams?"

Allen's first job in radio was at KOY in Phoenix, reports Ed Hider. "I announced, wrote, and produced several music and dramatic programs. I also got involved in man-on-the-street interviews and band remotes. For this, I was paid $125 a week." Allen left KOY because "I had been there for about three years and had gone as far as I could go in Phoenix, so I took my life savings of $1,000 and my family and headed for Los Angeles. The only station I could get work at was KFAC. And that's what I played—classical music, from midnight to 5 AM. They paid me $150 a week and I did so well I was hired away by a station that doesn't even exist today—KMTR in Hollywood."

Many, including Ed Hider, think that Steve Allen was the inventor of the ad-lib in radio, though Allen's script in those days was written for him. "In my early days of radio, I never ad-libbed a word. I wrote everything out." At KMTR, Allen was the announcer on Irwin Allen's program. "He was doing a kind of Walter Winchell news show. As you know, Irwin is now the producer of movies such as *The Towering Inferno* and *The Poseiden Adventure.* It was also at KMTR that I teamed up with a friend, Wendell Noble, who was working at KHJ at the time. We persuaded the Mutual Broadcasting Company to let us do a 15-minute, five day a week comedy and music show called *Smile Tonight.* It lasted a good two years on the network."

Then he was back on the street, but the street, fortunately, led to KNX radio in Los Angeles. "They hired me to do a half-hour show, five nights a week, from 11:30-midnight. I played a few records but did mainly comedy. Gradually, I talked more and played fewer records until one of the executives at KNX called me into his office and complained that I wasn't doing the show I was hired to do. I argued that since everyone else in town was playing records at that time, I wanted to offer something different. Comedy.

"I started playing less music than before and then came a very strong memo from the same man telling me to play more music or else." Allen continued, "I read the memo on the air several times and the audience reaction was predictable—I got tons of mail taking my side. So, with the help of a few friends, we carried five or six boxes of mail into the front office and asked him to take a look. A few days later, he admitted he was wrong and told me to continue what I was doing. I then started letting different friends of mine into the studio. They would laugh and the folks at home, thinking we had an audience, started requesting tickets. Within a year, we got such a demand for tickets that KNX expanded the show to an hour and moved me into a studio that held around a thousand people.

"It was during this period that I was forced to make the transistion from script to ad-lib. One evening, I had set aside a 25-minute segment to talk with Doris Day. Unfortunately for me, no one had bothered to inform Doris about it. And there I was with all that time with nothing written to read. So, I did the next best thing . . ."

"Went back to playing records?" asked Hider.

"That thought crossed my mind for a second. But, instead, I picked up a heavy floor mike and carried it into the audience and started ad-libbing with the people. That started it all for me. I don't think I depended on a record or a guest from that moment on." For instance, he announced wrestling. "There's a man down there in the third row giving out with boo's and catcalls and if I had that much booze, I'd call a few cats myself."

Some of the other disk jockeys around Los Angeles were Gene Norman now head of GNP Cresendo Records; Peter Potter; Ira Cook, and Al Jarvis. "By the way, actress Betty White was Al's secretary at the time.

"I got a lot of great reaction; Al Jolson, who was one of my guests, called it "the best show on the air." I was particularly touched by a personally handwritten letter from Phil Silvers, which was full of compliments. It seemed as though everybody who was anybody in the business world would stop by to either plug something or just talk. This went on for a good three years.

"Because of the reaction I was getting, CBS was impressed enough to give me the summer replacement show for *Our Miss Brooks*, which proved very successful."

Allen moved to New York where he substituted for Arthur Godfrey, became a regular *What's My Line* panelist and hosted a show called *Songs for Sale*. Then, in 1954 he was given a show to be seen locally in New York on the NBC-TV outlet. It was called the *Tonight Show*, and his announcer was Gene Rayburn. Eydie Gorme was a regular singer on the show. The following year, Andy Williams joined the show and shortly afterward it went network. Just for history, it should be noted that Allen did a husband and wife show with Jane Meadows 8-9 AM from their home on KHJ in the 60s. "After we had been on the air for about nine weeks, the manager called and said that he had just been fired. I told him I was sorry to hear that and he added, 'But that means you're fired, too.' KHJ had changed format and went all rock."

Today, it's difficult to obtain airchecks of the great radio people; for example, it's almost impossible to get an aircheck of the famed New York announcer Martin Block. You can obtain airchecks of Alan Freed if you scout around; at one time, someone was going to edit out commercials and try to syndicate the programs, but the project never developed. A very valuable study collection to obtain would be "Cruisin' the 50s & 60s: A History of Rock and Roll Radio" album series. This project was produced by Ron Jacobs and features recreations of some well-known air personalities, including Johnny Holliday–WHK Cleveland, 1964; Robert W. Morgan–KHJ Los Angeles, 1965; Pat O'Day–KJR Seattle, 1966; Don Rose–WQXI Atlanta, 1967; Robin Seymour–WKMH Detroit, 1956; Joe Niagara–WIBG Philadelphia, 1957; Jack Carney–WIL St. Louis, 1958; Hunter Hancock–KGFJ Los Angeles, 1959; Dick Biondi–WKBW Buffalo, 1960; Arnie Ginsburg–WMEX Boston, 1961; Russ Knight–KLIF Dallas, 1962; George Oxford–KSAN San Francisco (an AM station in those days), 1955; and B. Mitchell Reed–WMCA New York, 1963. Those disk jockeys and albums are a who's who of Top 40 radio, and were recorded on Increase Records, distributed by GRT Music Tapes.

It would be impossible to list all of the great Top 40, MOR, country, and soul jocks in the nation. Eddie Hill was great doing the all-night show on WSM in Nashville years ago and was the original (or at least the best) friend of truckers in the world, a type of show now copied by country music stations coast to coast. Rick Shaw and Dan Chandler were well-known in Miami on WQAM for years. Paul Berlin was a star in Houston in the early days of rock. Three generations grew up listening to Bob Van Camp doing a morning show on WSB in Atlanta; and two very popular morning show people are J.P. McCarthy–WJR Detroit, and Salty O'Brine–WPRO Providence, R.I., who has done the show several years and seen many format changes. Gene Norman and Al Jarvis were big names in Los Angeles. Some of the top people in radio have been: Russ Syracuse, Ron Chapman, Art Ford, William B. Williams, Ted Brown, Dan Daniels, Dan Ingram, Tom Donahue, George Lorenz, Jack McKenzie, Tom Clay, Peter Potter, and Ira Cook.

There's nothing better than listening to a good air personality, and nothing worse than listening to a station that either doesn't have good air personalities or who hampers their personalities with restrictive formats.

The program director, programming as a science, and ratings

Lucky is the program director who does not have to live—or sometimes die—with ratings. On the other hand, remaining in a small town where the only programming excitement of the month might be a lost dog report would drive most good program directors insane. They usually thrive on ratings, both good and bad.

Ratings are becoming the backbone of radio programming, and today's more knowledgeable program directors use them as guidelines. *Them* refers to Arbitron (better known as the ARB), Pulse, Hooper, and Source, plus a few others not too well known that deal in radio research. There are some other outside research firms involved almost exclusively in radio—DPS operated by Jack McCoy and Doug Herman in the San Diego area which provides computer analysis of the ARB ratings survey data; Entertainment Response Analysts in San Francisco, operated by Sebastian Stone and Willis Duff, which provides psychographic research on a market via the galvanic skin response equipment and services of Dr. Tom Turicchi; and Radio Index, an audience phone research firm operated by former program director Todd Wallace in Phoenix, Ariz. There are other firms such as the parent company of Source (Dimensions Unlimited) that will also do market studies for you.

However, of major importance to the program director and the general manager is the ARB. Without a good ARB, the general manager has trouble selling time, especially on a national level. The ARB has become *the* primary tool of timebuyers at advertising agencies in New York. Because of a small sampling base, in comparison to total population of any given market, an ARB diary's importance is exaggerated out of proportion. This can be extremely dangerous. In San Diego, Ron Jacobs, who was then programming KGB, received a phone call from a listener who had several ARB diaries. A ratings survey was then being taken, and the listener wanted to sell the diaries. Jacobs didn't want to buy the diaries, but he also didn't want them to fall in the hands of another radio station. The ARB was contacted; they said to buy the diaries and mail them to ARB headquarters in Beltsville, Md. The diaries were taken out of circulation by the ARB and KGB's money was refunded by the ARB, according to Jacobs.

One general manager in one of the nation's largest markets says that he buys diaries every ratings survey from someone who 'calls the station.' His argument is that everyone does it and that a diary means too much because it can count for several hundred thousand dollars of national business, as well as local business.

There's not much opportunity for ARB to control this kind of thing. Hopefully, it doesn't happen too often. ARB's computer now flags suspicious diaries. But the truth is that a larger sample needs to be taken to minimize misplaced diaries. In any case, because ratings are so important, the tendency today is to use them for programming purposes and average quarterhour maintenance has become the main drive at many radio stations. The idea is to drag people past the quarter hour—in that way they count double if they just happen to be filling out an ARB diary.

Here's how Charlie Van Dyke, morning personality and program director of KHJ in Los Angeles, explains it:

"ARB tricks?

"I think it begins early. You have to talk with the owner or manager first of all and you have to get very clearly assigned as to what your job is in delivering people.

"So, step No. 1 would be for him to say to you: 'I want you to be the teen king.' Or, in the case of KHJ: 'I want you to have 18-34 year old men and women in morning drive, 18-34 year old women in midday, 18-49 year old men in afternoon drive plus teens, and from 7 PM on, I want only teenagers.' And, you should make him break it down that far . . . because I think it's that difficult.

"That's part of it. Then, you're dealing with whether you should get cumes or quarterhours. Assuming that your cumes are all right—and, in the case of a lot of AM Top 40 dominant stations the cumes are pretty good and the quarterhours are pretty rotten—so I will only speak in terms of the last book . . . our maintenance worked really well. And we did a number of things, one of which was a contest called The Great American Money Machine.

"And the contest was really simple . . . it was simple in that the cash clock would begin counting off the seconds. You would hear the sound of the clock starting. This was a backsell—the ticking of the clock in the background—though the disk jockey would never refer to it, we considered it to be a subliminal sell for the contest. Everytime the guy rapped, you could hear a little ticking back there. When you heard the buzzer go off, which could be in the middle of a commercial, a record, or a newscast—anywhere in the world—you had to be first on the phone to win a Bicentennial silver dollar for every minute that the clock ran. Well, we did this obviously over a couple of quarterhours."

Van Dyke continued, "In the case of the night show, where I wanted to primarily build it up because there had been some erosion, particularly in teens going away, I ran the clock for as long as 240 minutes. Now, you have to understand that the only way to win was to be listening and hear the clock go off and be the first on the phone and be correct in the number of minutes. And we had loads of correct answers. Which means that they all had to listen 240 minutes. There's no other way. We didn't tell them along the way that the clock had been already running 18 minutes or anything like that. We did tell them what hour the clock would start in, which gave them that much of an advantage.

"The night show went from a five-something to an 8.7. And the quarterhours went tremendously high. We also ran the clock through all the dayparts. The clock always ran from one daypart—10 AM, 3 PM, 7 PM—into the other so we could try to get some carry-over.

"Another ARB trick is Jack McCoy's recycling ploy, which you can do yourself. I think this ploy is sensational. You will be able to locate pockets of listeners within an hour—highs and lows for any demographics. I experimented once. I ran a one-liner in what I graphed to be a high pocket of men. The one-liner said: 'Tomorrow morning at 7:30 Charlie Van Dyke will play the greatest song Elton John ever recorded . . .' And then I didn't play it. To see if anyone had noticed. But I did play it at 7:33 AM because the phone calls were incredible. That's just one recycling ploy.

"But you'll notice that I recycled some listeners from one particular time period to another. The same listeners. I think that the whole recycling concept cannot be taken lightly. You do have pockets of listeners. For example, have you ever gone to ARB and looked at a run? Have them do a run for you that shows every mention of your radio station. And also what it's shared with. You might learn, for example, that you have some guys who listen to you in the morning, but are at another station in the afternoon listening to sports.

"Now, you cannot make someone listen to your station that is not available to listen. If a guy is working at 3 PM, you're not going to train him to take his radio into the shop to listen to you. But, if he's listening to radio, you can get him back. So, if he's there in the morning, you give him something specific to turn back on in the afternoon so that he might at least begin sharing you with sports in the afternoon. And that way you build up your afternoon show.

. . . "I think you can find the pockets and move them across."

Cume is a station's universe of listeners; share is merely an efficiency factor—the efficiency with which the station reaches its universe—according to Eric G. Norberg, program director of KEX in Portland, Ore.

"We are now in the research era of radio programming . . . intuition seemingly counts for nothing unless numbers back it up." But Norberg points out that while research is a great tool, without a good understanding of "what you're researching, can really lead you down the garden path. Improperly designed or improperly evaluated research yields the wrong answers."

The best starting place for a program director to research his audience and market is a ratings survey. "First, though, a few things to watch out for. You've heard about the error factor—ARB prints a nomograph in the back of their book to help you calculate what it is. If you actually do, you'll be amazed at the size of the possible error when you get down to a demographic group in a daypart, where the sample size is tiny but rating services cannot substantially increase sample sizes without pricing their surveys out of the market. For that reason, not one ratings book can be considered gospel. For definitive programming research information, it's necessary to 'trend' with at least two and preferably three ARB books."

Norberg recommended concentration on cume rather than share. First, because it's more commonly used in selling radio time and second because it's more easy to manipulate share than cume by programming.

"One way of increasing share (time spent listening) is to increase the station's appeal to a minority audience, but that narrows the size of the total weekly audience.

"A station attempting to reach a mass audience must avoid that pitfall by programming to increase its cume base while maintaining roughly the same efficiency. That way, the share will increase as the cume increases." Norberg continued, "As for the greater manipulability of shares, well, if you can keep the same people listening an extra 5 to 15 minutes per daypart, your shares may increase up to 50 percent. Programming to the ratings, however, can result in cajoling, bamboozling, and bribing the listener to keep listening in a way that may eventually damage your station's image to him and result in lessening his loyalty to you and hurt your ratings in the long run."

Jay Blackburn, recently a principle in the radio construction/engineering firm of Hope, Bennett, Blackburn, San Juan, Puerto Rico, consulted many clients on programming; his experience as a program director ranges from Dallas, Tex., to Norfolk, Va. He targets listeners after figuring available time to listen. Available time to listen is obtained by going to ARB in Beltsville, Md., and spending approximately three days gleaning the information from a mechanical diary which can be requested for any given market. The information can be broken down however you want it—income level, age, geographical location, etc. Since average listening patterns within age groups vary little from year to year, Blackburn said the following information still applies to the Dallas/Ft. Worth market—the average available listening time for ages 18-24 males and females is 19.5 minutes between 6-9 AM, 27.8 minutes from 9 AM-3:30 PM, 20.3 minutes from 3:30-6:30 PM, 29.4 minutes from 6:30-9 PM, 38.1 minutes from 9-midnight.

"Remember, these are averages and could be broken down in any number of ways for various applications, i.e. record rotation, dayparting, etc."

Blackburn believes that in order to program by ARB ratings, you should understand what ratings are all about.

"Once an ARB diary is returned to Beltsville, two things happen to it: Justification and Computation. When a diary is justified, ARB makes sure that each station listed is clearly identified and that each entry chronologically coincides with every other entry. If a station cannot be identified, that entry is struck or red-lined and no one gets credit for it. If two or more entries do not coincide chronologically, then they are struck. Sometimes, the whole diary is thrown out," he said. "It obviously benefits the radio station to avoid all confusion. Constant and correctly placed identification is a must and to avoid confusion, a minimum number of *identifiers* should be used. In Dallas, for example, the call letters of KNUS and KRLD are different, but "The Zoo," or KZEW, is greatly different and easily remembered.

"In extreme cases, ARB even uses disk jockey names in the justification process. These should be memorable, exposed often, and mentioned one at a time. Crossplugging during a ratings period is not an intelligent thing to do."

In computation, ARB uses four arbitrary points on the clock: :00, :15, :30, and :45. Five minutes of listening in any quarterhour will get you credit for the entire quarterhour. For instance, 18-year-old Donna Alexander makes an entry in her ARB diary: KIKK for 4:10 to 4:20 PM. ARB would then give KIKK credit for two quarterhours.

By manipulating a listener to turn a station off or to switch to another station because of some kind of tuneout factor, and then encouraging them to come back a few minutes later for a contest or must-listen record, "it is wholly possible to milk eight quarterhours of credit from one listener in one hour!" Blackburn said.

"This makes it imperative to retain as many listeners as possible through the four points of the ARB clock. Logically, we then position all elements, other than music, within each quarterhour, avoiding the four main points of the clock. This should be the basis of your format structure and continuing quarterhour maintenance promotion."

It's entirely possible to hype a rating and it works. That's why radio stations during ratings periods tend to have more contests and larger prizes, advertise in local newspapers and billboards, advertise on television, and run promotions ranging from beach parties (even in cities that are hundreds of miles from the ocean) to bathing beauty contests. They will do anything and everything to gain attention and to force high visibility of the call letters so that anyone filling out an ARB diary will remember their call letters, in spite of what station they may actually have been listening to. Howard Kester, when he was manager of KYA in San Francisco, used to put up posters and even hold free concerts in areas beyond his signal reach.

Rating Woes

Hyping can take on many forms. John Gehron, the program director of WLS in Chicago, said that he was "concerned with stations using timewarping to hype ratings.

Timewarping is usually done at the most critical points in the hour, where two quarter-hours touch. A station will give the time as 2:20 PM when, in reality, it is 2:16 PM. Since ARB requires a minimum of five minutes of listening in a quarterhour to receive credit for that quarterhour, you can see how this hypes."

Gehron believes there are methods of capitalizing on the quarterhour programming principle without "having to lie to your audience. I hope programmers will think twice before using this practice. The Federal Trade Commission and ARB define hyping as 'activities calculated to distort or inflate such data.' Stations have received short renewals and fines for hyping during ratings.

"I think timewarping is consumer fraud and am concerned about this hype method being used against responsible broadcasters. This is certainly not in the public interest. WLS has made an official complaint to ARB about this practice in Chicago. If a station is aware of it in their market, they should protest to the ARB, too. You can be a professional programmer who wins with skill or you can program with deception and dirty tricks. Every program director should ask himself what kind of programmer he is.

"You can win honestly. We are at WLS."

Jay Blackburn believes that quarterhour maintenance promotions work on the same basis, "regardless of format. You tell the audience something is going to happen four or five minutes prior to :15, you tell them exactly what is going to happen two or three minutes prior to :30 and finally it happens five to six minutes after :45. This process is repeated on an hourly basis from 6 AM to 1 AM, seven days a week."

He feels that teeshirts (with the station's call letter on them) and free albums are decent quarterhour maintenance promotions.

Mike Deeson, program director of WNOR in Norfolk, Va., said that "while many program directors, general managers, sales managers, and disk jockeys curse ratings as a sword of Damocles hanging over our heads, ratings are, in fact, one of the most effective programming tools available. Besides telling a lot of folks that it's time to redo the old resume, what else does an Arbitron ratings book tell us?

"The first thing to look at is the 6 AM-midnight total persons 12-plus years of age. This gives you a general ranking of where your station stands in target demographics. You might have moved from fifth to third in total persons 12-plus years of age; however, your gain might have been exclusively in teens where you were trying to improve your men 25-34 years of age.

"Therefore, the next step is to figure out how you did in terms of target demographics; did your overall ranking increase or decrease in target demographics?" Deeson continued, "Next, compute your efficiency factor. What percentage of your audience comes from your target demographics? If, for example, you're targeting 12-34 and 65 percent of your audience is plus 50, perhaps your music is off target. The importance of the efficiency factor is that it gives you an indication of how successful your current programming is, no matter how large or small your total audience."

Deeson said that a station which moves from No. 3 to No. 2 in the market might still have cause to worry if it notices that its efficiency factor is drastically changing. At this point, the program director needs to determine if he still wants the same demographics or if the demographics he has are saleable and viable.

"It depends a lot on your station's general manager and sales manager. But having great ratings that can't be sold is as useless as having no numbers at all. Therefore, it is important to work with your general manager and determine what demographics he wants—consistent with good programming procedures in each time period—and then to program accordingly.

"To get a realistic view of how your station is doing in the marketplace, you must classify all of the stations in the market by format. If, for instance, your station experienced a heavy loss in men 18-24, you might have cause for concern. However, if in your format breakdown, you notice that men 18-24 are deserting AM contemporary stations in droves, then perhaps it is time to reassess your target demographics. It doesn't make much sense to try to program to an audience that isn't available for your format.

"Breaking out the market according to format gives you an overall view as to where the market is going and it gives you an opportunity to be on top of the trends."

The danger in breaking out the ratings via formats is that it can sometimes give false hope as to the answer to your station's problems. "For example," Deeson said, "you might notice that the country format station has captured a huge portion of your market, especially adults 25-49. So you figure all you need to do is change to a country format and your problems will be solved. However, in a report available from Arbitron showing the geographic distribution of raw demo mentions for each station, it may become apparent that the majority of the votes for country music come from outlying areas. If your station's signal doesn't adequately cover the outlying areas, then you will be supplying a format to people who can't hear it. Therefore, it is imperative to realistically assess your station's power, signal, and competitive strength in the marketplace."

To determine whether your station is successful, you also have to figure out how well the competition is doing. Although a radio station in the market may have a larger average quarterhour than another station, it is possible that listeners prefer the second station. So, to determine how successful your programming is, you have to determine the time spent listening. You do this by multiplying your average persons by the number of hours in the time period and divide this by the cume persons. This will give you a percentage of an hour figure. Multiply that number by 60 and you'll have the average number of minutes of time spent listening.

"If you are an AM contemporary station that is fifth in the market," Deeson said, "and your competition is first, determine how long the average listener listens to your station and to your competition. If there is a great disparity in the amount of listening time in your favor, perhaps the listeners are really more satisfied with your station than the competition, in spite of the ratings. It could be that not enough people are sampling your station, which indicates that you've got to work on your cumes through outside promotions. Cumes, by definition, cannot be increased through on-air product, because once a person listens five minutes or more, he or she automatically become a cume." Deeson added, "Henceforth, to increase cumes, you've got to concentrate on outside promotions.

"Of course, you can increase your cumes through recycling the listener; however, this gets into a semantic argument. Nonetheless, to determine how effective a job you are doing at recycling the listener, check your cume daypart combinations as reported by ARB. By adding the cumes separately in two time periods and then subtracting the corresponding cume daypart combinations from that, you can see what percent of your audience is not being recycled from one daypart to another. Then, do the same thing for your competition and see if there is a huge disparity between your recycled listeners and your competition's listeners.

"Getting trends from several ARB reports in the hour-by-hour breakouts can help you determine where the pockets of listeners are available to be recycled into various dayparts."

In working on listening time, it should be remembered that certain formats are going to get longer listening sweeps than others by nature of their format. A beautiful music station will have longer listening sweeps than an AM rock station.

"In dealing with competitors, are you sure with whom you are sharing your audience? It seems like a simple question," said Deeson, "however, you cannot be sure unless you go through the diaries in Beltsville or have a mechanical done for you, which is a printout available from Arbitron. You can see every diary that mentions your station and any other station that is mentioned. You actually might be surprised as to who your competition really is."

When you try to decide what programming decisions you'll make for each daypart, it is important to determine what the available audience is during each daypart. However, it is advisable to use many previous surveys to determine any listening trends in your market, since the hour-by-hour sample size is so small that in a one book period it may not be statistically reliable.

"Another problem with the Arbitron figures is that some programmers lose sight of how they relate to people in the real world," Deeson said. "I had a friend who couldn't understand why his women 25-49 dropped off from 3-4 PM. He was about to alter his programming drastically to keep his women during that hour. I suggested he first see what happened to other stations from 3-4 PM.

"He was shocked. The entire market had a loss in women 25-49 from 3-4 PM. He was befuddled and his conclusion was that no station was offering women 25-49 years of age the right programming in that time period, so he would come up with something revolutionary.

"I suggested that before he bothered, he should check what time schools let out in his market. He was again astounded. But the fact was that women 25-49 were busy each weekday afternoon at that time with their children coming home from school.

"Again, all too often program directors just see numbers and don't relate them to actual people."

It is important, Deeson said, to remember that the success that comes from programming "to" and "from" Arbitron is a combination of research of the ARB to gather the most information available about your market and then to relate that data to people.

Deeson concluded, "Ratings are a reflection of listening habits."

Most program directors have learned to live with ratings. However, Ron Jacobs protests about that necessity.

"I wish there was a federal hearing on ratings because I could come off as a really righteous witness. I mean, the best thing that could happen in the radio business or the media business in general would be a realistic approach to ratings. Having been on the receiving end of good, bad, and indifferent ratings, well, the problem doesn't just apply to radio. Everyone knows that the national Nielsen sample for television is a joke—that if the United States had to fly a man to the moon based on that kind of scientific data they wouldn't even have the astronaut's jockstrap on by now."

As far as ARB is concerned, Jacobs wants to know "why a firm which is owned by a data processing company uses a survey sample based on about 1,200 little paper diaries and then takes a month to add up and data process and cross tabulate those numbers. I mean, the day I went to Beltsville was an eye-opener for me, because I could see that this is a peculiar game that we're playing in radio if it's based on all this . . . if it's based on the ability of a lady with red ballpoint pen to correctly write down the call letters in her diary."

He said that before anyone programs a radio station or goes on the air as a disk jockey, they should look at a filled-out ARB diary. Otherwise, they'll have an entirely wrong and idealistic idea about the rules of this game as they presently exist—he said he didn't see one ARB diary in all those he looked through that was filled out from beginning to end.

"It just galls me that ratings have become so important. No one cares any more what a radio station sounds like or whether the programming is good or not, or whether the disk jockeys and the listeners are having fun, or whether the station is making a meaningful contribution to the community. All they care about is numbers. It's really insane."

Tom Yates, program director of KLOS in Los Angeles, feels more positively about ratings in general. He believes that competition between the different ratings firms has resulted in the program director being provided with more usable data than ever before, more accurately than ever before. He uses ratings as a programming tool, but like many other program directors, he also does other research.

Music Programming and Music

Programming a radio station is a nebulous labor. Though so-called rules have developed over the years, for one reason and another, radio programming is still essentially a fly-by-the-seatpants situation. Science has been applied to programming, sometimes in heavy doses, yet there are program directors and general managers who create radio kingdoms, generally by not following any carefully designed rules. In fact, any one of these program directors or general managers might find it difficult to tell you *how* they're successful. They might be able to tell you *why*—and talk for hours on the subject—but those why's would have little validity if attempted at another radio station anywhere in the nation.

A good example would be WSB in Atlanta. WSB is a great station—for years a leader in the market in ratings, earnings, audience impact—and its general manager Elmo Ellis is a great man. But listening to Elmo Ellis try to tell you how to program a radio station would be frustrating and maybe even a mistake. WSB features a "magazine" type of format that is not only difficult to achieve, but requires an enormous staff and enormous overhead.

Ellis once described himself at an annual convention of the National Association of Broadcasters as "a do-it-yourself broadcaster. In more than 30 years of programming, I've never bought a jingle or a promotion or a contest."

Radio programming, said Ellis, falls into three basic categories:

1. Pure entertainment;

2. Pure information; or

3. A combination of the two.

"All three categories offer a wide variety of options and opportunities," Ellis said.

At that same meeting, Ellis pointed out that "a great many saleable items can be developed by deliberately setting out to supply information and entertainment that you know a particular advertiser or group of listeners might like. For instance, if you have a client who is a golfing nut, create and sell a series of one-minute lessons of 'How to play better golf.' Any kind of popular sport lends itself to this kind of exploitation.

"If you know an advertiser who has a problem, why not develop programming to help him? We have produced informational campaigns on automobiles, real estate, and financial institutions that have been very successful—and very saleable. Let's think, for a moment, about some of the things the people of your city are concerned about:

1. How to look and feel better;

2. The cost of living;

3. How to lose weight;

4. How to be successful;

5. How to make more money;

6. How to save more money;

7. How to have a good time;

8. How to thwart robbers and burglars;

9. How to communicate with kids;

10. How to be happy.

"Any of these topics can be developed into a saleable, short report—possibly 30 seconds in length, leaving the other 30 seconds for the client's commercial."

Most program directors, at least in major and medium markets, wouldn't even attempt to try this type of programming. The fact that it works (and is quite profitable in audience and in dollars) for WSB in Atlanta doesn't mean that it would work in any other city in the nation. But it's obvious that many tactics of WSB *would* work anywhere and others might work somewhere. Ellis claimed that if a program director and/or general manager listens carefully to the people of his town, "they will clue you in on dozens of programming possibilities. The public can also help in developing and producing much of your programming.

"Listeners are only too happy to help select music, supply news and news tips, play games, contribute jokes and poems, personal experiences, and opinions. The more completely you involve your audience, the more loyalty and dependency they will demonstrate. It becomes a partnership of sorts." Ellis continued, "I recommend this because it has worked well for us in Atlanta."

Ellis said that the key to the future viability of radio lies in communicating "closely with the public" and developing new services as they are needed by the public "just as we had to develop new services when television came on the scene." He recommended that stations "seek out interesting songs wherever they may be. Don't limit your choices to a single category, which has no real validity. Try to develop your disk jockeys into knowledgeable communicators, capable of being informative, humorous, brief and breezy, and devise new and interesting ways to involve your audience."

Aside from WSB, other giant stations include WCCO in Minneapolis, WJR in Detroit, and WGN in Chicago. For the size of its market, WTIC in Hartford is a giant station, and WOR in New York isn't too bad as a total-market station. These stations command audience shares that many younger program directors simply can't believe. After all, these stations are different, they violate most sensible programming concepts. WSB, for instance, is more comparable to a small market station where the programming often has to cater to the potential advertiser. The only difference would be that WSB turns it into a programming plus through the efforts of an experienced staff, vast labor in production, good personal image of the station in the market, and abundant talent. The small market station usually doesn't have time nor the talent to turn a programming negative into a positive.

Personally, this type of programming that is done by a WSB is quite valid, but not necessarily wise to copy. It is useful to study, but not useful to imitate. Herein, we will discuss more applicable programming concepts. In any case, the WSB-type of programming can't be explained too well. It has to be experienced. When Bob Van Camp, the legendary (three generations of people had grown up listening to his show) morning personality on WSB retired, the station replaced him with a well-known personality and featured visiting celebrities (in other words, several people). Elmo Ellis never takes a step backward, it's always upward and better.

One thing should be noted: Several of the so-called giant stations have dwindled in popularity in recent years: WBT in Charlotte, WHDH in Boston, KSFO in San Francisco, KMPC in Los Angeles. This is not to infer that they are doing badly—they are, in fact, doing quite well. But they are no longer giants. They've gone modern, in effect, and no longer attempt to be everything to everybody. However, KDKA in Pittsburgh has made inroads towards becoming a giant, and so has WIRE in Indianapolis, oddly enough, with a country music format. (All of the other stations that you might call giants have been more MOR in nature than anything else. Though it should be noted that WSB plays Chet Atkins, Elvis Presley, and almost anyone else and they always have, even when rock stations decided that Elvis Presley was old hat). And one or two other radio stations may be on the verge of becoming giants. Once you reach this stage of radio, the audience seems to forgive, and even dote on, your programming mistakes because they know that you (the station) are on their side and out for their good.

In the soul music format, WDIA in Memphis is, without question, a tremendous station. What other station do you know that operates a school bus route, little league baseball teams, and more than the usual community projects? It's owned by Sonderling Broadcasting and is one of the greatest radio stations in the world.

Now, however, we're talking about stations that use a regular format approach. WOR in New York is mostly talk; at WCCO, you can find everything. WDIA uses a music format, on the whole, and it's music format (modern radio formats in total) that we are concerned with here.

9 Research

Research plays an important role in today's radio programming—as opposed to the ordinary audience ratings now being conducted by ARB, Pulse, Hooper, and Source. Magid in Iowa does market research, but is a little too expensive to use on a regular basis; Kent Burkhart, when he was head of radio for Pacific and Southern and later as a programming consultant, was always fond of Magid. Mike Joseph, the programming consultant who undoubtedly was the first in the field to do such, prepares an audience-flow survey as his first project at any station to find out who is available to program to and at what time of the day. Ron Jacobs, when he was programming KGB-AM-FM in San Diego, did his own music study in the market—he put several of his staff out on the street with a questionnaire.

Buzz Bennett, when he was helping with music at WMCA in New York, went out on the street personally to find out what records were being bought and by whom, in order to program with Terrell Metheny, the program director. Program directors today who're intensively involved in programming do enormous loads of market studies.

There is a danger, of course, in too much study, or studies that are not necessarily applicable, and that's how WMCA in New York went down the drain. Why? Well, Bennett was still flying on rather damp wings at that point (though he was later to evolve to a high level of programming relativity). His programming concepts hinged to a large extent on over-the-counter sales of singles. Unfortunately, the people who were buying singles weren't necessarily questioned by ARB or Pulse (even then, ARB and Pulse "adjusted" for Harlem and it was young blacks who were then buying most of the singles, especially anything with a blues sound). In any case, the people buying singles (who may have actually been listening to WMCA) weren't rated. WMCA eventually became a two-way talk station. They didn't realize that radio research had to be *tailored* to the individual market to be applicable for programming.

The object here is not to scare you against research, nor sway you totally in that direction. But the truth is that programming, while not a legitimate science per se, has become highly sophisticated and the wise program director of today does not ignore any research. All data about your audience is useful input. When Ron Jacobs finished his first research study in San Diego, he could tell you the popularity by daypart and by album cut for several hundreds artists, broken down by age groups.

Research can be broken into two different aspects. The first is audience research, the second is music research. Sometimes, these research tasks overlap. But audience research would entail more things than music tastes. It includes the time periods when people are available to listen by demographics, and information about the services the public might need. Jimi Fox, when he took over as program director of the old KGBS in Los Angeles, immediately began surveying the market to find out what people wanted to hear—their wants, needs, tastes. This type of audience research should be done sporadically.

Music research is something that should be done weekly or as often as possible. It can consist of obtaining data from visiting record promotion persons or those who phone; calling a few record stores to find out what's selling that week; checking a few national trade paper charts such as the "Hot 100 Chart" in *Billboard* magazine or any of the other charts in *Billboard,* and record tipsheets such as the *Gavin Report* from San Francisco.

Today, audience research is becoming more complex. For instance, in 1975, about 120 people were tested in a hotel out by the Los Angeles airport to evaluate five radio stations, only three of which actually existed in the market. Each of the test subjects, in one part of the experiment, was wired to galvanic skin response devices. The study (contracted by KPOL in Los Angeles) tested KPOL against two of its competitiors and two imaginary stations that KPOL operations manager Al Herskovitz created. Another part of the study involved tuneout factors—at random times through the experiment, the radio stations that are listed to by the test subject are scrambled in their ear phones, and the subjects must push buttons until they find that particular station or another station they might like better.

The galvanic skin response test—similar to a lie detector—judges how well people *really* like music, commercials, jingles, and air personalities. On another study of this type, Dan Ingram of WABC in New York scored higher than even Paul McCartney, who had an enormous worldwide hit going for him at the time. The news was rated last. In a study of the Cleveland market, one morning show disk jockey proved to be a tuneout factor; every time he started to talk the audience switched to another station! These studies were handled by Entertainment Response Analysts, headed by Willis Duff and Sebastian Stone, two former radio men. They contract for the services of CRI, a firm in which Dr. Tom Turicchi of Dallas is a partner; it's his system that's used in the experiments. At one point, ERA had research data of this type from more than 40 markets in which they had conducted experiments. All of the experimenting to date is highly complex. Some people in both the record and radio industries wonder if Turicchi's studies are sufficient judgments of records, music flow, air personalities, commercials, and other radio programming elements such as news, weather, and editorials.

"If Turicchi's thing works, it's a doomsday machine," said Jack McCoy, former research director of Bartell's radio operations. He is now head of DPS, San Diego, a research firm that analyzes ARB ratings for programming information and also provides client stations with programming data via closed circuit television.

George Wilson, now president of Bartell Broadcasters radio chain, once said that Buddah Records had CRI test five singles and that the Turicchi tests showed two of the singles could be hits. "And," Wilson said, "those two records were hits for Buddah." In some studies in the Dallas area, Turicchi found that some records suffer from fatigue—thus Turicchi can now tell a radio station how long to stay on a given record.

In April 1975, after an extensive ERA-Turicchi study in the market, KPOL gave up old music in its beautiful music format on FM. The AM station continued to program older material (it's also a beautiful music format), but general manager Pete Newel and operations manager Al Herskovitz had to find a method for appeasing younger listeners.

"The major problem with any beautiful music format," Herskovitz said, "is that the demographics are a little old because the formats always tended to rely on

Cole Porter tunes and other older writers. It's not that Cole Porter music isn't pretty—just that it turns off younger people who're not into bland music.

"Still, the average housewife doesn't want to listen to rock; she has enough noise around her in the house—the dishwasher, the kids."

ERA's research results, he said, proved that a gut feeling of his had been right; he'd felt that a beautiful music station could lower its demographics if it played music familiar to young adults—i.e., pretty music versions of contemporary hits. "The preference was toward newer music in all demographics outside of teens," he said. Eighty percent of the young adults preferred newer tunes, as compared to 75 percent of the older people—commanding portions for any radio stations.

It should be noted that Herskovitz didn't immediately run to the station and change the programming. First, he had to find some newer tunes. For this, he found a firm—Good Music Inc. in Los Angeles operated by arranger Ed Yellin—to produce for radio-airplay-only some records of hit tunes, all beautiful in arrangements. (The cost of these records were later offset when the radio stations around the country that bought them packaged special albums and sold them over the air—an excellent promotion for the station as well as a service to the listening community since you seldom can buy that kind of music in record stores anymore.)

In any case, Herskovitz altered the programming very slowly over several months in order not to disturb listeners. From the first, he expected no dramatic audience changes. "But, give us another one or two shares in the audience ratings surveys in the months to come and I'll be able to retire out beside the swimming pool." He pointed out that one or two share point increases in a market such as Los Angeles (on top of the station's present ratings) could result in enormous increases in advertising revenues for KPOL. KPOL-FM later switched to a soft rock format.

In San Diego (the firm is actually located in the suburb of El Cajon), the computer at Cyberdynamics Inc. (headed by Doug Herman) says: "Good morning you are No. 1. If KCBQ's audience had listened 32.5 percent longer, you would have been No. 1 with a 24.3 share. It is reasonable to expect your audience to listen 32.5 percent longer in this demographic." Thus, the readout comes back as Doug Herman, a computer expert, feeds in information gleaned from an ARB ratings survey. It's this information that his partner Jack McCoy, who operates the firm of DPS, markets. It was Jack McCoy, who when he was a program director, took over KCBQ in San Diego and programmed it to even greater heights than its former program director Buzz Bennett. McCoy built KCBQ into such a success that it was copied from coast to coast and the so-called Q-format grew. Essentially, the Q-format is based on the belief that adults don't even become aware of a record until it's about ready to drop off the national charts, so McCoy kept it on his total playlist (he had several lists) under the category of familiar. Later, stations came to have current lists and "recurrents." It was much the same thing as popularized by Jack McCoy. McCoy wasn't the very first to conceive of the idea, he just used it more effectively. For more than two or three years prior to McCoy's rise to fame, several program directors felt that records should be retained longer on the playlist. Most stations "retired" records that had dropped off their playlist for a couple of weeks, but were bringing some of these back early as oldies. McCoy, however, didn't bother to even retire them, just put them into a rotation pattern of their own.

However, radio will honor McCoy for more than just that, because he's undoubtedly a genius. George Wilson, head of Bartell Broadcasters and a veteran program director, admits without shame that McCoy is hard to understand, "but his ideas work." McCoy claims that a record company can tell him how many radio stations are playing a particular record "and we can find out the rotation pattern and tell you how many people have heard the record."

Under one service offered by Cyberdynamics-Recon, the program director using the service can ask the computer (a computer terminal is installed in each radio station) how many times he should play a certain record to reach an adult audience versus a teenage one. The computer will provide the rotation pattern, including the times to play it and when. Such stations as KLIF in Dallas and KYA in San Francisco went on line with the service, but at this time, it hasn't helped their ratings much.

One of the Recon services is a ranking system for records in a given market—the playlist. The station provides Recon with its store reports and requests, then the computer sums everything up and feeds the list back in order of importance. At this time, several radio chains are using one or more of the services of the two interrelated firms.

Other Research

The program director should be aware of all research that might pertain to his programming. Every six months, *Billboard* magazine reports how singles, albums, and cartridges are faring, based on chart actions, for each of the companies. It's interesting and educational to note which record companies are doing well in singles. In February 1975, the complex of Warner Bros. Records, Atlantic Records, and Elektra Records garnered 102 singles on the chart for 15.7 percent of the chart action. CBS was second with 83 singles and 13.6 percent of the action. Capitol Records had 50 singles on the chart and 10.5 percent of the action. Polygram was fourth with 46 singles for 8.1 percent of the total chart action during recent months surveyed.

But when it came to albums and cartridges, WEA was first with 29.3 percent, CBS second with 17.2 percent of the action and Capitol was a latecomer with 9.0 percent, while MCA Records had 6.8 percent. This is indicative of who is turning out the best and most popular records. Of course, the companies involved are all giants in the record business and no program director should ignore the fact than even a small label can produce a great and very popular single or album.

Several intensive audience surveys have been accomplished over the years. A few years ago, some two dozen record promotion executives (under the guidance of Jan Basham, a promotion executive with A&M Records) completed one of the most comprehensive studies of record buying habits ever attempted.

Store Study

Minority women 16-34 years of age were buying most of the new soul singles; and white girls 12-15 years of age were buying a vast majority of the pop singles. But up to the age of 24, it was neck and neck between women and men in regards to the purchase of singles. Before the age of 24, men usually spend more money on albums than singles. In fact, there were more than twice as many white males ages 19-24 buying pop albums (25.7 percent) than white females (11.4 percent).

This survey was the work of several Los Angeles record promotion people who devoted their personal time to interview customers throughout record stores in the Los Angeles area. The group interviewed a total of 1,030 record customers and ran all of the data through the A&M Records computer. Partial results of the survey were announced at an International Radio Programming Forum in Los Angeles.

The dominant record-buying ages were from 19-34 years of age, except country music albums were usually sold to an older white audience. Of the current country album sales, most were bought by white males and females 35-49 years of age, mostly by females (4.5 percent as compared to 27.3 percent). Other things noted by the survey included:

The dominant group buying soul were black and Latin-Americans between the ages of 16-34. On current soul albums, white minority males ages 19-49 made most of the purchases. But when it came to soul album oldies, the dominant buyers were generally white males 25-34 years of age. There were no significant sales of country oldie singles. Country album oldies were popular with minority females 19-24 years of age, but were mostly bought by white males and females ages 25-49. Other album sales were: classical albums—white males and females 19-34; cassettes—white males 19-49; cartridges white males 16-24; soundtrack albums—white males and females 19-34.

Radio Role

Without a doubt, radio was the major influence upon all record sales, though word of mouth was extremely important in the purchase of records, starting with white females even younger than 12 years of age and both whites and all minorities above 12 years old.

Though several stations have changed formats, it's interesting to note that the major stations influencing sales of singles of all kinds were: KHJ 20.23 percent, KGFJ 18.6, KKDJ 8.9, XPRS 7.6, KLAC 5.6. Since then, of course, KDAY went soul in format and is probably influencing singles sales. KKDJ, an FM station, has become the FM side of KIIS.

Stations influencing album sales were: KMET 17 percent, KLOS 10, KBCA 7, KGFJ 5, KNAC 4, and KHJ 3.9. KBCA was and still is a jazz-format station. KLOS later came up with huge ratings and today would fare better in a survey of this type. The most-listened-to radio stations were: KHJ, KMET, KLOS, KKDJ, KGFJ, KDAY, XPRS, KBCA, KIIS, KROQ.

The preferred disk jockeys of that time were: Wolfman Jack, Robert W. Morgan, the Real Don Steele, a tie between Dave Hull and Dick Whittington, and the Magnificent Montague. The most-listened-to FM air personalities in that particular survey were: Barry (Dr. Demento) Hansen, Steven Clean, Mary Turner, and B. Mitch Reed—all then with KMET; Rick Holmes, then with KBCA; and Rod McGrew with KJLH.

The study also covered listening habits. It revealed that white males 12-15 years of age are listening much more to FM radio than AM radio. This is true throughout the day, but even more strongly at night. And regarding male members of minority groups—78 percent might listen to FM radio 6-9 PM as opposed to only 22 percent listening to AM radio. During this same time period, more white females are listening to AM than FM and the gap is even stronger among minority females where 10 percent might be listening to FM as opposed to 40 percent listening to AM. Among those who worked on the survey besides Jan Basham were Chris Crist, Don Whittemore, Chuck Meyer, Dale White, Bill Pfondresher, and Sandy Horn. Though every market differs, many of the above statistics would hold true for other markets of similar size—or perhaps even medium markets. This survey has been recently completed; names and call letters have changed, but musical preferences remained fairly constant.

Late in 1975, a radio programming syndication firm in Los Angeles called Radio Arts Inc., paid for a national survey on music radio listening preferences and this survey is extremely noteworthy. Though Elton John and other rock artists may sell the most records, they often take a backseat on radio listening preferences among 25-69 year old listeners, according to the study of some 12,000 people by the research firm of Dimensions Unlimited. The 40 major artists among adult listeners are, alphabetically, Burt Bacharach, the Beatles, Glen Campbell, the Carpenters, Vikki Carr, Johnny Cash, Ray Charles, Chicago, Petula Clark, Roy Clark, Nat King Cole, Perry Como, Mac Davis, John Denver, Neil Diamond, the Fifth Dimension, Roberta Flack, Tennessee Ernie Ford, Robert Goulet, Al Hirt, and Englebert Humperdinck. Also, Elton John, Olivia Newton-John, Tom Jones, Henry Mancini, Dean Martin, Johnny Mathis, Wayne Newton, Tony Orlando & Dawn, Elvis Presley, Charley Pride, Helen Reddy, Charlie Rich, Simon & Garfunkel, Frank Sinatra, Barbra Streisand, Tijuana Brass, Bobby Vinton, Dionne Warwick, and Andy Williams were the artist most often asked for in the survey.

However, when the survey was adjusted to reflect population percentages in the 25-60 age group, such names as Eddy Arnold, Tony Bennett, Bing Crosby, and Sammy Davis Jr. leaped into the most popular 40 artists. When population percentages were applied, no heavy rock artist made the leading 40 circle, including the Beatles, Elton John, or any of the other expected names.

One of the more interesting aspects uncovered from this survey was that some artists are more popular in certain areas of the nation than in other parts, and this also applies to the size of the city.

Mac Davis was very strong among adult listeners in small and in medium-sized markets, but dropped slightly out of the top 20 ranking in major cities. On the other hand, Andy Williams was very strong in every market. Dionne Warwick faded a little in small markets, but was extremely strong in major markets and in the top 20 in medium-sized cities. Andy Williams is better appreciated in the Midwest, where he's among the top 10, but his popularity holds strong in the West, South, and East. Dionne Warwick is as strong in the East as Andy Williams was in the Midwest, but not very strong at all in the West. She's still in the top 20 ranking in the South. Mac Davis loses out in the East where he just barely makes the top 30, but is popular in the South, West, and Midwest.

By artist preference, the survey revealed some rather interesting points about likes and dislikes. Only about half of the people who like the Carpenters also like Frank Sinatra, and less than 10 percent of those same adults cared for the Eagles, who were at that time gracing the playlists of MOR, country, Top 40, and progressive rock radio stations. On the other hand, of the people who liked Frank Sinatra, a little more than half also appreciated the Carpenters and only about five percent cared at all for the Eagles.

About half of the people who like the Carpenters also like Charlie Rich and much the same thing was true about Sinatra fans and Charlie Rich fans.

This particular survey was launched by Larry Vanderveen, president of Radio Arts, to use as guidelines for his MOR radio syndication service for automated radio stations. Vanderveen, a veteran broadcaster, believes that: "All formats are moving to the center—toward that choice 25-39 age listener. But no radio station is actually programming for the middle age groups. The MOR radio format has been a wasteland for years. Frank Sinatra, for example, sells out at his concerts and in Las Vegas. But he is avoided as a programming element on MOR stations of today."

Vanderveen thinks that in the 1960s radio stations suddenly woke up to the fact that advertising agencies were trying to convince everyone that the listening audience was under 25 years old. Sales departments began putting pressure on the programming departments and slowly the classic MOR station became a mixed bag. Today, MOR stations usually stand out on the radio dial as a mixture of incompatible music. He pointed out that record charts in trade publications were based largely on sales.

"Essentially, singles buyers are under 25 years old. And for a radio station that aims its programming at the over-25 listener to program strictly from charts is incongruous."

Vanderveen added that advertisers are again looking at the total audience group, regardless of age, usually that audience ages 18-59. "But as advertising agencies moved back to reality in their time buys, they left the typical MOR radio station out in left field."

The Radio Arts format fits that void which Vanderveen believes exists. And, it does exist in many, many markets. Vanderveen claims that as MOR deserted its listeners, they were forced to listen to country and beautiful music stations, thus in those formats, the audience has increased in the past few years.

Audience studies abound. Statistical Research Inc. has done a Radio All Dimension Audience Research (RADAR) study for ABC, CBS, MBS, and NBC radio networks—a measurement of individuals listening to all radio, i.e., AM and FM network affiliated radio stations, and network programs. The report covers radio network audiences and radio usage data nationally, regionally, by market group combinations, and for demographic groupings of age, income, and education. In 1976, Arbitron revealed a study that showed ethnic radio wasn't as dominant (either soul or Latin radio) among their own target audiences. In a study of 15 markets, including such cities as New York, Philadelphia, Louisville, Washington, Los Angeles, and Detroit, ARB found that the listening time of blacks was 47.5 percent devoted to soul music stations and Latin people spent only 45 percent of their listening time with Spanish-speaking stations.

In soul radio, black teens are the largest audience, but their parents back off extensively and listen to some other format. It's the reverse in Latin radio, where adults seem to listen more than teens, perhaps because younger people are becoming more Americanized. In any case, the first choice in radio among Spanish-speaking teens is contemporary radio formats with a 61.3 percent share.

A demographic breakout across 15 cities regarding station format showed that 45.5 percent of black women 18 years and older listen to soul radio while only 41.0 percent of the men 18-plus listen. The black teen audience was 68 percent. Of all the cities, Kansas City experienced more loyal black listeners than other markets; here 59.2 percent listened to the soul station. In Cincinnati, only 36.8 percent of the blacks spent their time listening to soul music radio. In Louisville, local contemporary stations had a large audience of blacks with a 44.5 share to rank first and the soul format in the city was second with a 17.7 percent share. In St. Louis, MOR radio formats scored first with blacks with 39.7 percent and soul radio was second with 32.8 percent. The next most-popular format with Latin people, aside from Spanish-speaking stations, was contemporary format with 23.5 percent, soul 5.3 percent, and beautiful music with 4.4 percent. While soul-formatted stations ranked first, black teens spent 24 percent of their remaining time listening to contemporary stations.

News, talk, jazz, and religious formats have higher shares among blacks than among the total population. Soul radio was the second most-listened-to format among all teens—blacks, whites, etc.—but ranked fifth among men 18 years old and older, and third among women 18-plus.

Latin teens spend almost as much time with soul radio—11.8 percent—as opposed to Spanish radio at 13.8 percent. Blacks listen to fewer radio stations than the general population. The average number of listed stations in the 15 markets surveyed was 17, compared to 29 in the standard ARB radio report for the same market.

Concerning reported audience, not actual audience, speaking before an annual meeting of the American Forces Radio and Television Services, Chicago, 1976, Rick

Sklar, director of operations at ABC-owned and operated AM stations, said that besides internal guidelines and FCC regulations, the program director of today "also has to program to try to compensate for some of the peculiarities and biases that may be built into the rating services—the methodologies they employ. Do you think, for example, that the full impact of popular music radio—which goes everywhere and is heard by people on the move—can be captured by the sedentary act of people who will sit and write in a diary?"

The program director has very little margin for error, Sklar said. Research, knowledge about how to use that research, and the experience that comes from competing for ratings, are necessary. The kind of person who fills out a diary is different from the ordinary radio listener, believes Sklar. He pointed out that today's program director has learned that in order to survive, he has to program to a very specialized audience.

"The wider the audience target, the more difficult it is to hit in radio."

So, there are studies available—from Arbitron, the National Association of Radio, Advertising Bureau, and various trade publications. And the program director can do his own or have it done through several research firms, including Dimensions Unlimited.

Programming Research

There is a type of research that only a program director and his staff can do. Lee Abrams is considered one of the brightest people in programming today and he works as a consultant to several stations coast to coast in a format using mostly album cuts. Years ago at the International Radio Programming Forum in New York, Rick Sklar, then program director of WABC in New York, spoke about the album cut problem in programming. Several program directors, including Tom Yates at KLOS in Los Angeles and Lee Abrams, of the firm Kent Burkhart/Lee Abrams and Associates in Atlanta, seem to have found the answer. Here, Abrams talks about his psychographic grid theories:

"The core of the contemporary audience is 12-34 years of age, right? Yet this demographic grouping is the most fragmented, elusive, changing, undefinable audience in broadcast history. It's getting out of control. We must begin to understand this critical area, or else we may find ourselves in a situation of over-specialization or under-efficiency, which could be economically disastrous to contemporary radio in the future.

"To better understand the matter, I've created a 'psychographic grid'—this breaks out the 12-34 audience into different listener types, in this case determined by music preferences in regard to radio listening."

The purpose of his psychographic grid study technique, Abrams said, is to "very precisely evaluate all of the different fragments of the 12-34 audience and relate that to far more effective music targeting.

"Each type on the grid is referred to as a cell. In 1963 there were about 25 different cells making up the 12-34 age group. In 1973, there were more than 175, each with different characteristics. By looking at the different cells, you can determine compatibilities between certain ones. In other words, a mass-appeal radio station should search all of the cells for absolute compatibility, to ensure maximum audience response and maintenance.

"Conversely, a wrong cell interjected among right cells would lessen efficiency. What I'm trying to do is target music more precisely than ever before to maximize quarterhours in a situation of fragmentation. The whole thing is complex and must be preceded by and maintained with a great deal or research because the cells making up the grid are constantly multiplying, making programming more difficult, and the results less fruitful.

"Here's an example of multiplication: At one time, 1967-68, there was one cell for progressive type music listeners. You could keep them intact with just about any, then-released, then-referred-to as underground album—Buffalo Springfield, Jimi Hendrix, Joni Mitchell." He continued, "Through the years, this one progressive cell has multiplied into about 45 different cells. For instance, the following artists are considered progressive by 1973 standards—Deep Purple, Bob Dylan, Mahavishnu Orchestra, and Traffic. Yet, each artist is represented by a different cell. Some of the above are far from compatible."

Abrams pointed out that a progressive station playing Deep Purple, Mahavishnu Orchestra, and Bob Dylan back-to-back is playing Russian Roulette with maintenance of quarterhours because, although all three acts are progressive, they represent three completely different listener types.

"Generically speaking, the Deep Purple fan will tune out Bob Dylan. The Mahavishnu fan will tune out Deep Purple, etc. These are tolerance factors which can be computed into each cell. Very basic, but an example of how one cell multiplies into others and how the reaction can hurt the ratings of the station."

The album area is definitely the hardest to graph effectively, Abrams said. "And even more difficult to reach. The more involved an individual gets in music artistically, the more difficult it is to program to him. Eventually, the musical super-active person becomes so involved in what he likes—the only programming that will keep him intact is his own record player. But that person, too, represents a cell and by looking at an effective psychographic grid, a programmer would instantly spot the futility in trying to reach this type of person.

"But Top 40 formats are the ones which really need a psychographic grid application, since volume of listeners is more important there than highly specific demographics. What should a Top 40 station play?"

Top 40 radio today has little to do with reaching a mass audience, since album sales have, in effect, created a new listener, said Abrams. "Should a Top 40 station play Jethro Tull? Does black music tuneout white audiences? Why do 25-34 year olds move to MOR music approaches?

"The answer is on the grid you devise. The grid maximizes efficiency of programming by pinpointing audience availability in relationship to music."

The final makeup of each cell, Abrams said, contains this kind of information in the psychographic grid theories:

1. Which cells are 100 percent compatible as far as combining with other cells for airplay;

2. Which cells are 100 percent incompatible as far as combining with others for airplay;

3. Specific music type, given cell represents a main factor based on predetermined music types;

4. Music-buying habits of given cell;

5. And radio-listening habits of given cell.

You'd also want to know: under-listening radio habits of a given cell, minutes per week listening, station mix listened to, trends of individual habits in members of given cell, and when members of given cell listened and their comprehension factors. You'd also want various demographic information to be reflected.

"Although many agree that it would be impossible to make a grid because of the many different types of listeners there are, that is wrong," insisted Abrams. "Research will show that there are really no individuals. And everyone falls into a cell, primarily due to the standardization of the music and radio presentation in our society." He added, "The primary information on the grid is psychographic. Simple demography means little here, as it does in any fragmentation situation when relating to its execution. The final result from the grid, though, is demographic simulation, since ratings are demographically based. However, if one wants to target only 18-24 year olds, rather than the entire 12-34 audience spectrum, or to only target black people, the secondary category of cell information would be critically important."

Building a psychographic grid to use as a programming tool is a lengthy process, but Abrams insisted it can be rewarding. However, a thorough researching of all segments of the 12-34 population is necessary, or the demographic age group the program director wishes to reach.

"This means going into the ghetto, as well as the upper-class downtown appartments. You must research every possible element of the 12-34 age group, not only what you perceive as your potential audience. As a prerequisite, you must weigh the individual elements you research, which should be based on U.S. census data. If you research five percent blacks in an area of 58 percent blacks, the grid would be ineffective. Each cell should contain weighting information. After all, it would be senseless to program toward a cell that represents only five percent of the population, especially if that cell conflicts with a cell that represents 5.6 percent. It's like a puzzle—once you're finished, you just fit the cells together and program accordingly."

The sample size, however, must be effective.

"I've found," Abrams said, "several methods of researching:

1. *In-home interviews*—face to face contact is good, although it is time consuming, sometimes dangerous, and occasionally an appearance compensation occurs, where the person being interviewed will modify his answer to be as 'hip' as you appear to be, etc.;

2. *Telephone*—time consuming, and occasionally not as comprehensive as it could be;

3. *Diary study*—the best, I've found—do an ARB-type study where the subject logs music information, listening information, etc.

"But there are dozens of other methods; the best thing to do would be to read as much as possible about market research and sample different approaches. The point is: the information must be thorough, truthful, bulk, and effective. The usefulness of the grid depends on statistical accuracy, volume of response, weighting, and proper translation."

The initial research for the grid should take about six to eight months, Abrams said. You need a solid, accurate base of data. The second step (after really researching and translating the raw figures) is to classify. With each classification, the data must be super accurate, and again weighted. The third step is classification into specific cells, and grid construction. Its-practical use is super-targeting.

"Actually, the whole thing is far more complex and a bit more mathematical than I've explained here, but the outcome can potentially give a programmer an unapproachable knowledge of the 12-34 group, and the true beauty of it is the organization. With a series of glances, you can zero in on absolutes regarding music and people and open up a new era in audience and music targeting."

Audience research on a market must be done. But there are pitfalls. Dr. Herbert Kay, president of Herbert Kay Research, Montclair, N.J., stated at the International Radio Programming Forum a few years ago that "when we undertook a study for a radio station in the Midwest, the station manager pointed to his afternoon drive disk jockey as the reason why the station did so well among 25-34 year-old women. And, it is true, the disk jockey sounded first-rate to us, too. Then we finished our research and after a careful analysis came to the unmistakable conclusion that the good ratings which the station got in that time period had nothing to do with the disk jockey—in fact, the disk jockey was something of a negative. His fans were mainly women over 50 years of age. What attracted the younger women was the music—it was great music to do housework by. The disk jockey was merely the fifth wheel on the car for them.

"Moral: The audience which comes to a given station at a given time got there for one or more of many different reasons—your disk jockey's personality, the music, the strength or weakness of the competition, whether or not you include news, and how long it is, the overall image of your station, and so on.

"Don't assume that you can guess which of these is giving you the good or bad numbers, there's at least a 50-50 chance you're wrong."

Gene Nelson, vice president of WLCS in Baton Rouge, La., has always believed in his own personal research as a method of achieving good ratings. At a recent International Radio Programming Forum in Chicago, Nelson said that the impact on the radio industry of the new research techniques then coming into use widely "and the fractionalization of the radio audience by the professional ratings services has been absolutely devastating. Back in the late 1950s when Hooper was the bible of the industry, we built our formats and staked our programming fortunes on raw audience figures. Why, demographics wasn't even a word. Then, the whole thing blew up in our faces. Studies were made, new sampling techniques tested and refined. The age of the computer hit us like a tidal wave and, within a period of a few years after the mid-1960s, left a programming shambles in its wake.

"Fractionalization of the ratings into basic demographs blew the foundations out from under the old Top 40 format concept, and one ratings giant after another began to slip. Programmers who had smugly waved No. 1 ratings at their competitors woke up a year or so later to find that teens counted for zero, and that in basic adult categories they were sadly lacking. The truth of the matter is that most of us who were involved in the pioneering of the Top 40 concept built our little programming castles on the quicksand of a shallow and basically unscientific rating method. Raw audience just wasn't enough."

Nelson said that after a visit to Pulse to examine field sheets, and then by using a map of the metropolitan area of his market which had previously been broken down into economic, social, and ethnic units, "it became obvious to me that the addition or deletion of small numbers of selected interviews would perhaps have a drastic effect on the outcome of the survey.

"Not being able to experiment with the sample through Pulse's computer, I did the next best thing. I secured a complete Pulse supervisors' manual together with all forms, procedure, and control data, and using a professional survey company exactly duplicated the Pulse survey in the city."

Later, he did the same for other ratings services. However, he eventually refined the method so that he could use in-house people on the phone. Thus, he was able to find the information before the professional ratings firm's surveys took place, and then he could compensate in his programming and/or his promotions to strengthen his weak spots. From 1958 to 1962, WLCS made basic listener telephone surveys at the rate of about 6,000 calls a month. The calls were made intensively over a five-day period by a battery of trained survey operators and "enabled us to get a look at the audience ratings six weeks ahead of time."

Tabulating about 100,000 of these phone calls showed him "audience flow."

"Audience flow can be changed by the most minor program adjustments and the rate of its increase or decrease is far greater than anyone ever dreamed. Audience flow is affected by the weather, the time of day, and the intensity of the individual air personality."

From his 1962 study, Nelson knew for the first time that "radio audience is compositive by its very nature and is manipulative by composite techniques." By changing the intensity of the personality and promoting him, Nelson was able to accelerate audience flow to his station's air personality and listening spans were increased; and the audience was increased up to 20 percent. He also found that teens and young adults tend to flow more than older demographics.

"As radio programmers, we live in a world in which there are no easy answers anymore. Those freewheeling days are gone when our format structure alone held up our ratings. Who would have imagined 10 years ago that a country music station in a major metropolitan market would knock off a good Top 40 station?

"We are buffeted by changes. Basic changes in music itself and improved programming techniques have made it almost impossible to find differences between MOR, good music, chicken rock, and Top 40 stations. Our programming options are more limited than ever before. We talk a new language. We think a new way. Research, sometimes our greatest tool, paradoxically becomes our greatest enemy. Our audience is more knowledgeable, more sophisticated, and more difficult to manipulate. We can't con them. We can't hype them. We can't fool them.

"The answer, I am convinced, lies in basic theoretical knowledge—knowledge gained by research and study. We must become more knowledgeable than our competitors and our audience. We must out-think them, out-know them."

Weekly Music Research

Research for a radio station's playlist can go to any depth that the radio station wishes and can include any or all of these facets:

1. Check local sales;

2. Checking requests;

3. Personal surveys both in record stores and elsewhere about what people want to hear;

4. Checking playlists of other radio stations in other cities of similar population makeup;

5. Compiling information provided by record promotion executives;

6. Checking record tipsheets such as the *Gavin Report* and the weekly record report edited by Betty Breneman, Los Angeles;

7. Checking charts of national trade publications.

The record playlist is a very unusual entity in itself. One of the first playlists ever printed as a promotional item for the radio station may have been that of WIND in

Chicago in 1942. However, CHUM in Toronto has been printing one and distributing it to listeners via record stores probably longer than any other radio station on a continuous format basis, according to CHUM air personality Roger Ashby. CHUM started its playlist in May 1957.

Outside the station, the playlist serves several functions: it is a great promotional item for listeners, it helps the record stores stock records, it gives the record industry some form of feedback on how well their records are doing in your market, and it informs other radio stations in other markets about what you're playing that might also be viable in their own market. Within the station, it's a programming guideline.

A playlist is the current list that the radio station prints and distributes to the public. But for programming purposes, the radio station may have several lists:

1. Current records;

2. Recent hits (sometimes called recurrents);

3. Oldies;

4. Psychographic records;

5. Local hits from other format stations in the market that could be crossing over in your format in popularity;

6. New records;

7. Extras;

8. Album cuts;

9. Humorous records;

10. Balance records

A program director might use one or two more categories and have two or more lists within any given category. Oldies, for example, might be broken down into different groups by years (such as records that were hits between 1970 and 1975, records that were hits between 1965 and 1969, etc.) in order to capitalize on the nostalgic value of those records for the purpose of attracting a specific demographic at a specific daypart.

Psychographic records are those records that might have phenomenal appeal to a certain audience segment. For instance, "Teddy Bear" by Red Sovine in the country music field is a good psychographic record to appeal specifically to truck drivers.

Extras are records that a program director might wish to try out on a limited basis; normally, these would be limited to a given time of day.

As for album cuts, they're increasing their impact on today's programming. From a hit album, the program or music director might pick as many as four cuts viable for programming, especially by a name artist. There seem to be about four or five good cuts on any album turned out these days by Carole King, Neil Diamond, Elton John, or Johnny Cash.

Humorous records (or any other specific category of this nature), like balance records, are used to counter a trend on the current list. For instance, if all of the bigger hits during a particular week are sort of down, a balance record would be a bright, happy tune. Or it might be a slow record as opposed to a current list massed with fast, hard tunes.

There might be other lists, of course. Buzz Bennett was noted for the "goof record" invention. This was a record designed to get people to tune out in order to build average quarterhour shares in ratings.

Jay Blackburn, a former principal in Hope, Bennett, Blackburn of San Juan, Puerto Rico, and Bruce Earle, an engineer buddy of his, were coming back from the annual convention of the National Association of Broadcasters a couple of years ago.

"And we had 13-Q (WKTQ in Pittsburgh) on a skip, right? We were listening and we heard Mark Driscoll, who was calling himself Marcus Aurelius. He had a liner for all of his goof records, Buzz Bennett did, and it was: 'A memory or two from 13-Q.' We heard Marcus do his basics and roll a memory of two and he rolled Dodie Stevens' 'Pink Shoe Laces.' We fell apart. Got down on the floor!

"I guess the goof record was Buzzy's idea, goddamn, he's smart as a whip, there's no doubt about it. We've stolen so much stuff from him—research methodology and whatnot. A lot of that stuff he pioneered and there's no bull about that.

"Here's your stopset on the hot clock, right? If you can get a Frances Irving in her little ARB diary to go through 4:10 PM to 4:20 PM, that's 10 minutes of listening but your station will get credit for two quarterhours because she went past this arbitrary point on the hour, :15. What you want to do is make her leave, but be back between :20-:25.

"So, you tune her out a couple of minutes before the :15. Now you have to be careful, you have to know what your competition is doing. For example, the competition in this case is running 20-20 news (news at 20 minutes after and before the top of the hour). So, if you *goof* her just before they go into their news, she'll punch over to them and wait a minute or two before she punches back. Then you hold her through several minutes with good records.

"What you've actually done is—if she'd listened straight through, she would have given your station two quarterhours; but by getting her to punch out once, you've given yourself three quarterhours. If you can carry her past the break point, you've got four quarterhours for the same listener.

"It's because of the way the ARB does things—the arbitrary setup. But an effective and efficient program director can get eight quarterhours out of an hour, with one listener.

"It's possible. It's hard to do, but it's possible. You can also do this by timewarping. You want her to think you're rolling the record past :20, but you may not be; it may be only :17 after the hour. When she fills out that ARB diary, however, she doesn't bother to look at the clock to see what time it really is. Anyway, most people set their clocks by radio. They believe radio.

"Timewarping is universal. It applies to all formats across the board and you'll find many stations using the theory, live and automated. Those guys aren't dumb."

Records might also be played for tempo reasons—fast vs. slow—for season, for relevance, and to accent a mood or feeling such as "Stormy Weather" on a rainy day. How these records are played varies from station to station, depending on the hot clock.

Some stations don't use a hot clock. Progressive rock was devised under the concept of programming music in thematic sets, and also records with musical or lyrical merit. A few stations still let their air personalties play the music by ear. But most stations use a playlist and most use a rotation pattern, regardless of the format. And many slate every record for the disk jockeys, in order.

The Tight Playlist

For several years, the tight playlist has been a bitter complaint of many record company executives. In April 1970, a survey showed that the tight playlist was a myth—at least among small and medium-market stations. A survey showed that playlists ran anywhere from 45-80 singles. Unfortunately, as of February 1976, the disease of the tight playlist had spread from major markets through medium markets and into small markets. According to a survey conducted by the radio section of *Billboard* magazine, of the small market Top 40 stations surveyed, 53.6 percent of the program directors stated that they believed the tight playlist (less than 30 records) helped build a listening audience. "Nothing we don't play hurts us," remarked Jack Raymond, program director of WEIM in Fitchburg, Mass.

The tight playlist had been a very big factor in medium markets as early as three years ago, but its role in small market Top 40 radio wasn't proven until this survey. This survey spelled out bad news for the record industry and the promotion man, who recently had been plumbing the smaller markets to get that initial record exposure and sales reaction (not that any small market radio station could account for many sales, but it could serve as a thermometer on a record and serve as proof to a larger radio station that a record had merit).

John Mitchell at KERN in Bakersfield, Calif., said he believed in the tight playlist because, "it's necessary to play familiar music." Christ T., program director of WAKX in Duluth, Minn., said he also believed in the tight playlist, "but this depends, of course, on the individual market. Our market had been without a station that really did any research or played from a tight list for over five years. And we have found a great deal of success with our list, establishing WAKX as a station that plays the best music all the time."

Denny Luell of KLWW in Cedar Rapids, Iowa, said about the tight playlist, that "a constant dose of unfamiliar material produces tuneouts." Jon Horton of WTTS in Bloomington, Indiana, felt that "audience listening spans continue to be short and repetition of established hits assures a positive reaction."

Harley Drew at WBBQ in Augusta, Ga., said, "A basic tight playlist keeps the hits coming and that seems to fit best with the tight schedules of today's lifestyles. Listeners want to hear something familiar promptly when they tune in. We supplement the basic list with oldies, album cuts, and midday and night extras for variety without compromising the basic tight playlist idea."

On the other hand, Jerry Riley at WAAM in Ann Arbor, Mich., said, "We're up against CKLW of Detroit, which has a tight playlist and so does WDRQ there. We get a lot of calls complaining about them and how many times they repeat songs! Audiences here like us better because we have a better music spread. We also daypart, which tends to add to our total record count."

Ray Quinn of WAMS in Wilmington, Del., believes in the tight list, as does Bob Charest of WHYN in Springfield, Mass. But Mike Novak of KYNO in Fresno, Calif., said, "No—not with two FM stations in our market with three-plus hour rotation of the hits."

Chris Conner of KAFY in Bakersfield, Calif., also felt that the tight list became "stale very easy." Thus, competitive reasons, as you can see, sometimes force a station into a longer list just in order to be different in air sound.

At WIOO in Carlisle, Pa., however, program director Ray Thomas thought the tight list was fine "because every time a listener turns on the radio, he hears a familiar hit song. Familiarity keeps listeners."

Lee Thomas at KLMS in Lincoln, Neb., said that the length of the playlist in his opinion should depend on the competitive situation. "We have encountered audience complaints, both directly and in ARB diaries, about repetition of records—and the complaints usually come from young adults. In our area, the really tight playlists aren't really working. And they seem to be the most vunerable to FM, because people flee to FM to escape them."

Regardless of the length of the playlist, the survey showed that small market Top 40 stations are not adding many new records. The average of 2.68 new records were added per week, but only 1.18 of these had not been played elsewhere. The station involved was just getting to the rest. About half of the program directors— 53.6 percent—let their air personalities have some say in the selection of new music. Jim King at WRIE in Erie, Pa., commented that he listened to between 50 and 100 new singles a week, but only added two to nine of these and only three or four of those were really new. In regards to the playlist, a below-30 list works "if you're after teens. They can take, and want, the repetition. But for over-18 year old listeners, the tight list is a burden."

Considering markets of all sizes, large to small, the consensus was that 32.33 records was about the right length of playlist for a mass appeal station targeting teen and young adult demographics. In major markets surveyed, there was only one station that sometimes went up to 45 singles; another one focused on 40; most had playlists ranging from 25-35 singles and one major facility plays only 20 records. When you add in a few extras and recent hits (also called recurrents or new gold) and a few hit-bounds (new records just added to the playlist)—the typical playlist of a rock radio stations goes to an average of 37.67 records, all market sizes.

In reality, however, only about 12.59 to 14.03 of these are receiving concentrated airplay. These records in higher rotation are usually, of course, the biggest sellers in the market. Larry Ryan, then programmer of KEEL in Shreveport, La., said that his playlist features 35 records, plus "about 10 other records that are restricted to evening airplay."

Bob Davis, program director of KELI in Tulsa, Okla., doesn't hold to a consistent number, but lets his playlist range anywhere from 28 to 45 records. In regard to a tight playlist (below 30 records), he pointed out that it doesn't always work "because while familiarity is a plus, familiarity can also breed contempt!"

Neil McIntyre of WPIX in New York ran with a list of 25-30 records; Bob Christy of WVBF in Boston reported 27-35; Jim Davis at KIMN in Denver held at 35; Mark Driscoll, then programming KSTP in Minneapolis, went with a list ranging from a low 28 to a high of 31; John Gehron at WLS in Chicago used about 20.

Bobby Rich at B-100 (KFMB-FM) in San Diego lets his list float between 25 and 35; Les Garland at CKLW in Detroit liked 30 records; Michael Spears at KFRC in San Francisco used 25-35 records; Jim Dunlap at WQAM in Miami said he used a list of 25-35, depending on commercial load; Ed Kaye at KOMA in Oklahoma City had a list of 20 records, plus five extras.

In major markets, playlists tended to be slightly smaller than in medium markets, but on the other hand, the range was great. For instance, playlists ranged from 28.41 records to 36.82 records in major markets, while in medium markets playlists went from a low of 29.15 to a high of 33.60 records. There was a strong tendency for medium market stations to have fewer records in high rotation patterns. Program directors in major markets said they had between 11.06 and 14 records in high rotation patterns, based on how long or short their playlist was at that particular time. In medium markets, program directors had between 10.63 and 11.62 records in high rotation patterns, also depending on the length of their playlist at that moment. The longest playlist mentioned in the survey in a medium market was 40 records, the shortest was 18. The general rule seemed to be about 30 records.

Charlie Parker, vice president and program director of WDRC in Hartford, Conn., has a playlist ranging 30-40 records, "but I think market size and competitive factors play a part in this question. We work with a 30 list. I do not subscribe to a high rotation pattern."

Pat Patterson, then programming at WKIX in Raleigh, N.C., used a playlist of 35 records, with 20 in a high rotation pattern. Mark St. John at WISE in Asheville, N.C., said he used a playlist of 30 records, with five to seven extras for night play only and a few album cuts. As far as rotation is concerned at WISE, 10-11 get extra on-air attention, "but it is not so much how many you play as how often you play them, i.e., two-and-a-half hours to two-and-three-quarter hours rotation."

Jay Thomas, then at WAYS in Charlotte, had a playlist of 25-30 singles and 8-10 were in high rotation pattern. Steve Kirk at WING in Dayton, Ohio, plays 45 singles, with extra air attention devoted to 25 of these. Gene Nelson at WLCS in Baton Rouge, La., plays 30 records and five get heavier airplay. Bob Savage, program director at WBBF in Rochester, N.Y., said that he plays 35-40 records, "depending on availability of product." John Randolph at WAKY in Louisville, Ky., said that the best length for a playlist of current tunes is 33 and that seven of these get heavier attention on the air at his station. John Long at WAPE in Jacksonville, Fla., liked a 30-35 record playlist, with 10 getting extra airplay.

Gene Rump at KAKE in Wichita, Kan., said, "even with adults, I think repetition is important—a list that is too fat just permits you to play a bunch of junk. The discipline of a 30-record playlist is good for a station." He plays 30 records, with 12 receiving stronger airplay.

Bob Klieve, known as the father of Top 40 radio in Spain (he advised installation of the format years ago there) and general manager of KLIV in San Jose, Calif., slates anywhere from 27-34 records each week and 8-10 of these get stronger attention on the air; "a tight playlist is the basis for Top 40 programming." Roger Collins at KTKT in Tucson likes 35-40 records for a playlist and 8-10 of these get stronger play. Tom Barsanti of WOW in Omaha plays 20-25 records, with 8-10 getting stronger airplay.

Joe Monteith at KTOP in Topeka, Kan., said that he used a playlist of 30 records, with four or five of these getting heavier airplay.

"Generally, radio listening is done on a brief period basis at various times of the day. The short playlist gives the audience what they want to hear. It reduces your chances of playing something that most of them do not want to listen to. It's what most of the audience wants to hear most of the time. Rick Sklar of WABC in New York said it first and it works."

Monteith, who doubles as operations manager, added: "Since our last audience survey, we have made a number of changes in our approach to programming and the results have been great. When I got my start in radio, I never had anyone really sit down and work with me and give me the opportunity to learn what radio is all about and how it works. In the last year, we spent about $1,000 in phone calls to some major market program directors that I have had the chance to meet and they were good enough to give us a lot of help and generally teach me the basics of radio.

"We also sorted out all of the trash records and made oldie lists that are put into dayparts. We play just the biggest oldies dayparted in rotation with our current hits, which are also dayparted. We use a clock rotation on the top four songs in town and the rest of the current list are rotated depending on playlist position. The music is great now and you never hear a bad record on KTOP."

Gary Osborn of WIBM in Jackson, Mich.., said, however, that he felt Top 40 stations were getting away from the tight playlist. "Our playlist turns over approximately every three and a half to four hours. I feel the audience gets tired of hearing the same records every couple of hours." Dan Martin at WTRY in Troy, N.Y., plays 30 records, plus three new records and normal rotation features five records of the top 12 and five of the bottom 18, plus two holdovers and four oldies. Jerry Rogers at WSGA in Savannah, Ga., features 30 records with 10 in high rotation. "Your average Top 40 listener does not listen much more than one hour per day. When that person is listening, it's important to play something familiar. However, this does not preclude breaking new records."

According to the study, in the small markets, a typical Top 40 station rotates 15.21 to 16.10 of the records more often; the typical playlist ranges 33.38 records to 37.52. Record companies protest this short playlist, with the exception of Russ Regan, president of 20th Century Records in Los Angeles, who stated a few years ago that he thought the current length of the playlist was okay. "One thing that the tight playlist of Top 40 radio does is provide concentrated exposure, and that intensified exposure may be the difference between a listener merely liking a record and loving it enough to rush out and buy it."

What a tight playlist means is that the record promotion person has to work a lot harder than in the old days and it takes a record company a lot longer to break a record. Regan should know. He got his start in 1960 as a promotion man for Buckeye Record Distributors in Los Angeles and still gets deeply into promotion even now. To some extent, the "fun has gone out of record promotion work. You don't see smiling faces so much any more among promotion executives. Everybody is more serious and businesslike today. In the old days, people used to have more laughs. What has happened is that promotion and the record industry have become big biz. A record represents thousands of dollars at stake.

"It is true that today a record promotion person has more places to go to in order to get radio exposure. By that, I mean the AM stations and the FM stations with all of their various formats, and don't forget college radio stations have become increasingly important in not only their capability to break records, but also establish artists. This also means that the promotion man cannot afford to concentrate his effort like in the old days when you could sit around and have coffee with the disk jockeys at a station. No, today the promotion man has to stay on the road. Thus, the product has to speak for itself most of the time.

"And the promotion person today has to have more details available to present to the radio stations. Radio personnel are more informed these days and are taking a greater interest in product than they used to take. On top of this, a lot of the time a program director will say that a given record doesn't fit his station's sound. That's why it takes longer to make a record happen than a few years ago."

But the wise promotion man doesn't give up. "If you have a No. 1 record in any city in America, you just keep pushing and trying to spread that record. For example, it took us six months to break 'Gypsy Woman' by Brian Hyland. That record almost died twice."

10 The record promotion person as a viable source of information

There was a time in radio when the promotion executive was a finger-snapping loud-mouth. Perhaps a few may still exist somewhere. However, over the past few years the promotion executive has grown and developed into a promotion scientist in the record business. Some are former radio program directors; some came up through the record business with the sole desire to be excellent in their craft—Jan Basham at A&M Records, Chuck Thagard at Columbia Records, Mel Turoff, Steve Resnick, John Fisher, George Furness, Jerry Morris, Tony Richland (who always seems to win every competition for the best independent record promotion executive in the nation), Dickie Kline at Atlantic (who once leaned a little to fingersnapping, but is a man who knows what he's doing), Ray Anderson, Don Whittemore (who would have been a fingersnapper but could never manage the stunt and had to revert to being good), Del Roy (who always knew more than most, but few knew it), Ernie Phillips (the god of Texas), and men such as Jerry Sharell, Neil Bogart, and others who are rising to become chief executives of labels. Bogart owns Casablanca Records; Sharell, who once was head of promotion for Bogart at Buddah Records, is an executive of Elektra Records. Out of radio came Joe Smith who is chairman of the board of Elektra Records; Smith, a former rock disk jockey in Boston, hasn't lost his wit and is still one of the best after-dinner, during-dinner, before-dinner speakers in the record or radio industry.

Scott Shannon, vice president of promotion at Casablanca Records, Los Angeles, was a former disk jockey and program director whose last job was at WQXI in Atlanta. Bob Sherwood, promotion expert for Columbia Records, was a leading program director and has brought that same expertise to his duties at Columbia. He replaced Steve Popovich, who moved into A&R at Epic Records which is closely affiliated with Columbia; Steve really did well in promotion, and became an expert in using the sales information provided by daily computer reports as a promotional tool. Popovich later left Epic and returned home to Cleveland to become an independent record promotion person.

There are several promotion executives who should be mentioned, if for no other reason, because of their flair—Ernie Farrell, Don Graham (who once was rated the best promotion person in the nation when he was at the helm of the promotional force at A&M Records, according to a *Billboard* survey), Matty Singer, Larry Baunach, Bobby Robins, Pete Wright, Dutch Holland on the air and Gary Edwards off, Billy Bass (out of radio and now working with Chrysalis Records), and LeBaron Taylor, one of the best air personalities and program directors that soul radio ever knew, now head of special projects for CBS Records. And there are many others. Promotion people, as a rule, are dedicated to their business. You won't find a more dedicated man than Vince Cosgrave at MCA Records, Los Angeles. He heads the promotional "air force" at MCA. He's a former disk jockey, and also a record buff. Can you imagine a guy with several ancient jukeboxes in his house and one of them featuring nothing but Hank Williams? He has several jukeboxes in his house—all collector's items. He's as big a record nut as Barry Hansen, alias "Dr. Demento" on syndicated radio, or Bob Kirsch, a former *Billboard* reporter who now works at ABC Records in Los Angeles.

Chuck Meyer at MCA Records is one of those good-ol'-boy types of promotion executives. But he knows what he's doing.

Jim Davenport, owner of WFOM in the Atlanta suburb of Marietta, believes that record promotion men are basically the lifeblood of the radio-music industry and "most of them are uppers." He said this long before he retired from radio and started a promotion firm in the area. At that time, he felt that many radio stations, regardless of who's at fault, had gotten burned from poor information from promotion men. "They get scared after getting burned, so cut to a 20-record playlist."

Today, the successful record promotion man or woman has to be professional. Jan Basham, a promotion executive at A&M Records, has long fought to improve the image and status of the record promotion person. She helped start an informal group of promotion people in Los Angeles a few years ago.

"It was started because we wanted to upgrade our image and not be what some people might consider a necessary evil. We feel we perform a vital task. We, like no other person in the business, are into nearly every aspect of the music business. We deal on all levels.

"And we are a little tired of people thinking that all we do is pick up our records, snap our fingers, and run to the radio station and say: 'Here, baby, here's your latest hit'. A radio station is vitally important to us, but our job doesn't end there. We have to nurture every record we handle, making sure it's in stock in the record stores and that our salesmen are aware of them and where they are on the air, then feed this information back to the trade papers and the record tipsheets."

Bruce Wendell, head of promotion at Capitol Records and a former radio man, said that a promotion man "has to work closely with the A&R department and sales—communicating closely about stock, advertising, and marketing plans. From A&R, I get feedback on records."

The record company sets up merchandising, marketing, advertising, publicity, and promotional campaigns behind certain acts. "We have lots of money invested." Then, when a record shows sales results, the label follows "with a blitz campaign. We give our artists full commitment. We chase when we see daylight. What it all boils down to is exposing singles and selling albums."

Russ Regan, president of 20th Century Records, noted that sometimes records do not get exposed or sell as well as you'd like. He estimated that about a third of his records reached the charts.

"In some instances, I think the records never got the proper exposure. For example, I think we lost the No. 1 record in the nation with 'He' by Today's People. That record went to No. 1 in nine markets. It went to No. 1 on KLIV in San Jose, Calif. We just couldn't get . . . well, we couldn't put it all together. I feel very badly about that. I hate to see No. 1 records go down the drain. Needless to say, where we got airplay, the sales were fine. The phone requests were good. It had tremendous response. I think it was a tune-in factor for any radio station that played it. The record just needed a good location; it couldn't just be put on a night rotation pattern at a radio station; it had to be given a full shot at a station. Where it had been given a full shot around-the-clock at a radio station, it usually went to No. 1.

"I like to feel that I know a little bit about radio programming. Needless to say,

I don't tell anyone how to run their station, because I don't want anyone telling me how to run my record company. But I do respect an awful lot of radio programming people. People who are creative. And, hopefully, there will be more.

"There are a lot of programmers who take a great deal of pride in their radio stations . . . pride in playing the right records. Like I say: The one thing I believe in is people who have confidence in themselves enough to say: I don't care if it's not on the charts, I don't care if it's not being played anywhere else, I'm going to play this record because I like it, and I'm going to break it—make it a hit. Now, that's what I think is needed today, in fact, it is necessary for the survival of radio as we know it—for the health of both industries. New artists are always exciting on a radio station as well as within the record industry. If radio stations don't develop new artists, they've got to wind up hurting themselves. I think their listeners, every once in a while, are going to think: Gee, I've heard that record so many times—like some of those bad commercials on television—and I wonder if there's anything new out there. I think we have a lack of development going on right now in radio."

Several years ago, there was a station in a little market—WLOF in Orlando, Fla.— that always got excellent record service and had more than one record man, men such as Charlie Fach of Mercury Records, who credited WLOF program/music director Bill Vermillion in those days with breaking national hits. Vermillion said that he had "found that the promotion man has been one of my most valuable sources of information. If you are like most of us in the smaller markets, you have often noticed that there are hits on the national charts that get little or no response from your audience. You have to learn your market. To do this successfully, you can make your job much easier by learning to use the promotion man.

"Too many stations make too little use of the promotion man and his information. Many seem to discount anything he says and regard him as a man not to be trusted. And I've talked with many promotion men who tell me of program directors who refuse to see promotion men. Do this and you lose a quick and (if you are careful) reliable source of information." Vermillion said that to use a promotion man effectively, you had to build a mutual respect and trust.

Harvey Cooper, now executive vice president of marketing at 20th Century Records, Los Angeles, said. "It's really sad. In the old days, radio stations used to respond to local promotion people. The record distributors were also involved." It's more difficult to go to a station today. "Because you don't get the cooperation you used to. Radio management is at fault here, I think. Their image of the music business is so horrendous. And they're so obvious about not wanting us around, they're insulting."

Johnny Rosica, head of promotion for RCA Records, New York, points out that determination is a key asset of a promotion man. When Rosica was a fledgling promotion man in Philadelphia, in the days with Dick Clark's television show was based there, Rosica brought Clark a record and played it for him. "He (Clark) said it was a terrible record and he'd never play it.

"The next week, I played it for him again. He said: That's the record you played for me last week. Get it out of here. Don't ever play that record for me again! The third week, I go in and play the record for him again and he yells: 'That's it! Get that record out of here!'

"Almost a week goes by when I get a call from one of his secretaries to bring the record over because they were going to put it on the air. It was 'Tell Laura I Love Her' by Ray Peterson. Right? It wasn't a terrible record, but he was basically right.

"The mistake he made was in saying never."

There's another view, of course. Jacqueline McCauley, music director at KLOL in Houston, complained when in April 1976 another Houston station received several albums first—product by Led Zeppelin, Rolling Stones, and Bad Company.

"A situation of this sort creates difficulties for everyone involved—the record company, the local rep (who, in this case, has been most helpful), the stores (who sometimes don't have product until weeks after it is first leaked), and, of course, the rest of the programmers in the market.

"We had considered pulling Atlantic product in protest of this situation. However, since we are an open-format album rock station, we are committed to providing our audience with a wide range of excellent music that, in many cases, cannot be heard elsewhere. Excluding Atlantic product would be a disservice to our listeners.

"If we are to be effective in programming and marketing product, we must take a responsible attitude toward our individual and collective action. It is a necessity that our major concern be for the functional operation of the industry as a whole. This concern should never be overshadowed by personal relationships or attempts for personal gain, which allow leaks of this sort to occur."

The Radio Station and Promotion

Now for a different view. One national promotion director for a record company—who wouldn't dare have his name mentioned for fear of radio staions not playing his records at all—had this to say a few years ago about the "superiority complex" of program and music directors at many of today's Top 40 stations:

"I can understand when Rosalie Trombly in Detroit says we can't call her on the days she does her record store survey. She's fine. But what about WQXI in Atlanta telling us we can only call on Monday. And at WLS in Chicago, record promotion men are seen every other Thursday for five minutes. Now, WOKY in Milwaukee won't take any calls at all. Bill Young at KILT in Houston—you can only call him on Tuesday. Rick Sklar at WABC in New York—I haven't seen him in three years. Even KAAY in Little Rock—you're not supposed to call except on Tuesday and the problem is that music director Johnny King does the evening show and comes into the station late so you either can't reach him or he doesn't have time to talk to you.

"I'm not crying, but it's very difficult to promote records today and it's getting worse. For example, I've just tried to reach Robert Collins at WRIT in Milwaukee and Lee Gray at WKLO and John Randolph at WAKY, both in Louisville. But I can't reach them. They know I'm not a hype artist. I haven't had anything to tell them in a year, and now I do—I've got a record breaking in Miami and I can't alert them because they won't talk to me. It's frustrating! It's not fair. It's kicking the hell out of our industry.

"Now take Tex Meyer at WOKY. We've always been candid with each other. Tex is more than a radio man to me and I've always thought I was more than a record man to him. We used to be buddies. But I didn't know that hits were only made on certain days! What really gripes me is that if this particular record becomes a chart item, I'll get calls from radio stations asking why they didn't get it and why I didn't tell them about it—and I saw those records go out of here to those stations.

"I recently sent WLCY in St. Petersburg, the same record every day for a week. When I called, they not only hadn't heard the record, but didn't even know if it was in the station!

"Now this is not just sour grapes about these stations—these violations—that's what I call them, but I think it's terrible that we can't call a station and tell them when we have a hit. One music director I was talking with recently said he didn't care about hits, that he wasn't in the record business. I asked him why he bothered to print a playlist, why he bothered to call record stores to find out what was selling, why he didn't just program the station by the seat of his pants. Let him see how long he'd last!"

Now, because of the nature of the industry, most of the radio people mentioned above are at different call letters in different cities. But, essentially, the same problems exist here and there throughout the industry. It's not necessarily the fault of the program director or the music director at a radio station. Today, the program director's job is often a 24-hour, seven-day task and, while it may be a labor of love, finding that extra hour to answer just one more phone call from a promotion man or two is sometimes difficult. It's not that there's just one phone call, it's that there are several. While record promotion does have a problem, it's really because the economics of operating a radio station do not allow the station to hire someone to do nothing but talk to record people.

Pat O'Day, when he was general manager of KJR in Seattle, generally always had No. 1 ratings in the market and part of the reason may have been that he used the aid of record promotion people in the market. O'Day held weekly record listening sessions in which all of the local promotion people not only participated, but discussed each other's product.

"I think it's gratifying to know that no record on the station is simply there because I personally like it," O'Day said. "A lot of people derive their livelihood from records. Our credo is we're very indebted to them. Admittedly, it would be almost impossible for a music director to maintain an equal relationship with all of them. Too, the scope of music is broad and there's more product today than ever before. I think that greater care has to be taken with music today. You can't just follow someone's list anymore."

O'Day plays the product, the promotion people comment, and, generally, by the time a promotion man or woman comes out of the KJR meeting they know whether or not their product was going on the air. At one session, David Krause of Elektra Records spoke of needing more than just two or three weeks of airplay on a given record "because we just now got it racked." O'Day pointed out that co-music directors Gary Shannon and Norm Gregory just didn't have enough information on the record, that it had been a "calculated risk, being that far out in front on the record. But, just because a record is off the list doesn't mean we can't go back on it." He told Krause to keep working the record and bring any sales information to KJR's attention. The record went into a "considering" pile.

Steve Fischler presented some information on the Spinners' "I'll Be Around." The record was already being played on KHJ in Los Angeles. Fischler was fighting for "accelerated airplay" on KJR. Other promotion executives, all local, had their chance to make their statements about their product. A few times, O'Day asked other promotion people in the room what they thought about the chances of a given record.

The meeting lasted two to three hours. Such meetings have been used at other radio stations. Several years ago, WCFL in Chicago was in its heyday as a rocker and the station offered promotion executives coffee and a chance to air their information once a week.

Generally, the rapport between a record promotion person and a radio person is all one way; everything is in favor of the radio person. In some cases, the promotion executive has created his own monster. One of the talents of a promotion person is the ability—consciously or unconsciously—to build up the ego of the radio program director or music director. In many cases, the program director or music director eventually begins to believe he's as great as the promotion people tell him he is. He's certainly willing to be treated to lunch, dinner, or a free show by the record promotion man. There's nothing legally or morally wrong with it. It's just that the ego of the program director or music director continues to ascend. Sometimes, he/she becomes too great to bother talking to the promotion man.

This is an exaggeration, of course. The type of promotion person who uses "ego building" as his only promotion will eventually lose touch with the very person he used it on.

There are some program and music directors who abuse their power with record companies. Not too long ago, a situation came to light in Los Angeles where the practice of free concert tickets to disk jockeys, music directors, and program directors was being abused. Record companies have to pay full price for tickets to concerts, as a rule. Normally, giving free tickets to disk jockeys and program directors is considered good promotion and well worth the price to record companies. But it was found that a huge number of the tickets were going to secretaries or being passed to babysitters and garage mechanics.

Jan Basham, on behalf of record promotion people in Los Angeles, stated that it was not wrong for a record company to first ask program directors and disk jockeys if they wanted tickets and then tell them they could have tickets if they'd show up personally.

Dell White, a promotion person, pointed out that she'd given out 30 tickets to a Gladys Knight concert and only a few of the people who were supposed to show were there.

What is needed to settle a long battle between programming and record promotion people (though it's not on the surface, it is a war—the very promotion person who builds up the ego of a radio man and tells him how great he is often laughs at him behind his back) is more honesty and respect for each other. The good promotion executive is as much an artist in his craft as is a program director. Together they are a better force than when at odds with each other. And, while the program director and music director might exist without the promotion executive, they can do much better in their job because of him.

Perhaps a wise thing would be for the radio station to clearly state its music policy. The following policy statement was made by Ted Atkins, general manager of WTAE in Pittsburgh. Though not an absolute guideline, it does have a lot of merit to it and is applicable to a medium or major market station, regardless of the format.

1. All record promotion personnel (local, regional, and national) will be seen by Chuck Brinkman without appointment every Monday and Tuesday afternoon between 2-5 PM. In Chuck's absence, please leave product with his secretary. Under no circumstances are records to be furnished to disk jockeys or attempts made to influence them in the amount of airplay given to any particular record. This does not, however, prohibit you from furnishing disk jockeys with new releases for their own personal use.

2. National promotion people and company executives may visit the station on Thursday or Friday, by appointment only, between 2-5 PM.

3. All promotion people are encouraged to drop off hot new product (established artists, awaited product) at any time, without appointment, by asking for Chuck or his secretary or, in their absence, by leaving it at the switchboard. We never want to find ourselves in a position of not having new releases when our competition might have access to them, so we ask your cooperation in insuring that we are serviced

promptly. The WTAE switchboard is open 8 AM-midnight, seven days a week, and they have been instructed to call Chuck or me immediately, at any time, when records are dropped off.

4. Because of my many commitments it will be impossible, for the most part, for me to visit with any promotion people. Chuck Brinkman is the WTAE music director and you should work through him at all times. This, however, does not preclude my joining you in the evening hours on a social basis if you would like and my schedule permits.

5. Wednesday is music day at WTAE. Chuck and I screen all product and compile the weekly WTAE music list. On-air adds and deletions are reflected by 8 PM each Wednesday evening. In any given week, we will probably, on an average, be deleting and adding as many as eight to ten individual titles. WTAE policy does not prohibit our adding new releases on any day of the week (records of merit will be added to our list at any time). When a record is added for station airplay, you will be asked to service the station with an additional 10 copies so that we might guard against breakage and insure ready replacement for any scratched records. We will also be programming a considerable number of albums and we ask that you service us all new album releases.

6. All new records added to the WTAE weekly list will, for the most part, receive a minimum of four weeks airplay. We will play records for a sufficient time until we are convinced they have no potential. All new songs will receive equal airplay (approximately three or four times per day). WTAE will not publish a weekly playlist for stores, distributors, or record companies. A copy of our list will not be available at the station. However, individual promotion people and record companies may inquire through Chuck or his secretary as to whether their own records were dropped or added. National music trade publications will be furnished specific record information, including all titles deleted or added in any one week. WTAE will not be a "numbers" station and will not rank songs in order of popularity.

7. Please do not assume anything regarding our on-air music policy, please service us with all of your product including rock, MOR, R&B, and country music as well as any oldies series your company may release. Our station will best be defined as contemporary MOR, featuring the greatest hits of all time, plus the best of today's hits. We will try to play what most of the people want to hear most of the time and will be programming a wide range of music appeal.

8. WTAE policy prohibits any staff member from accepting gratuities and favors at any time from members of the record industry. This includes, but is not limited to, out-of-town airfare and lodging for any event. This does not preclude local social occasions that might include cocktails and dinner.

9. Our plans call for a well-defined, and well-structured on-air music policy. Commencing Sept. 1, the WTAE music department will be involved in wide-scale local music research via on-the-street and in-store interviews as well as several other areas that will not be defined to the industry. I make you one promise—WTAE will become a vital force in the Pittsburgh area and will play an increasingly important role in the selection and influence of Pittsburgh's musical tastes.

The beauty of the music policy that Ted Atkins laid down was that it clearly spelled out guidelines for the record industry. It let them know where they stood. There was no doubt left. True, the guidelines that fit WTAE might not fit your station—or even most stations. But a good program director, once he takes over the programming at a station, should set similar guidelines that apply to his own format and his market size. A program director in a small town might immediately think: Why? After all, he hasn't seen a promotion person in his life except at the International Radio Programming Forum or once when he went to Los Angeles on his vacation.

Such guidelines are even more important at the smaller market level, if for no other reason than to let the record industry know you're personally alive and that your station is alive. And, of course, the weekly playlist is a good tool that the small market station can use to draw attention to itself from the record industry.

Other Format Playlists

The typical playlist at MOR stations has been dwindling and even the country music station doesn't usually boast about the 100-plus playlist as it did a few years ago. The MOR station's playlist may be as short as 40 or 50 records; the theory is that while familiar records win, the adult (25 years and older) gets turned off by repetition. However, some MOR stations have gone to playlists the length of Top 40 stations and are augmenting their on-air sound with oldies—rock oldies, no less, since today's adults grew up listening to rock. Overall, the country music list seems about 55 records. The feeling is that country fans are more loyal and stay tuned for longer periods, thus familiarity has to be balanced with repetition, but not overdone.

The soul music stations have also drifted toward a tighter list. In spite of a poor signal, KDAY, Los Angeles, grew to prominence under program director Jim Maddox.

"How long should a playlist be? I really have no opinion. The playlist at an R&B station is a little different from that of a Top 40 station, aside from the kind of records played. The playlist of an R&B station should be a little longer, if for no other reason than there's no vast supply of oldies to draw upon, and you're left mostly with new product, plus album cuts.

"However, I believe in a disciplined format and that the most popular songs should come back at you more than the also-rans. Here at KDAY, we have two lists— one for the record shops to give away to record buyers and the other for the disk jockeys in the control room. I would never put anything on the printed list for the public unless we've played it. But the printed list is longer. Sometimes, the list in the control room is down to 15 records." He continued, "In regard to tuneout, I think that people listen to a radio station for a given thing and when you give the audience something it doesn't expect, they turn the dial. We're very cautious about what we give the listener."

The typical soul station playlist might be 30-50 records, depending on the market; today, more than ever before, the soul format station has to compete in the general market place more than just for ethnic listeners.

Even album cut stations are formatted, to some extent today, though the playlist may be quite long because of longer listening spans on FM radio in general. Classical music stations have moved further toward format; several program directors have given serious thought to what effect a playlist would have in the classical format.

Incidentally, the more successful all-news and all-talk stations are also formatted. Shortly after it hit the air with news in a Top 40 approach to the genre, WINS in New York was an excellent example. Oldie stations have formats, but because of the boredom factor (an oldie can quickly become a tuneout factor if heard too many times too soon), a playlist is hardly feasible. All-request stations, however, have used playlists, though this kind of format (WORC in Worcester, Mass., under former program director Dick Smith, achieved excellent success with an all-request format; the format was later copied by several stations nationwide but has since faded) isn't viable in large markets. This is because the phone company would have difficulty installing enough lines to handle calls; the people who call would not necessarily be the ones the radio station would like to reach; etc.

It was the all-request format that led Bill Weaver to launch the first all-oldies format with KLOK in San Jose, Calif. The station achieved excellent results for several years, and even did well in San Francisco ratings. Some while ago, Weaver added a new touch to KLOK and to KWIZ in Santa Ana, Calif. He called it Music Information Radio and the concept was to provide listeners with stories behind the hits. The information is brief and is casually worked into the disk jockey's rap; it can deal with the song, the artist, the producer, or the record company.

"I've always felt," Weaver said, "that just playing music did not make for a complete music station. For this concept, I've thought of going into recording sessions, getting interviews with various people involved with the song or record, getting into areas that will make us a distinct station." Weaver also felt that radio could not go on forever with the short playlist.

The direct opposite of the all-oldies or solid gold radio format is the all-new records format. KFRC-FM, billed as K-106FM, in San Francisco had used an oldies format for three years, but then over a year ago went to a Northern California top 20. They did this by using a revolving top 20 countdown starting at 9 AM and running until midnight (the other hours, it simulcast the Top 40 format of KFRC-AM). This playlist was changed daily, based on sales at about 15 retail stores in the area, and twice an hour the station played a new record. Dave Sholin guided the format, and handled music chores at KFRC-AM. Each of five new records—an acetate, an LP cut, or a new single—were played five times daily and phone response requested from listeners. The top-requested new single was added to the playlist the next day. Any record company could pay for air time to have a record retested and get the results of the re-test via registered mail.

"We could expose 100 records a month this way," said Sholin. "That's a lot of new product." History won't have a chance to prove whether K-106FM found a niche in the San Francisco market or not, the station was later sold before the format could prove itself.

Other formats that are still experimental in nature, though all three have shown fairly decent results already, are the black progressive format, the progressive country format, and the disco format.

WHUR, an FM station operated by Howard University in Washington, D.C., was the station that launched the so-called black progressive format, which depends upon album cuts by blacks, most of them hard rock in nature.

KOKE-FM in Austin, Tex., launched the first progressive country programming (the music has been called redneck rock, country-rock, rockabilly, etc., and Willie Nelson and Waylon Jennings probably did more than anyone else to popularize the movement; their way of doing a country song was largely rejected by Nashville's musical clique). However, KAFM in Dallas, programmed by Chuck Dunaway (who'd been one of the early rock jocks at WABC in New York), was the first full-time progressive country station and probably did more to spread its glory, if not its programming viability. The station eventually shifted, somewhat, away from a pure progressive country format.

In April 1976, Bob Henabery, president of Bob Henabery Associates, a New York research and programming consultant firm, claimed that "country music is about a year away from being the next big format, specifically the progressive type of country music—i.e. Willie Nelson, Waylon Jennings, the Eagles—those acts that aim at a younger audience."

Henabery was the first programmer to delve into psychographics of listeners. He also innovated the disco format and launched it on WKYS, an FM station owned and operated by NBC in Washington, D.C. Several stations then jumped on the disco format; WSRF in Miami dropped off after a few months claiming the commitment was too great. So, the disco format hasn't proved itself yet either.

As FM stations shift toward their own programming formats, fragmentation of audiences increases and more stations are forced to hunt for their own programming niche—thus the possibility of even more new formats and/or "twists" of formats in days to come. The FCC has ruled that, effective May 1, 1977, the AM-FM duplication limit in cities of more than 100,000 population is 25 percent. In markets 25,000 to 100,000, the limit that stations are allowed to simulcast is 50 percent, and on May 1, 1979, (even in cities of 25,000-100,000) AM-FM simulcasting is to be limited to 25 percent. This has to force ownership to endeavor to be successful with their FM, or at least encourage them to sell it to a broadcaster who will do something viable with it.

Hot Clocks I've Known and Loved

There is nothing mysterious about the hot clock. It's simply a pie graph overlaid over an hour.

Jay Blackburn has consulted and programmed many stations. In his younger days as a program director he once designed hot clocks for every hour of a radio station. As he grew older, he realized his mistake. The reason for a hot clock is merely to establish consistency, so that each hour features the same programming elements in the same order as any other hour. If you're programming for dayparts, then you would probably have one hot clock for morning drive, one for midday, one for afternoon drive, and another for evening (though the same midday hot clock might be used with just a different playlist involved).

Blackburn described a hot clock he designed for KEYS in Corpus Christi, Tex., a few years ago:

:00—MUSIC, two-record sweep

:06—COMMERCIAL SET

:07—MUSIC, one record

:11—WEATHER, MUSIC, two-record set

:19—COMMERCIAL SET

:20—MUSIC, one record

:25—COMMERCIAL SET

:26—MUSIC, one record

:30—STATION ID JINGLE, MUSIC, two-record set

:36—COMMERCIAL SET

:37—MUSIC, one record

:41—WEATHER, MUSIC, two-record set

:46–COMMERCIAL SET

:47–MUSIC, one record

:50–COMMERCIAL SET

:51–MUSIC, two-record set

:55–NEWS

The structure of this format clock tells the disk jockey several key things:

1. They have to come with a two-record sweep out of the news;

2. At least a two-record sweep out of the weather, the point of this sweep is to cover :13 to :17 (or past the quarterhour mark) at least;

3. The next required sweep is the half-hour mark, with a three-record sweep (excepting the jingle) :27 to :36.

4. The :43 to :46 period is covered with music.

The above hot clock is not as complex as many today. News might be in another position, for competitive reasons. For example, if your main competition features news at five minutes before the hour, you might have yours on the hour, or :20 past and :20 until the hour. Kent Burkhart, now a programming consultant, tried to popularize floating news—which means the news was shifted around at no set point during the hour. This is not advisable; your station might have listeners who listen to it expressly for the news.

The hot clock might also show other programming elements, for instance, public service announcements. As far as public service announcements, KHJ in Los Angeles uses the back-sell technique. The disk jockey might mention that there will be a sensational arts and crafts show that weekend at the beach, the weather is going to be great, everyone's invited, and it's being sponsored by the local heart fund. Therefore, according to program director Charlie Van Dyke, the listener is more inclined to feel the disk jockey is tuned into the market and "we get PSA credit on the thing, too."

In any case, the hot clock concept applies to just about all formats, including (or perhaps it should) progressive rock. The idea is to demand consistency and the hot clock is a programming tool that any disk jockey should be able to follow within reason, regardless of the music played. Elements within the graph might change, and the time scale where those elements are to be aired might change. But a hot clock can prove beneficial.

Eric Norberg, program director of KEX in Portland, Ore., an MOR station, has this to say:

"Hot clocks are very misunderstood and often used to counterprogram rather than program a station. It should be noted that a radio station which concentrates mostly on counterprogramming is unconsciously informing listeners that another station in the market is better than itself." Norberg added, "And it's very hard to win that way.

"Slotting your double-play against the other guy's news is a destructive idea unless it makes sense within the totality of your format structure to have that double-play at that particular time. The correct function of a hot clock is to establish a specific sequence of records. The sequence, in turn, is determined by the desired balance of records.

"The first step is to formulate an idea of what kind of repetition you desire. To cite an example of how this works, in structuring the station I was with at one time— KMBY in Monterey, Calif., in 1969—I wanted to have a relatively long list at this Top 40 station since considerable variety is important to attract and hold a large adult audience. High repetition of familiar records, on the other hand, was necessary to maintain the youth audience. The solution I arrived at in this particular case was to establish a list of roughly 50 titles, divide them into two categories—the top 15 hits and the remainder—and rotate the two categories on a one for one basis.

"The top hits were determined by local sales and requests mainly, and the list was lengthened to this level not by increasing the programming of picks and secondary records, but by retaining the former top hits until they had stopped selling and being requested in the market.

"The top hits had a two-and-a-half to three-and-a-half hour repetition pattern, with the remainder of the list cycling every six to seven hours, depending on spotload. The result was a relatively low (for Top 40) repetition of individual records, but an extremely high familiarity factor on records played."

It should be noted that many program directors have designated time slots for oldies, balance records, psychographic records, or they might specify on a given hot clock: "Play oldie from list A" or "Play oldie from list B." It all depends on how regimented the particular program director is.

Some program directors, after briefing disk jockeys on general guidelines, leave the decision of what records to play up to the disk jockey, only specifying that the key hits have to be played at given times.

Profit and Loss and Programming

Of course, there's more to programming a radio station than being able to pick a hit record. Today's program director must be versed in all aspects of the station, including the profit and loss picture.

Al Herskovitz has a career in programming that extends through rock radio and beautiful music radio formats. As operations manager of KPOL in Los Angeles for Capital Cities Communications, he was also often called upon to advise on other radio operations throughout the chain. He suggests that program directors should put themselves through a brief test not unlike the ones you see in magazine articles about your personality. Just answer these questions *yes* or *no.*

1. Do you know how to use your radio station's ratecards?

2. Have you ever seen your station's profit and loss statement?

3. Have you ever attended a sales meeting in which you were not a specifically invited participant?

4. Have you ever gone out on a sales call?

"If you are involved in the programming of a radio station and have answered *no* to any of the above, then you had better make some fast moves to turn those negatives into affirmatives," Herskovitz said.

The most beneficial of the four acts would be to make sales calls with one of the radio station's account executives. "You may think this is odd advice, but it probably is one of the most important acts you can take to put your entire broadcast career into proper perspective. You see, that is what radio broadcasting is all about—it is a business! It is not an educational institution. It is not an instrument for social change. It is not a charitable foundation. It is not some kind of game or sport to be played for fun.

"This is not to say that it cannot be educating, socially useful, charitable, or enjoyable. However, there is only one major purpose to the whole effort and that is the making of a profit.

"And there is nothing wrong with that. It is at the core of the free enterprise system and our entire way of life. It allows the individuals working in the radio station to feed and clothe themselves and their family. If you believe otherwise, teach, be a social worker, do volunteer work, or play amateur hockey."

The radio station's license is a franchise from the federal government to do business under a certain set of rules, said Herskovitz. "As basic as this description is, it seems that it becomes forgotten. The concept is not that far removed from opening a Kentucky Fried Chicken stand. If you do not sell enough chicken to enough people, you close down and go out of business. That is why it is so important to understand this aspect of broadcasting with which you have the least directly to do."

Making a sales call with an account executive to a potential client might give a program director or even an air personality a perspective of his radio station that he probably never had before. It dramatizes vividly what keeps the broadcast industry functioning—the aspect of making a profit.

Herskovitz also recommends that the astute program director should call on an advertising agency that is deeply involved in the utilization of research material, ratings, cost-per-thousand, efficiency, reach and frequency, demographics, psychographics, and market-targets. "And all of those other words that are tossed about relative to the effectiveness of advertising. What makes this aspect of the battle so unusually bruising is that the struggle for success not only involves your direct radio competitors, but every other forum for an advertising message—television, newspapers, magazines, billboards, direct mail, posters, handbills, skywriting, up to and including messages handpainted on rocks along the highway."

Herskovitz said that much too often he'd talked with program directors who had veered miles off course. They had constructed a wall between themselves and the realities of the business by immersing themselves too deeply in the frills and fringes of their responsibilities ... associating with music entertainment people ranging from record artists to record company executives. It's okay to enjoy this aspect of being in radio, but radio is also a job. Fractionalization of the marketplace by FM radio coming to the forth and the growth of competition in programming has brought about several interesting facets in radio. Being No. 1 is no longer necessary, "but being competitive is. What this means is that the station has to be worth what it charges for advertising and the station's programmer has to make it worth it."

Herskovitz considers it wrong to let a disk jockey kiss-off a live commercial, claiming that the sponsor has paid for a sincere, believable delivery. He also feels that public service programming is good business. "Every radio station is in a community from which it takes; therefore, it is obligated to give. Imaginative public service programming builds goodwill, excellent business contacts, and audience involvement with the station. There are no negative aspects."

But it's the financial side of a radio station that the program director must also master in order to be a rounded radio person and do his programming job better. "If a program director wishes to demonstrate the ultimate in creative skill, let him effectively prepare, then handle, his department budget. It is remarkable the profit contribution good budgeting can make."

Doing a program project cheaply, with the results being ineffective, is bad budgeting. But also each expense should be measured against the result it will bring.

Herskovitz also recommends that a program director can achieve a better perspective of his duties by mentally exchanging places from time to time with the general manager, the sales manager, the business manager, the chief engineer—by looking at the entire radio station and its programming from their viewpoint.

In any case, it's clear that a good program director should be acquainted with the P&L of his radio station in order to give his programming goals stronger meaning.

11 Those crazy hazy days of radio promotions

It's not only music, or fantastic disk jockeys, or fantastic programming that makes a radio station successful. Many (perhaps too many) program directors think that giving away money is the way to get listeners. Then they pray that they can keep them with good programming.

Buzz Bennett at WKTQ in Pittsburgh and then at Y-100 in Miami gave away $50,000 for a phone call—the old Cash Call promotion that has been used and reused not only by a countless number of formats and stations, but even by stations overseas. It has been proven, however, that you can't really *buy* an audience.

But promotion continues to be the forte of most program directors and over the years has taken many forms. For instance, one promotion was as follows: In order to win several thousand dollars and a Thanksgiving turkey, all the contestant had to do was find the turkey.

To make certain that everyone in the town had a chance at the prize, the general manager and one of the disk jockeys at the radio station took the turkey and pushed it out of a plane at 2,000 feet. Unfortunately, Steve Bellinger, the manager of WDZ in Decatur, Ill., had forgotten that domestic turkeys can't fly. The big bird crashed through the roof of a local dry cleaning establishment.

Instead of awarding a listener the prize, Bellinger ended up presenting the owner with several thousand dollars for a new roof. Little did the bird know—as he gave his feathered all—that he was helping save radio for the world.

You see, in the early 1950s everyone knew that radio wouldn't survive. After all, it didn't have pictures. It was a dying medium. Even most of the radio greats like Red Skelton, Jack Benny, and Bob Hope had abandoned radio for television. And radio station owners who also owned fledgling television stations began to cut back on their radio operations and plow the extra funds into TV staff and equipment.

Some radio men sold their radio stations for any price they could get. Thus, most men who stayed in radio were considered slightly aberrated, or nuts, if you prefer. A few of these radio men weren't crazy. Maybe they were just too stubborn to admit radio was dying—if they were even aware of it. And they began to change radio.

For example, Bill Stewart and two other disk jockeys locked themselves into a radio studio in New Orleans and played the same record over and over for days. Gordon McLendon arranged for a disk jockey to stand on a Dallas street corner and give away money. Chuck Blore, a program director with a flair for show business, had several of his disk jockeys push balloons out of windows in Los Angeles. Steve Bellinger dropped ping pong balls out of a plane over Decatur. Each ball had a number representing money that was obtainable by presenting the balls at the radio station.

All kinds of crazy things were going on—disk jockeys broadcasting from flagpoles, welding themselves into cars, burying treasure for zany treasure hunts, doing a show on the air while nude—the stunts got wilder and crazier.

Within a few months, radio—especially rock (or Top 40) radio—became the most exciting stimulus in the United States since the invention of the martini. Rock 'n' roll became the *new* sound. Instead of dying, radio and a large majority of broadcasters literally went crazy.

Disk jockeys climbed into Ferris wheels with microphones and spun around dizzily for days, speaking in their machine gun-like style while playing records by Clarence "Frogman" Henry, Chuck Berry, Bobby Vee, Little Richard, or Buddy Holly. The roller coaster was a favorite haunt of deejays. One deejay even climbed to the top of the Astrodome in Houston for his radio show.

The disk jockey who first climbed a flagpole is still a broadcast mystery, but Tom Clay, once known as "Jack the Bell Boy" and maybe other names (deejays often changed names from town to town and no respectable city was without its own Johnny Dark or Johnny Dollar) may have done it once. In Buffalo, he did climb on top of the roof of a rock radio station and then up a billboard with his mike on a long cord. As he continued his radio show, traffic slowed to a standstill for blocks, then police and firemen converged on the scene. Clay refused to come down. The fire chief climbed up the truck's extension ladder.

"Get off of there you crazy son-of-a-bitch!"

"Folks, that was a message from your local fire department," Clay said, and continued broadcasting, thus also stirring up trouble with the Federal Communications Commission for airing profanity. He was thrown in jail, and later fired by the station; management often didn't understand what was really going on in rock radio.

In New Orleans, Bill Stewart locked himself in the control room and played the same record—a bad one—over and over for days to herald the new format of WTIX. Irate citizens protested, but his radio station soon went to No. 1 in listeners. In St. Louis, one deejay—Johnny Rabbitt, otherwise known as Don Peatromonaco—could do his show to magic tricks.

You had to have a gimmick. Arnie "Woo Woo" Ginsberg at WMEX in Boston used cowbells and train whistles. Gary Stevens at WKNR in Detroit had his "Wooly Booger." Anything and everything was used to attract attention.

In Miami, disk jockey Dick Starr of WFUN had himself welded into a Toyota for several days. Listeners didn't believe he was staying in the car day and night. Starr had to elude fans in order to get a few hours of sleep. And because there really was no other way out than a blow torch, you can imagine Starr's problems when he wanted to go to the bathroom.

In Philadelphia, record hops were so much a part of disk jockey Jerry Blavat's life that he'd hit as many as four a night, traveling from one place to another by helicopter. Several thousand dancing, music-stunned kids screamed at his soft-shoe antics whenever he duplicated his radio show by playing records with overlays of "Geator-with-the-Heater" patter.

Cleveland's Ernie Farrell tried to hold a summit meeting with Khrushchev at a record hop. Farrell heard that Khrushchev was visiting Cyrus Eaton in Aurora. With tongue-in-cheek, Farrell, a record promotion executive, sent an invitation to Khrushchev to come listen to American rock 'n' roll, specifically a group called the Cadillacs that he was promoting. Surprisingly, Khrushchev accepted Ernie's invitation. All of a sudden, WJW's usual Saturday night record hop—hosted by Casey Kasem, now an actor—assumed international importance. The story made the wire services.

"Are you crazy!" yelled Kasem. "Some kid with a zip gun will shoot him and you'll end up starting World War III."

And because a U2 plane was shot down at the time, Khrushchev backed out of attending the Cadillacs' record hop at the last moment. But it was this atmosphere of "anything can happen in our town right now" that gave radio much of its early vitality. And, while such stunts saved radio from the death clutches of TV, older adults at that time wondered if it was worth saving.

Other factors, of course, helped rescue radio. For example, the transistor opened up a whole new audience. Music suddenly became extremely portable for everybody, anywhere, at a low cost. A teenager might not be able to afford a television set of his own, but he or she could take his transistor radio to the beach, to school, even to football games. Then Elvis arrived with a touch of sex and blues to excite music, the same as those mop-haired kids from England were to do later when the "British Invasion" of music hit the United States and the world. Persistent men such as Gordon McLendon, the late Todd Storz, and Chuck Blore made great contributions in reestablishing radio as back in command of the air waves.

Today, McLendon and Storz are considered the fathers of Top 40 radio. Radio station owners, managers, program directors, and disk jockeys, even today, confer their adulation upon them. You see, though TV may have taken away the bulk of radio's creative people, those who were left were fanatically devoted to the medium. They were young, eager, highly inventive, and aggressive, often to the point of being ridiculous. They were out to promote themselves and their stations in any manner possible.

Today, a radio station could lose its broadcast license for some of the zany stunts that were pulled 15 years ago. Many of the wilder radio promotions were geared to announce the arrival of a new disk jockey or a change in format for the station. In Dallas, Gordon McLendon at KLIF welcomed new disk jockey Jimmy Rabbitt by turning over cars alongside the freeway and painting "I flipped for Jimmy Rabbitt" on bottom. Everyone coming into town—or leaving—got the message. Rabbitt was a celebrity before he even hopped past the city limits sign.

Another time, a man appeared on a Dallas street corner giving out one and five dollar bills, and occasionally a ten or a twenty. Local newspapers featured stories of the "eccentric millionaire." He made the news on TV. You can imagine how embarrassed the newspaper and TV reporters were when the "millionaire" announced live on TV that he was the new disk jockey for the morning show on Gordon McLendon's KLIF. The same stunt has since been pulled by radio stations in Jacksonville, Fla., Hartford, Conn., and elsewhere.

When Chuck Blore announced his new Top 40 format on KFWB in Los Angeles (now an all-news station) for weeks before the new format, secretaries, engineers, and disk jockeys blew up balloons in rooms all over downtown Los Angeles. On New Year's Day, the day the new format went on the air, balloons were pushed out the windows. Attached to every fifth balloon was a dollar bill and a fifty dollar bill on one out of 50 balloons. Traffic was tied up for hours over about 200 square miles. But everyone quickly knew about rock 'n' roll music on KFWB. It became the No. 1 station in Los Angeles as fast as people could switch radio dials.

Radio promotions took many forms—raising funds for hospitals or orphanages; marathons and walkathons; bicycle races and go-cart races; and the ever-popular 'How Long Can You Stay On The Air Without Stopping' promotion. Don French, now programming a radio station in Alaska, probably holds the sleepless nine-day record. In 1961, the program director of KTKT in Tucson, Ariz., even threw his disk jockeys out of an airplane (he, being a kind program director, did allow them to wear parachutes). Only Jay Lawrence, now afternoon disk jockey on a country music station called

KLAC in Los Angeles, refused to jump; Lawrence broadcast the event live from the ground.

There was often a carnival quality about the goings on. Although fiercely competitive, disk jockeys, program directors, and station managers were addicted to outlandish pranks. And nothing was sacred except audience ratings, i.e., being No. 1 in listeners.

Watche Konochee, for example, once roamed the south from Glassboro, Ky., to Tucson, Ariz., offering radio stations the opportunity to bury him alive in a coffin with rattlesnakes. L. David Moorhead, now general manager of KMET in Los Angeles, knew Watche Konochee well.

"He was immune to rattlesnake poison. I used him at five different radio stations. Watche used 28 rattlers, 28 cottonmouths, 2 boa constrictors, and a python. I don't remember what his real name was," Moorhead said.

"The reason I used him a lot was that I always worked for losers," said Moorhead. Losers were stations at the bottom of the ratings battle. The radio station would charge 25 cents a head for people to see Watchee buried.

"In Tucson for KTKT, we were trying to break a record, because he'd been there before the past winter. I don't remember what year it was, but Kennedy became president about that time." He continued, "Unfortunately, this time it was summer and, to say the least, the snakes were uncomfortable."

Moorhead and the KTKT staff took the snakes to an outdoor museum near the city to "let the snakes clean themselves out. Can you imagine what that coffin would have been like with all that snake crap?"

But the truck that they rented had been sitting in the sun. The truck bed was about 125 degrees. "When we tossed those rattlesnakes on that hot metal truck floor, they started striking, killing each other." KTKT had to, literally, dig up some more rattlesnakes.

Then other problems developed. "Watche was bitten six times by those wild rattlesnakes before we could even get him into the hole," Moorhead said. "The poison didn't bother him, but one of the rattlers had cankermouth. Watche had a hell of an infection problem for a while."

"But the snakes did their job," Moorhead said. "We sat there in the market with a 64% average share." He added, "It was only much later—after I became a general manager myself at a radio station—that I learned it was much better to have 28% of a market and make money."

In the early days, the rock 'n' roll hotshot program directors and disk jockeys usually worked for losing stations. After they took a station to No. 1, the owner would sell it to some sucker. The FCC didn't require an owner to keep his station three years in those days. There were a lot of owners who made quick money building losers into winners and selling them fast. Owners would call in what George Wilson, now head of radio for Bartell Broadcasters, referred to as "a circus." A circus was a group of guys who traveled together from town to town working over radio stations. Several such circuses existed, some with phenomenal success, some with only minor achievements. But Terrell Methney, known in those days as Mitch Michaels, remembers going into several markets and transforming "dogs" into "instant wonders" in 60 to 90 days. Methney rose to become national program director of all Southern Broadcasting's radio stations reaching from Winston-Salem, N.C. to Phoenix, Ariz.

L. David Moorhead was sometimes known as Guy Williams in his disk jockey days, "because six of us worked together for 10 years under 30 different names."

He was fired as McShane by one station in Omaha, then hired in Denver as Guy

Williams, and later hired back at the previous Omaha radio station as "the sensational Guy Williams." Moorhead worked a total of seven radio stations in Denver during one period of his career under six different names.

"At one station I forgot who I was one night on the air. It was about the time— 1958 or 1959—that 'El Paso' by Marty Robbins was a hit. Marty had done a great record for late-night disk jockeys because it was exactly 4:35 minutes long. A great bathroom record—to play while you headed for the john—maybe that alone got it enough exposure to make it a hit.

"I was at KTLN in Denver (now KTLK) and George Wilson was program director. And I hadn't been told where the bathroom was."

Moorhead left the studio to call one of the other staff members about the john, first putting on "El Paso." Finally, he reached Rick Flight. He ran back up the stairs from the phone only to discover that the door to the studio had snap-locked; his keys were in his coat laying near the control board. He thundered down seven flights of stairs to the main floor elevator and zoomed back up, hoping to get in the front doors of the studio, but they, too, were locked.

There was nothing else to do but crawl out a window and walk along a ledge toward the window of the studio. But the studio windows were also locked.

"Ever try to break a window seven floors up over Denver?"

Sweating, he took off a shoe and banged it against the window—just as the last bullets thudded musically into the million-selling Marty Robbins. He lost the shoe, and cut his arm as he went through.

But as the record ended and went clunk, clunk on the end grooves, Guy, alias whoever-he-was-at-the-moment, hit the chair scared and out of breath and shouted into the mike, "That was 'El Paso'," and then spun another record.

J. Paul Emerson, now a newsman at KGMQ in Honolulu, believes Pogo Pog was the king of radio stuntmen. "Pogo Pog worked at KIMN in Denver from 1955 until 1965. He wore a fur hat, racoon-skin coat, drove a three-wheeled auto, carried a pogo stick as a cane and used the name Weird Beard. Anyway, during the time at KIMN, Pogo once did his show from the storefront window of Zales in downtown Denver. And, get this, he did it while sitting in the middle of 150 snakes (75 were killer snakes). On the 13th day, while on the air, his chair broke and fell into the snakes . . . A cottonmouth jumped out and bit him on the arm three times. Pogo (Morgan White) Pog was in the hospital for several weeks after that stunt."

Moorhead said that perhaps it happened differently. Watche Konochee climbed into the jewelry store window surrounded by rattlesnakes. After weeks of publicity, the final day arrived. The station had climbed to No. 1 in the market. The program director wondered what he would do for an encore? And this program director wanted fiercely to stay No. 1 in the market. The promotion was almost over. Watche Konochee was being interviewed on radio about the deadly snakes. Then, suddenly, the radio audience and the people milling outside the jewelry store realized that something had gone wrong. A rattlesnake was loose. A disk jockey appeared to be bitten. Two men slashed at the DJ's wounded hand to prevent the venom from spreading.

An ambulance was called. The DJ was given anti-venom and rushed to the hospital. That "snakebite" proved itself worth extra mileage; the disk jockey ended up being interviewed by local newspapers and eventually by most of the press in the West and Southwest.

To this day, only two or three radio people know that truth, according to Moorhead. Secretly, the program director whacked the DJ with two nails on a board. By the time his hand was cut up and he was rushed to the hospital, no one knew the small difference. The "big" difference was in the even-greater ratings the radio station achieved the next few months resulting from the publicity.

"Watchee was okay," said Moorhead. "A real pro."

Pogo Pog was also a real pro. In Ogden, Pogo once jumped on a pogo stick for 35 miles to raise money for The March of Dimes. He also holds the world radio record for riding a Ferris wheel 17 days without getting off (he used a porta-potty supplied by the U.S. Air Force). As for his name, Weird Beard, Pogo Pog may have used it first. And once while playing the record "Bonapartes Retreat" over and over for 24 hours on KIMN, he was kidnapped from the studio by some college dudes who drove him out to the boonies, stripped him, shaved his beard with a dull pocket knife, and left him standing in the snow wearing only his racoon coat and the weirdest weird beard you've ever seen. He had to walk back to Denver, since it was past midnight and no one would stop and pick him up.

Another incident that will go down in the annals of radio was "Formula 63." In Minneapolis, few people ever tuned in as low as 63 on the dial. But Chuck Blore, hired to work magic on the failing KDWB (ever notice how some stations in city after city not only sound alike, but have similar call letters?) thought that the power of advertising could solve the problem. Chuck persuaded the man who made Hadacol famous to create a series of commercials advertising the new Formula 63 which was guaranteed to relieve ennui. Drug stores throughout Minneapolis were stocked with little packages of Formula 63. It was free "for a short time only."

A major advertising firm bought mass time on most of the radio stations in town; only a couple of stations turned down the heavy ad dollars. None of the radio stations bothered to really find out what Formula 63 was. Listeners were merely told to run down and pick up a packet of Formula 63.

"And they went into drugstores by the thousands," Chuck Blore said, "because we'd bought guaranteed spots, so that on any given moment, regardless of which radio station you turned on, all you'd hear would be this colonel saying: 'I'm the fellow who brought you Hadacol and I've got something good for you.' "

When the listeners hit the drugstores, they were given a packet that told them all they had to do was "tune in to 63 on the dial" to solve all their problems. Some of the competing radio stations were furious, but by then, KDWB was on its way to becoming the No. 1 station in town.

"I guess I wouldn't have thought it funny if someone had done it to me . . . I'd have been furious too," Blore said.

The extravagance of radio promotions was dazzling. Station managers were wholehearted in their rivalry. And often there was an innocence about their tricks that is appealing in these post-Watergate days. In Denver, for example, two Top 40 radio stations were deadly foes. During those days KIMN was managed by Ken Palmer and KTBR was managed by C. Edward Little, now head of Mutual Radio Network. When Little announced that KTBR was going to give away "lots and lots" of records, Palmer announced that KIMN had bought a record store and would give away every single record in the entire store. Little announced that KTBR was going to give away three Mustangs. Palmer bought a used car lot and gave away every car on the lot. Palmer won that particular battle and later made more millions in real estate.

Promotional Backfires

Not all the radio stunts worked—some backfired. One of the classic radio stories of all times was the Fresno, Calif. programming battle of Bill Drake—later to revolutionize rock radio by limiting commercials—then program director of KYNO, and Ron Jacobs, then program director of KMAK.

Story has it that the staff of KYNO figured out the clues to a KMAK "treasure hunt" and dug up the prize. Drake points out that he "played a lot of psychological games" with Ron Jacobs. "He thought that I had his treasure. It was a dog-eat-dog situation."

Ron Jacobs, once program director on KGB-FM-AM in San Diego, declared, "There was never a promotion that I was involved with where they didn't find the treasure. There was one where they didn't find the treasure when we thought they were going to find it. We almost had to give listeners the answer, and we had to get the thing found before the next morning because the Highway Patrol was about to take us all away. There were about 8,000 people in a field about the size of a supermarket in the middle of the night. It was cold—about 20 degrees.

"Everyone was searching for the Magic Key or whatever the hell the prize was, even using bulldozers, which can be a little hazardous, right? The goddamned thing was out there where a disk jockey named Frank Terry and I had put it a couple of months before in the middle of the night, a foot below ground, and nobody could find the goddamned thing. After a while, hell, you run out of clues, how can you make rhymes anymore? You know, 'Here it is and here it's not; now, goddammit this is the spot!'

"We had all these people in the field and they began to think we were putting them on. We kept coming up with more and more clues. The competing station, KYNO, was going crazy because they thought we'd screwed up. Finally, someone found the thing. There was just a while when it didn't look like the treasure would be found, that, I think, probably started the rumor that we had a contest where the treasure was never found."

One station in Miami got into trouble with the FCC because of a non-winable contest.

KYNO ended up with 40 percent of the listeners in town, KMAK had 20 percent. Between them, rock radio literally controlled 60 percent of the listeners. In any case, that treasure hunt contributed to the later demise of KMAK as a Top 40 station. It now programs country music.

The major purpose of giveaway contests in radio is to keep the call letters of the station in the minds of everyone who turns on a radio. In Denver, KMYR in 1956-57 gave away the entire Denver Symphony Orchestra to raise funds to maintain classical music in the city. The winner knew he'd won the grand prize when he awoke at 6 AM to the symphony playing "Oh, How I Hate to Get Up in the Morning" outside his window.

Then and now, stations gave away tee shirts, belt buckles, beach towels, tennis hats, posters, record albums, trips, cars, and money, and often, a deejay-for-a-day.

One of the biggest, most complex giveaways was launched by Cecil Heftel, an entrepreneur who now lives in Hawaii, and his gifted program director-of-the-moment, Buzz Bennett, in the amount of $50,000 that made all rival program directors blanch. Programming teeth gritted from coast to coast when they heard the $50,000 contest hit the air. It had to be an audience winner. Heftel had just purchased several radio stations for millions; $50,000 was only some additional pocket change compared to his basic costs. How could a rival station compete? After all, $50,000 represented a year's promotion budget or more, at many stations.

The complex contest required many phone calls back and forth between listeners and the station. Unfortunately for the station, the contest was not complex enough. Some listener won it in less than three weeks.

Sometimes promotion stunts have a way of creating adverse publicity. For example, in one of the flagpole sitting contests in El Paso, the disk jockey got lonely and talked a cute, young girl into climbing up and crawling into the little house he was broadcasting from on top of the flagpole. He was no longer lonely, but when they got caught it was a bigger scandal than a promotion. Also, identification with a radio station may be so strong that a stunt can backfire. There had been a three month's drought in the Los Angeles area. KFWB ran an Indian rain dance every hour. Twenty-four hours later, it rained. The station received several letters blaming them for the foul weather.

But the strangest radio stunt to backfire was the Los Angeles "amoeba" stunt. An honor student had been shot by a doped-up kid. His friends and schoolmates went to radio station KFWB asking for help. They wanted to visit the state capitol in Sacramento to plea for tighter anti-drug abuse legislation. Chuck Blore, then program director of KFWB, went on the air several times with public service announcements, hoping to raise funds so the kids could charter a bus. He ended up with only $300 in donations. Blore got angry and created the greatest radio event ever; in fact, it almost ranks in the same ballpark as Orson Welles' legendary radio show *War of the Worlds.*

A KFWB news reporter interrrupted a hit record for a special bulletin. An amoeba was reported to have been seen on a residential street. Nothing more was known at this time. Further information would be forthcoming. KWFB reporters were rushing to the scene and would report live.

A few moments later, another bulletin hit the air. The situation was much more serious than anticipated. There were reports from the law department that some homes would have to be evacuated. Police cars were speeding to the scene. Another bulletin at the end of Fats Domino's "Blueberry Hill" reported the progress of the amoeba down the street and into another area. The army was being alerted. More news would be given in the newscast at the top of the hour.

Occasionally, KFWB would run a disclaimer. But college students caught on to the gag and began phoning in reports.

"The army with tanks and bazookas were being brought in to confront the amoeba."

Chuck Blore received the attention he wanted for his anti-drug abuse campaign. There was only one minor problem. Everyone knows what an amoeba is, right? Wrong! Ordinary citizens became frightened—much the same as during the *War of the Worlds.* Soon, phone calls from frantic citizens literally blew out the switchboards at police and fire stations. Other radio stations were swamped with phone calls from hysterical people. And, since those stations were not aware of what KFWB was doing, that added to the mass confusion.

KFWB finally finished the promotion and succeeded in gaining enough donations to send several buses of students to visit Governor Brown (father of Governor Jerry Brown); stiffer laws were passed. Though irate citizens and other radio stations protested, Chuck Blore and KFWB got away with the amoeba invasion because it was for the public welfare. Unfortunately, when George Wilson, then program director of a Top 40 station in Denver, tried the same stunt he didn't bother to "amoebatize" the city for a public service campaign. Wilson admits "stealing" heavily from Blore—"he was the greatest"—and admits the same promotion in Denver raised more public ire than public good. Wilson, who now heads radio for the Bartell Broadcasters which runs from New York to San Diego, and one of his disk jockeys spent a night in jail until lawyers could rescue them.

One station in Los Angeles actually lost its broadcast license because of "misrepresenting" a contest and other such governmental no-no's. The contest was a "find the man in the street" search. Actually, the man—Perry Allen—was a deejay who was then still living in Buffalo. The station had declared they would give a prize of $10,000 to the listener who found him in the streets of Los Angeles. All you had to do was ask everyone you met if he was the new disk jockey on KRLA. A program director at a competing station, Don French of KFWB, knew that the deejay was still on the air in Buffalo. French got on a plane, flew to Buffalo, and forced the disk jockey to fly back with him. KRLA's red-faced general manager had to pay the rival program director the $10,000.

Radio Today

Radio people, for the most part, are reluctant to discuss fraudulent contests. They usually avoid the topic of KRLA losing its license by shifting the conversation to some good public works their station is currently doing. Perhaps the castration power of the Federal Communications Commission is always in their subconscious. The FCC's authority is something that a radio man knows he must live with, deal with, and overcome. The FCC, audience ratings, audience tuneout commercials (Preparation H, for example), a weak broadcasting signal, and other such flaws are simply threats to the radio man's programming expertise.

In the search for publicity, goodwill, and brighter promotions, radio station personnel will sometimes risk physical jeopardy. They will participate in skydiving, bullfights, ostrich races, golf cart races, and fly hot air balloons. (Gene Rump, program director of KAKE in Wichita, Kans., broke his leg a few months ago trying to land a hot air balloon.)

KTKH in Tucson in 1960-1961 ventured its disk jockeys against baby bulls in the 'south of the U.S. airwaves' city of Nogales, Mexico. The disk jockeys trained with the aid of tequila. The bullring was packed.

"But the so-called 'baby' bulls we were to fight sported horns that went from there to there," said David Moorhead, holding his hands as far apart as possible. "If you ever go to Nogales today, you will find my claw marks left all over the walls as I attempted to get out."

A deejay's life is very insecure anyway. He usually doesn't know that he's been fired until he walks into the door and finds a new man before the mike. Gary McDowell, known as Gary Mack on stations such as KLAC in Los Angeles and WNEW-AM in New York, and at WSGT in Atlanta, once said that you could tell the size of the city a disk jockey was working by the size of the U-Haul trailer behind his car.

George Wilson commented, "We didn't want security." And this is true of Wolfman Jack, Larry Lujack, Gary Owens, and Don Imus—deejay's who are now so famous that they have actually achieved a measure of security in a business where security is as fleeting as the words they broadcast.

One promotion that was so successful that it was given special consideration, especially in audience ratings, was devised by Jack McCoy when he programmed KCBQ in San Diego. It was a very complex contest which gave away expensive prizes like four $30,000 foreign sports cars, and four of this and four of that. The contest overwhelmed cities. Everyone listened. McCoy ended up syndicating "The Last Contest" coast to coast, and Puerto Rico. Ratings went up so high and so suddenly at the stations, that the ARB rating survey put an asterisk beside their audience ratings, stating that its numbers were not necessarily the result of good programming.

Radio promotions have usually one basic purpose: Winning. A good ARB rating can mean that a disk jockey or program director gets to keep his job until the next ARB survey, and that the radio station makes money. One FM station, KMET in Los Angeles, at a conservative estimate, made more than $2,000,000 in profit this past year. And, the station does a lot of promotion—last year it offered all listeners who were living in sin the chance to be married at the La Brea Tar Pits. Several hundred couples showed up.

For a while, broadcasters thought that radio's only job was to transmit today's music and news. But the swing is back to entertainment and "colorful" radio. Radio programmers such as Paul Drew, vice president of programming for RKO Radio; Ron Jacobs, once programmer at KGB, San Diego; Bill Tanner at Y-100 in Miami, national program director of the Heftel radio chain; and Bill Young, program director of KILT in Houston, are constantly looking to create audience excitement through good programming contests, and giveaways. True, the old kinds of zany stunts are virtually outlawed.

"All of the rules today are much more stringent," said Chuck Blore, now head of the commercial firm of Chuck Blore/Don Richman Inc. in Los Angeles. "You can't do a lot of the things we used to do, nor would you want to.

"One of the glories of radio is its maturation, I think. Back in those days, we were very flamboyant—like a kid of 17 or 18 years old just about to experience adulthood. But by the time you're 27, you're wiser and you don't do things that you did when you were younger, but what you do is a lot heavier and has more consequence."

Perhaps radio stations don't have deejays climbing flagpoles anymore, not so often anyway, but they are doing promotions.

"You don't see balloons dropped into main streets. Instead, you see radio stations involved in community activities like WDIA in Memphis buying buses to get kids to school," said Blore.

"Because radio, as we knew it, did die. People will say: What do you mean? Radio isn't dead. Well, bull manure; it died. Because we now have a whole new medium. Only the name remains the same. Radio used to broadcast to a mass America. Today, it broadcasts on a one-to-one basis. Me, communicating with you. And it's a totally different concept. Absolutely different."

Also, one of the things that changed radio was new government regulations. For example, the always-used, always-successful Cash Call is now tough to do because of new FCC rules; no longer can radio stations quickly give away vast sums of money to listeners who say "I listen to . . ." when they phone. But it's absolutely true that the wild and wooly promotions in early Top 40 brought public attention away from TV, helped give radio new life, and created the dramatic radio of today for all kinds of formats from rock to country music.

Where have all the zany stunt men of radio gone? The wacky souls who stuck with radio are the "giants" today—Jack Thayer, president of NBC Radio; Ruth Meyer, at WMCA in New York; George Wilson; David Moorhead; Rick Sklar, of ABC Radio; Bruce Johnson, Starr Broadcasting; and Chuck Blore. Their love and devotion for the medium has helped produce a prestigious multimillion dollar radio industry. No one today can call radio a dead medium. Television, after all, is not a threat. As every radio man will tell you, the weakness of television is that it "needs" pictures.

Modern Promotions

Turn on any radio station and you'll find that promotion hasn't died (though it may seem awfully dull in comparison to yesteryear). However, radio stations today use promotions more for quarterhour maintenance than just for glory, and for establishing call letters rather than disturbing a populace.

Bob Hughes, program director of WASH in Washington, D.C., took advantage of the format change of WRC in the market from music to all-news. He took full-page ads in both major newspapers announcing the fact that: "This weekend WASH is accepting new listeners." The ad described WRC's format change to all-news and invited music lovers to switch to WASH.

"We opened phone lines and asked listeners to call in and pledge to 'WASH with the stars.' And every person who made the pledge got one of our new WASH With The Stars teeshirts. Our personalities assisted by making 17 personal appearances, handing out teeshirts, and tape recording pledges from potential listeners in shopping centers, tennis courts, and even a Georgetown watering hole."

That type of promotion, taking advantage of a given situation, resulted in both television and newspaper exposure for WASH. And, of course, the station aired the taped pledges; what better way to promote your station than putting your listeners on the air?

While searchlights combed the sky, WUBE in Cincinnati had a young married couple climb a ladder to a specially constructed platform beneath a billboard on Interstate-75. There, the couple entered a fully equipped $15,000 motor home where they were to live around-the-clock for four weeks. Their purpose? To prove that WUBE is the station "that's fun to live with." They weren't regular listeners of WUBE and had agreed to listen only to WUBE for the four weeks in order to win $1,000. WUBE program director Johnny Bridges reported that the couple spoke with disk jockeys via CB radio as well as with all other CB operators who were driving down I-75.

KHJ in Los Angeles presented a concert one Christmas, with all benefits going to the Children's Hospital of Los Angeles and to other charities. The "Cavalcade of Stars" featured Tony Orlando as host, Captain and Tennille, Cher, Mac Davis, Freddie Fender, Tony Orlando and Dawn, Donny and Marie Osmond, Freddie Prinze, and Helen Reddy. What a great lineup of stars!

WAYS in Charlotte, N.C., did the same type of concert every year for the same purpose, the same as WDIA in Memphis, a soul music station. This is the type of promotion that all stations have been involved in, whatever the format, at one time or another. Country music radio stations make extra money out of country music concerts, and they are also excellent promotions.

Rick Leibert III, program manager at KGB, San Diego, caused a stir when he sent Secretary of State Henry Kissinger an official KGB Chicken Shirt. Leibert received a letter from someone else in the department, he then made copies of the letter and sent them everywhere to reap the promotional value.

Another excellent promotion achieved by KGB was an album featuring local singers and groups who won a talent contest sponsored by the station. The "Homegrown" album has become an annual event and sells more than 30,000 copies, with proceeds going to charity.

KIOI, owned by James Gabbert in San Francisco, does an occasional amateur show, broadcast live. The result? Considerable news coverage in the *San Francisco Chronicle,* which Gabbert then made copies to send to national and local advertisers, national trades, etc. WKGN in Knoxville, Tenn., had a short film made of its stations to use as promotions at high schools and civic clubs. Bob Baron, then program director, claimed that the film helped the station's ratings.

Since launching its country music format, Chicago's WMAQ has been giving enormous amounts of money away via Cash Call. On Feb. 27, 1976, the station gave away $13,257 to a listener for knowing the exact amount in the jackpot, and the check was presented by weekend air personality Rich Renik.

The wildest promotion of any radio station was the American Revolution Bicentennial questionnaire run by KCBQ in San Diego. One of the 200 questions was: On Jan. 30, 1774, Benjamin Franklin was informed that he was dismissed from a public office. The office was:

(K) Delegate from Massachusetts;

(C) Deputy Postmaster General;

(B) Ambassador to France;

(Q) Music Director at KCBQ.

The questionnaire was distributed through local clients. Clues were to be announced on the air. And since the promotion happened during an ARB ratings survey period, some other stations in the market protested bitterly.

That promotion was the brainchild of Gerry Peterson, program director of KCBQ. But Russ Wittberger, general manager of KCBQ, created a "Visible Vault" promotion that was copied coast to coast in 1975. The station had a Plexiglas vault containing $10,000. To win, all you had to do was punch a series of numbers in the proper sequence on a device similar to a push-button phone, on the door of the vault. The odds of discovering the series were slight, so the station gave out clues on the air. To dramatize the promotion—and this was the most important part—the vault was moved each day from one area to another in San Diego, with the call letters of the station as visible as the greenbacks. Armed guards gave the whole promotion credibility. Wittberger arranged the clues so that someone had to win in three weeks.

However, to illustrate how some promotions can backfire, when KHJ in Los Angeles attempted the same promotion, something went wrong with the push-button device and the vault opened on the wrong number. Instead of giving out the $10,000, and then fixing the vault door, the radio person on duty simply announced there had been a mistake.

KHJ, of course, was sued by the woman who claimed she'd won the money.

Starting in January 1977, WLS in Chicago gave away a total of 30 roundtrip tickets for two to Hawaii, which included lodging and meals for a week. To enter the contest and qualify for one of the trips, all you had to do was send a postcard or fill out an entry blank at any one of several travel agencies throughout Chicago. The promotion, in conjunction with Aloha Hawaii, was part of the on-going "Musicradio Game" on WLS, which in the past has featured such prizes as 20 Chevrolets, 31 Kawasaki motorcycles, a $42,000 home, 100 trips to Disneyworld, and $40,000 of stereo equipment.

However, promotions may be more of a burden to radio than an attribute. This is the opinion of many radio men, but George Wilson, president of Bartell Broadcasters, voiced it firmly during a general session at the 1976 annual convention of the National Association of Broadcasters in Chicago. In essence, he felt that radio stations were spending too much money on promotion and he was intending to experiment to see how much of those funds could be applied to community service without losing either ratings or advertising revenues. In Canada, radio stations are limited monthly in how much they can spend on promotions. Perhaps some such sort of guideline might be adopted in the United States—programming skill should be the major criteria for winning audiences, not the depth of the pocketbook.

One major market music syndication firm spent more than $150,000 in advertising on television, billboards, magazines, newspapers, taxibacks, bus sides, park benches, and even Sparkletts drinking water bottles (some competitors claim the figure was more like $400,000) to insure that a radio station carrying their programming service did well in ratings. The station did extremely well and the programming firm offset the cost of the promotion by selling the syndicated programming in other cities. After all, they could point to enormous success in a major city; they didn't tell San Angelo or Wichita Falls *how* those ratings had been obtained. Sometimes the ability of a station to buy ratings, either through huge giveaways or advertising, gets a little ridiculous. But who knows what the perfect answer or solution is?

12 Music—that weird stuff they insert between commercials, jingles, etc.

The popularity of mass music today—or since the advent of Todd Storz, Gordon McLendon, and the countless program directors who were their conceptual children—has not been accidental. There have been musical accidents on the mass appeal genetic tree, but even these have been relatively rare. As a rule, the music that appeals to the masses has been a direct result of radio programming.

A cliche so time worn among both radio and record men that no one today would use it without ducking their head in embarrassment because it's so obvious is: A record will sell if it has it in the grooves. The claim is that all the airplay in the world will not cause a record to sell if it doesn't have it in the grooves.

Bull!

Because it's so expensive to produce a single record today, let alone an album that may march above $100,000 just in studio costs—and the songwriter, artist, producer, engineer, and promotion and marketing divisions of most record companies have become so skilled in their craft—only a marginal number of records today do not have it in the grooves. Thus, the processes of what sells and what doesn't sell are usually left in the hands of the program director at radio stations. We speak not only of records that sell in the United States, but American product that sells in countries abroad, with all sales generated, swayed or influenced by program directors in the United States; even, to a large extent, the foreign-born product. For instance, it's doubtful that the Beatles would have had the worldwide influence they did without American program directors playing their records. And Helen Reddy and Olivia Newton-John were not that popular in their own country of Australia until they became popular in the United States. British product, for example, generally doesn't make it overseas in markets like Australia, Brazil, Peru, New Zealand, Japan, until it has met the programming acceptance of American program directors.

In countries like Spain, Belgium, and even Brazil, some local recording artists learned to sing in English in order to have a better chance at that "international" hit, because that's where fame and fortune lie. Brazil is so dominated by English-language product on radio that some local artists (whose native language is Portuguese) adopted American sounding names and recorded in English to get local airplay. Several countries—Australia, Canada, and others—have set up limitations on radio station airplay of foreign artists in order to force radio stations to give native talent a better chance in the local market.

Though it is true that program directors do influence what music becomes popular, it is also true that a lot of factors have influenced the program director. These factors are numerous and each has made contributions to the overall effect. The growing strength of FM radio, both in earnings and ratings, has played an enormous role in musical tastes giving rise to longer records, more depth in the music itself, more complex musical forms, plus acceptability on one level or another of more types of music. In May 1975, a 10-year study by the ratings firm of Arbitron showed a 55 percent growth in FM between the Oct./Nov. 1966 ARB and the Jan./Feb. 1975 ARB. San Francisco had 11 new FM stations that showed up in the survey; Los Angeles went from 12 to 18; New York from 11 to 19; and San Francisco from 9 to 20.

In September 1975, Arbitron reported that FM radio's share of the listening audience was up 81 percent in the top 10 markets in just the past five years. FM listening increased 138 percent in Chicago, 108 percent in Boston, 103 percent in Pittsburgh, 102 percent in Philadelphia. Washington in 1970 had been the No. 1 FM market with total 27.5 share of the audience. But in this study, Detroit was the No. 1 FM market with a 41.1 percent share of the total listening audience.

Here's how the top 10 markets fared in FM listeners in that survey: New York City 36.4, Los Angeles 35.3, Chicago 31.6, Philadelphia 39.7, San Francisco 32.6, Detroit 41.1, Boston 38.8, Washington 40.7, Dallas and Fort Worth 38.2, Pittsburgh 29.8. The average share for FM in the top 10 markets was 36.4 percent of all listeners in 1975. And the evidence since that time has been that FM is still growing. KLOS, an FM station in Los Angeles, competes neck and neck with KHJ, the RKO Radio AM operation, sometimes whipping it in one demographic or another at some daypart.

In 1974, T. Mitchell Hastings Jr., president of WBCN in Boston, an FM progressive station, told the 15th annual convention of the National Association of FM Broadcasters (now the National Radio Broadcasters Association) in New Orleans that FM radio would overtake AM radio about 1981. And "the percentages of FM revenues to total radio revenues will grow at 23.3 percent annually through 1981, based on the average growth rate from 1963 to 1972."

The truth is that FM is growing faster than anyone had expected. In July 1976, WIXY general manager Nick Anthony, a veteran program director, changed the format of the AM Cleveland station to reflect FM programming trends—in other words, he virtually imitated the rock programming concepts that had become popular on FM. His reason: FM programming had changed what the radio audience wanted in the market and he was trying to meet vast FM competition by adopting the same programming procedures.

FM programming has already affected musical tastes around the world. Though KSAN in San Francisco was the first full-time progressive station, the station that made the world sit up and take notice was WNEW-FM in New York, then managed by George Duncan. It was WNEW-FM that began to influence record sales of album rock groups that were farfetched from the typical rock singles being exposed on AM Top 40 stations. In fact, many of those same groups—the Vanilla Fudge, the Cream, the Paul Butterfield Blues Band, and the Blues Project—were virtually taboo on AM radio. As sales were generated by FM, more artists moved in that direction musically, and more groups of that musical bent sprang up on the streets of New York's Greenwich Village and in San Francisco—groups like the Jefferson Airplane and the Grateful Dead. In Forest Hills, N.Y., Bob Dylan was booed when, after intermission, he stepped onstage with a rock group backing him up, and then he slowly was accepted because of FM radio. FM programmers liked what he was doing electrically, more than they had liked his folk music approach.

Adults didn't comprehend the music at first, just as they hadn't appreciated the Beatles for a long time, and before that Elvis Presley. And way before that, jazz. It's always been that way.

During a contemporary music workshop at the 1976 annual convention of the National Association of Broadcasters in Chicago, Mardi Nehrbass, then music coordinator for the RKO Radio chain and then west coast manager for Big Tree Records, pointed out that "there is much evidence to support the notion that each generation, as it accepts new musical forms, must contend with the criticism and general disapproval of the older established generation before it is able to indulge its tastes and image openly.

"At different points in time, this generational conflict over popular music centered around the cakewalk, ragtime, jazz, rock 'n' roll, and even progressive rock. We are experiencing these conflicts today with disco music and with sex-oriented music. As these changes occur, we as radio people must remember that people still seek organization in their lives and demand and need to be directed to a fulfillment of their emotions. We have to create a trust, have the listeners love us so much as a radio station that they are comfortable with what we are doing, then, if we play a bad record or run a bad promotion, they won't leave us because they still trust us.

"The youth information network is still incredibly effective, because they are willing to take chances in making changes. If we could tape this area, we would be able to program our radio stations six months in advance, but the problem is complex."

She also said that she felt surveys and chart analyses had been "typically" overworked as research techniques, not only in the study of popular music, but in other areas as well. "They are just tools."

Other things were affecting musical tastes, of course. Marie Gifford, manager of KEEL in Shreveport, La., said that as far back as 1962 or 1963, she had eliminated the term "rock 'n' roll" for KEEL, "It's a mass audience station." She maintains good music control, though "every so often I feel that the music is a little off from my philosophy. We have a music meeting. The music sounds better, though only for a few days—to please the boss, I suspect—and then the air personalities and the program director get back to what they wanted to do in the first place."

Actually, the music trend changed as a direct result of other factors rather than because a few stations like KEEL were aiming for "everybody" instead of just young adults. One of these factors was MOR's "music stealing" from the playlists of rock stations. This came about in two different ways. First, several leading MOR artists started doing MOR versions of contemporary hits. MOR program directors eventually decided that rather than play the "cover record" they'd play the version that had already proven most popular, especially if it wasn't too hard musically.

And, slowly, records had been getting softer. The reason? Well, the tight playlist of Top 40 stations played a very important role in this. Several rock acts of the past 10 years found it difficult to get new records played on Top 40 stations. Top 40 program directors were demanding that a record have "proven" results of popularity before they would put it on the air—in other words, the records had to start somewhere else. For a time, Top 40 playlists were comprised of black artists, since the only stations playing new product in a given market (especially the larger cities) were the r&b or soul music stations. WABC's playlist in New York grew heavily soul-oriented at one point because WWRL, the r&b station, was influencing so many singles sales. You could actually get 30,000 sales of a single by airplay on WWRL; WABC had to recognize that kind of sales. There was no viable country music station in the market at that time and the MOR stations were going through their "cover" period In order to gain some initial airplay, a few rock-type groups started producing softer records. 'ou suddenly had several artists spring up who, only a few years before, would have been rock artists but were now broad-appeal artists like the Seekers, Joni Mitchell, Carole King, and Simon & Garfunkle. MOR radio exposed these artists and, after the initial exposure, Top 40 stations carried them over the top in sales and national popularity.

Eventually, this trend led to a melding of formats. More about that later.

Another factor that affected music programming was the Federal Communications Commission. The FCC claims that it doesn't decide formats. However, pressure or fear of pressure have played vital roles in the formats of several stations. These include WGKA in Atlanta, WEFM in Chicago, WGMS in Washington, D.C., and WNCN in New York City. All were and still are classical. Owners wanted to change format. Citizen's groups who had not been listening (to judge by radio ratings) rose up in protest. It didn't seem to matter that WNCN was losing money and there were WQXR-AM and WQXR-FM in New York fulfilling classical programming needs. Starr Broadcasting tried to change WNCN to WQIV, a rock format. Today the station is classical, owned by GAF, and general manager Bob Richer is out to put it in the black.

WGMS in Washington stayed classical (RKO wanted WGMS rock on AM and classical on FM) on both AM and FM and is making money though, without question, RKO Radio could have made more money by going rock on AM and turning the FM into a profit-making structure.

Concerning format changes, Alan Shaw, vice president of ABC owned FM stations, New York, said recently, "We at ABC feel that entertainment programming involves so many subjective values that the public's interest would be best served if broadcasters were allowed to continue making changes in programming based on the free market place wherein listeners 'vote' for the programs they really want to hear by voluntarily tuning in the radio stations they enjoy. Anything less than this kind of freedom would set dangerous precedents for outside arbitrary tampering with the creative and economic freedom of the American system of commercial broadcasting.

"Furthermore, we also feel that if this kind of policy were extended to license renewals, broadcasters would be economically discouraged from attempting to create new program formats that might someday be characterized as 'unique' and thus be bound to that format forever, even if it was not popular enough to allow the broadcaster to avoid operating an uncompetitive station. We feel that the net effect of this policy would actually be to discourage rather than encourage innovative or special program formats."

Make no mistake about it; the FCC does affect programming. Fortunately, the result has not been totally negative and the involvement has, to date, been actually very limited. The melding of formats is playing a very great role in musical tastes and in programming's future. It has, of course, been happening for a long time—dating back to the popularity of r&b on Top 40 stations, the trend of rock artists to softer MOR-style records, and the growing popularity of country music.

Record companies for the past few years have been striving hard for the so-called "crossover" record—a record that starts in one market and bridges over into the pop market in sales. For example, a record that starts on r&b or country music stations, and is then picked up as a pop record by MOR and/or Top 40 stations. Also, a lot of MOR stations are now programmed by former Top 40 program directors. The result has been that a station such as KMPC in Los Angeles now can play all kinds of records; it's an adult contemporary station now as opposed to being an MOR station.

This melding of radio formats may have ramifications throughout the radio and record industries in days to come. Record promotion executives have strongly urged radio stations to take the "tags" off records, especially when they were trying to convince some Top 40 music or program director to play a potential crossover country or r&b record. However, promotion executives may not like the final result when all playlists squeeze to a minimum, highly detrimental to the record industry and the music of the future.

LeBaron Taylor, vice president of special projects for Columbia Records for many years, had a phenomenal career in r&b radio. He believes that black radio may suffer because of the "tremendous exposure major radio stations are giving to black music. Habitually, black music stations always had a limited signal. But now WABC in New York is fighting for its life against strong competition from many directions. WABC even tends to go on black music records before WWRL, one of the traditional soul music stations in the New York market. Perhaps WWRL is even losing its audience because of this.

"I feel it will be good for the music business, but it may prove costly to black radio in the future."

The melding is a strange situation and very unpredictable.

"Some black records," said Taylor, "are still treated as black records. Earth, Wind, and Fire came off a million-seller and we still had trouble getting pop play on their next single, 'Can't Hide Love' which sold more than 500,000 copies from black radio airplay alone. So, while the music is coming together, the pattern is not consistent. It's not coming together as we'd like."

As stations continue to meld formats, MOR, Top 40, country music, and soul music stations have taken on the same sound with almost the same records. Thus, it's clear that someday record men may long for "the good old days" when there was a soul music, a country music, an MOR, a progressive, and a Top 40 station in almost every market, instead of stations playing similar records, and oldies, the same oldies. This will shape music drastically; record artists, producers, and companies tend to create what they think will get played.

Another factor that will affect music will be the growing importance of radio syndication. A recent survey of radio syndication firms revealed that about 17 percent of all vaible radio stations today feature automated programming syndicated by several firms such as Drake-Chenault Enterprises, Los Angeles; FM-100, Chicago; Peters Productions, San Diego; Stereo Radio Productions or Bonneville Broadcast Consultants, New York; TM Programming in Dallas; and Broadcast Programming International, Bellingham, Wash. Radio Arts in Los Angeles, just over a year old, is nearing 40 stations on its MOR programming package at this point. There are many other firms in syndication. Drake-Chenault has more than 200 radio stations, AM and FM, using its programming services, which range from rock to country and even beautiful music.

Syndication is growing. The equipment field is growing for automation. Moffat Communications, CKXL in Calgary, Canada, has a computer-assisted automation system whereby the disk jockey never touches a record. His playlist appears to him on a small television screen. He punches one button to cue a record, another to put it on the air. He can make his own choices from his playlist, but if he makes a mistake, the computer will tell him: "No. 17 was played this hour yesterday; suggest you try No. 15." The computer even runs off a printed log for the station of what was played when. Keith James, vice president of programming for Moffat, said that the computer operation "doesn't do the show for the disk jockey, it merely helps him do his radio show better." The system, developed by engineer Gordon Kyle, is being installed at other stations. Solid automation is now being used on stations such as WCFL in Chicago, now a beautiful music station, once a live Top 40 giant.

Other types of programming in syndication are also having phenomenal effects on radio. For instance, Tom Rounds, president of Watermark Inc., Los Angeles, brought modern program syndication to fame (as opposed to the early days of radio when syndication of music shows were in wide vogue via ET (electrical transcriptions). *American Top 40,* a three-hour weekly program hosted by Casey Kasem, is heard around the world. And it was *American Top 40* that opened the doors for countless other programs and musical documentaries. (*The History of Rock and Roll* by Drake-Chenault had done well, but it was really Watermark that paved the way for all syndicators of today.) *The History of Rock and Roll*, the greatest documentary in radio to date, has been revamped and placed in syndication again.

What automation does is centralized programming. It also stabilizes it, meaning that even more radio stations will be exactly the same in city after city.

Jerry Wexler, former executive vice president of Atlantic Records who is today involved in record production, once commented, jokingly, that sooner or later every radio station in the nation would be playing the No. 1 record over and over. He may not be very far from the truth someday.

Other Factors Involved in Programming

It is imperative for the program director to become more aware of radio production, engineering, and all facets of a radio station.

Production deserves a whole book in itself. And Jay Hoffer, vice president of programming for KRAK in Sacramento, Ca., has written a book on it, *Radio Production Techniques,* Tab Books, Blue Ridge Summit, Pa. 17214, $12.95. Today, a good radio station will hire at least one extremely knowledgeable production person who may or may not be called upon to do an on-air show. Don Elliot, production chief and operations manager at KIIS, Los Angeles, does weekend and swing work on the air, but most of his time is spent in production—doing everything from commercials to special programs. Bobby Ocean, production director of KHJ in Los Angeles, does a regular air show on a Top 40 station, but his expertise is in production. Shadoe Stevens, a former program director (KMET, KRLA, and KROQ in Los Angeles), now operates his own production facility and studio, Big Bucks Creations, Los Angeles.

Engineering as a Way of Life

Bruce Earle, past chief engineer of radio for Sterling Recreation Organization, is one of the new breed in radio today. He believes that AM sound can be improved, and he has done so. Earle also spends a lot of time improving signals of FM stations to make them sound clearer throughout their signal coverage area.

John Harvey Rees, director of engineering for Hope, Bennett, Blackburn, San Juan, Puerto Rico, finds that many radio transmitters are not matched to their antenna systems, thus the stations aren't performing effectively.

James Gabbert, owner of KIOI-FM-AM in San Francisco, is a man who believes in sound in a definitive way; he builds his own broadcasting equipment—everything from transmitter to antenna. He helped build the transmitter for the CD-4 discrete quad broadcasting experiments. The system was the Lou Dorren Quadracast Systems Inc. quad unit.

This brings up several other points about radio. At this time, several stereo AM systems are vying for the attention of the FCC. If AM stereo follows the same pattern as discrete quad broadcasting, it would benefit greatly. And it does work well.

FM discrete quad (4-channel) broadcasting is one of the greatest potential contributions to modern radio that has ever been developed. It's to stereo as stereo was to AM monaural radio. In real quad, music sources can be placed on a record anywhere or everywhere in a 360-degree spectrum. The first station to broadcast in quad was KIOI-FM in San Francisco with permission from the FCC, using the Lou Dorren CD-4 (compatible discrete 4-channel) system. Then, the big industries got involved and five systems were later tested at KIOI (GE had tested its system out in between at its station WGFM in Schenectady, N.Y.). The systems tested at KIOI-FM were by Quadracast Systems Inc., Zenith, RCA, GE, and Nippon Columbia. Mountains of data were collected for the FCC.

Until FCC approval, FM stations around the country, and even some abroad, were using matrix encoders to achieve a simulated type of quad. Principles involved in this were the CBS SQ matrix system and the Sansui QS matrix system. Without question, discrete quad would be a vast step-up in acoustics for FM radio, just as stereo would benefit AM.

Meanwhile, engineers such as Bruce Earle believed that the amount of intelligible audio that is transmitted via the FM band usually exceeds that of AM stations "because of the wider pass band. But it is the 'apparent' frequency response, rather than the stereo format, that has hurt AM stations the most with deserting listeners."

In any case, it's obvious that many AM stations are using outdated equipment or unmatched equipment and their acoustics could be enormously improved. FM stations could also stand some shaping up. Many were built several years ago when all that was necessary was that they be on the air to retain the license (they were usually simulcasting the AM programming); they were low-power, multi-antenna-bay installations. Fewer bays and higher power can improve multi-path distortion and improve the sound. As FM stations move to viable formats, either live or via automation, stations are improving acoustics.

The Future of Programming

Radio programming is going through rapid changes, a *future shock* all its own. Because of automation, syndication, economic influences, music tastes, and the computer in general, radio is forced to make constant adjustments almost on a day to day basis.

Fortunately, it is improving. This is a direct result of the dynamic, energetic people involved in radio, and also involved in the music industry itself—up to and including the record artists. No one can deny the worldwide radio impact of Elvis Presley or the Beatles.

Because of these rapid changes, it's impossible to write a book about radio programming without going directly to the people who've made it happen. And that's what this book is about.

PART II
INTERVIEWS

Editor's note

The following interviews were done over an extended period of time, but because the people who were my subjects had contributed so much to the craft of radio programming in various formats and markets, none of the interviews have become dated. They are each an important part of Radio History.

For example, Bill Stewart was a witness to the birth of Top 40 radio as we know it. Chuck Blore gave Top 40 radio the show business appeal that it needed; he is considered to be both a genius and one of the radio giants. In two separate interviews you'll discover that even giants are sometimes human in regard to their dreams about radio. Bill Drake took away the clutter of radio and as the programming consultant for the RKO radio chain, he was responsible for building several market-leading stations coast to coast. He became known around the world, and even today he is probably the most copied man in radio other than Todd Storz and Gordon McLendon.

These interviews were often emotional; it soon became a high honor only accorded to the very top people in radio. And, because this was the one chance in a lifetime for most of them to put down all of their hopes, dreams, successes, and failures, they were unusually frank and honest. George Wilson told of his drinking problems so that radio generations now and in the future would understand the causes of something like that and avoid, perhaps, the same pitfalls. Ron Jacobs told of his month's jail sentence. Chuck Blore revealed why a programming concept that he loved and which everyone thought was sensational didn't work out.

Sometimes, one interview contradicts another interview—you'll have to make your own decision about who was right . . . or more correct.

Essentially, these interviews all have important lessons that should be beneficial to anyone interested in radio today and in the future. They represent the disk jockey, the program director, and the general manager at his creative peak. They represent a highly productive and influential era of radio.

The interviews were taped in various locations. Once, I taped Bill Drake in a bar on La Cienega Boulevard, Los Angeles; once or twice more at his home on Bedford in Beverly Hills. Bill Stewart's interview was taped in a restaurant at the top of the 9000 Sunset Boulevard building while disk jockey Paxton Mills sat by. Bruce Johnson and Dwight Case were taped in their offices. In the case of one program director, he flew from New York to Los Angeles just for the interview.

To understand the real significance of these interviews, you have to realize how deeply involved in radio I became.

I had joined *Billboard* magazine in New York about 1964. When the radio editor left, I was suddenly given his position. Fortunately, I'd listened to radio with some passion for years—DXing all of the radio stations I could pick up from my west Texas home on a small table radio. I used to lay awake half the night listening to the

"Sleepwalker's Serenade" all-night show on KVOO, Tulsa. And Eddie Hill on the all-night show of WSM, Nashville; Frank (Gatemouth) Paige and Horace Logan of KWKH, Shreveport, La., were my heros.

So, being radio editor was a natural for me though I doubt that anyone on *Billboard* or even myself realized it at the time.

Also, I had only landed in New York two or three months before from a reporter's job on the *Times-Picayune* newspaper, New Orleans, at an opportune time (I had previously worked at Fawcett Publications on *Cavalier* Magazine in New York). The Beatles had just invaded and some exciting things were about to happen in both music and radio, artistically and scientifically.

I lived in New York just when Murray "the K" Kaufman on WOR-FM (an upstart FM operation programmed by Tom Reynolds, a television man) started progressive radio with his nightly show. In truth, Kaufman caused a massive increase in sales of FM radios in New York, but he did not invent progressive radio. What really happened was that Murray the K hired Bobby Calendar to help him screen records; and Calendar liked the flipside of "Cherish" by The Association. That record was "Requiem for the Masses," and once Murray the K got audience feedback, he continued to feed that reaction. To hell with the hit "Cherish," his audience preferred "Requiem for the Masses."

Oddly enough, it was Bill Drake who almost destroyed the progressive rock format. In those days, it was called underground radio, a term that sprang out of San Francisco—more than likely, from the brain of Tom Donahue. (He was soon to remake a radio station—KMPX, an FM operation—into a full-fledged format catering to the crowd that was fed up with the Ohio Express, the Music Explosion, and the moon, June, and spoon rhymes that usually flooded out of the so-called Tin Pan Alley in New York.) Donahue's listeners much preferred Bob Dylan and the Paul Butterfield Blues Band with Mike Bloomfield on guitar. (It was no accident that for a long time progressive radio carried a heavy blues flavor—that's what Donahue had been playing mostly on his KMPX show.) On the other hand, in New York, Bob Dylan was booed at Forest Hills, when after intermission he came back onstage with an electric band (his first set had been guitar and harmonica); and he wasn't really accepted as a rock artist for some while.

Drake couldn't stand progressive rock—often called "acid rock" because it was wrongly believed that you had to be dropping acid to dig it. I had, in a series of articles and editorials, criticized Drake. By then, I had boosted *Billboard* subscribers from less than 1,500 in the radio field to a healthy readership; even more, I had the readers that counted. I'd been working as many as 16-20 hours a day to build up a rapport in radio. I would even track down program directors in bars or at home just to get a few comments from them about programming. My stories on Drake even inspired a college student at WTBS in Cambridge, Mass., to do a show on the air parodying both Drake and myself. He called it the "Joe Schmo Go-Go Show," and in the show the disk jockey, on a "more music" station, is always just about to get to that next big record. That was what most people thought of Bill Drake in those early days.

About that same time, the disk jockeys at WRKO in Boston laminated one of my editorials to a filing cabinet in the disk jockey lounge; either Alan Gates or Dan Tucker was the culprit. In any case, I soon found new jobs for some of the men, including Chuck Knapp, who went to work at WIXY in Cleveland, as I recall, a couple of days after leaving WRKO. Needless to say, Bill Drake wasn't exactly friendly to me when we met one afternoon in the cocktail lounge of the Americana Hotel in New

York. Drake was trying to be friendly; from Georgia, he's actually a very warm and friendly person by nature.

But me, I had a dream. I saw WOR-FM as something totally new and different. It was an excellent avenue for the exposure of a new product, especially a new kind of music that was not being played anywhere—except in the second half of a concert by Bob Dylan, or during a sporadic thing promoted by Albert Grossman at Town Hall in New York (which might feature Tom Paxton, Odetta, or Gordon Lightfoot). And how many of you remember a group called Lothar and the Hand People that performed at the Electric Circus in New York? And whatever happened to Sky Saxon, lead singer of the Seeds from Los Angeles?

Bobby Fuller also had a group that jammed well in the breaks; however he died before he could even take credit for what he must have instinctively felt was happening in music. The music — which I later tagged as progressive rock — was slowly beginning to happen.

Al Kooper and a few other guys were blowing their minds in what was really the first progressive group of all—the Blues Project. I will never forget going backstage at a little club in upper Manhattan (I was always the kind of music reviewer that stayed backstage more than out in the audience) where I saw Kooper lying down exhausted, and one of the other members of the Blues Project explained to me why they were seeking a sudden replacement for the session.

I witnessed the Blues Project and later the first Blood, Sweat and Tears when they jelled at the old Cafe A Go Go in Greenwich Village in New York. (How many remember Howard Solomon who operated the club that was so important to music in those days when the Cream from England did their first United States public set there?) I recall going backstage and asking Kooper, the organ player who'd formed the group, if he was going to also let this group go down the drain, and he told me no.

My wife and I were there at the Cafe A Go Go the night the second Blood, Sweat and Tears premiered with a new lead singer and without Kooper (the horn men were still undeveloped in those days). Shortly afterward Clive Davis, then chief of Columbia Records, walked in with his entourage. My wife said something about the atmosphere that Clive Davis created—like that of a minor god walking into a palace on the back 40 acres. He became a star, as much as most of his recording artists did. Later I got to know him better; he could be warm and human. In any case, he certainly had a flair for discovering recording artists. I don't think he deserved all of the adverse publicity that surrounded him during the infamous New Jersey "drugola" investigations. Everyone within the record industry thought he was a scapegoat and felt badly for him. Then and now, I always thought Clive Davis was a good guy rather than a bad guy.

In any case, I must have been a bad guy to Bill Drake that day at the Americana. To him, I was probably putting a stumbling block into all of his drives for good radio, as he saw it.

To get a steady sound Drake used to do the disk jockey announcements for his stations. Anywhere from Los Angeles to Boston to New York to Memphis, you could hear him saying: "Here's the Robert W. Morgan Show" or "Here's the Bill Wade Show." He taped these personally, to give the station a consistent sound. Drake, above all men in radio in the early and middle 1960s, believed in consistency; he never changed things (at least, not in his own mind), he merely made refinements.

We drank a few that day. I think I had Bloody Marys; Drake was probably drinking Seven and Sevens, (a horrible drink no one else, to my knowledge, drinks). He was leary of me, and mistrusted me. And he had every right to do so. During that drinking bout (and many of my later meetings with Drake were to be drinking bouts, which I consistently lost) I was trying to impress upon him my own feelings about format. What right does a mere reporter have to try to achieve formats? Well, that never worried me. In fact, it was my own term—"progressive rock"—that I had affixed to WOR-FM. I hammered it home, and "progressive rock" replaced the word "underground" for the format, especially on Madison Avenue. And that had been my intention all along. It's difficult to sell something that is cult-induced—at least, on a national basis. Madison Avenue eventually accepted progressive rock; I realized this fully when one day I interviewed (if you can call it that) a long-haired, fat-faced kid who'd been hired as a vice president at J. Walter Thompson because he "understood and liked" albums. So much for the world of commercials on radio and television.

So, essentially, I faced Bill Drake that day at the Americana as a fighter on behalf of WOR-FM. I thought I'd won. In fact, Drake renewed Murray the K's contract. Then, because he couldn't stand that kind of music, at that time, he soon afterward dismissed the entire staff, including Murray the K. He sent in Gary Mack to hold the station together, recruited Sebastian Stone, sent Stone and an entirely new staff in and, consequently, progressive radio almost died.

About that time, George Duncan asked for and got a loser—WNEW-FM. An old friend of mine, Harvey Glascock, was managing both WNEW-AM and its FM counterpart. Glascock had tried his own version of WSDM in Chicago, a jazz station that used sexy all-girl announcers and did a lot of promotions. I still recall one of the girls dressed in leopard skin tights strolling down the streets of Chicago with a real leopard on a leash. Unfortunately, Glascock hired girls who appealed to him; he was above 40 years of age. The girls were great—Glascock always had excellent taste in everything—but they weren't exactly the same as WSDM, nor was the music. Glascock was trying to give New York women something to listen to, but they didn't listen.

Duncan had been in sales on WNEW-AM; the FM job was an improvement. He was named manager. I remember walking with George Duncan several blocks crosstown to eat, on a tradeout, at the China Door. We were good friends from the start—both of us were hungry—not for Chinese food, but for radio. It's not surprising to me that he's now president of Metromedia Radio. He deserves it. He won it over countless battles of chop suey and chow mein. I often told Duncan what to do; to his credit, he never listened but went ahead and did what he'd planned to do all along. We became very good friends—and I later got to know such men as David Moorhead, George Wilson, Chuck Blore, Don Imus, Pat Patterson, Gary Owens, Keven O'Donohue of Australia, Luis Brunini and Guilherme de Souza (and Titto Santos) of Brazil, James Gabbert, Lou Dorren, Jay Blackburn, Bob Bennett, Rick Sklar, Jack Thayer, Rod Muir, Jim Long, Bill Meeks, Harry O'Connor, Tom Rounds, Casey Kasem, Chuck Dunaway, Scotty Brink, and hundreds of others. It always pleased me when they confided their personal problems to me. I have, at the same time, been looking for a new general manager for a radio station, a new program director for that station's general manager, and at least one new disk jockey for that station's program director—each, without telling any of the others that I was privy to information that they did not know. Once, I called David Moorhead, then program director of WOKY in Milwaukee, told him to call Ruth Meyer, then program director of WMCA in New York, and tell her that the management was already interviewing prople for her job. (Management of WMCA hadn't confided to me about her replacement, thus I was under no ethical obligation to them; what management or ownership never knew was that about 98 percent of the people they'd been talking to had been calling me to check out the station and the ownership).

The one man who didn't check things out with me was Terrell Metheny, otherwise known as Mitch Michaels. He became program director of WMCA and when ratings didn't measure up to his expectations he eventually left the station; what is interesting is that his music director was Buzz Bennett, who later grew to fame. Metheny had been national program director of Southern Broadcasting, and he gave up security for the challenge of New York . . . and lost. I always liked him and felt that he might have won, but . . . .

I respected and liked Bill Drake, too—more than he ever liked me. But I never became as close to Drake as I was to others. His changing of WOR-FM didn't help things, especially after he'd led me to understand that he wouldn't.

Fortunately, the format was saved by George Duncan, who was willing to take a chance with WNEW-FM (actually, he didn't have much to lose). Duncan sort of backed into progressive rock, as a format. I think he actually wanted to hire Murray the K. But Murray the K wanted to capitalize in dollars on the format that he'd spurred, fed, and developed; he demanded too much from Metromedia. In any case, his image was not that of Metromedia (image is just one of those things that's difficult to define—it may change from station to station and market to market). He was never to become a part of what he had played a role in creating. Instead, WNEW-FM hired Bill "Rosko" Mercer. Mercer had been the midnight-6 AM man on WOR-FM. He used to play a lot of Motown Records—soul stuff—that was his forte.

After I mentioned to Tom Reynolds that three Motown records back to back didn't sound very good (I later heard three Motown records back to back in Buenos Aires and thought that was lousy programming as well), Rosko got into playing the same thing that Murray the K was playing . . . and did well at it, weaving in poetry, not talking much. Rosko benefited much more from progressive radio than Murray the K. Especially after he left WOR-FM and went to WNEW-FM. When Bill Drake tried to format WOR-FM, Mercer discovered it wasn't his kind of radio.

Murray the K called to tell me that Rosko was resigning on the air one night from WOR-FM. I listened in. Personally, I was pleased that someone thought enough of what I was dreaming to put their life on the line. Professionally, I was against a disk jockey resigning on the air; it should never be a public event. Let the station quietly find a new man on the air for when the disk jockey's last time period rolls around on the clock—no muss, no fuss, no waves. The professional doesn't whimper at losing a job, nor does he whine about giving one up. His duty is to the listener and to his craft, even if the station or someone at the station has done him wrong. Fade out. Don't cause any problems. Your reward will be at another station, in another city, in another time. George Wilson once had his furniture waiting for him on the sidewalk when he came home from work one day (what a way to find out that you've been fired—to see your wife and kids sitting on your furniture in the middle of the sidewalk). But today the man who had his furniture moved out of the company house onto the street is still striving for a meager buck in radio, and . . . well, read the George Wilson interview for yourself.

My hope with these interviews is to not only give you, the reader, a sense of pride in your craft (if you are a radio man like I am) but to instill in you a sense of craftsmanship.

My wife, Barbara, remarked that in the interview with Gary Owens he was "only doing a show in print." That's true, to a great extent. Gary *works* most of the time, on or off the air. But, since I play basketball with him almost every Sunday morning and try to block his swinging 40-foot layup (Gary has an unusual shot, but generally makes it) and have the pleasure of fouling him a lot, I know what a great craftsman he really is—in more ways than one. He never stops working. Even dribbling down the court, he's also dribbling one-liners.

The most popular interview that I've ever done was with Charlie Tuna, who was then with KHJ in Los Angeles, though in the process of leaving. Tuna was not emulated as much as some of the others on KHJ (you'll still find several Robert W. Walkers and Roger W. Morgans around), but he became the pinnacle of what a good disk jockey should be—and perhaps could be if you just knew what made him tick. I guess the interview was read by just about everybody. Several disk jockeys have told me since that they've kept clippings of that interview and read it over from time to time. To illustrate how good Tuna is—and was—Bill Stewart became national program director of Fairchild's radio operations for a while. Ironically, one of those stations was KLIF in Dallas. Stewart put his morning man, Paxton Mills, on a plane, and they flew to Los Angeles and spent a few days listening to Tuna. Stewart's comment to me was that he was hoping some of Tuna's magic would rub off on Mills. Whether it did or not, Mills is having a very successful radio career in Cleveland at the time of this writing. I think the interview with Tuna reveals what makes him tick as an air personality; I received more than 300 letters commenting on the interview—all favorably.

The second most popular interview was with Ron Jacobs; he'd already left the Drake-Chenault organization (he programmed KHJ in to a giant station for programming consultant Bill Drake) and was doing something totally different in his programming at KGB-AM-FM in San Diego. It was such a change that it was as if the south pole had suddenly become the north pole; from a rigid and extremely tight playlist of singles, Jacobs had switched to a very long list of thousands of LP cuts. He was eager to play good new music. Everyone questioned his wisdom in trying that kind of format, but no one doubted his intelligence. Everyone watched closely to see what was happening with the man who'd coined the term Boss Radio at KHJ. The Jacobs interview here reveals two different time periods—the first when he was still striving to build KGB's audience, and the second when he'd decided to return home to Maui to ponder radio rather than work in it on a day-to-day basis.

The interview with Don Imus and Robert W. Morgan—Imus was morning man at WNBC in New York and Morgan was morning man at KHJ in Los Angeles—was strictly a fun thing. They'd just violated format at KHJ that morning on Morgan's show (Imus joined him on the air and did a live grocery store commercial that has to go down as one of the funniest commercials in radio. That show was later part of an album by Imus called "10,000 Hamburgers to Go" on RCA Records), both had been kicked out of the studio shortly before Morgan's show was supposed to end. (Morgan always denied they'd had the plug pulled on them, but, in any case, the last part of the show was just music without even an intro to a record.)

Morgan is one of the best ad-lib men in radio; you'd swear that it's impossible to come up so spontaneously with the things that he says and does, but he does. Imus prepares like crazy; when he's really working on his show, he has that unique ability to make everyone talk about him—listeners and advertisers alike. They may not enjoy his show, per se, but they don't dare turn him off.

A number of these interviews were printed in segments in *Billboard*. However, many have been updated for this book. I spent three more hours with Drake and two more hours with Jacobs, putting stuff on tape—material that was not printed in *Billboard*. And, of course, some of the interviews are entirely new. These interviews are basically intended to be educational—whether they concern a general manager or program director or disk jockey. They're part of the lore of radio programming.

They're part of what is and what will be in radio. They're things that have happened to me, and to radio.

I wish that I could have included all of the interviews I've done through the years; I can't. I've interviewed people like Gordon McLendon, one of the fathers of Top 40 radio as well as a pioneer in the beautiful music format. And I've interviewed Sam Phillips, the man who discovered Elvis Presley, Johnny Cash, Jerry Lee Lewis, and several other major recording artists. I've interviewed Buzz Bennett, Gene Autrey, Bill Randle, Mac Allen, George Carlin (a former disk jockey), and others. But those interviews will be another book, perhaps, at another time.

You'll notice that in the interviews names and call letters are mentioned. Radio is a rapidly changing field, and those men have most likely moved on to other call letters in other cities. For historical purposes, I haven't tried to update the interviews to point out where the people mentioned are right now; they probably wouldn't be there either by the time you read this.

For now, suffice it to say that I hope you enjoy the interviews here, that you benefit from them, and that radio will benefit because of your interest in the science and art of radio programming.

Claude Hall

BILL STEWART

Bill Stewart

INTRO: Bill Stewart deserves more credit than he realizes. In fact, it's debatable that Top 40 radio would have become the viable medium that it is without his contribution to it. Gordon McLendon, head of McLendon Corporation, paid tribute to Stewart for the success of KLIF in Dallas, one of the pioneer rock stations, then owned by McLendon Corporation. Stewart not only initiated several programming practices himself, he also incorporated the innovations of men like McLendon and Todd Storz, whom he worked for more than once during the formative years of Top 40 radio. Stewart was the first real program director in modern radio as we know it. An outstanding family man, Stewart later worked in sales for the music syndication division of Susquehanna.

Hall: When did you get started in radio?

Stewart: I guess about 20 years ago in Boston, on what was then a classical music station—WBMS. I was a classical disk jockey, of all things.

Hall: What are the call letters of the station now?

Stewart: I believe it's a soul station—WYLD.

Hall: Then what did you do?

Stewart: Well, I worked around Boston for several years. Then, I guess it was in 1954, that I made my initial foray into the South and went to work for Gordon McLendon in Houston, at a station that was then KLBS and is now KILT. He wanted to build the station up a little bit and then unload it, which he did. He later bought it back for a while. Then I went to KLIF in Dallas; that was about 1955, I guess. We had a lot of success there. The station went from 10th or 11th in the market to No. 1 in 60 days. So, Gordon sent me to New Orleans to get another station off the ground, WNOE, which his father-in-law, James A. Noe, owned. At that time, Gordon was running that along with a Monroe, La. station his father-in-law also owned. We got that New Orleans station rolling. It was about 20th in the market and it went to about No. 2 in two weeks. That was the time that I personally, along with a couple of other disk jockeys, played the same record for four days straight.

Hall: Do you remember the record?

Stewart: A record called "Shtiggy Boom." The name of the group eludes me. But it was on Capitol, I think. It was written by Al Jarvis, a disk jockey. And this was in the early days of rock 'n' roll when anyone who could carry a tune, even if it happened to be only in a wheelbarrow, was put into service. This song was recorded by three people who happened to be janitors in the Capitol Building at the time. Literally, they were

162

janitors. They brought them in from the hallway and they sang the thing, "Shtiggy Boom," and it was lamentable. But because we played this thing over and over for four days, it was a phenomenal promotion and made the front pages of the newspapers. That was about the last thing of that type that the newspapers carried in print and television gave exposure to.

Hall: What did you do? Did the disk jockey announce the record every time?

Stewart: There were three of us, two other jocks and myself, who did the air work. And we would announce a different record every time.

Hall: Who were the other jocks?

Stewart: Bill Stanley, who's now a newsman at WDSU in New Orleans. And a guy by the name of Bill Elliott, who's now in the agency business in New Orleans. The promotion really caused a stir—in New Orleans, it made WNOE overnight. That was in 1955 or '56, I guess.

Hall: Didn't you get pretty tired of that record?

Stewart: Very tired of it. And all three of us stayed up all four of the days. And then, as the final thing, we flew Al Jarvis in from California and he asked us to stop playing the record. We had people who were coming up with all kinds of petitions and everything else, asking us to please stop playing it. That was the first of the locked-in-the-transmitter type promotions.

Hall: The first?

Stewart: I'm sure it was.

Hall: When Elvis Presley came along there were some stations that tried that type of promotion.

Stewart: But Elvis was after this. There have been other stations since that have played a record longer—broken our record—but I think that was the first such promotion.

Hall: How can you be sure the station went to No. 1?

Stewart: It didn't go to No. 1; it went to No. 2. I want to be factual. Todd Storz was in the market at the time, and that was the second station that Storz owned. They bought WTIX, which was then a 250-watt station, way up in the jungle at 1490 or somewhere on the dial, and Storz put on what was really the first music station in town. It was singularly successful because no one else was doing anything even remotely like it. At that time it had like 35-40 percent of the audience. But we put a big dent into them and, in time, began running neck-and-neck with them.

Hall: Where did you go from New Orleans?

Stewart: I went with Storz. He figured that if I was giving him that much competition, I was good enough to work for him. So I went to Omaha, which at that time was his home office. That was early 1956, I guess. And we lived there for about four years.

Hall: You became national program director there, didn't you?

Stewart: Yeah. We had KOWH in Omaha, WTIX in New Orleans. Then we bought WDGY in Minneapolis. Went up and kicked that off. Then WHB in Kansas City.

Hall: Did you put WDGY on the air?

Stewart: Pretty much. I think it had been on the air for about 60 days when I went with Storz. And I pretty much shaped it, I guess. Then after that, we bought WQAM in Miami, and I went down and put that on the air. I left Storz about 1959 after the second deejay convention.

Hall: You put on both of those conventions, didn't you?

Stewart: Right.

Hall: The first was done in Kansas City, wasn't it?

Stewart: Yes. The Muehleback Hotel. That was the headquarters. I would say that we had, my memory is bad, because in those days, particularly with Storz, we always had a ratio figure. We arrived at it like most disk jockeys arrive at their pay, or what they claim they get paid—we took the base figure, multiplied it by two, and subtracted a third. I would say, to the best of my knowledge, that we really had about 500 people at the first convention. But it was very, very successful. It was the first time it had ever been done. It was a step that you, Bill Gavin, and Bob Hamilton have followed up on and done very well with since then, I might add. But this was a very bold step in those days. In 1958, when we held the first disk jockey convention, the image of the disk jockey was at an all-time low. Our image was only about two steps above the cleaning man's. And most station managers, well, that was the start of the first disk jockeys, period. Before that, everyone was a radio announcer rather than a disk jockey, and their main stock-in-trade was coming in and reading their five minutes of news on the hour, or whenever they had to read it, and doing a record show that was probably scripted by some woman who was the music librarian, the notary public, and everything else around the station. She would write out these ad-libs for the guy; he would do them and then retire to the nearest bar, sit down, and get loaded. That was the main stock-in-trade of most radio people at the time. The public thought of them as drunk people who had deep voices and made a lot of money.

I think the first disk jockey convention did more for the image of disk jockeys around the country than anything that had been done before that or has been done since. And I think the second convention, because of the success of the first one, was even more successful. We had about 1,500 people at the second meeting. And that was the meeting that really gave the disk jockey a lot of credibility. I say that, in spite of the fact that we had an awful lot of adverse publicity at the convention. But in those days, well, times have changed since then. If you remember, in those days we were just an upstart industry—the independent radio industry. Everybody was after us. People feel today that FM progressive radio is *something,* and that they're in an elite bag because people look askance at them for doing something different. But I can tell you that the feeling that pervades about FM radio is not half as bad as that which existed in those days for "rock 'n' roll" radio.

I can remember in those days when you'd go into a bank and try to make a loan, and the guy would say: "What do you do?" and you'd say: "I'm program director of KOWH." He'd say: "You mean that loud music station that no one can listen to?" Rock 'n' roll just had a very, very bad image. Consequently, when Top 40 radio became successful everyone was out to get us, particularly the newspapers—in view of the fact that most newspapers also owned radio stations in those days. Since that time a lot of them have split up, but then in almost every market you could find a radio station owned by a newspaper—radio stations that had been big for a lot of years during the great rise of network radio. And they were on their way down because television had literally taken over the whole industry. Were it not for people like Gordon McLendon and Todd Storz who had the foresight to think that maybe they could arrest the decline of radio, I think radio would have died. Right then and there.

When we had the other convention down there in Miami the press was really out to get us. This guy came in and wrote a story on the convention for a national magazine. He also wrote a story for the local newspaper that appeared the following Sunday—the final day of the convention—which was headlined "Booze, Broads and Bribes" across the front page of the newspaper. Alliterative, but not actually true. It sure did cause quite a lot of consternation for me, for instance, because my wife came down—we were to go on vacation—and we had a Storz rule that said no wives were allowed down there, because we were going to be very busy. She came into town—we were going to go down to the Bahamas with Paul Berlin and his wife. When I picked her up at the airport I was a few minutes late, and she'd already bought a copy of the morning paper. She was sitting there reading it.

"Booze, Broads and Bribes." That took an awfully long time to explain to her, and I might say that since then, it's amazing how things grow, like Topsy, over the years. That particular disk jockey convention has grown like Topsy. I run into people in radio now who don't place my name as being a part of that. Somehow during the course of the conversation something about the disk jockey convention will come up. I hear more wild stories about what's supposed to have happened there that are so far from the truth that it's unbelievable! But those kind of stories do grow over the years.

Hall: How many people were at the Miami meeting?

Stewart: I would say that there were maybe 2,500 people. They were all heavy people; they were the people of that day. Your recent convention—I don't know what the total number was but I thought the people you had there were really representative of the industry, and I think you are to be commended for keeping this thing going. I know that you've been on a continuing campaign over the years to improve the image of the disk jockey.

Hall: Well, I've certainly been trying to avoid the image of the Miami convention.

Stewart: But you've been on a campaign to upgrade the image of the disk jockey, and I think that's an important thing. A lot of people have a grave misconception about disk jockeys. And I'm sure that a lot of them have good reason to have grave misconceptions. But the average disk jockey is just a real hardworking guy who, I think, performs a great service every day. I think that most people in radio don't realize the valuable service they are performing. I believe that sometimes they themselves began to do their jobs in a lackadaisical manner, and maybe this is part of the problem. I don't believe most people in radio have confidence in the importance of what they're doing. But then, it is hard to keep in mind what an important medium radio is.

Recently, we did a thing in Dallas which reminded me what a fantastic medium we have—a medium that can really, literally, reach out and touch people. Now, it may touch some of them in the wrong way—some people may get angry—but at least radio has the ability to *touch* them. We put on KLIF, a Bill Ballance type of program. We didn't take the syndicated Ballance show because we wanted to localize our show. When we did it, we really released the flood gates. In all of the days I've been in radio—and I've been through some fairly big promotions over the years—playing a record four days straight, like I mentioned earlier, we did the first really big money contest in Omaha and Minneapolis when we buried $110,000 in cash, or check. And that was the first time that had been done anywhere. Now that got a lot of reaction; we got letters from people in Alaska and Wyoming who wrote to the station when they read about the promotion in *Time* magazine, wanting to know exactly when the promotion was so they could schedule their vacation around that time. Take all of the things that I've seen over the years and multiply them by five, and they still wouldn't equal the reaction we got in Dallas.

Hall: Back to the Miami convention. Your basic aim was to bring the people in radio together, wasn't it?

Stewart: Right.

Hall: And it just sort of backfired.

Stewart: Radio at that time was in a very advanced state of disorder. We, and by *we* I mean the people with Storz and McLendon, were thought to be rebels. We were doing something that had never been done before in radio. It was very illogical to the old-line radio people. They couldn't believe what we were doing. We were sort of upstarts in the industry. After what we did was successful, then other people started copying it. There were a lot of people who joined us almost as the social outcasts in radio. So we got all of those people together and got some of the opposing factions together with us—that was the main thing we tried to do at both of the conventions. We had the head of Hooper at both conventions as a panelist. We had advertising agency people who were directly involved with our kind of radio, but who actually added a lot of stature to us at a time when we needed it badly. Because our kind of radio at that time had very little stature, we were below the level that underground radio is at today. There may be people looking down their noses at underground, progressive, radio and saying it's not for the masses. Well, people thought the radio we were doing wasn't for the masses either.

Hall: What kind of man was Todd Storz?

Stewart: Storz was probably the most incisive man I've ever met in my whole life. I had a great deal of respect for Todd. If there's any man I had hero worship for, it would be him. He was a man's man. There was no bull about him. He told you what he felt. You always knew where you stood with him.

Hall: How long were you national program director of his firm?

Stewart: Well, I was national program director for about four years at that time. I'd gone into the consulting business, primarily, for about four years, then came back. By a strange coincidence, between my leaving and coming back, the home offices had been moved to Miami.

Hall: What caused Storz's death?

Stewart: He died from a massive stroke of some kind. I'd joined the company and was supposed to start work on a Monday in Kansas City where the home offices were going to be. While having breakfast at the Hilton Inn, I was paged. From Miami the message was that Todd had died in his sleep that night. So, anyway, that time I spent about two and a half years with the company. Getting back to Storz, because we've digressed a little, I think that Storz has done an awful lot for the radio business, done an awful lot. And I don't think he gets the credit today that he should. Most people today think that radio was discovered in Los Angeles when KHJ went rock in 19-... whatever year Drake brought it there ... 1960 something. I remember hearing Ron Jacobs at an annual International Radio Programming Forum talk like he was there at the birth of Top 40 radio—that he was sort of a "junior Marconi," and he never mentioned the guy who really was Marconi ... I guess he was alluding to Bill Drake. Incidentally, I almost sat down and wrote you a letter about that. I think over the years I've had some minor quarrels about things you've put in print, but I had a major quarrel with you selecting Ron Jacobs as a keynote speaker for a major meeting of radio people. I just don't see it—it would be like putting Mayor John Lindsay of New York City as the keynote speaker of the Republican Convention. It doesn't make any sense at all. I think that it set the whole tone of the convention off on the wrong leg. Fortunately, you had other speakers who were more positive and knew much more about what they were saying. And they, at least, got the meeting back on the right track. I was very disillusioned in the things that Jacobs had to say. I thought it was a very anti-radio pitch. And I think if he devoted a little more time to watching KCBQ, San Diego (Jacobs programmed KGB-AM-FM at the time), he'd be a lot better off. I just don't feel his particular track record, as of now, is that great. I think he ought to devote more time to building that track record instead of tearing down radio. Radio at this time doesn't need anyone tearing it down.

Hall: Who *really* invented the Top 40 format? How did it happen?

Stewart: The way it happened, actually, was that one night Todd Storz and I were sitting in a bar in Omaha, Neb., and . . . .

Hall: Do you remember the bar?

Stewart: Across from Gilpatrick's on 15th Street. That was where our studios used to be. And we were sitting there and the jukebox was playing. And it kept coming up to the same song. And I can't even remember what the song was, but it was a rock 'n' roll type song. We must have sat there four or five hours talking about various things. They got ready to close—I guess it was midnight or whatever time they closed—and everyone was gone. They were kind of giving us motions like we were supposed to leave. The waitress went over and put a quarter into the jukebox, and lo and behold she put her own quarter into the machine and played that same record three times in a row—the same record we'd heard all night long. So that sort of tripped a lot of . . . well, it was in both our minds. I don't know whether you could say that Todd literally discovered Top 40 or whether I did or whether someone in the company did. I don't know. I know it was not Gordon McLendon; I can tell you that for sure, because Gordon's experience with that kind of radio came after Todd's.

Hall: What year was the bar incident?

Stewart: About 1955.

Hall: Tell me, had he been successful with rock radio before that?

Stewart: He had been successful, but the station seemed to be on a downgrade.

Hall: What station?

Stewart: KOWH in Omaha. That's why he went looking for me to come up there.

Hall: This was the first time you went with him? You'd been in New Orleans?

Stewart: Right. And the station was on a downgrade at that time in ratings. And I went in and put in a closed music list for the first time it had ever been done anywhere. Cut it down to about 30 records. We got the station turned around—back up the chart.

At that time Don Burden was starting to make a lot of noise across the street at KOIL. He was giving us fits, but we got KOWH turned around. I think it was the last daytime station to be No. 1 completely in a decent-sized market, which is still a fairly hard thing to do. Storz sold the thing in 1957, I think to Bill Buckley for $822,500, which, to this day, is still pretty much of a record for a daytime radio station. Since then prices have skyrocketed, but I don't think there's a daytimer that's gone for a price like that in any comparable market. We kept the station afloat, and when we sold it we were still No. 1.

Todd was the kind of guy I greatly admire because—and I think this is the sign of a successful person and, to an extent, the reason for the success of McLendon—if management feels that the person working for them knows what he's doing, they'll let him do his thing. That's the problem with radio today. I don't think that enough owners or general managers give people their heads. Now I realize that everyone who calls himself a program director doesn't necessarily have the gray matter to make all of the final decisions. But I think there are a lot of guys who could make some great decisions if enough people would let them. But the trouble is that they get beaten down too often; when they go in with a hot idea that seems far out and the manager says, "Well, no, let's wait on that one," and the next time around the program director gets the same story—after a while their creative instincts are dulled. And this is the reason, I think, for the success of Storz—and McLendon—because I don't think that either one of them came up with *all* of the great ideas in radio over the years. No one has. Everyone has contributed a little bit to it. But they had the ability to be able to *see* in people a creative talent, and direct them to do whatever it takes to get the job done.

Hall: Programming is a creative talent, isn't it?

Stewart: Absolutely.

Hall: Sort of a unique field all of its own. There's nothing to compare with it?

Stewart: It's much rarer talent today than it was in the old days. In those days, you could come up with a format and say: "This is the format, and we're ready to go. We're going to be No. 1 for five years." But you can't do that today. Today, radio programming is a real day-to-day operation. You don't even say to yourself that you have the format, or that you'll even stick with it for five months. Or five weeks, even. You have to look at it in the hard, cold light of day and be willing to say: "Well, maybe we'd better change that." And I think that's why so many Top 40 radio stations are in trouble today—some of them are trying to go with the old format that worked so well for so long, without any changes. They're in trouble. And some other stations are in trouble because they made the mistake of trying to change the basics.

What we really need in Top 40 radio is to give people the opportunity to try new things, and I think that's really the big problem. Take Bill Drake, for instance. I think Gene Chenault had enough faith in him to say: Hey, go ahead and do your thing. Otherwise, Bill Drake might have been picking strawberries now in Georgia. What Drake did was not any different than what had been done in the past. This is not a knock at Drake. I said at one of your International Radio Programming Forums in New York several years ago that Drake took a bunch of old formats and added to them a psychological effect—the "more music" concept, a flow pattern to music— that had not been used in any of the other formats. But if Gene Chenault had not given him opportunity to do that, no one would have known what Drake had to say. There are a lot of guys like that out there in radio today. What we need are program directors who'll let air personalities who have something to say, say it, and we need more managers who'll let their program directors who have something to try, try it.

Hall: How did the first jingle come about? That is, a real, professional jingle?

Stewart: Well, I've seen many stories and just read another two or three months ago that said Bill Meeks cut the first jingle in Dallas. But I don't think that's really so. To the best of my knowledge, the first jingles cut in Dallas were jingles that we did for KLIF in 1954. I had these melodies in my mind, and I knew the lyrics that I wanted. I contacted Tom Merryman, who's now the head of TM Productions. I said: "Hey, Tom, I've got an idea for some jingles." He said that he played the piano, his wife sang, and he could get a group together. He came down to the KLIF studios. We cut the jingles and put them on the air. Later the jingles became the first package of—I forget what the name of the company was—the forerunners of TM, but those jingles were in the first package that went out in syndication. That was the first commercial jingles package, as far as I know. Bill Meeks, in those days, was in the agency business and doing some very interesting things in commercials. He was one of the first guys in the United States to come up with gimmick commercials. In those days all commercials were straight. Bill was among the first to put in voices, sound effects, things like that. He was doing a great job at that time. But it was later, much later, that he went into the jingles business.

Hall: Do you think that the Top 40 format has any way to go? Or is it locked in now?

Stewart: Well, I think the Top 40 format is always going to be a viable format. It has to be, because Top 40 radio is radio *of the people.* This is why men such as Gordon McLendon, who's probably one of the great leaders in radio—both then and now—have been able to make valuable contributions. Gordon recognized—either instinctively or somehow, I don't know—what the people needed, or wanted. Look at the types of radio he has been responsible for developing: The wall to wall KABL format, the classified ads format, the all-news format. And without doubt, Top 40 wouldn't be the success it is today without Gordon McLendon, because he had the guts to risk his radio station, to put it on the line. As I pointed out earlier, Top 40 radio wasn't very respectable; at least it wasn't respected in the business community in those days. Gordon never let anything deter him from taking a good idea and heading for the goal line. And he usually scored with it, too.

To get back to Top 40 in general, I keep coming back to an old cliché that I used in the mid-50s because it's as applicable today as it was then: If people want to hear Chinese gong music, that's what Top 40 radio stations should play. The problem, I think, with Top 40 radio today is not that the general format is waning or losing popularity, but that programming people tend to digress too far from it. I think that most program directors fall into the "trick" bag—feeling that they are playing their music for the record promoters; or the people who live in the same apartment building; or for the people who they meet in places where you don't run into average people. For instance, I keep reading everywhere about "bubblegum" music. Well, you ask the average person what bubblegum music is and he won't know. Try it sometime. Stand on a street corner and ask the first ten people who pass: "What do you think about bubblegum music?" They won't know what the hell you're talking about. And yet this is one of the most accepted terms in our industry, mainly because it has been tagged on to certain kinds of music by record people and by disk jockeys. That type of music has become so disliked by program directors and disk jockeys in this day and age because they feel that if they're playing bubblegum music they are not hip, that they are square. But that itself is really a violation of Top 40 radio, because Top 40 radio should be playing the music that the people want to hear. I think what is happening is that somewhere along the way, when the music or program director is totaling up the votes or sales reports that he gets from the record stores, if he sees a thing by Donny Osmond, the Partridge Family, or someone he considers bubblegum, that record gets a little lower rating than it would otherwise. Consequently, what should be the major staple of our product, isn't. It's amazing.

Hall: The consensus is that the people these program directors want to reach with their programming aren't buying those records.

Stewart: But whose consensus is that? The only guy who really knows what's happening today in the radio business is George Wilson, national program director of Bartell Media stations. He's really down-to-earth. I think George is very aware of what's happening. And the stations that George has under his wing—the Bartell chain—play bubblegum music. If it shows up on the survey, they play it. He's very adverse to LP cuts, as I am. I just think it doesn't do much good. First of all, the average person doesn't have access to a lot of LP's. It isn't just black people who're buying singles. It's the poor people, and there are an awful lot of poor people in this country. Those are the people we're really aiming at. We're not aiming at the people who live in the rich section of town and go down and buy six albums with their allowance every week. We're aiming at that 15- or 16-year-old kid who gets his/her buck allowance once a week. She or he is lucky if their father doesn't get loaded on payday and come home broke. The kid gets a dollar, and has to figure out how best to spend that dollar, and goes down and carefully invests that dollar in a single. Well, I'm exaggerating, of course, but what I'm trying to point out is that the particular purchase of a single may represent a whole lot more than just one sale or one choice.

A jukebox, to me, is the greatest proof in the world of what's happening in music, because people put their money in. Go into a jukebox location in an average neighborhood and watch the guy who's drinking boilermakers at the bar. He gets a quarter change, and to him it's a big decision to go over and put that quarter into the jukebox, because in doing that, he may not be able to buy a pack of cigarettes tomorrow, the day before payday. The average person in the United States today still lives from payday to payday. We keep forgetting that, because most of us don't live that way. We're a little better off than that. But a half-dollar to the average person is still a considerable amount of money, and when he puts a half-dollar into a jukebox to play a record or three records or whatever it is, he is very selective about his choices. That may be the biggest decision he's going to make all of that week.

Hall: Let's go back to the bar in Omaha where Top 40 was born. When you realized that the barmaid was playing a record over and over that had been virtually worn out during the evening, what did you do then? Did you or Todd Storz immediately cry: "My God! Why don't we do that?" What actually happened?

Stewart: First, we were kind of amazed at it. We were getting sick of hearing it over and over. I guess it dawned on us gradually that people wanted to hear the records they like often.

Hall: When did you realize this? The next day? A week later? A month?

Stewart: I think it was very soon. It was in the next few days that we did something about it. We'd already gone to a closed music list.

Hall: By "closed," you mean there was a list and everybody played from the list?

Stewart: Right. Then we originated the idea of taking a record that was big and playing it more often than the others, and that was where the Pick Hit started, in Omaha, Neb. We started playing a Pick Hit once an hour, and the No. 1 song once an hour. That's where that started.

Hall: Ah, you put in the rotation pattern!

Stewart: When I first got there, the guys could play pretty much what they wanted to play within reason. I put in the closed list, and if memory serves me correctly, I think it started at 40 records, and we gradually got it down to 30 records. The tradition at that time always was: The deeper the trouble, the shorter the music list, and it always seemed to work. If the ratings went down, if you were playing 30 records, you went to 20. I can remember when Johnny Barnett was programming our station WTIX in New Orleans, we got down to 15 records at one time. And it worked. The full reason that Top 40 radio came about—and I'm not saying that I was the instigator of all of Top 40 radio, but I was responsible for a lot of the elements—in those days, in the early 50s when I first started in radio, radio was a very strange thing. The mid-50s, I guess I'm talking about, 1953 and 1954, I taught Speech and English part-time at Emerson College in Boston, while I was working as program director of this classical radio station. I decided I wanted to go out and see what made radio tick. So I took a trip to Cleveland around 1952 or 1953. Bill Randle was on the air at WERE. He really owned the city of Cleveland at that time. It was the strangest thing I've ever heard, because those were the days of cover records. Most guys in radio today don't even know what cover records are, but in those days the minute a record sold 150 copies—I think that was the magic number—somebody else would cover it by recording the same tune, and a radio station would end up with maybe eight versions of the same song. Well I went to Cleveland and spent about three days there, because besides teaching English I also had a radio class that I taught. My students wanted to hear some of the people that were good around the country, and Randle was a real hot rod.

That was probably the first time that anyone ever sat down and listened to a radio station as programming consultants do today, with a pen and pencil, writing things down on a yellow pad. And what was happening absolutely amazed me. If memory serves me right, Phil McLain was doing the morning show. The title may be wrong, but the idea should get across to you. He'd come on and play "Tennessee Waltz." Then, Tommy Edwards, who was doing the midday show at that time, would play another version on a different label. Of course, he would say the record was the greatest record of all time, because he'd got a hot dub of it. In those days, guys would have their own record boxes—records they'd gotten from the record companies—and when they went off the air they'd lock up their boxes in their closets so nobody else could play those records. Anyway, Edwards would play his version of the cover record, and then Randle would come on the air with a third version. And *his* was the greatest of all time, the greatest ever cut. Whoever was the evening guy might even have another version, and the all-night guy might have a fifth version. I said to myself: Wow, what kind of believability can radio have with so many straining points? And that's when I made up my mind that if ever I got to a station where I was given my head, I'd eliminate those problems so there would be some kind of credibility.

Those days were really the start of an exciting era in radio, and a lot of people today don't give credit to them. There's a guy who didn't actually start Top 40 radio, but a lot of people don't realize what an immense contribution he made—a guy by the name of Bill Randle. He was the first really exciting personality in independent radio. What he did was what Bill Drake did many years later. So, I've got to reverse my early stand. It was Randle who introduced the psychological effect to radio. If memory serves me right, he did the 2-7 PM stint. He'd come on the air, introduce himself, and say: "At 2:37 PM this afternoon Columbia Records is going to record a song at 1619 Broadway in New York. It'll be called 'Tennessee Waltz'. Mitch Miller is going to personally take this record out to LaGuardia Field and put it on an airplane, and I'm going to have that record here in my hands and play it at 4:47 this afternoon." So, he plays his records and does the commercials and makes a pitch again: "Don't forget, I'm going to play this new record this afternoon. It isn't even cut yet, but I know it'll be fantastic, because Mitch Miller is doing it and he told me so." Randle would do this after every record and he would build up the suspense . . . it would become almost like a fever. Then when 4:47 PM came, he would say: "We were going to play this new record, but some people have phoned that they're just getting off work, and they'll be between their office and home at 4:47 PM. So we're not going to play it until 5:03 PM this afternoon." And he would keep building this up and finally play the goddamn record, whatever it might be, at 5:30 PM. It might be the worse record of all time, but he would say: "That's fantastic. That *is* the greatest record of all time. Mitch, you're a genius. I'm going to call him up and tell him that, too. But first, I want to play the record again." He'd play the record four or five times in a row, and he might even play it a couple of times later. Then, when he went off the air, he'd put it in his box and he had the only copy in the world and the next morning the distributor would have 5,000 orders.

Every day it was the same thing—the greatest record of all time, and whatever record it was, he'd build it up and up. The psychological factor really worked. That's where the idea for the closed music list came because WERE was doing fantastically well in the Cleveland market and Randle was unbelievable. Well, he was the forerunner of Dick Clark . . . the radio version. But WERE sounded like six different radio stations, because everyone had their own little hot dub. So, that was the thing I wanted to avoid if ever I got the chance. If three versions of a record came out, someone—and it turned out later to be me—decided which of those versions the radio station would play. That's probably the very reason cover records died.

Hall: When you got into programming you also had final responsibility for the music, didn't you?

Stewart: Right.

Hall: Do you think this is a function of programming, or the function of a music director?

Stewart: It's absolutely a function of programming. A program director, in order to become a program director, should have enough knowledge of music so that he can be the final judge because he knows what he's trying to do with the station. I don't think the music director does. I think the music director lives in a completely different world. He has no concept of the commercial responsibilities that a program director has. All he's aware of is whether the record is a hit in the first eight bars, or whether the record is No. 7 in Bowling Green, Ohio. Well, I don't think those things really matter. I think the program director can tell about a record because he knows exactly what he's trying to do with the radio station, what kind of a sound he's trying to build, what kind of an image he's trying to create. When you get two diverse people, such as a program director and a music director, I don't think it's there. Some program directors say: "Well, my music director thinks like I do." That isn't true, because when you take a guy who doesn't think like you do and you make him think like you do, you run the risk of the guy second-guessing you. The music director will say to himself: "Well I don't think Charlie is going to like this record because he didn't like the last one like this, so I'm not even going to play it for him." So what happens is that the program director winds up missing an awful lot of good records. In other words, in most situations like this the music director screens the stuff, and he brings the best of the product to the program director. But if he is second-guessing, the program director is running the risk of blowing a lot of good records.

Hall: What do you think are the greatest attributes a disk jockey can have?

Stewart: Two things: Being himself and being aware of what's happening in the world—being aware of what's happening in the strata of society that he chooses to live in. George Wilson said something in one of your interviews—that he misses going into the bars and sitting down and drinking with people. That's the best way of really finding out what people are thinking. People are vulnerable when they're drinking.

I think a disk jockey has to be aware of what's going on around him. Not just aware from reading *Billboard* and *Vox Jox,* or reading the *Bill Gavin Report,* but aware from the newspapers, aware of his surroundings, aware of keeping topical. Because, in the final analysis, the single most important thing that makes or breaks a disk jockey, a good disk jockey, is his ability to be topical. I could cite all kinds of instances. I could show you on television where there's a guy who probably has less talent than some of his competitors, but murders them. I'm talking about Johnny Carson. Dick Cavett certainly is a lot more intellectual than Carson ever was. He's basically a lot funnier than Carson. But he lacked two things—the ability to be topical, and the ability to really get to the level of the people the way Carson does. And that's why Carson is so successful and always will be. He'll eat everybody's lunch seven days a week. Because Carson has the common denominator and the common denominator is really topicality.

You have to be able to grasp, in your mind, what people are talking about, and then talking about that very day. If Roman Gabriel threw six touchdown passes that day and that's what people in your town are talking about, then that's what you should be talking about. If there was a 12-car collision on the freeway and that's what people are going to be talking about on the way to the office or the factory, then that's what the air personality should be talking about. I think Charlie Tuna is the voice of the people. Somebody asked me if I had a radio station, and I had my choice of any five air personalities, well, Charlie would be No. 1, and there wouldn't even be a close second at the moment. Really, because he's got the *feel* of what he's doing. I don't think he's got a really good shot right now, but if he did, he could eat everyone for lunch. (Tuna was at KROQ at the time.)

Hall: There have been some good shows done by air personalities.

Stewart: But day in and day out, Tuna is consistent. He does his homework.

Hall: His preparation is phenomenal. He works like hell preparing his show. But then, so does Don Imus of WNBC in New York. People have the idea, from his air work, that Don's a zany, irresponsible rascal. That's not true. That's merely his public image. Pat Patterson at WKIX in Raleigh, N.C., is a damned good personality. I enjoy listening to him, and he has a standing order to send me some tapes every few months just so I can keep up with what he's doing on the air. Larry Lujack in Chicago works like hell on his show. But, getting back to Tuna, what do you think makes him so successful?

Stewart: I think that Charlie knows the kind of people he's aiming his show at. I think that a couple of years ago a prominent disk jockey had that same feel. But when you get on the Martoni circuit and the type of people you're aiming your show at is the bartender, well, those aren't the people you should be aiming your show at. You should be aiming your show at the people who're outside waiting at the bus stop to go home. And Charlie Tuna, I think, has never forgotten that. I think he spends more time in preparing his show than anyone I know. And there's no way today, particularly on a morning show, that you can do a good show unless you go in well prepared. The days of winging it are gone, I think. When you're winging it, people can tell that you're winging it. And that's basically the first crack in the credibility gap.

OUTRO: The disk jockey convention in Miami undoubtedly affected Stewart's career adversely, although he can't be blamed for what happened there. Adults attended that meeting and they played adult games, the same things that go on at any convention whether it's a convention of doctors or grocery store managers. It's a pity that Stewart was identified too strongly with the meeting, which he helped organize in his position as national program director for Todd Storz. That convention, too, affected the careers of every radio man for years to come—especially the disk jockey.

Bill Gavin edits a weekly record news report, operating out of San Francisco. Bob Hamilton, who was mentioned here with Gavin, edited a similar report at that time; today he edits a radio information quarterly.

The International Radio Programming Forum is an annual convention of radio executives who come from all over the world. Ron Jacobs gave a keynote speech at more than one of these meetings.

Bill Randle, highly praised here, retired from radio after doing a daily talk show a few years at WERE in Cleveland; he is now head of broadcasting at the University of Cincinnati.

The Martoni circuit mentioned here is a reference to certain watering holes frequented by radio and record people. In Los Angeles, Martoni's is a very popular watering hole; in New York, you can usually find radio and record people at the bar in Al & Dick's. San Francisco and other cities also have popular hangouts for the industry.

CHUCK BLORE

Chuck Blore, first interview

INTRO: No one (though several outstanding program directors tried over the years) ever created a total success of KIIS radio station in Los Angeles. Without a doubt, the man who brought it near the top was Chuck Blore, president of the commercials production firm of Chuck Blore/Don Richman Inc., Los Angeles. Here, Blore delves into his early career in radio; he discusses the promotions (he later grew to resent his fame from these promotions that set the radio world on its ear) such as "Formula 96" and "Amoeba," and his dreams for KIIS to have a totally new radio format. Blore is considered a genius in the world of radio.

Hall: Why did you decide to get back into radio?

Blore: Well, I've only had three programming ideas in my life, one of which was the KFWB format. That was the first thing. The second thing was years later when I created the Bill Ballance "Feminine Forum."

Hall: Was that your idea? I thought Bill Ballance sort of stumbled onto that idea.

Blore: They bought it from me. Paid me a lot of money. And my third idea . . . .

Hall: The "Feminine Forum" concept is now monstrous around the country. I've listened to Bill the past couple of days to see how he was doing, and he's sensational at that type of thing, he handles it with just the right touch.

Blore: He's really good. The idea was called "Cosmopolitan Los Angeles" when I gave it to them. He changed the name—"Feminine Forum" is much better. But I'd original-ly intended to cash in on the word "cosmopolitan," to get the ruboff from the maga-zine, and it still sounds nice—"Cosmopolitan Los Angeles." Anyhow, that was the second idea and the third one began to *happen* to me.

Well, I think everyone's lifestyle has changed in the past three or four years—yours has, mine has, everyone, at least, who is alive, vital, right? And anyone who is at all aware of what's going on in the world. It's a marvelous thing. I think we've had greater changes in lifestyles, attitudes and in the honest expressions of love and emo-tion in the past five years than we've had in the previous 500. Men's clothing, for in-stance, has changed much in the past five years. At any rate, there's this freedom, this change which is going on. And I, because of my commercials company, have to keep in tune with what's going on at this instant. Because if I'm going to sell things on the radio—which I believe to be the most avant-garde form of communication—I have to be ahead of the audience I'm talking to. You have to keep your fingers on the pulse. Well, this is an exciting thing to do, providing that you take part in it. And it changed my life; my having to pursue that knowledge of lifestyles changed my life totally. My response to these changes was like a light inside me, a fire. Wow! It's so great that people can be themselves, be independent, do what they want, and express themselves truthfully without society getting in the way. You can meet a girl today and say: "Gee, I'd like to live with you," as opposed to: "I'd like to marry you," and it's equally acceptable. Had you said that to a girl—what, five years ago? Maybe 10? I don't know—it would have been a tremendous affront. It's a much more honest thing that's happening now. And, of course, my whole background, since I was seven years old, has been in radio—there's been nothing else in my life. So, when these lifestyles, patterns, attitudes, and morals change, I don't have any choice but to put them into the one area I know, radio. I began to think, how would you do this? Because I had no desire to go back into radio. I really enjoyed the role of . . . the god, you know, the retired king crap. Nobody could touch him, right? I enjoyed that. I'd go to the conventions and everybody would point and say "Wow," and they'd talk to me, and I'd come down off my cloud and talk to them and say, "Yes, that's true." That's a nice role.

Hall: You realized then that you were a god in radio?

Blore: Of course. You cannot have people react to you the way they were reacting to me without assuming you're a thunderhead! I mean without feeling . . . I'll tell you something interesting though: Five years after I left radio, I was a much bigger man than when I was in it. Because people like record promotion man Ernie Farrell and others were keeping the myth going, which is fine. I enjoyed the myth and I contributed to it. I would dazzle everyone at a Bill Gavin conference with a produced tape, but they never stopped to think that I might have spent a full year creating 30 minutes of stuff, right? They always thought: "Wow, everything he touches is fantastic!" And it might not have been me who even did the show; it might have been a couple of writers I have. The point is: I did enjoy that god role. But to take that image back into the field of battle and hold it up to be shot at is . . . .

Hall: A challenge?

Blore: And something that I really didn't care to do. I've had an awful lot of radio offers in the past ten years.

Hall: Were you scared about getting back into radio?

Blore: No . . . well, maybe so. I probably was, but I would never admit that to myself. I might admit it to someone else, but never to myself. In fact, the question hasn't come up until right this moment. Certainly, not within me. So, anyway, I had that role and didn't want to get back into radio, just stay on the fringes. But then I began to have this idea: How would I reflect these new attitudes and changes in lifestyles, love, and honesty? In radio? So this format began to develop in my head. KIIS came to me about six months ago—no, eight months ago. They said: "Can you come over and help us?" I said: "No, but let me tell you what I would do if I were there." They said: "Wow, it's perfect; come and do it." I said no. I guess it was trepidation. But then for a while I had a programming company with Ken Draper. I was never active in the company; I was just a name. My whole role in that company was to discuss philosophy with Ken. If there was a problem, we discussed the philosophy of it.

Hall: You're not connected with that company now? You're free?

Blore: I had to get out of that company in order to do this. I obviously couldn't program KIIS and lock Ken out of Los Angeles. So Ken and I parted. I think he's about to have two stations in Los Angeles now, an AM and an FM. And it's good for us, too, since the more things that are happening in radio—the more energetic things—the more people will be aware of radio and tune it in. It's really terrible to have a city the size of Los Angeles and have only a 14 percent tune-in. And that's a high estimate.

Hall: Why don't more people here listen to radio?

Blore: Because they're bored with it. And it's not just this market. But you get a market where radio is exciting. Well, I could go back to the days of KFWB. Of course, that was 12 years ago, but nonetheless there we had 17-, 18-, and 20-percent tune-in. Now, that doesn't sound like a hell of a lot, but think: At any given moment 20 percent of the people who owned radios had them playing. That's immense. In Los Angeles, that means at any given time you'd have 10 million ears available.

Hall: If you had that percent?

Blore: Yes, and then, of course, you want to go after your share of that percent. Anyway, I had this idea for a format. The people at KIIS went away and then came back and made me an offer I couldn't refuse. I'm doing it for nothing at the moment. Unless it works, I get nothing. I'm getting absolutely zero—no pay at all.

Hall: You're kidding.

Blore: No, no. Because it may make me rich at the other end. If it doesn't work, I get nothing. Of course, I know it will work.

Hall: How was this station doing? Was it in the black or was it marginal?

Blore: I don't think that should even be a part of this story. The fact that we're bringing in all of these new people should indicate they have money.

But the idea about not being paid was mine. I said that I didn't want to be paid for my format unless it worked, that I didn't want them to invest that much money. In fact, I don't think any station could afford me at the price I would put on myself. In order for my ego to accept it, you see. So doing it for nothing is a better way. It's an investment in me, an investment in this format, which I really, really believe in. And I know it will pay off. In fact, I predict this: In less than a year from now, there'll be a KIIS format in every major market in the country. I promise you.

Hall: You mentioned it to me once before, but tell me again what happened in Minneapolis that time. That was a tremendous feat.

Blore: But we're not through talking about KIIS?

Hall: No. We'll come back to that.

Blore: Because I haven't said everything yet.

Hall: Let's go to Minneapolis. The year was?

Blore: About 1960, I guess. KDWB was way down at the end of the dial—63. And up until that time all of the radio stations were above 1100. People didn't even know that the other end of the dial existed. What we had to do was figure a way to get listeners down there. So the answer was, advertise on the other radio stations. Well, though it's an obvious answer, it wasn't that easy to bring off. What we did was get the fellow who invented Hadacol . . . .

Hall: Remember his name?

Blore: Colonel something-or-other. He was from New Orleans. We got him to record these commercials for Formula 63. It was free and guaranteed to remove boredom.

Hall: I heard that you made the stations guarantee to run the spots.

Blore: No. Had any of the stations bothered to check into the situation, they would have found out KDWB was behind it. But they didn't. They got the spots from the agency and put them on the air. They would not do that today, of course. All of the rules today are much more stringent. They'd find out; it's a rule now—it wasn't then. You couldn't do a lot of the things today that we used to do in radio, nor would you want to. One of the glories of radio is its maturation, I think. The fact is that back in those days we were very flamboyant—like a kid, 17 years old, just about to experience his adulthood. He runs and plays and does all kinds of wonderful things. By the time you're 27, you're wiser and you don't do things with quite the old flamboyance, but what you do is a lot heavier. It has more consequence, and it means more.

So you don't see balloons being dropped into main streets anymore. No, you see radio stations involved in some community activity—like buying buses to get kids to school—consequential things, which are really the best kinds of promotions. Movies were flamboyant in the early days, and these were the early days of radio. Because radio did die. People will say: "What do you mean? Radio wasn't dead." Well, bull manure; television killed it. Radio, as we knew it, died. People to this day are trying to resurrect it and it's dead—it's a ghost. And they ought to leave it alone, because we have a whole new medium. Only the name remains the same. Radio used to broadcast to mass America. Today it doesn't do that; it broadcasts on a one-to-one basis. Me communicating with you. And it's a totally different concept, absolutely different.

Hall: When you hit in Minneapolis, you created quite a stir, didn't you?

Blore: Yes, we did. The product was available in the drugstores. People could go into drugstores and pick up these packages of Formula 63. And they went into the drugstores by the thousands. In these little packages was a message that Formula 63 was a radio station and if they tuned it in they would never be bored again. But yes, it caused quite a furor. We'd bought guaranteed time so that on a given moment if you tuned completely across the dial all you'd hear was that one spot. There would be the colonel saying: "I'm the fellow who brought you Hadacol, and I've got something good for you now."

Hall: Did the other stations get mad?

Blore: Some of them were furious; others made us finish the contract. Most of them thought: "Hey, we've been duped, but what a great thing to have happen for radio." But there's one giant station in the town who didn't think it was funny. I guess I wouldn't have thought it was very funny if someone had done it to me—I'd have been furious.

Hall: Going back over these things—because those are classic stories—the next stunt you pulled was in Los Angeles, wasn't it?

Blore: The Amoeba promotion wasn't a stunt. I wish I could clear that up. It was to raise funds for a charity project after all other pleas had been relatively unsuccessful.

Hall: It was copied in several markets.

Blore: One of my pet peeves is that human beings were given a brain in order to think.

Hall: Meaning, the program director?

Blore: And all they're doing is copying what everyone else is doing. It's tragic—one of the great problems in radio. Program directors don't know how to use the medium; they don't have the slightest idea. I really learned to use the radio medium when I got out of radio and into commercials where I was forced to deal in 60-second increments. I had to sell an item in just 60 seconds. Most program directors have 24 hours a day to sell their radio station, and it *sounds* like they're using all 24 hours. Sounds sloppy. Their stations are not programmed concisely and beautifully. But when you have only 60 seconds, you have to do everything in that 60 seconds. You can't do a little bit this 60 seconds and a little more the next and so on.

Hall: Was KFWB one of your original programming ideas?

Blore: KFWB was the original concept. From Gordon McLendon's policy book, we took his attitudes about local news, and from Todd Storz we took his views about playing the same records over and over again. And we were not the first with KFWB to bring these things together. I'd done the same thing in El Paso, for example, and both Todd and Gordon were spying on each other. I guess spying isn't the word, but they'd send their people into the other's market and bring back ideas about what the other was doing. So, there was already a music and news programming concept.

Hall: What was the news concept? I know about the music bit.

Blore: To *localize* the news. People in those days thought there was no way radio could compete with the national coverage on television. But McLendon realized that he wasn't watching "news" on television, he was seeing newsreels of something that had happened perhaps three days ago, because they didn't have all of the sophisticated equipment for TV then. Gordon realized that television couldn't, in those days, move those heavy cameras around and cover local news. And a newspaper couldn't report fast enough. He saw a way to make his mark with local news. So he sent local news units out all over Dallas, and almost instantly had like 85 shares. This was at a time when nearly every other radio operator had given up, and they were trying to sell their radio stations and/or get into television.

Hall: Now, the Todd Storz music concept did not consist of just playing 40 records, but in playing certain records more often, isn't that true?

Blore: Todd Storz . . . his initial concept was in playing 10 records. That was it initially, until Bill Stewart got into it and began to develop it. But his original idea was to play 10 records—the 10 records most played on jukeboxes. Not the top 10 records that were sold in the market or anything like that, because he didn't think he had any way of getting that information. The information he got initially was from the jukebox operators, and they were telling him which records were being played most. He took the top 10 records and played them over and over and over again.

Bill Stewart took that concept and said: "Let's play the top 10 a little more, but let's expand the playlist and play some of the other records, too." Now the 40 idea happened because we were on the air three hours, some guys were on for four hours. This was McLendon now, not Storz, because Storz was repeating those few records and getting huge ratings with a little daytime station in Omaha, and beating everybody. But at McLendon's station we had a music policy, the first music policy in the history of man, I think. We would play just so many records an hour, I think we decided on 13 records. Now, how were we going to do that? Well, we figured that 10 of these should be hit records, okay? Two of those should be oldies because Gordon liked Glenn Miller, right? And one . . . well, you'd play a new record every hour. So that was our initial thing. And because each deejay shift was four hours and we had to have enough records to fill up the show—you wouldn't think of repeating the same record in the same show—you multiplied the 10 hit records per hour times a four-hour shift and that's where the expression Top 40 came from. And when I came to KFWB we changed it to "The Fabulous 40."

The thing we added at KFWB to the music and the news was the showmanship element. The flash. The dash. We added show business. It's always been my theory that radio is an *entertainment* medium, and what we did was bring entertainment back to radio, but in a totally different way, We didn't do Jack Benny. We had deejays who were really sharp professional performers. We had newscasts with production—of a five-minute newscast, two and a half minutes would be: "Bom! Be bom! Bom bom! Watch out for the news." Took that long to get into it, but goddamn it was thrilling! KFWB did that spectacular stuff.

Other things happened at KFWB. The logo. Before, there'd never been a logo for a radio station. There had been jingles in the past, but never a constant repetition of the call letters in melodic form. Because of the success of the Lucky Strike jingle, they kept hold of something for years and years. I thought: That's a good idea—you could just hear the melody and know what the message was. So I incorporated a logo for the call letters KFWB, and suddenly the logo was born.

The jingle package that I did—well, I'd just seen *West Side Story* and I said: "That's the kind of music I want in a jingle." My theory was that the jingle should be something totally different from the music we were playing so it would stick out and be something super that the jock could just jump on. So we had this big band and some exciting people singing. The jingles played anywhere from 30 seconds to a minute and a half. Yet in those days that was great, because people accepted the jingles as if they were hit music. Today, of course, if I were doing them, the concept would be different, like the prototype tape of KIIS that you heard. Our jingles on KIIS sound like mini-hits, and we even program them that way, as if they're another hit record. It's on for a while and then it's gone, and later it comes back as an oldie. But they are made to complement our overall sound . . . be a part of it rather than stick out.

Hall: So, the next stage in your career would have to be the commercials industry and the third stage, since you mentioned earlier three stages, would have to be KIIS.

Blore: Yes.

Hall: Well, in the commercials field what did you try to achieve?

Blore: When I was at KFWB one of the things over which I had no control was bad commercials. We had a continuity acceptance department, and we didn't accept any commercial, of course, which had double entendres or which yelled at the audience. We didn't put those on, but we couldn't keep off just dull commercials. They'd say: "What's the matter with it?" And you'd say: "Well, it's dull." It's a judgmental decision, and their decision is just as valid as yours. The client would say: "It isn't dull, it's *my* product." We would spend hours and hours trying to amass this audience, you know, and 60 seconds of DULL would drive them away sure as hell. Of course, Stan Freeberg was doing a campaign every now and then, and he'd prove that commercials could be audience grabbers. Yet it wasn't happening. Nobody in the advertising field ever cared about radio. More than likely, radio used the audio portion of the television spot, which was dreadful, but that was what was happening nonetheless. Someone once said that if you wanted to be a success, find a void and fill it. Well, I was certainly aware of the void, though I wasn't aware that I could fill it. But I had a noncompetition clause in my contract when I left Crowell—Collier Broadcasting which owned KFWB, and I couldn't work in radio for 18 months. So I thought: "Well, I'll give commercials a try." By the end of 18 months, I couldn't afford to quit.

Hall: Where did you start that commercials firm?

Blore: I was born in Los Angeles, so this is my home. I started the firm, as a matter of fact, because I was married then. And I had to have an office to work in—I just couldn't get up and go to the dining room table—so I built a little shack on my garage. Just a kind of lean-to. I'm not a builder, but it had a floor and I put a desk and a telephone in it. And that was where I started the company. My first expenditure was $13 for a file cabinet. I thought: "Wow! Do I really want to invest in this company? Do I believe in it that much?" But, to show you how much of a void there was in radio commercials, we'd only been in business about eight months when I entered our first competition—the international broadcast awards—and we won in every single commercial radio category. Not that we were that good, it was just that nobody else was even trying. That was 10 years ago, and the firm became immense. I would never have thought it possible, but I became a much bigger name in advertising than I was in radio.

Hall: You told me a while back that you had won more than 500 awards.

Blore: Yes.

Hall: And the firm is still going right now even though you're here at KIIS?

Blore: My thing at KIIS is very temporary. Sonny Melendrez is the program director, not me. I'm program supervisor, or something. What I'm doing here is trying to translate all of my ideals to Sonny. And the best way to do that, we feel, is to do things together. So, everything we've been doing here has been in tandem, so he can hear me talk. When the questions come up, we answer. Then, more and more, as questions come up, he'll be answering rather than me, because this format didn't exist anywhere except in my head. It was at an International Radio Programming Forum that Sonny and I talked about this thing—history was born then. Anyway, he was the one person I talked to who responded. He was as excited about it as I was, and excitement is the one criterion. The one prerequisite about this format is that you have to like it. You have to be excited about it or you can't do it. Another thing that's got me so excited about this format is that I think it can't be copied. I said earlier that there's going to be a KIIS format in every market—the truth is that it's probably going to be the worst station in those markets. Because this format is so fragile that it can be saccharine— just plain crap—if you don't watch it every single second. We have to have a staff of writers, for example. You heard the prototype tape; that's what the station is going to sound like, but it's behind-the-scenes that's really critical. That staff of writers is writing stuff . . . those little "delights" that you heard. We have two production rooms going 24 hours a day. We're doing six and seven of those "delights" an hour, because this format just eats them up. And, man, we don't want to repeat them. So, we'll have a library of thousands and thousands of these things in a very short time, on tape. When we have that then we'll go back and repeat one or two of them, and people will never know because they'll be three months apart. As you know, some are only 20 seconds long . . . or as long as 90 seconds.

Hall: And those little features are going to be a major part of this format?

Blore: A major feature of this format is the fact that it is preproduced. I would guess— Sonny can help me on this—I would guess that 60 percent of this radio station is preproduced; it will be born in the production studio.

Hall: Does that include putting the music on tape?

Blore: No. We're not talking about music. The music is "live" . . . "live" in the sense that it comes directly off the records.

Hall: Yet the rest of the sound is mostly preproduced?

Blore: The deejay . . . and deejay is a word that we've got to stop using, because he's *not* a deejay, he's a *catalyst* for all of this information.

Hall: I prefer the term *air personality.*

Blore: Well, yeah, that's fine. But even that now has a different meaning here at KIIS, because these guys here are also producers. We supply all of the information, all of the programming elements. And these fall basically into what we call the "delights," little things which are just produced to make people say, "Yeah . . . ." When they say, "yeah," we've done our job as far as the delights are concerned. It's our goal that when this station gets to where we want it to be, a person will not be able to listen for a half hour and not feel better. Feel better about being alive. I don't mean hearing a joke, but feeling better about living, about the earth on which they live, about human beings being human . . . we are constantly recalling to their attention that this is a very nice place in which to live. The best of all possible worlds, you know? The best of all possible life times. The best of all possible Wednesdays. Or Tuesdays. To put the format into one sentence, it's a celebration of life. We encourage the listener to come and celebrate life with us.

Hall: The disk jockey—I mean, the air personality—blends these things?

Blore: What he does is . . . well, we have these delights, he has his music list, obviously the master log would have commercials and things on it, and we have features that we put on—we're doing a study a week on something. The one we had on the prototype tape was "Sex Isn't Funny, or Is It?" which is an interesting psychological study. We're doing one on bio-feedback, one on Satanism. We're also doing one about polls because a pollster can ask you any question and get any answer he wants—while both of you are being honest. We're doing many, many fascinating things. The air personality, emcee, or catalyst, has to bring all of these things together and then supply a great deal of himself. And that falls basically into two areas. One is the area of fascination. All that means is something in which he's fascinated. If he's only interested in something, that isn't good enough, he has to be fascinated. And how many things do you run into during a day about which you're fascinated? Probably few, very few. You really have to search.

Hall: Well, I'm always getting to talk to people like Sonny Melendrez and Chuck Blore and people like that, so I'm always meeting fascinating people.

Blore: But the average guy? Our biggest problem with the jocks—I mean the air personalities or whatever you want to call them—is that they come to us and ask: "Is this really fascinating or is it merely interesting?" And normally, if they have to ask the question, it's only interesting. Interesting is not good enough—we don't want things that are only *interesting* on our radio station. I think today that radio generally . . . well, *any* radio station is fascinating. At some given time of the day. Dave Garroway used to sign-on his program with: "I promise you that during this three-hour show, there will be at least one moment of fascination." Well, if you listen to his three hours, there probably was. But we're going to have that every time we open the microphone. And that is really difficult. It requires the people, the air personalities, if they're on the air three hours, to spend at least six hours—at this time they're spending much more than that—just gathering the material.

Where do they find these fascinating things? They find them from life, magazines, their own heads, or perhaps something they might remember as a little boy. Anyway, they find them. Once you start digging these things up and get your sources, they're easier to find. But we say: "Don't be interesting. Be fascinating!"

I think that every radio station has areas of fascination. The thing is that the listener has to wait too long for them. Generally, when you listen to a radio station, they're not fascinating except for that little period—they're not even interesting. But, with KIIS we're bypassing *interesting* and going right to *fascinating*. Everybody here has been warned that if it's merely interesting, we don't want it on the air. And that's only one aspect of what the air personality does. The other is to contribute to the image of the radio station, that image being the celebration of life. If what he does makes people say "Ah! Yeah," or, "Wow!" if it helps them realize that life is good, life is love, that this is a great place to be—then he brings to radio—to this produced mass—humanness.

Hall: When I listened to the prototype tape of the KIIS sound the music was rock in nature, but it seemed more bright and melodic than hard. I sensed that you were being careful on the music selection.

Blore: If someone asked us what our music policy was, I'd have to say that it was a policy designed not to have any mistakes in it. Because if 60 seconds of a bad commercial could chase an audience away, than two to five minutes of music they don't care about could really drive them off. We don't want any mistakes, that's the thing. Now, we have to be a little more general in our music selection than you would be if you were programming a Top 40 station. A Top 40 station is the easiest kind of station to program in regard to music because you just go with the sales figures of the records. Such stations never have a problem about the top 20 records. But we have to be much more selective than that, because . . . well, everybody in this room—and we're all connected in radio or music—can listen to a rock station and, say, every 45 minutes hear a record that they don't like . . . can't stand that record . . . so they go away. I think that the public generally—and this is so obvious that no one ever thinks about it—does not have the same interest in radio that we people in radio have. It's as simple as that. But we always figure that everyone is fascinated by radio because we are. You tend to judge the entire universe by yourself, which is the normal thing to do. But if you stop to think about it, you realize that the public doesn't care about radio the way we do. It's not vital to their lives. It's nice to have it on, but that's all. It's merely a pleasant companion and friend. But it's no big deal to them. They may develop habit patterns, like listening to the same air personality in the morning for years. He would be missed, but he isn't critical to their lives. If they go one morning without turning the radio on, they haven't missed a thing.

My whole point is that when listeners get to a spot on the dial and stay there, they've given you, the radio man, everything you could possibly ask from a listener. They have done you the ultimate service by tuning in that spot on the dial. We don't ask a listener to write us a letter, participate in a contest; we don't ask him or her or them to do anything except give us their ears, and attention, hopefully. And once they've done that, that's the ultimate service they can do for us. They've given us everything they can. We must give them everything we possibly can, which means: Reward after reward after reward, constantly giving them something that makes them say, "Wow!" Or a delight, something of fascination, something to reward them for tuning us in. And that means a hell of a lot more than just playing records and giving them the time of day and the weather. These are the factors that will make KIIS different—the rewards and the things that other people who imitate the format will try to do but probably will not be able to bring off.

Hall: The music, though, will be carefully selected?

Blore: Very, very carefully selected. What we do . . . well, at home at night I love to play "Nights in White Satin." I've had the Moody Blues album a long time. But I'm not going to play it on KIIS because it's too rocky. That doesn't mean we're not going to program rock records, as you heard on the tape. But there's something—I guess you'd call it visceral communication—between program director Sonny Melendrez and David Pell, the music director. We all look at each other and say "no" or say "yes," and if we all say "no" or "yes," then that's the answer, but if one of us says "no" and the others say "yes," then "no," too, is also the answer.

Hall: The record has to appeal to the entire trio?

Blore: Everybody. And we don't make a big deal about a record, you know? Even if a record is the No. 1 record in the country and we're still shaking our heads about it, it doesn't go on the air. Because we're striving for one thing. Well, anyway the people who listen to radio for hit records won't be listening to us. KHJ and KROQ will have no problems from us. They're after a different audience—they're after the record-buying audience. We're not. We're after people who're in love with life. I don't care if they ever buy a record; it really doesn't make any difference to us. They obviously will, because they're people who're living, and a great part of living today is music and having a vital record collection. It is. It's critical. You can't spend a night . . . I can't . . . without music.

Hall: Is that because TV is so bad?

Blore: I don't think so, I think it's because they're different rewards.

Hall: Well, why is music so important today? More important than it has ever been in history?

Blore: First, because it's better. Also, to hear music the way we hear it today and take it for granted, in our living room . . . heck, as little as 20 years ago you had to go to a concert. You physically couldn't hear it in your living room on the scale we have today. And today you even have better a quality of music than at a concert. I really think that music isn't any more important to a person than it's ever been, it's just more readily accessible. Recording artists are satisfying a hunger that was probably there before, but wasn't satisfied.

Hall: But aren't various lifestyles being dictated by music?

Blore: I think they're being heavily influenced. I really, really believe that the Beatles changed the world. So, yes, lifestyles are really heavily influenced by music. And, of course, vice versa, because a lot of music is dictated by life.

Hall: And so the music that goes on this station . . . how do you picture it, how do you explain it?

Blore: It's difficult to explain what kind, because . . . .

Hall: I heard "My Sweet Lord," and I heard Three Dog Night.

Blore: Yes. Of course, you could hear those particular records on almost any radio station. But if you looked at our playlist right now, you wouldn't see a hell of a lot of records that aren't also being played on other radio stations. Maybe some of the newer ones would be an exception. Since we aren't going after the hit record audience, we can play a new record merely because it adds to the image of KIIS. Not because we think it might be a hit; that's of no concern. If it adds to our image, then we can play it.

Hall: Are you playing new records?

Blore: Sure, quite a lot.

Hall: How many records are on the KIIS playlist at this time?

Blore: Our playlist is broken up into A, B, C, R, and G categories. The A's are all the big hits. There are about 25-30 records on the A list. The B's are unproven records, but records that are moving up or that we have reason to believe will be hits. The C's are records that we feel either fit the image of the sound of the station or enhance the station itself. We'll play records on KIIS that you might not hear on any other radio station. The rationale is that it's a two and a half minute cassette, if it was done musically. We also have something called "entertainments" which are tiny, little features to break up double spots. It occurred to me that to shove two commercial spots at listeners in a row was a little pushy. So, we've found a whole mess of delightful little things which we call entertainments, which earn their right to be on the air by being totally entertaining. And they will break up the two-spot clusters. They can be 10 seconds long, they can be 20 seconds long . . . even a minute. A great example would be Carly Simon's "Hotcakes." Plays a minute and 10 seconds. Zap, it's in there and gone. Really nice. So, we've got all of these little entertainments happening all of the time.

Hall: How about your R list?

Blore: The R list is composed of recents, records that are about a year old. Not old enough yet to be considered an oldie. And yet you'd still like to hear them one more time. I tell you that I was so sick of "Tie a Yellow Ribbon 'Round the Old Oak Tree" that I wanted to vomit. But I heard it again about three days ago as an R record and I said: "Wow! I haven't heard that for such a long time." But, there you get that little bit of delight by hearing it again, whatever the record is. If we'd continued in the first place to play that record, our station would have taken on the sound of an *old* radio station. People would have said: "My god! Are they still playing that thing?" So, you can't just leave records like that on your playlist in the A category.

Hall: Then you have the G's, the golden oldies.

Blore: And even those come in two classifications, because we have the solid golds that go back to about 1962—well, maybe 1965. But, from that period back, they're the real giants, the classics. And we play at least one of those classics every show. But the regular golds, well, we put them in a regular rotation pattern. A classic comes up at least every four hours.

Hall: Do you have a mini-drama for every gold record?

Blore: Not every one, no, because we have so many. We have about a thousand. But we're doing about three mini-dramas a week for the golds, so we may have 100 of them by now. Something like that.

Hall: Now, has the station reached that feeling that you wanted initially on the air?

Blore: Pretty much. Not totally. I'm still making changes in staff. Still looking for the new and better things. We still have the same financial problems that we began with—it's a very expensive format to run. The creative department, for one reason. We haven't gotten to the point, for instance, where I can say, "well, I'm going to get an all-night guy." We don't yet have an all-night personality—we're either taped or we're playing records all night back-to-back, with some little inserts. We're certainly at a point where we're about to have an all-night man. But, frankly, we'd arrived at the point some while back where we could say: "Now look at this son-of-a-gun start paying off!" And that's when the economy just fell on its butt. The condition of all radio at this moment is just dreadful.

Hall: Nationally speaking.

Blore: Yes.

Hall: The national dollar is virtually dead.

Blore: It's not just any one station in any market, it's everywhere. And so, once we had everything where we thought they ought to be, the dollars flowed in, but not as fast as we thought they would. Yet we're a very healthy radio station, but not to the point where we say: "Now we have everything we want." That will be a little while yet. We still have to pay back all of this money we spent in developing the format.

Hall: For example, you haven't started paying yourself yet, right?

Blore: Well, I'm not working on a salary. But now we're getting into a situation where we are syndicating our material that we created for KIIS.

Hall: Why is it that program directors have never really capitalized on the medium of radio . . . never used the medium to its full potential?

Blore: I think it's kind of like the question: Why haven't we been to space before? We just never got that far. We were just unaware of the possibilities. For example, in the old days of radio they talked of the "theater of the mind." Well, for example, "The Shadow" . . . scary as hell, but they told you every single thing they were doing on the show. The creators of the show weren't doing what I'm talking about right now. If they said, "Stop the car, Cato," then you heard the car brakes squeak. Then you heard Cato say, "I'll open the door" and you heard the door noises, then you heard him say, "Now I'll close the door" and a clunking sound. Then, "Now I'll walk," and you heard the footsteps; "up to the house and knock on the door," and you heard a knocking sound. They explained everything they were doing while the sounds were being heard. And so, even then they weren't *using* the media as we now know it could be used.

Once you start thinking about the possibilities of radio, it opens up door after door in your mind. I was telling an air personality here yesterday—he said it was difficult to tell something fascinating every few seconds—and I said: "Well, you're trodding down this long hallway marked Deejays of America, right, where a lot of talented people have walked before and a lot more will tread the same direction. The only way you can become significant among all of those going down that hallway is to open some of the doors along the way that are marked *No Admittance.* Go in there, in those rooms, and have a peek around." So, what we're trying to do with the air personalities, what we're trying to get them to do . . . well, we've made up a list of clichés which every deejay in the world leans on, and they're absolutely forbidden. Whenever a guy catches himself saying one of those things you know, he's suddenly aware: "My god! I'm a cliche!"

Hall: How many of them are taboo?

Blore: There are 50 million of them and to start naming them . . .

Hall: You mean the "Hey, dig this, baby" sort of thing?

Blore: Not so much the jargonistic things as "The time right now is . . . " sort of thing.

Hall: I recently heard on a major station in Los Angeles: "And now we'll play some Hank Mancini to lead us up to the news."

Blore: Here's the biggest cliche of all: "Hello. My name is so-and-so and I'll be here until six o'clock." Who cares that he'll be there until six? If you sat down you could think of hundreds of them. We're just trying to get rid of the clichés. And the jock says: "What can I put in its place?" They feel that those clichés were born because they had to get from here to there in their show. Again as you heard, Claude, in the prototype tape, we don't care about transitions anymore, not on the station. By leaving out those transitions, the station takes on a new energy—a pace that goes bang-bang-bang. Then I could tell you about another area we're into at KIIS, which is the psychology of juxtaposition, but that would take a year. Yet it's a very important part of our programming.

Hall: Putting things together that belong together?

Blore: Or those that don't belong together depending on . . . well, on the prototype tape you heard Jack Angel referring to a record about hurting each other "and it's a shame people do that." And the next thing you heard on the tape was something that had nothing to do with the statement. It was a little girl and boy talking about Santa Claus, the little girl saying that Santa Claus doesn't exist. And, just because Angel said "hurting each other," the concept is that the little girl is trying to hurt the little boy, telling him that there is no Santa Claus, that Santa Claus doesn't exist. That thought would never have entered your mind if it hadn't been juxtaposed against Angel saying that people try to hurt each other. If you'd heard anything else prior to the little girl and boy, it would have changed the whole meaning. That's what I mean by the psychology of juxtaposition.

We have, for example, coming out of the news, this fellow shouting: "Damn everything but the circus!" Thus, he's referring to all of the things you just heard in the newscast. Right? But if you'd come out just previously and said: "That was so-and-so and the story of a broken-hearted love affair" then the statement about the circus refers to the broken heart and the guy saying: "Screw everything."

Hall: On the tape I heard earlier, I heard a word like "damn." That's no longer a taboo in radio, is it?

Blore: I don't think so, but it wasn't used just for the sake of honesty. If we came on the air and said, "Darn everything but the circus!" or, "To heck with everything but the circus!" it wouldn't be saying the same thing. There's nothing wrong with "damn" in the right context. We're trying to be more adult in everything we do. I didn't mean . . . well, this has nothing to do with sex. When I say adult, I'm talking about sophistication. I'm talking about us treating our listeners as though they were *thinking human beings.*

Hall: Now that you brought it up, I did notice that the prototype tape was sexy.

Blore: Yeah, but that was only because we were doing a report on: Sex isn't funny. Well, we had all of the teasers in and so forth. If we were doing a report on . . . .

Hall: So those are the "elements" that surround the report?

Blore: Yes, and if the report was on polls then you'd think we were a very political station, because we'd be promoting our feature with items of similar nature. And if the feature was on bio-feedback, you'd say: "Wow, they're into all of these physiological things." Whatever report we're featuring during the week, the station takes on that particular image so we can get people interested in that report when it arrives on the air on Thursday, Friday or whenever it is. We spend several days building up to the report. You see, when we do the research on a report, we obviously can't put all of the information into the report itself. There's just too much information. So, all of this information is filtered down to the writers and the air personalities, and thus a lot of their "fascinating" items—a lot of their programming elements—take on that particular flavor. So the whole station, for example, might be pushing toward bio-feedback.

Hall: This report comes once a week?

Blore: That all depends. They could come more often or less often. Here's a critical thing about this format: Our actions are not dictated by the clock. We dictate *to* the clock. I mean that if a report is ready to go on the air Thursday—and by ready, I mean everything is ready—then it goes on the air. But if it's not perfect, we don't put it on the air merely because the clock says it's time to go. We can put it on the air a week from Thursday. It doesn't make any difference. We don't say how many records we're going to play an hour. That, too, makes no difference, because we use records to fill up the areas where we don't have any fascination. If we have a particularly fascinating hour, we might play only three records, but if we have an hour with nothing in it, we might play 15 records.

Hall: In other words, you're not going to have an air personality saying: "Here's Glenn Miller leading up to the news?"

Blore: Right. The most important aspect is that we don't have to have any particular thing on the air—so much of this and so much of that—because if we did, the quality of what we're trying to accomplish would suffer.

Hall: A lot of program directors are worried about where the next single is coming from, what album cuts to play and how many—all of that doesn't concern you at all, does it?

Blore: No. Again, we are not after the record-buying audience. The people who're listening to us are not primarily interested in hearing hit records. The people who'll be listening to us will primarily be those who respond to our way of life. Or, we respond to *their* way of life—that's a better way of putting it.

Hall: To me, well, from what you've said of this format, it's very complex.

Blore: It's incredibly complex. It's immense. And that's why . . . well, when I would sit for hours and hours dreaming up a little thing to put on KFWB in the old days, and then put it on the air, and the next day it would be all over the nation, I'd be really irritated that other program directors weren't thinking those things up for themselves. But I'm not too concerned about that here with KIIS. They might be able to copy the surface of it, but if they only copy the surface, then their radio station is going to be saccharine, and it's going to be in a lot of trouble. So, there won't be many successful KIIS formats, though they'll all try it. For a while. Like KABL when it went on the air in San Francisco. We had a KABL in every city; they all tried it until they went broke. Now those stations are back rocking or they're all-news. Only KABL and a few others, like the one in Dallas that I think KABL was patterned after—it's been there forever and is really a good radio station—have been successful.

Hall: That's where Gordon McLendon got the idea then, that Dallas station?

Blore: Gordon McLendon has enough ideas of his own. He doesn't get them from anybody. If there really is a god in this industry, it's him. He's the one, boy . . . he did it.

Hall: You once worked for McLendon, didn't you?

Blore: Yes.

Hall: Did you help build KELP in El Paso?

Blore: Yes.

Hall: Did you work for Todd Storz, too?

Blore: No. I just knew him, and respected him, back in those days everybody knew everybody, because there were only 10 guys in the business. I mean, about 10 guys in radio who were doing things. And when you had a chance to talk to one of them, that was super. Wow. And when Todd Storz put on his deejay conventions, that was the most miraculous thing that happened in the industry. The deejays and the record companies screwed it up for people, but the idea was a super one in the first place. And the first one in Kansas City . . . remember that? Were any of you guys around then? [Both KIIS program director Sonny Melendrez and MGM Records promotional executive Ernie Farrell were in the room during the interview.] The first Todd Storz meeting was in Kansas City. We were snowed in, and there just wasn't the crap that went on in Miami the next year, which really had to kill everything, you know. Anyway, it was a good idea. Todd Storz was a brilliant man. I talked to him many times, but never did work for him.

Hall: Are you worried about this new format of yours at all?

Blore: I'm scared to death. Not that it will work. It's just that it's so immense that . . . well, it's so fragile. Any time you say the things that we're going to say on this radio station—we have so much God, and love, and kindness, and goodness on here—that any time you do that, you face the possibility of becoming a plastic greeting card. You know? And that's one thing we have to guard against. I'm fearful of that. But fear is good. It keeps your guard up. And, if we were all that confident about the format, then it would probably be dull.

Hall: Who were the best program directors you've ever known in your life?

Blore: Other than me? Gordon McLendon, although he was never really a program director; he was the best. Don Keyes. Bill Stewart, although he was a bit of a dictator. Yeah, Bill Stewart was brilliant, but he was pretty dictatorial. Ask some of the people who worked for him. Ted Randal is a good program director. Let me see . . . now those were the older guys. One of the newer program directors who I've come to respect is Ron Jacobs, probably one of the best in the world. At least, while he was at KHJ.

Hall: He's having a tough time right now. [Jacobs was then programming KGB-AM-FM, San Diego. He later did well with the station.]

Blore: He's having a tough time because it's a totally new concept. And it doesn't make any difference with his concept whether he get to be No. 1 or not. That's not what he's after. He's after . . . well, he's doing something remarkable. Every other station in the nation is concerned right now about changing FM call letters to something other than their AM call letters so the FM station can have a dignity and an identity of its own. Ron is doing the opposite—he changed his FM back, as you know. So his AM and FM stations are simulcasting, and he's programming FM concepts on AM, which I think is kind of unusual, and a gutsy thing to do. If he believes in it that much, it has to have quality because he has a quality brain. He's a good guy, a super brain. Tom Rounds is another good program director. That fellow who programs the Drake station in San Francisco . . . Sebastian Stone. I understand—and from everything I've heard about him—he's a brilliant guy.

Hall: You haven't heard his station?

Blore: I don't think so. Wait, didn't he do WOR-FM in New York? Then I've heard his work. Another young guy who's going to be a really strong part of this industry is Jack McCoy, program director of KCBQ in San Diego. Jack and Sonny Melendrez are the only two program directors I considered for KIIS. And Gary Allyn. Gary Allyn, working with zero, has created the His and Hers and Ours formats in San Diego, with one guy helping him. Then, of course, the best program director of all, Sonny Melendrez.

Hall: What about air personalities you've heard or known over the years?

Blore: The best one of all, and there's no question about it, was Don McKinnon.

Hall: It's weird, but a lot of people say that. Why?

Blore: Because I trained him. No. I don't know why, unless because he was so perfect ... everything he said was relevant. You never heard him say anything that didn't matter. And yet, he always said it in such a witty way. He had an incredible brain. He was very, very funny about things that mattered. And that's the thing. Many deejays today can be funny, but so what, you've heard a joke. However, when you're funny about things that matter, wow! And that's what Don McKinnon was.

Hall: Have you heard Don Imus of WNBC in New York?

Blore: Yes. I think he's certainly one of the top guys around today.

Hall: He doesn't crack jokes.

Blore: Right. He and Robert W. Morgan don't use jokes; they use humor and today's the time for humor instead of jokes. A good example is Bob Hope, who could not sell a comedy album. And you love him, he's funny. Hear him and you laugh, but you don't want to hear the jokes again. But as for George Carlin—not in his television appearances but in his album—you hear him and you say: "Wow, that's humor." Or Bob Newhart, where you want to hear the things over and over again. They're not jokes, they're humor. Listen, for example, to Don Imus on those telephone calls—you can hear him again and again. Because they're funny. And the reason you can listen to them again is that they're humor, not jokes. The difference between jokes and humor is humanism. If it doesn't have any human qualities, it's a joke.

Hall: What would you say the program directors of the nation need in order to improve their radio stations? To bring Top 40 radio back to life, for example?

Blore: Well, let's not think even about bringing Top 40 back to life ... because maybe that's had it. Maybe we shouldn't bring it back. To bring a station that plays records back to life could have nothing to do with Top 40 ... it might be something totally new. I think that program directors should be less concerned—again, this is so obvious—with their audience than they are with their staff, and more concerned about what records they're going to play. If you think about your audience you have to think about them in deeper terms than just what records they like. They must have other likes and dislikes. If you start considering whether or not you can supply his other likes ... well, then suddenly you're doing the listener a favor. You're complimenting him for being more than just a record listener. Although there's been many "record" radio stations done, and successfully, there's none today that I'd like to be a part of, although I admire the success of the stations that are just there to play music. That's all they're for, and they do it very well. Though they don't happen to be my cup of tea, that doesn't mean I don't respect those kinds of radio stations.

Hall: What percent of importance would you put on the records of your radio station?

Blore: At KHJ here in Los Angeles, I would say that records are 90 percent of the station. At KIIS, I would say that records are only 10 percent of the station.

Hall: Why was KFWB so important? Why was it so unique? What made it such a copied station across the nation?

Blore: Number one, its success. It was the first time that rock 'n' roll had been programmed in a major market.

Hall: The first?

Blore: Well, there are others who'll say that Dallas was a major market. And, indeed, it is. And was. But in the top five markets, boy! You just didn't dare put on rock 'n' roll.

Hall: Oh, I see.

Blore: Because that was where the heavy advertisers were.

Hall: San Francisco was then a major advertising center—much more than it is now?

Blore: Right. So that's what was holding rock radio back in the larger cities. But what we did at KFWB was take all of the theories—that I had developed, that Bill Stewart had developed, along with McLendon, and Todd Storz—theories that until that time were just theories, and we made them laws. You know? Because of the strength that I had in those days, I just had to say, "This is the way it is," and everyone said: "Okay, fine." Also, the programming concepts were not being bent by the sales department, which was one of the huge problems then throughout radio. I could say, "This is the programming concept," and that was the way it was, and the sales department had to work around it. Of course the salesmen were happy to do it, because of the tremendous amounts of dollars flowing into the radio station. But counting more than all of the theories, was the showmanship of the station. Bill Gavin once said about me that I brought show business to radio. And that would have to be what KFWB added, and what everyone began to sort of copy. Today I go around the world making speeches on behalf of radio—I've spoken in every country where there is English-speaking radio except South Africa—and in every one of these countries I still see things that I created for KFWB. That's true. And what has it been, 10 years?

Hall: Still being used?

Blore: XXXX [name of radio station], I gave them that format and they're still using it. Which is a criticism, incidentally. I'm saying: Isn't it a pity that they're still using it?

Hall: But there's hope for radio, isn't there?

Blore: Radio is the most magnificent medium ever. Because you're dealing with people, you're dealing with their head and their heart. There's nothing in the way in the communication between you and the listener—radio is a direct pipeline to the heart. ZAP! If you do it right.

Hall: Well, then you're still excited about radio?

Blore: I didn't know how much. Because people used to ask if I missed radio and I'd say, "Nope!" I didn't miss it. I was very happy doing my commercials; I was into a lot of public service stuff. You know. Like the Love spots which I really enjoyed doing. And I was doing more for the community, really, than I had been programming a radio station. I had the time and the inclination to do something for my community. The

Martin Luther King thing you heard was a thrilling thing to do, but I did it mostly for me, and I would like it to be on the air as a public service thing.

Hall: Do you consciously realize you created a masterpiece in the Martin Luther King bit?

Blore: I realize . . . I like it a lot.

Hall: How long had you had this vision of a radio station like KIIS?

Blore: A couple of years, I imagine. But I didn't realize I had it so completely. When Ken Draper and I used to talk philosophy, I used to mention love a lot. But I didn't realize until now how totally I had thought out such a format, until I sat down to put it on a piece of paper one day. And two or three hours later I had 14 or 15 pages about what this station is and should be. And we have changed it many times, visibly, since then, as we get into the format and find that a particular thing doesn't work, but another does. And we're still working.

Chuck Blore, second interview

INTRO: Here, Chuck Blore explains why all of his dreams in regard to the new KIIS format hadn't succeeded as quickly as he had planned.

Hall: How come it took a year for you to reach your present level of programming with KIIS?

Blore: There were just so many problems that I had no idea existed. I had thought it was going to be like several years ago when I ran KFWB in Los Angeles, when all I had to do was say something and all of a sudden magic happened and it was a fact. But at KIIS—I'd say something and it went off into this giant sponge, never to be heard from again. It kind of seeped away.

Hall: And that was because the people there didn't know?

Blore: Because none of us knew what to do. I'd say, "Let's do this." And they'd say, "What is that?" Because they'd never done it before. In everything we did, there was no place to go to learn. We had to do it right there, learn it on the air. So, the lessons were very expensive, because we'd work on something for two or three months and then the new ratings would come out and we'd say, "Ah Ha! Here's where we goofed and here's where we didn't." We had to wait, for the ratings services to tell us whether we were right or wrong. For example, we got very big, very quickly, in the women-only area. But that's not what we wanted, so we changed our radio station considerably. In the beginning, we had sounded like we were owned by Hallmark greeting cards, all lacy and frilly. We had so many things on the air about the basic thrust—the celebration of life, the positive attitudes toward everything, the looking at love over and over again in its many aspects—we had these little cassettes that we would drop in to continue the mood—sustainers. We have found out now that we should have three or four every hour. But we didn't know what to do in the early days. We'd put on six. We'd put on two. We'd have to put them on and listen. We had no reference about how to program them. Or any standard by which we could say, "This is good and that was bad." Back in the old days of rock when Todd Storz was doing his thing in one area, Gordon McLendon in another, and I somewhere else, we could all relate to each other—and we all did. We talked together a lot. Discussed things that worked and things that didn't. And when KFWB was going strong, it was a combination of all those proven things. Gordon proved the value of local news; Todd proved the value of repetitive music. I proved the value of the show biz aspect of radio, you know? But at least you had a point of reference, because many things had been proven over a period of time. But the things that we were trying with KIIS had not been proven elsewhere.

As a matter of fact, you may recall that one of the things I was trying to do was make the station totally clichéless. Well, we'd put things on the air and the listeners would very quickly tell us whether they agreed with us or not. We could see in the ratings that they were acting positively, negatively, and forcefully. It was a very reactive audience, what I call the "collective genius." It's not an idea as much as putting into words the feelings that a lot of people have. There exists a collective genius—it's the mass audience. Now, you and I could sit here and listen to a record and we might like it, but we don't know if it's a hit record or not. Nobody knows. Name the top record producer; they do not know. Nobody really knows except the audience. Put that record on the air, and the collective genius says yes or no. And they're never, ever wrong. You could go to a movie and enjoy it or not enjoy it, and you'd never know if it was going to reach out to the masses and be a hit or not. But if you fill that movie house up and sit there and pay attention, not only will you know if it's a good movie or not, but whether it's funny or sad. All these things will be told to you by that audience, and you are a partner in that collective genius during the movie. But, move those people out of the room and sit there alone again and you will suddenly lose your barometer. It is that collective genius that is never wrong.

A Broadway show is the same thing. You can get the very best people as writers, actors, stage managers, costumers, lighting technicians, musicians—really experts. And what they do is go out of town to open the play because none of those experts are really sure that they have anything worth a damn—not until they bring in these untrained, theatrically-uneducated people to tell them whether their theater is any good or not. That audience will say this part is good, that one is not so good, but it's done collectively. Well, this same type of collective genius works on radio formats. They say: This is good; that is poor. But in order to fully exploit the collective genius and use it as a barometer, you must use control. You can put on only one thing at a time for them to judge. You couldn't, for example, put on a sports program and then change your music policy, because you wouldn't know what they would be reacting to. That's obvious, of course, but nevertheless using this collective genius as a gauge takes a long, long time.

Hall: What have you been doing—manipulating this collective genius?

Blore: Constantly. Well, not manipulating, because I don't think you can manipulate them. But exposing things to them. Asking: "Do you like this? Do you like that?" The things they like, we leave on. The things they don't like no longer exist. This is a good time for this interview because it's only now—and it's been damned near a year and a half—that this station is coming together. I wanted so much not to sound like a typical radio station—I wanted people to know it was a different station the instant they tuned in. Well, they knew that . . . but the fact of the matter is that it wasn't a radio station. It was just a collection of programming stuff, you know?

Hall: Who helped organize it into a radio station?

Blore: One of the happiest associations I've had in radio is when Ted Atkins came to spend six months with us. That's all he had to spend, and that's all we knew he could spend with us. But in those six months he put much organization into the station; he built programming foundations that we are still using. We needed something to build on, and he put down all of those bricks, and all of the mortar.

Hall: You were the theoretical man and he was the practical?

Blore: The people at the station used to call us the poet and the picayune. I was creating all of these beautiful, ethereal things, but it was Ted who picked at them and put them in place. He would say: "This fits here, and this relates to that and fits there." But once the foundation was there, it was fairly easy to put the other things on . . . to see if they worked. Because all of a sudden things were working in concert. Once we had a foundation for the format, things didn't seem to be quite so breakable. The things that we put on the air that worked were solid and pulled their share of the load. And we got into much more contemporary thoughts and ideas and language. An example would be the cassettes—the mood sustainers. They used to be like this: "Love looked at hate, and cried." A lovely thought—and it fits. But they were all like that. There was just too much of it! The station sounded dainty and feminine, which was not what we wanted. We brought in Don Richmond for a wry look at a sports type of program—not reporting sports, but giving an amusing look at things in sports. And we began to toughen up the other things. The cassettes, for instance, became more like: "You cannot leave footprints in the sands of time while sitting on your butt . . . ." After all, who wants to leave buttprints in the sands of time? And another one, very contemporary and earthy, was: "They made a movie of my sex life and it was rated G." These kinds of things. And even today we're very careful not to be ethereal.

We now know that we must create, write, and produce—because of the music rotation pattern—41 little "cassettes" each week. We create, write, and produce eight little mini-dramas, which are the intros into the records—things which expose those given records in a new light, put a new viewpoint on the lyrics of a song, reveal the song in a different aspect so the listener might really relate to it. These mini-dramas to a record are like act one and act two of a play and the record itself is act three. We now have one of those an hour. We had tried earlier to have two of those an hour. We even tried with just one every four hours, but one an hour seems to work nicely. We've now begun to produce those mini-dramas for the oldie records. They make listening to radio a nice surprise for the listener when the curtain goes up and you hear Dusty Springfield with "There's a Brand New Me," for example, which we just did the other day. Anyway, those are a valuable part of the format.

Hall: Do you do different ones for the same record to give variety?

Blore: Yeah. For example, "The Way We Were" was so big for so long that the first mini-drama was about a guy talking to a girl painter, telling her that her paintings are all misty, and that she should be more contemporary. She says no, and the vocal on the tune starts out: "Memories . . . ." That's only a brief explanation of that particular mini-drama, but you get the idea. We did maybe five different versions for that song . . . it was an especially easy record to work with. Little plays. The most we've done on any song so far is five. Normally, just one is all that's needed. And sometimes, two.

The problem we've found so far is that today new hits are not born fast enough. We'll spot a record coming onto the *Billboard* magazine Hot 100 Chart and say, "We've got to watch that one." When it gets up above 50 on the chart, we'll do a mini-drama, because we know it's a strong, moving record. But there may be only two of those fast moving records a week that were not already in the top 50 last week, you know? And the top 50 doesn't change that fast. The bottom 50 changes furiously. Records are not coming into the top 50 fast enough for us to keep the kind of rotation pattern on the mini-dramas that we would like. I would like to have 10 a week if I could. If there were 10 new hits every week, we'd really have it made, because there would be all of these nice musical things happening for the KIIS format.

Hall: You have the cassettes and the mini-dramas. What other features are involved in the KIIS format that have developed since you first started it?

Blore: We have something called "90 Seconds," which is very interesting—a feature that takes a vicarious look at something you would not or could not do. For example, we spent a day in a patrol car. Then we come on the air with the statement: "KIIS spends 90 seconds in a patrol car"; "KIIS spends 90 seconds backstage"; "KIIS spends 90 seconds in a nudist colony"; Or: "KIIS spends 90 seconds with a hooker on Western Avenue."

Hall: Is that where hookers hang out in Los Angeles?

Blore: Would you like an address? Anyway, we have a man spend a day doing it, then edit the tape down to about 90 seconds. The patrol car bit: the first thing you hear is a guy saying, "All right. Lay down, flat on the ground." It's really a dramatic scene where they're arresting this guy. There's a little time-passage sound effect, then a woman runs up to the car yelling, "They're after me!" And the feature dramatizes how the policemen handle the situation. We go through their whole day like this and you hear just as they're going off shift, one of the policemen saying, "Whatta ya bet, we're going to hear them call us on the way back in." Then you hear the two-way radio with, "Car 385 . . . calling car 385." We've gone through a whole exciting day with these people. They're awfully hard to cut down to 90 seconds because the events are so intense and dramatic.

We also have another feature that has stayed with us since the KIIS format went on the air called "Out of His Mind." It's a feature where significant people say things you'd not ordinarily expect them to say. Our interviewer asks not what is your next record, or how did you get into show business, but like: "Do you pray? What's your favorite childhood story? Tell me about your dreams." You come up with a lot of really interesting insights into people which you never hear anywhere else. The feature states: "This is Roger Miller . . . out of his mind." Then Miller says something and the feature ends: "That was Roger Miller . . . out of his mind, over KIIS." They're fascinating little things.

Hall: What about the big features?

Blore: Those are our proudest deals. We have a research department that spends eight weeks researching a feature. Well, what is a feature? On Easter, we did a feature called "The Miracles." What we did was dramatize contemporary miracles. The biblical ones, we just said they existed. They were easy to deal with because they were distant. But how do you explain the contemporary ones?

We used to have one feature a week. It was just too often, because we couldn't do the quality things we liked. Often we were getting features on the air merely because it was Tuesday, not because we had a good feature ready to go. Now, we may go six weeks without a feature, because we may do research and find out we haven't anything valid, and we have to start over. But, normally, features hit the air roughly every 10 days. We're doing one on the brain, another on psychosurgery. When everyone was talking about the movie *The Exorcist,* we did one on exorcism. Our feature on Halloween was narrated by Vincent Price.

Hall: You say now that the format has more or less jelled the way you wanted it to?

Blore: Yes. Of course, there are still constant changes. It must never sound like the same radio station two days in a row . . . no, I'm sorry, it must *always* sound like the same radio station, but you must never hear the same things.

Hall: How are you going to start syndicating the features, the mini-dramas—all the special things within the KIIS format—to other radio stations?

Blore: John Wolfe, manager of the station, will do it. He's taking some time away from his regular job to syndicate the KIIS content. And all it's called is: "The Concept." Some of the stations—we already have four besides KIIS—are only using parts of The Concept. Ted Atkins, who now manages WTAE in Pittsburgh, was our first customer. He's playing different music on WTAE. His station has a much harder on-air sound, because KIIS doesn't have any real extremes in music . . . no audience chasers. Ted's station, on the other hand, is heavily into oldies and plays a lot of harder hits. I frankly didn't know if the KIIS concept would fit. But it fits beautifully. In fact, he's developed into one of our greatest boosters. Ted gets everything, but he ignores our music and plays his own.

Hall: Is the price to the station based on a rate card?

Blore: I'm not really sure. Based on the size of the market, I guess.

Hall: And the production firm for the concept is at the station?

Blore: Yes. I produce them. I write some of them, but I produce them at KIIS and they go out, arriving at the other stations the day after being aired, because we're about a week and a half ahead.

Hall: What's the name of the syndication firm?

Blore: The Concept.

Hall: Are you a partner?

Blore: I'm personally a partner in the syndication with KIIS and John is running it.

Hall: Is the music provided, too?

Blore: It can be. It is on the mini-dramas. In any case, everything that is on KIIS is a part of the syndication package. Except for the progressive rock stations, which made it very big in many markets and not so well in others, this is the first time that I can recall that a philosophy has been designed into a format.

Hall: Was there a philosophy behind KFWB when you programmed it years ago?

Blore: Sure.

Hall: Larry and Toni Greene once told me that they thought you orchestrated the KFWB format, even the air personalities.

Blore: That was the big difference, I think, between KFWB and other stations of that kind in its time. It was a well-put-together station. KIIS is getting to be that way, too.

Hall: Do you feel that it was worth your while to get involved with KIIS?

Blore: Probably had I known how hard it was going to be, I would have hesitated a little longer. But this format just had to be born. And it's developing. It's so exciting now, because it isn't where we were a year ago . . . it isn't quite what we set out to do. It's better. It's changing and constantly evolving. And it's constantly creative . . . .

OUTRO: Ratings at KIIS were better than ever in its history when the station was sold. Thus, the dream for a new format ended. Blore today produces and syndicates the mini-dramas mentioned in the interview, often performing himself. They are currently being featured on more than two dozen radio stations. Sonny Melendrez, mentioned in this interview, is now a disk jockey with KMPC, Los Angeles. KIIS now simulcasts part of the day with the FM station previously known as KKDJ, now also called KIIS. KROQ, a station with an excellent staff, but a lousy signal, went off the air for a while. Blore, incidentally, continues to produce the best commercials in radio. If you've listened to a radio for more than 15 minutes in your entire life these past 10 years, you've undoubtedly heard at least one of his commercials.

GEORGE WILSON

George Wilson, first interview

INTRO: George Wilson, today president of Bartell Broadcasters with headquarters in New York, may hold the distinction of programming more No. 1 radio stations than any man in history—and those stations included formats ranging from Top 40 to r&b. Just recently, he sought to become owner of WADO, an all-Spanish radio station in New York. Once a relatively shy person, Wilson today is an outspoken defender of programming as a respected craft—worthy of a respectable salary. He was a featured speaker in Chicago at the 1976 annual convention of the National Association of Broadcasters, and at Radio 77, an annual radio/record industry meeting in Sydney, Australia, in June-July 1976. Wilson is the type of person who believes in developing the industry; he devotes a considerable part of his time—without fanfare, without praise—to helping others build a radio career. Here, he talks of his own career with its ups and downs, and he discusses his radio philosophy.

Wilson: I don't know if you've got stock questions.

Hall: No, I ask things like: When did you start in radio?

Wilson: Do you think people care about that?

Hall: Yeah. Everybody has to start out someplace small and .... anyway, I'm interested. Where did you start?

Wilson: Charleston, S.C., for WOKE—the call letters then were WHAM.

Hall: When and where did you first become a program director?

Wilson: My first actual program director's job would have been, I guess, at WMRB in Greenville, S.C.

Hall: At how many stations have you been program director? You told me once, and all I remember is that it was something like 15 or 20.

Wilson: I really don't know, Claude.

Hall: Well, then you became manager in ... ?

Wilson: This is my third manager's job. I managed WMBR in Jacksonville, Fla., and WSHO in New Orleans, La. Now, WDRQ-FM in Detroit, Mich.

Hall: And how many of those have been No. 1?

Wilson: All of the stations I've programmed except one—WITH in Baltimore, Md., the only station that didn't make decent ratings. That was funny because I probably had the best crew there that I've had at any radio station. Bob Foster, Paul (Fat Daddy) Johnson ... in fact, one of the things that used to make me laugh was when

202

WMCA in New York made all the hullabaloo about having a full-time black disk jockey, Frankie Crocker, on a Top 40 station. We had Fat Daddy way before that.

Hall: That was around 1967?

Wilson: Maybe 1965 or '66.

Hall: When did you work at WOKY in Milwaukee?

Wilson: April 1, 1968, I went there to help David Moorhead, who's now general manager of KMET-FM in Los Angeles. He was program director of WOKY then. He started with me back in Denver in 1959 as my all-night man. He was succeeded by John Rook, a consultant for a while with WCFL in Chicago. That was Rook's first job.

Hall: What were the call letters of the Denver station?

Wilson: KTRN, which is now KTLK. Anyway, at WOKY in Milwaukee, after Dave left to go to the West Coast, I became program director. We've had great success.

Hall: Before WOKY, you were where?

Wilson: WHAT in Philadelphia. A black station. I was program director.

Hall: So, you've actually programmed just about all of the major formats—country music back in the South, and . . . .

Wilson: And I've done middle-of-the-road—though my station would probably have been called all over the road—and black programming, but mostly Top 40.

Hall: How old were you when you first became a program director?

Wilson: I've been a program director or manager the past 18 years. I'm 43 years old now.

Hall: A program director 18 years! A while ago we were talking about the pay scale of most program directors.

Wilson: I've had a big campaign just by myself, and I've been trying to find ways to . . . well, it's an unfair situation for a program director, who's responsible for building ratings and, if he's a good program director, he's also worried about the profit-and-loss picture of a radio station—the bottom line. He gets the ratings and then, because of the ratings, the sales manager is able to sell time on the station. Because of the sales, the general manager and the sales manager earn a commission, which gives them added income. I've always felt it rather unfair that a program director couldn't be involved in some kind of incentive program so that he could participate in the extra earnings that come as a result of his good ratings. In my opinion, most program directors are very underpaid.

Hall: Have you ever worked on a point basis—where, if you get higher ratings, you get paid more?

Wilson: I have personally . . . and it didn't do anything to make me work harder, but it certainly was nice. I remember on some stations having it so that if the jocks increased the ratings, they got X number of dollars. It was good for the jocks and good for the programmer. But today, in a much more competitive situation, the program director loses his job if he doesn't make ratings, yet if he does well in the ratings, the sales manager and the manager make all the money. And I just don't think it's right.

Hall: Using the point basis, did you get a higher salary?

Wilson: It wasn't a higher salary. It was a bonus. If the ratings went up so many points you got a bonus.

Hall: Do any program directors today get that type of bonus?

Wilson: Not that I know of. But there should be something set up where by they could profit as the result of their work. It's not that they would or would not take a specific job because of that type of thing, because most program directors are in this type of work for the love of it. The ones I know, they'd do the job if you paid them in green stamps, as long as they could be creative. I think anybody who's a program director is an egomaniac . . . anybody in radio for that matter . . . and maybe the record industry. Money doesn't matter really, until you get to a certain age. And maybe that's why it's beginning to bother me. I'm getting older.

Hall: Do you know of any station where they reward their air personalities with a bonus?

Wilson: I don't know of any offhand, but I'm sure there are some.

Hall: Because I'd heard that Larry Lujack was only going to stay with WLS in Chicago until he got his bonus. I don't know what kind of bonus that was, though.

Wilson: If he got the bonus, maybe he could afford a suit.

Hall: Do you have any type of reward system set up at your stations yet?

Wilson: (Laughs.) If they do well in the ratings, they get to keep their jobs.

Hall: You've taken some men . . . men who weren't ostensibly program directors before . . . and put them into good positions.

Wilson: Well Rook and Buzz Bennett were two of my men . . . and, of course, Jack McCoy, who in my opinion is the best program director in the nation, bar none. Now, he has the opportunity at KCBQ in San Diego. Well, while I think Bennett did a good job there—he's dynamite, no question about it, and it's very difficult to put a man into a position following Buzz Bennett, but so far Jack McCoy has shown that he can handle the situation. We'll just have to wait and see about our other choices. I guess what I look for mostly is dedication. When you talk about Rook, he works 18 to 24 hours a day. The first questions Jack McCoy asked about KCBQ was: "Is there a cot in my office so I can stay there?" The program directors that I like are the ones totally dedicated to radio. I think that's the way to win. Some of the older guys have gotten into a money-worry situation, but most of the younger guys are not really worried about making money. They're worried about doing the job.

Hall: The Bartell chain is now beginning to put more and more of its emphasis in FM, isn't it?

Wilson: Well, we've felt . . . actually, Dick Casper, who was the head of Bartell when I joined it, had always felt, far more than most people I've known, that FM was not on its way, as everybody else thought, but *here.* He started the whole ball rolling, as far as we're concerned, with WMYQ (now called 96X) in Miami. We program not just for gross numbers, and in the new ARB ratings that just came out, we did very well in the areas where we were trying to win. We feel we still have a way to go, but we're very definitely already a factor in the market—No. 1 in midday with women, which is the most saleable; No. 1 with teens at night, which is a category that's very important. Overall, I think the station is rated about top three, but I don't have the actual figures with me.

Hall: Where are your next FM stations slated? I know that you lost the Milwaukee FM you'd planned to buy because of an uproar from classical music fans who wanted to keep that particular station classical.

Wilson: We're waiting on Federal Communications Commission approval now for a station in St. Louis. (KSLQ is now on the air there.) And, of course, we just recently took WDRQ in Detroit to a rock format. Dick Galkin, who's president of Bartell Broadcasting now, believes that FM radio is a viable force.

Hall: Why is it that many broadcasters still do not place much value in FM, even today?

Wilson: I don't know. I remember that last year at the International Radio Programming Forum in Chicago someone asked James Storer why he sold us his FM stations in Miami and Detroit. His statement if I remember correctly was that he was in the broadcasting business to make money. But obviously if he were to check the billings of WMYQ in Miami this year, he'd be rather shocked. Because it's definitely making quite a bit of money. But I can't answer why people still haven't put more faith in FM; people just have different opinions, I guess. If people don't believe in FM, maybe they ought to call Jim Schulke. He could give them some pointers. He's keeping the wolf away from the door pretty well, and via FM too.

Hall: In the stations that you've programmed over the years, how does the playlist differ now from then? Was it longer in the old days?

Wilson: I don't think we've ever had a definite number of records. Even today we don't hold to a given number at WOKY in Milwaukee or KCBQ in San Diego. We do at the FM stations, because of the nature of their formats. We only play hits on the FM stations. We don't try to play new records; we let the other stations make them hits first. That way we keep a more familiar music sound on the air. But in Milwaukee, we don't have a given set number of records. Any station like that which does put a limit on the number of records it will play is silly. You play what the station needs, what the market will bear.

Hall: But don't you at least repeat the bigger sellers more often?

Wilson: Oh, we have systems. All of our stations have systems of play. All operate on the same systems as to how the records are exposed.

Hall: Even the FM stations?

Wilson: Well, there are places in the system for the exposure of new records that aren't on the FM stations. The stations sound different, of course, because we adjust the records to fit the market. San Diego is much more progressive than Milwaukee, which is kind of an old-fashioned area. Everyone teases about Milwaukee being the bubblegum capitol of the world, but that isn't true either. We play country records, for example. We were the first one to play Lynn Anderson's and Charley Pride's hit singles.

Hall: Do you still play bubblegum records?

Wilson: Sure. We'll play anything the people want to hear.

Hall: Why are some Top 40 stations backing off from that type of product?

Wilson: I think—of course, maybe I shouldn't talk about this—but I feel very strongly about stations that *judge* records ... well, that's the reason some "program directors" are losing Top 40 ratings, because they don't do what Top 40 *is*. Top 40 is a reflection of your community's musical tastes or whatever else you put on your radio station.

And now, all of a sudden, we've got a few people who would like to lead and teach, and that's not Top 40 radio.

Hall: But they claim that the crowd that goes out and buys an Osmond record is not the type they want listening to their radio station. Is that a fair decision on their part?

Wilson: They don't want them listening to their radio station? Well, then they shouldn't be in Top 40 radio. Because Top 40 is gross numbers. And if those numbers want Osmonds, play Osmonds. If they want Led Zeppelin, play the Zeppelin. Whenever you try to judge what the other man wants and does not want, then I think you get out of Top 40 radio. Then you have to get into some other kind of radio. Because around the country, if you'll check ratings, stations that are trying album cuts and not playing this kind of record or not doing this and not doing that are the ones that are suffering. I read articles about Top 40 radio dying. It only dies when the program directors try to be smarter than the listeners are. They are not doing what they're supposed to be doing.

Hall: They're actually limiting their scope of audience then?

Wilson: I feel that if you're a Top 40 station, you mirror the community as best you can. That way, you don't judge anything about what people feel or want to hear in music.

Hall: Are you finding that MOR stations are crossing over into the Top 40 realm?

Wilson: I'm sure that they are in some cases. But, where there's a legitimate Top 40 station, I don't think they've made any inroads. Of course, the only areas I can talk about with any great knowledge are our markets. KOGO does well against KCBQ in San Diego, but only because of baseball. It's not because of any great programming techniques that they have, although KOGO is a very good station. But in Milwaukee there isn't any MOR station that's making us have any worries at WOKY at this point.

Hall: Even in demographics?

Wilson: In ARB, our stations will lead in listeners ages 18-49 in almost every case.

Hall: That includes both men and women?

Wilson: Well, at our stations we only program toward women in the middle of the day. We don't care if we get men and teens; we're after ages 18-49 in women.

Hall: You mean that all of the records are oriented toward women?

Wilson: Everything we do.

Hall: How do you orient the records toward women? Keep the sexy male vocals flowing?

Wilson: If I told you that we'd soon be out of business. But it's no big thing. There are just certain records we believe are offensive to women and some that aren't. We keep paid research people on the phones. We check quite thoroughly to be sure we're playing the right kind of music for the people who're available to our station for each particular daypart.

Hall: Then your research people are calling up the homes and . . . .

Wilson: We have research people who go to homes. They not only ask about music, but what the people are interested in, what's going on in the community, and how we can be better involved in the community. We do an awful lot of research.

Hall: In Milwaukee?

Wilson: Everywhere . . . at all of our stations, on a continuing basis.

Hall: So then you're able to better target your music and your promotions.

Wilson: Right. I've found that it's very difficult for most program directors, as a rule, to do what they have to do. In other words . . . well, as you know, I'm an alcoholic. And without drinking the past couple of years I've felt that although this helped in other areas of my life, as far as programming goes—and I've said this before—I really regret having had to stop drinking. I don't get into the corner bars enough anymore with the shot-and-beer people to find out what they're thinking and talking about. Now, I have my lunches in the decent uptown restaurants, and I'm not talking to our listeners. So I have to regroup my thoughts from time to time and go back and study our people, the average everyday people. We aren't trying to attract the country club set.

Hall: Do you think that you're a better program director now that you've stopped drinking? Or were you better before?

Wilson: Well, I've never thought of myself as a good program director, but I've always felt that I did well at motivating people. They made me *look* like a good program director.

Hall: Then, how come you didn't win at WITH in Baltimore? Was it the signal?

Wilson: The signal wasn't that good, but I think you can sometimes overcome a poor signal. I don't know if you can be a dominant station in a market on a bad signal, and I certainly would never take one on with my eyes open again. But I don't think the signal was our problem . . . that was just one problem. To be honest, probably the biggest reason why we didn't do better was because that was one of the bad times of my life. I was drinking very heavily and I didn't keep tight enough control over the ship, and didn't have total cooperation from management which, of course, is most necessary. That's one of the beautiful things about working with Bartell. The top management people in New York allow us to do our thing. I felt that at WITH we were never allowed to do what we had to do. But there are a lot of reasons why WITH didn't make it under our regime. It did make it at one time under Bob Adams a few years before we got there, so the major problem wasn't the signal. We were doing—or *I* was doing something wrong. But more than that, the ownership of the station at that time jeopardized us, and some of the things we had to do, we couldn't do. Everybody kind of got discouraged, and then the station just went downhill.

Hall: Sometimes, failure starts at the top, doesn't it?

Wilson: In that case, it was definitely true.

Hall: Have you run into many problems with managers over your career?

Wilson: Constantly. Most of the problems in programming come from above. First, a manager goes out and hires a program director from his track record or whatever, and brings him in and then tells him what to do. In these times, a program director must get everything settled before he goes into a station because he *has* to have control. And there's no way that a program director can be told what to do and still accomplish his goals. Why should a manager hire a program director to begin with if he's not going to let him do what he has to do in order to win? If you examine most of the radio stations today that do not have good overall track records, you can usually look at the top management and see why.

Hall: Have you met some good managers, too?

Wilson: Sure. In fact this group that I'm working for now is ideal from the top right on through the air personalities. We probably have a better understanding—at least of any company I've worked for or heard of—about radio. Our managers understand programming, and they allow us to do our job.

Hall: You once mentioned appreciating the talents of Jack Thayer, currently general manager of WGAR in Cleveland.

Wilson: Whatever I know about radio, I learned from a man named Don Burden. He's just the greatest. And when I first got to know about Jack Thayer ... before I really knew him—I've just really gotten to know him well this past year—there were so many Don Burden-isms in Jack Thayer. Or vice versa. Jack is such a warm, relatable person that it has to come out of the radio for him. He gets his people going. He knows how to turn them on and motivate people to do what they have to do. You just can't be around Jack Thayer without being caught up with Jack Thayer. He just has that magnetism to make you want to be a winner.

Hall: Are there a lot of men like that in radio today?

Wilson: Unfortunately, no. I think we've come to a point now where maybe because of the times or maybe because of stricter FCC rules, we don't have all of the fun that we used to have back in the old days when managers could be a little flamboyant and we could do fun things. Managers have a lot more on their minds—or so it seems—than they did in the old days.

Hall: Or maybe you weren't so aware of them then.

Wilson: That's very true. We kinda had a devil-may-care attitude about radio. Again, I sort of think this may be one of the things wrong with Top 40 radio stations today. I remember talking to Kent Burkhart, head of Pacific and Southern Broadcasting. He used to go into a hotel and lock himself in his room and listen to his radio station all day long. I would imagine that if some of the Top 40 operators today had to go into a room and listen to their station 12 hours they'd be climbing the walls in just four, because their stations aren't fun. They're just music machines. Not that I think music machines aren't okay—don't get me wrong, I do. But there has to be more to good radio. Good radio has to be run for the people, get the audience involved. People love to be part of anything. Most Top 40 stations don't make their audience a part of anything.

Hall: Why is it that in spite of the fact every good program director believes in the "personality" approach for radio, the stations that aren't personality prone seem to be the winners more often than not? You can look at market after market, and it's usually the station that does everything by rote, like a jukebox, that's winning.

Wilson: For example?

Hall: Well, I was going to say the typical Drake station, but Bill Drake always argued with me that he had great personalities on all of his stations, and to some extent he has had some very exciting personalities on his stations.

Wilson: I think one of the greatest Top 40 personalities—I don't think so anymore, but I did until a year or so ago—was station KHJ in Los Angeles, one of the greatest personality stations anywhere. Whether it was a hard Drake station or not, it was a dynamite radio station with phenomenal personalities. The only radio station that I can think of which didn't have personalities as such, in my estimation, was WABC in New York—my favorite station in the country other than my own. I've always felt

WABC was the best Top 40 station in the nation, yet it's not a personality station in spite of the fact that anybody who listens to radio in the afternoon in New York knows Dan Ingram, and he does things between the sets. In Chicago, Larry Lujack, lately of WLS, is a personality.

I think Top 40 has changed in the last few years, especially in the morning where you've got to have a personality who does more than just play music. On all of our stations in the morning, we're heavily personality—not the typical Top 40 station. WOKY in Milwaukee, for example, is quite middle-of-the-road in the morning. And to an average radio man, I would assume, Charlie Tuna, both when he was in Los Angeles on KHJ and on our KCBQ in San Diego, is a very good personality.

Hall: In other words, a Drake station can have personalities?

Wilson: Definitely.

Hall: And they were fun to listen to. Is that why he was a winner?

Wilson: Well, it was a combination of many things. If you listen to a radio station that just plays the hits, it's a very dry sound and obviously you can't listen to it for a very long period of time. People like to be entertained, and that's why we're there. Radio has got to be an entertainment medium and not just a music machine.

Hall: How do you feel about women taking a stronger role in radio?

Wilson: As long as it's not forced. There have been two girls who've worked with me who I felt could have been program directors. Mardi Nehrbass is very aware of radio.

Hall: Who is she?

Wilson: She's Jack McCoy's secretary now in San Diego. She was in Milwaukee.

Hall: One woman who has always impressed me as being pretty good in radio was Gini Hobbs, who's married to Ron Nickell in the Drake organization. There are about 20-25 women program directors around the country.

Wilson: Betty Breneman was always very aware. She used to take phone requests at KTRN in Denver when her husband Tom was my nighttime jock. Back in about 1960, I guess. Another woman who has worked for me and is very good is Rochelle Staab.

Hall: Well, I've helped bring about the move of more blacks into Top 40 and MOR radio. Maybe I should try to push women into general radio a little more. Do you know there are about five black jocks in country radio now?

Wilson: Well, certainly Charley Pride has opened some doors in country music for more black jocks. Maybe the reason there aren't more black air personalities in country radio or other kinds of radio is not so much they weren't wanted, but that they didn't want the job.

Hall: A good point. Back to Top 40 radio, what do you see happening in the future? Any trends developing, any problem areas?

Wilson: If there is a problem, and I don't know if there really is one, it's that the people who're programming the stations aren't sticking to Top 40 formats. In other words, everybody's getting so specialized that they're scared they'll rip off some 18-24-year-old men if they don't play album cuts, and if you don't do this you're going to lose those, and if you don't do this you're going to lose these. Everybody gets worried about everything except what they should be worried about and that's mirroring their community. If there's any problem at any Top 40 station, it's because they're not doing what they're supposed to do.

Hall: This is your third venture into management, and you're also national program director. Isn't it difficult to do both?

Wilson: Yes.

Hall: Which one are you going to give up?

Wilson: If I had to make a choice, I'd prefer to stay in programming. We have a unique situation in our company. Although I'm the group program director and we have meetings on basic philosophies and formats, I let each program director program his own station. It's not like they have to do anything—it's not all Wilson. They operate their own show. Gary Price programs WOKY in Milwaukee, Al Casey programs WDRQ in Detroit, Kris Stevens WMYQ in Miami, Jack McCoy KCBQ in San Diego. For example, I spend very little time in San Diego now because we don't have any problems there. Jack McCoy is handling the station very well. He's been with me before; we know each other very well. He knows what to do. Our only problem right now is in Detroit, but Al Casey is in there, and he did quite well in Miami with WMYQ.

Hall: Do you get on the street much to sell?

Wilson: I do some, but selling as such is not one of my strong points. The fact that I'm so familiar with what we do—the audience we're attracting—I can help with sales calls and I do make calls. But I feel very strongly that the manager of a radio station has to delegate authority. The sales manager's job is to make the sales, and I help him whenever I can, but that's his ball game and I let him play it. I do that with everybody. I have a very strong feeling against people interfering. I feel you hire a man to do a job and, if you go in and interfere, it just doesn't work out. In any case, where there has been someone at a higher level who was overbearing, you just don't succeed as well.

Hall: How much involved are you in the music now at the radio stations?

Wilson: I keep very involved. Well, I don't do the actual playlist, although I did that last week in Milwaukee—but please don't put this in there. Our playlist was screwed up, so I went in and straightened it out . . . made store calls and did the whole thing myself to make sure we were playing the right records. Music is the backbone of our radio station, so if I feel we're not playing the right records or if we're staying on some records too long or too short or whatever . . . .

Hall: Can I put some of this into our interview?

Wilson: Well, okay go ahead and use it. I'll call the guy at WOKY to make sure he doesn't get upset.

Hall: How were you able to feel that they weren't playing the right records?

Wilson: I don't know . . . just a feeling. I added 13 records.

Hall: In one week?

Wilson: And they were all chart records. We just weren't playing them. One I noticed immediately was the Bill Withers record. I don't see how anybody could not play the Bill Withers record. And there was an Elton John record I added. And all of the 13 records were selling records.

Hall: Do you still have as good a rapport with the record industry as you had in the old days?

Wilson: You think I had a good rapport? I believe my situation with the record industry fluctuates. I've learned, maybe as a program director or music director or whatever category you want to put me in, that the guy promoting records is doing a job, making a living for his family and so, as long as they're honest ... well, this fellow walks in and says: "Hey, man, I'm getting heat from New York on this record." Well, as long as there's a place to play the record, I'll put it on for him. But if we find out he's just shucking and jiving and it isn't true, then the next time he comes in, he's cut off. But I feel that most of the guys out there in the field are just making a living, and we try to treat them all as nicely as we can. It's very funny. Sometimes you're up with one company for a year, and then you're down, for whatever reason. Basically we try to keep a pretty good rapport.

Hall: I've always thought that, contrary to the old cliché about a record having to have it in the grooves, a radio station could influence sales of any record.

Wilson: I don't think so at all. Very definitely no. If it doesn't have it, you could play it all day long and nothing will happen. If a record is a hit and you're on it early, then you can sell it, meaning that you don't have to wait until it's a proven hit before you play it, but you certainly can't make people buy a bum record.

Hall: How much of a shot does a record get on, say, WOKY?

Wilson: It depends on the type of record. If it's a slow record, we tend to play it a little longer. If it's an upbeat type of record and it doesn't catch on with the public in a couple of weeks, well, we'll probably quit playing it. But I think we're pretty lenient about going back on a record if it makes it somewhere else. I think that many program directors feel against going back on a record, thinking: "Well, we tried it here and it didn't make it." With Billy Joe Royal records, they're usually slow starting in Milwaukee but strong finishing. We go on them, go off, then go back on them again. As long as the people want them, why not?

Hall: Do you think that WOKY is a big factor in record sales in Milwaukee?

Wilson: It is in the total sales of a record. If a record is a hit and we don't play it, we will affect the sales. I don't think we break that many records. Sure, we've broken some records, but most of the time we don't even try. Occasionally we'll try to break a record, but it's not our thing to break records, really. As far as the total potential sales of a record, though, if WOKY doesn't play it, it's not a hit.

Hall: Are you playing many album cuts?

Wilson: Never have played an album cut and never will. Not unless I go into a different kind of radio. Biggest waste in the radio industry is to play album cuts on a Top 40 radio station. I'll take that back. We did play a couple of the longer versions of singles at nighttime, if they were requested enough.

Hall: Like "In-a-Gadda-Davida?"

Wilson: Right. Right.

Hall: But those cuts were already out as singles?

Wilson: Right.

Hall: You don't think that programming album cuts achieves anything?

Wilson: Yes, I do think they achieve something. They achieve losing ratings for you. People who're into album cuts—listeners—aren't into Top 40 radio.

Hall: But doesn't that FM progressive station in Milwaukee do okay?

Wilson: WZMF? They do okay, but only in 18-24-year-old men, like any progressive station.

Hall: But doesn't WOKY, your station, do well in that demographic?

Wilson: We're No. 1 in that category. We're No. 1 in every category in Milwaukee. I'm sure we're No. 1 in every category in San Diego, although I don't have any figures with me. Even so, I'm sure that KPRI in San Diego gets some 18-24-year-old men.

Hall: Looking back over the old days, what was the most fun you ever had at a radio station?

Wilson: Well, I guess when we did the amoeba thing at KTLK, which was KTLN then. I've always had fond memories of that. It was originally Chuck Blore's idea. We just had the afternoon guy go on the air and—I said it was fun, it really wasn't fun after it was all said and done—we just had a man go on the air and say: "There's an amoeba loose in Denver. Don't panic." The college kids picked up on it right away and they started phoning in reports of an amoeba marching down Colorado Boulevard in hip boots and waving banners. It was really funny. Well, it wasn't funny at the ending because we just demolished the phones for two hours, and finally the chief of police came to the radio station and got me.

Hall: What did he do?

Wilson: Kind of carried me off into the night, I guess. He wanted us to stop—to make an announcement on the air. I said we would stop the amoeba thing on the air, but I wouldn't make an announcement. Naturally, the Federal Communications Commission frowns on this sort of promotion quite drastically now. It was bad in that we had so many people upset, but . . . .

Hall: Didn't the listeners ever learn what an amoeba was? What year was that?

Wilson: 1959, I think.

Hall: This was before KIMN became the monster in the market?

Wilson: KIMN was a monster then. They were bigger than we were. KIMN has always been a big station.

Hall: Did you ever beat them?

Wilson: We never beat them totally, but you know, we had segments. We did okay. But we were never the dominant No. 1 radio station in Denver.

Hall: What happened to cause the demise of KTLN?

Wilson: I don't really know what happened with KTLN. I got fired.

Hall: Because of the amoeba stunt?

Wilson: No. For drinking. I was doing KRIZ in Phoenix and KTLN at the same time . . . for Dick Wheeler . . . and my drinking became a problem.

Hall: What caused you to drink?

Wilson: We don't have enough time to discuss that. But a while back, I spent 35 days in the most wonderful place I've ever seen, called Hazelton, in Minnesota. A place for alcoholics and dopers. Just a magnificient place.

Hall: What did they do there?

Wilson: It would take a long time to really explain it. I don't know that I could tell you everything that they do except that they help you understand why you drink or why you take dope or whatever it is that your hangup is. But any person who I feel any warmth toward, whether they ever drunk a drop in their life or took anything, I'd like them to have the chance of spending 30 days in Hazelton, because I'm sure they'd come out a much better person.

Hall: I only have this problem with beer, especially Newcastle Hunter Ale from Australia or Brahma from Brazil. But I'm curious, do you think you program better now than you did then, or do you know?

Wilson: Like I said earlier, I don't know if I've ever been a good programmer, but I've been able to get a lot out of my people. If you motivate people so they get the most out of themselves, then you're a success.

Hall: I want to ask a weird question. Do you think you could make a country music station work in New York City, where it failed before?

Wilson: I think you can make any type of format in any city successful as long as you have your sights set properly going in. If you're saying: Could I make a country station No. 1 in New York? I would doubt it seriously. If you're saying: Could we make it financially worthwhile? Well, that's one thing all of the people in our company strive toward . . . we program for the bottom line. We're not interested in being No. 1 in all categories . . . we're interested in being No. 1 in the category for that time of day that is salable for our sales department and our advertising representative. I think we could make a profitable country station in New York, yes.

Hall: Well, could you do the same thing with a progressive rock station, say an album-oriented station, in a major market?

Wilson: Sure. You could make any format successful that you set your mind to, to some extent. The thing that bothered me about the progressive format stations—in spite of the fact that many of them are good and there is a market for what they do—I think that people thought they were more than what they really are. Sure, you could make a profitable progressive rock station in a major market. There's one in Cleveland, WNCR. They're very successful. They don't make the gross dollars that maybe the big AM daddy station makes, but the criterion of success of any station is the profit margin. Any station, if you set your mind on it, can be made profitable and I think that's the whole ball game. For your ego you'd like to be No. 1, everybody likes to be No. 1. Anybody who says that being No. 1 is not important is either crazy or lying. But you have to realize your limitations and adjust to become a successful and profitable operation.

Hall: You let the air personalities at WOKY pick their own music out of the playlists?

Wilson: They have categories. I guess there would be three categories from which they make choices, but the choices they can make are limited; they can only choose from records that are there for them to choose from.

Hall: The records are pulled from the library for them?

Wilson: Every record that's in the control room has been put there for them. They can choose from A, B, C, or D, possibly, depending on the hour of the day.

Hall: At night, those records would change.

Wilson: No. Those records change all day long. I'm telling you some trade secrets. We program strictly for dayparts—who's available to listen to your radio station—and go after them.

Hall: Well, that's Mike Joseph's theory. And one of his stations is now a competitor of yours—WZUU in Milwaukee.

Wilson: I think his philosophies are much like ours. I have a great deal of respect for Mike Joseph.

Hall: The comment that I hear from men in middle-of-the-road radio is that their format is *the* format of the future. Because they play all of the records that a Top 40 station does except the ones that irritate. In addition, they have stronger personalities. Does that argument hold up?

Wilson: Certainly doesn't hold up in Milwaukee and San Diego, where our stations do quite well. And partially in Miami.

Hall: Why have so many Top 40 stations gone to shorter and shorter playlists?

Wilson: I've thought that the short playlist was caused by program directors who didn't bother to do enough research on their market.

Hall: They feel the long playlist won't work anymore.

Wilson: I don't even feel we should think in terms of short or long. There are two very specific reasons why we don't play new records on our FM stations, but I don't want to discuss them because I believe it would affect the stations. But, regarding our AM stations or any Top 40 station, if a music director gets a record and he feels it should be on his station and he doesn't play it because his station is only supposed to play 30 or 35 records, that's completely stupid. If he feels it belongs on his station, he's silly not to play it. Whether it's by a new untried artist or not.

Hall: Bill Drake has the theory that you should never play a new untested record unless you can sandwich it in between two proven and familiar hits. He feels that you would lose your audience.

Wilson: I feel that way. There's at least the possibility. But regarding theories, Buzz Bennett has the theory that you should try to eliminate as many tuneout factors as possible. And one of the biggest tuneout factors, far above everything else, is a commercial. So . . . ? A sales rep would dearly love reading that. There was a theory a year ago that jingles were a tuneout factor, but I never believed that. We've never stopped using jingles. I think the problem was that in almost every market you heard almost the same jingle. All of the radio stations were into that "more music, KCBQ" jingle thing and that probably offended people in the long run—the overuse, not the jingle itself.

Hall: Whose jingles do you use?

Wilson: We use some from everybody. The latest set we bought from Tom Merryman, TM Productions in Dallas.

Hall: How often do you change jingle sets?

Wilson: About every six months we freshen up. But we don't actually change them per se, because we want to maintain the same sound.

Hall: Do you believe in clustering commercials?

Wilson: Absolutely not. But we try to hold to a 70-second limit.

Hall: How come you don't cluster, when clustering commercials seems to be the trend?

Wilson: I'll answer that with a question. Do you know of any stations that improved their ratings because they went to clusters? Do you know of any stations that went to clusters that lost a lot of ratings? I'll tell you why I never went to clusters—because it doesn't work.

Hall: You mentioned earlier about having some great managers at your stations.

Wilson: Yes. The manager at WMYQ in Miami is Russ Wittberger, whom you know. Hap Trout is manager of KCBQ in San Diego. Ralph Barnes at WOKY in Milwaukee. Joe Kelly will manage the new KSLQ in St. Louis when it goes on the air. A fine group of managers.

George Wilson, second interview

INTRO: At the time of this interview, George Wilson had been promoted to executive vice president of Bartell's radio operations, and the fortunes of one of their stations—WMYQ, an FM station in Miami—had ebbed. He was deeply concerned about the station, from both a programming and a management standpoint, and he was on the verge of changing the format to all-Spanish, if necessary, to improve the bottom line.

Hall: Programming today is becoming more and more of a science, it seems to me. It's becoming highly sophisticated. Is that because new research techniques have come along?

Wilson: With the number of FM stations coming into the market that you have to contend with today, in order to be successful you have to eliminate as many of the variables in our business as possible to make sure that you stay on your target, whatever your target may be. There used to be one dominant factor in each market and then there was a middle-of-the-road station, a country station, and there was an r&b station. Today, you switch on the dial and there are all kinds of different stations, all vying for the same type of audience, only doing it in a different manner.

Hall: Because you are not only just the head of the chain of the radio division but also a programmer per se, do you have to rely upon a team effort?

Wilson: If I had to go back and become an active programmer today I would have to hustle. I am just out of touch. The added duties that I now have just do not allow me the time to be as involved—I don't know if I could tell you the top 10 records in any of our markets.

Hall: Have you tried to keep up with it?

Wilson: I used to know who was on the air at everytime slot on all of our stations, and now I have the most competent man in our industry in charge of programming—Jerry Clifton—and that's Jerry's duty. One thing I have always maintained through the years—and why I have also been able to have some decent people around me—is that when I hire a person, I let them do the job that I hire them to do. I have said in front of our board that if Clifton is the right guy he will make me look good; if he is the wrong guy I will take the punches for it. My life in programming is now in Clifton's hands; whatever he deems to be the right way to go, he will get the leeway to do whatever he wants to do with our chain. I will not interfere with him one iota. Certainly we watch and we discuss things and when he thinks he needs advice from me he asks it; if he doesn't think he needs it, he doesn't ask it.

We have professional managers who run their radio stations, and I try to leave them alone as much as possible. If I see something that I don't like particularly, I talk to them about it, but I try to allow everybody to do the job that they are hired to do with the least amount of interference from me. I think that if you will look at the stations in the country that have been unsuccessful on a regular basis, and the stations that were successful and aren't doing so well today, it is because of the upper management who doesn't know what-the-hell they are talking about and what they are doing. They've lost touch with the times or maybe they never had touch with the times, but the people who interfere with those they hire are the people who are not successful.

Hall: After Jerry, is there a music coordinator?

Wilson: Yes. That's Rochelle Staab. In all honesty, I really don't know about how their systems work and how they are doing it. Probably one of these days I will ask them exactly what they are doing, in case I ever have to go back to programming again. Rochelle reports to Jerry. She works under his guidelines. When I was the national program director, she worked directly with me, and at that time I turned the music over to her. She knew what she was doing and, of course, my opinion is that she is one of the three best there are in the country. I think that Marti Nehrbass, who works for RKO Radio, and Rosalie Tromley are the other two. There must be some guys that are great with music, but it seems that these women have come to the top of their particular field. They are phenomenal people; they do their job very well and they live it. That's the whole answer for anybody ... whether you're music director or program director or whatever your title may be. In order to be successful, in my opinion, nothing else matters. You have to live your job in order for you to be a success. It causes many problems with your home life and with your personal life, but in order to be a success there is no question that ... at least, everyone I know that is a successful person lives, eats, sleeps, and is totally involved with their job.

Hall: In programming do you see any trends developing? There has always been a leadership complex like when the "Q" format came along that ostensibly started in San Diego on KCBQ, then you had all the other stations that jumped into the Q ... is that copycat syndrome bad?

Wilson: I don't know that it is necessarily bad. Like anything else, when the Drake thing was big, it certainly wasn't bad to follow because most of the time when you followed and copied it there was, indeed, something to copy. I think that's a great myth with the "Q" format; I don't think there is such a thing, but people seem to think there is and they follow it, and if in doing so they become successful, fine. Look how many people followed Bill Drake. The whole industry followed him for years. How can you fault people for following something that's successful if it helps them to become successful?

There is nothing wrong at all, in my opinion, with being a follower. I have been criticized my whole career for following, but I don't really care because the people that criticized me through the years are now only program directors in medium-sized markets, while, on the other hand, I can happily eat steaks almost every night if I choose to.

Hall: Is radio programming different today than when you were programming?

Wilson: Oh, sure, it's a lot different. The whole ball game changes regularly, you know, every few years ... it all turns around and changes. Just look back. It was not many years ago when the Drake thing was the whole industry, right? And in the last couple of years the so-called "Q" format has been the big thing. Radio always keeps changing and it always will.

Hall: But how is a program director different today than when you were involved?

Wilson: In my day, everything came from my belly and the seat of my pants. Today, everything is done from research. I am not necessarily convinced that it's the best way to go all the time, but it seems to be the successful way to go at this time. So I am certainly not going to ignore it.

Hall: Do you still fly by the seat of your pants occasionally?

Wilson: Not occasionally—I do that probably 90 percent of the time. That's just the way I am. I talk to people. I get a good feeling from people. I think that the one talent I have is the knack to be able to read people well and get a good feeling about who is right and who is wrong. I have been very lucky in that area.

Hall: You weigh all the information and then act on it?

Wilson: And sometimes act before I have any information at all, and that's not just in programming. I believe very sincerely that you've got to be a dice shaker, and if you are going to be successful you've got to take a chance. The only thing you can do is eliminate the possibilities of failure as much as possible in your own mind. When you do take a chance, if you've done all your homework as well as you can, then you just go ahead and do it. If you're right, fine, and if you're wrong, live with it. I think that there are people born to be winners and people born to be losers . . . is that a strange thing to say? I think that there are people just born to be winners, and no matter what setbacks they get through in their lifetime, they always end up landing on their feet somehow.

Hall: Recovery power?

Wilson: Look at Jack Thayer. Can you think of a better example than Jack Thayer? He is the greatest example of that. I mean no matter how bad things got for Jack— bingo, back on his feet again.

Hall: You program a lot of different stations today, although you have been basically a rock man in the past.

Wilson: Well, I did rock a lot of times because it was the only way I could get a job . . . I had to take any job I could get a lot of times. Maybe that was the reason I worked so many different radio stations. But I don't think that the format itself is important. I would never want to be a party to or part of a progressive rock station, no matter how successful it would be. I wouldn't want that, and yet I do understand and realize that it is a very important part of our business. I can appreciate and respect the guys that do well in it.

Hall: Do you think you could program a classical station?

Wilson: Sure, I could program a classical station—with the same basic philosophy that I have always used. I would go get the best classical music guy that was around and put him in charge of it.

Hall: Now that Bartell Media is contemplating expansion, what do you foresee doing?

Wilson: Well, I know exactly what we are going to do in the future. I have a game plan of my own in mind, but I have to get approval before I move. I can say very definitely that the Charter people who own Bartell are interested in expansion.

Hall: Do you have programming concepts that would apply for any of those markets?

Wilson: Yes. We have specific markets that we want to go to, and we have specific things to do with the stations after we do acquire them.

Hall: Have you also considered the people you will need?

Wilson: The people for the most part will come from within our own organization. We will promote from within whenever possible. I hope that it will always be that way. I don't like to go outside and get people.

Hall: Over the years you have been fairly instrumental in the careers of a lot of disk jockeys, helping them develop as people. Is that because you were a disk jockey once yourself? Because you know their problems?

Wilson: I think that I was associated with many who have been quite successful. I would never be presumptuous enough to think that I caused their success or taught them. The only thing that I think I did was give a lot of people the opportunity to do what they can do well. And back in the old days when I was drinking, I wasn't always able to function properly. Consequently, in order for me to be a success, I had to surround myself with people whom I considered to be the best I could get, to be with me at the time to do the jobs that I wasn't physically able to do most days—areas like production. I was never a good production man, so I had to have the best. In each radio station I worked at, I had the finest—the guy who I thought was the best available man to do the job. For example, in that area Jack McCoy is the best, in my opinion. There were two guys—David Moorhead and Jack McCoy—who worked with me through the years at one place or another. They were the two best that I've ever seen in production, and I did everything in my power to keep them with me as long as possible because they made me look good. In my being selfish in that area, it gave them the opportunity to come forward. I never had to go looking for a music director much because music always came rather easy to me, and so, no matter how screwed up I happened to be at the time, I could always handle the music portion of the job okay. It wasn't any big thing to do. But, looking at it realistically, if you're a program man, you're only as good as the people around you, and being a very selfish, self-centered person with a tremendous ego, in order for me to continue to look good I always had to have as good a disk jockey or production man or whoever was available, and I tried to always have those kinds of people around me.

Hall: What makes a good disk jockey?

Wilson: Somebody who can relate to the audience. There are two different kinds of good disk jockeys. There are people who don't have the God-given talent to sit there and ad-lib and do all the things naturally that have to do with their job. There are also guys who are willing to pay the price to prepare. For example, the best is Bob Berry, who in my opinion is the best Top 40 morning man in America. He worked at WOKY in Milwaukee—he works on the air three hours a day, he also works every day three hours preparing for the next morning's show. He has to do that because he doesn't have the God-given talent to just wing it, and there are many other people in this world who do have that kind of talent.

In my opinion, your best overall morning man in America is Wally Phillips, WGN, Chicago. It's obvious listening to Wally that he does a lot of preparation. But not only does he do his preparation, he also has the ability to wing it and ad-lib and make it come off just phenomenally—he's just one hell of a talent, but he also does his homework, so he's a sensational disk jockey.

Hall: I listen to Gary Owens.

Wilson: Oh, Gary Owens. There is no question Owens is a . . . the amount of preparation he does, I assume by listening to him, is minimal. But he is sensational because he has that God-given talent to . . . .

Hall: He works, he prepares like hell. Most of the time anyway.

Wilson: Does he prepare? Well, then he is a greater talent than I realized, because he doesn't sound prepared, he just sounds great. If he does prepare indeed, and then pulls it off on the radio so he doesn't sound prepared, then he's absolutely sensational, better than I had ever anticipated . . . and I think he's one of the best there's ever been.

Hall: He spends up to two or three hours in the studio. They tape a lot of stuff; he doesn't want to take a chance on it. But he feeds it in so damn well you'd never know. One day I caught him in the act of taping something. I wouldn't have known. I said, "You son of a gun! I thought all of that was live." Well, there aren't many any better than he is, that's for sure. The other kind of disk jockey is the one who can wing it?

Wilson: Yeah, the Larry Lujack type's a . . . there aren't many of them. You can count them on one hand in the whole country for the last 10 years. They are able to walk into a studio on any given day and come off with a great show. But what the heck, how many great movie stars are there or how many great talents do you know in other fields that just can walk in and do things? There aren't many.

Hall: Were you a good jock?

Wilson: I was probably the worst disk jockey who was ever on radio in the history of the world. I used to have a hell of a lot of fun, but a great disk jockey I'm not.

Hall: In the old days, when the so-called "circus" existed?

Wilson: Our traveling circus?

Hall: Yes.

Wilson: That changed from time to time, but there were a lot of guys who got on the bandwagon from town to town. But it changed a lot. Lee "Baby" Simms was an integral part of it. There was a fellow named Bobby Dee who spent a lot of years with me from town to town. Buzz Bennett was on the wagon for a while—that's a funny expression to use for Buzz. Bob Foster did a little tour duty with us. David Moorhead was in there. The fellow who is now the head of UPI News in Washington—the head of the news bureau believe it or not—is Bill Greenwood who was with us for quite a while. There's been an awful lot of jocks. John Rook was in for a while . . . .
There's just been so many of them and there's so many fond memories that I hate to mention names because you leave some of them out, and you put some of them in different brackets than the others. That really isn't fair because they at the time were important to all of our careers and we all appreciated each other. One of the great examples is Paul Johnson in Baltimore. I'll never forget WITH in Baltimore because it was, without a question, the best crew that I was ever privileged to work with. Yet we did the worst of any radio station that I ever had a part of. We, we just . . . can you imagine? I worked mornings, this guy I was talking about earlier—Bobby Dee—worked in the midday. There is a fellow named Bill Taylor who was with me for three or five cities. I guess . . . Foster was on in the afternoons, Fat Daddy—Paul Johnson—was on at night, and you talk about a circus—there was a circus. Some weeks we'd never hit the bed for five or six days. It was just an incredible bunch of guys having a hell of a lot of fun, but the fun just never came off properly on the radio.

Hall: What was the circus? What was the function of the circus?

Wilson: Well, we had a bunch of guys who . . . we called that. I refer to it sometimes as "traveling circus" just because it was kind of a town to town kind of thing, but I don't know if that is a fair term to use. We all had our particular time slots that we worked on the air, we all knew each other, we all loved each other. We all could talk about each other on the radio. There was total communication between all of us all of the time. That's what radio is all about—communication—and that's the thing we all fail the most at inside our industry. We are in the communication business, but we are all the worst communicators to each other in the world. The people that used to travel with me in the old days . . . we all just loved each other, and we were all out for each other's good and each other's success. Without anybody even knowing about what we were doing, or anything else, it was just a feeling of total togetherness, and we had a hell of a lot of fun on the radio. We had a lot of fun off the radio, too.

Hall: That was the day when a manager/owner would buy a station and build it up and sell it fast.

Wilson: Yes, indeed.

Hall: But this doesn't . . . .

Wilson: Well, there is a three-year rule now that prohibits that. Some of them try today to still do it, only on a three-year term. But it's much more difficult today—the interest rates, the money that it takes to do it, and so forth. You just can't do it like you used to do it, like you did in the old days. People are still trying, but it certainly isn't working like it used to. There are a lot of people who have bought radio properties recently—and I say "recently" meaning the last five years—who have had that game plan in mind, but when the interest rates jumped and the economy dipped and what have you, that put a different outlook on their approaches, I'm sure.

Hall: So, the circus type of thing is . . . .

Wilson: When you say circus, I know what you mean. Bill Drake had the same thing. He had his key people who were with him through the years. Maybe they weren't the same insane, crazy people that, perhaps we were. But, by the same token, look at what he achieved against what we achieved. We were nothing compared to Bill Drake. We were just little guys having a lot of fun in small markets while Bill was workin' and doin' great things and making a fortune in the big markets. But the same basic principles applied; I'm sure their guys loved each other just as much as our guys did. The only thing—they were a hell of a lot smarter than we were because they were making a lot of money and we were just having fun.

Hall: Is the life of a disk jockey a difficult one?

Wilson: Well, probably not at the time to the guy involved, because although it is under the norm, I guess to the people involved it isn't. It is the only way of life they know and probably the only way of life they care to live. We're all egomaniacs; we're all vagabonds. I hope maybe part of that's over for me, although I wouldn't trade one minute of my life. If I were to die tomorrow I could die totally satisfied that, no matter what happened in the past or whatever, I wouldn't trade a minute of my life, except maybe for some of the grief that I gave my wife. I would like to trade that . . . but, as for my own professional life, I wouldn't change a thing. And I don't think any of the guys who are out there now would. Although they go through a lot of trying times, they also go through a lot of great times, have a lot of fun from time to time, and I don't think any of them would change. But I also don't think we're a normal breed of person; I don't think anybody—if this is "show biz" as some people call it—I don't think any show biz type would do anything any differently. They enjoy doing what they're doing . . . and they have good times and bad times, and they're just made up that way so that they accept it and they don't get upset if things are bad for a while. That's part of the game that we play.

Hall: Your son . . . what's his professional name?

Wilson: He calls himself Andy Carpenter now.

Hall: Are you pleased that he's in radio?

Wilson: Sometimes yes, sometimes no.

Hall: You didn't mind this thing happening to you, but . . . .

Wilson: I think that personally, my opinion of my son is that he is just much too nice a person to be in our business. I don't think that there is a lot of room for successful radio people being nice guys.

Hall: One of the things, George, that has always depressed me about the radio industry was the lack of security.

Wilson: There *is* no security, but we all know that going in; whether we know it in the beginning or not, we learn it quickly and it's really not an important thing. Security is not what we're looking for; that's not what makes the animal function. Security is for the people who are the pinstripers of the world—the bankers, and the lawyers, and those kinds of people. Our people aren't interested in security, as such, until they get to an age when they realize, "Hey man, I guess I got to worry about paying bills and taking care of this that and the other thing."

But that's just not in us—security is not one of the things that's important to people like us until we get older. Certainly, it's much more important to me today than it ever was before, because I'm no longer a kid. But in the old days I wasn't worried about getting fired or buying clothing or anything else. I didn't give a damn one way or the other. And maybe that was good, and I often think that it *was* good, because if you're going to be a creative type of person . . . I'm not saying that I was a creative person, I certainly wasn't, I was a follower . . . but in order to be a creative person you can't worry about what's going to happen tomorrow, you've just got to do what you think is *right* to do at the time and let the chips fall where they will.

Hall: You said you were a "follower." Who did you follow?

Wilson: Well, I followed Chuck Blore; I guess I probably copied Chuck more than anybody else. The only one whom I never followed and for whom I had a lot of respect was Bill Drake. I respected what he was doing and I respected the successes that he was having, but I didn't agree with his philosophy always, so I watched his career with great admiration and a lot of respect, but I was not a follower of his type of radio.

Hall: You said "follow," but what you really meant, it occurred to me, was that you took ideas or successful ideas and combined them.

Wilson: I'm of the opinion that there are no new ideas, that the only thing you do is take a good idea, twist it and then make it better. And that's what I always tried to do—take something that I know worked and then . . . see. That's why Blore was always kind of like my hero and I always thought when I grew up—I still do, if I ever grow up—I would like to be like Chuck Blore. He's kind of my ideal in that area; Bill Stewart used to be, too, if you remember Bill in the old days . . . in the old days Bill was a hell of a man. Kent Burkhart, too. There's a lot of guys who were very instrumental, whether they cared or didn't care—I'm sure they didn't care—but there are a lot of people who were instrumental in my thinking, whether they knew it or not. Blore used to have phenomenally great ideas. I would just try to find out what he was going to do next week and then I'd do it.

Hall: Do you think the air personality is going to be improving?

Wilson: I think everything improves, Claude; I think that's a pretty easy question to answer. I think that everything always get better and better and better. I'm of the opinion that everything always works out for the best, no matter how bad it looks at the time, and the young person who might be reading this should remember that no matter how bad it seems right at this very moment, he/she'll find that in the long run everything always works out for the best. No matter how dark it looks right now.

Hall: In spite of the economic recession, radio seems to be doing fairly well overall. Do you find that true with Bartell?

Wilson: Yes, except in Miami where we haven't been privileged to have good ratings at WMYQ, so we haven't had good business there. But in all the other properties we're doing very well. In fact, we're right on target with our projections this year, which are naturally over last year, and we had a very good year last year. Everything looks very good. Unless the bottom just falls out of everything, we're going to have a very good year.

Hall: How much more do you project when you projected your budgets over last year, six percent?

Wilson: I think the average was probably eight percent.

Hall: For each station?

Wilson: For the group. Some stations will do better. WADO will be our biggest profit maker. That's the one station that doesn't fall into the Top 40 type category like the others. It's Spanish-speaking.

Hall: Speaking of WADO, how closely do you watch that station?

Wilson: Very closely. Of course, we don't get involved in the programming of it like the rest of them, because we have people specialized in Spanish who do that. Nelson Lavergne is the manager and has total control of the station, pretty much with complete autonomy. And he does a phenomenal job. In programming and in sales, Nelson Lavergne is WADO.

Hall: Is it going to make a lot more than even WOKY in Milwaukee?

Wilson: Not a lot more, but the profit there is substantial.

Hall: Do you know what Bartell made last year?

Wilson: For the radio division, of the gross dollars that we take in, we do about 23 percent profit.

Hall: What do you foresee for radio? I know that you're striving to make the radio operation a totally active, very profitable venture, since this is, in effect, your first year as head of the radio division, even though you've been involved in the programming for a long time. But what do you see overall for radio, not just at Bartell?

Wilson: With the way business is going—and from conversations with other broadcasters . . . . For example, last week I talked to Stan Kaplan who runs WAYS in Charlotte and WAPE in Jacksonville, and an FM station in Charlotte, and all are having a great year. But, of course, Stanley Kaplan is probably one of the two best, if not the best, radio salesmen in America today, so that probably figures into it, but they're having a hell of a year.

Hall: Do you think that the financial success of radio depends upon the man who sells?

Wilson: I think that the salesman has a very large influence on what happens, but it's becoming more and more obvious that you do, indeed, have to win ratings books in order to get to the big gross dollars that are available. You have to be a dominant factor in the ratings. You can, on a local basis with a good salesman, do more maybe than another radio station, but in order to get the big national buys and in order to get the heavy gross dollars, it's very obvious that you do indeed have to have large ratings.

Hall: Even today?

Wilson: Even more so today, I think, than before. Where they used to have national buys made in markets five deep, today buys are only three deep. You've got to be into that category to get the dollars.

Hall: This brings up Miami again. Of course, right now the station is sort of at a low level. It has been a winner in the past. What causes the up and down swing of a radio station? Did someone change the programming on it? Change a winner?

Wilson: No, we didn't necessarily change the format of the radio station, it's just that we were willing ... or I guess I should say *I* wasn't willing to spend the promotion dollars to keep it where it was. I thought maybe we could be competitive enough without giving away the radio station and still make a profit, but that's not the case. Now, it looks like sometimes you get to a point where it costs too much money to be No. 1 which makes it almost impossible to make a profit. If you look at the radio stations that are now in the high-rated categories in Miami—if they are public companies and you're entitled to look at their bottom line, you'll find that being No. 1 in ratings isn't necessarily also being No. 1 in billings and No. 1 in making a profit. I think that this is one of the things we have to look at in Miami very carefully, especially regarding what we're going to do in the future. Is it important to be No. 1 and lose money? It isn't to me. I'm in business to make money, pure and simple, and Bartell is in business to make money. We are a public company, and they don't want to know about being No. 1, they want to know what's the bottom line. So that's what we're looking at now. Whether or not it's the right move to be competitive and be No. 1, with what it costs to be No. 1, and after you're No. 1 still not being able to make a profit, which is what I think is . . . .

Hall: Where do you draw the line?

Wilson: We're working on something now that I think may be the answer for us in Miami, but I'm not privileged to say at this point what we're going to do.

Hall: When it comes to a radio station in general—your chain or any other chain—what percent of the profits should be fed back into promotion in order to be No. 1?

Wilson: That's very definitely an individual city situation. In some cities, it just doesn't cost as much to be competitive as it does in other cities.

Hall: In Los Angeles, I understand that a beautiful music FM station supposedly spent $150,000 in promotion—billboards, newspapers, TV.

Wilson: If you're limited to six commercial minutes or eight commercial minutes an hour and you have to spend large promotional dollars to be competitive and be No. 1, sometimes it's not worth it because you can't make a profit. That's where you have to decide how much your ego or your pride is worth. I have to do everything possible to make a profit, and not worry about being No. 1. No. 1 is good for your ego, but not necessarily good for the bottom line.

Hall: There was a time when you were a program director when pride would have probably won out over profit, wasn't there?

Wilson: No question about it. Back in the days when I was an active program director, I was interested in being No. 1, first probably for my ego, and second because it's what everybody strives for. We all want to be No. 1 at something. We all want to be the best or whatever. When you're not worrying about the bottom line, that takes precedence over everything. I think that's where the program people may be growing up a little today. They have to realize that they are, indeed, businessmen. The thing that stands out in my mind is that most of the time the program director who honestly cares anything about the radio station works 18 hours a day; he's not worried about anything else except having a great radio station. He really cares about his radio station—the people that work under him, his disk jockeys, and so forth. He's not necessarily looking at the bottom line, but I think today that more and more program directors are beginning to realize that they are the backbone of the station and if their careers are going to improve, and grow, they have to not only worry about being No. 1—they have to worry about making a profit for the station. And they are the key to making the profit. They have to get the numbers, but they have to do it in a manner where it makes sense, so that there is a possibility of making a good profit for the station.

I'm of the opinion that you can have a good salesman who, if he is indeed a good radio salesman, he could be a good print salesman, or outdoor advertising salesman, or whatever field that he chooses to be in. But programming type people are dedicated radio people. In order for them to become managers out of programming they have to realize—and I think they are more and more—that they've got to be interested and involved in the bottom line.

Hall: How do you tie the two together, tie the programmer closer to the manager?

Wilson: It's an impossible task, in my opinion, to have compatibility between the sales department and the programming department, and I don't really think that it's necessary. In fact, it might not be healthy. I think that this competitive situation is good, because if you let one or the other take over, then the radio station doesn't benefit from it. As long as you have meetings on a regular basis between these departments and they all try to understand each other's problems, you have a chance. There has to be a bending from both parties on what you can and can't do, and what makes good programming sense. You can't just be running promotions and contests for advertisers to help the salesman make a sale. It has to work for the benefit of the radio station. But I think sometimes program directors will arbitrarily not do something that would help the sales manager make a sale; just say, "Oh, you can't do that because it's not wise programming." There has to be a meeting ground somewhere that's good for both, and they have to have a mature, intelligent approach to the situation, so that the station can benefit from both of their positions.

Hall: In Miami, do you think that the programming has a lot to do with the fact that the station is not making money now?

Wilson: To a degree, I think so. I think that we made—I shouldn't say we, I should say

I—made some very bad choices in Miami about what we would do there. But I don't know that even if we had succeeded at what we were trying to do, it would have been right. Things usually work out for the best for whatever the reason. Maybe the reason we've done badly there is that we were on the wrong track all along. Maybe we shouldn't have been in the rock 'n' roll business in Miami all this time. Maybe there was no way to make a big profit in Miami with the rate structures and the competition that's in that market. Maybe we have been shooting at the wrong star all this time. That's what we're looking at now.

Hall: There seems to be a trend back to a longer playlist just for that reason on some of the so-called "Q" format stations, that perhaps the format was successful, but unsaleable.

Wilson: Teen listeners are not a saleable commodity today like they once were. You have to reach the 25-49 demographics to get the major buys. You cannot be just a teen-oriented radio station any longer. Of course, when you start out in a market, you have to win the teens first because they're the peer music leaders, and they're the ones that are the most fickle. When they switch, they bring you some older demographics, but you have to eventually win the 25-plus demographics in order to make substantial dollars at this time in the radio business. The 18-to-24 category is not the big gross dollar biller that it used to be. Not that it isn't an important category—I don't mean that at all. But you have to win more than teens in these times than you did in the old days.

Hall: And in order to win those specific demographics at a viable dollar, I guess it's programming that is the focal point—the product itself.

Wilson: No question.

Hall: Is changing the programming always the answer?

Wilson: I don't know how to answer that question. I guess if you're not doing well, changing the programming is the answer. If you're doing well, you're certainly not going to change your programming. So I guess the answer to the question would be yes.

Hall: Do you see a continued growth in radio, not just from the money standpoint, but overall as an industry?

Wilson: Oh, no question about it. To operate a magazine, you have certain costs. Now, you get your basic cost structure set, and the next thing you know, ink prices go up, paper prices go up, postage goes up, and no matter how efficiently you run your operation, you have no control over those areas. So in a year's time, although you're right on target with your sales projections, your profit is going to suffer dramatically because of the situations that you have no control over.

With radio, once you hit a certain level of operating costs, that's it. The air doesn't cost any more than before. If you do more business than you anticipated doing, it falls immediately to the bottom line. In the other industries there are so many intangibles you have to deal with that even if you might write more business than you have anticipated in your projections for the year, cost factors that you have no control over can kill you. Radio is much better as a business. Radio will continue to progress in both quality programming and profitability.

OUTRO: The WMYQ problem, George Wilson later decided, was an image problem, and the call letters were changed to WMJX (called 96X on the air).

Things have changed: Jack McCoy, mentioned here as a program director, now operates DPS in the San Diego area, an audience ratings analysis firm that deciphers ARB's. Ralph Barnes is now managing an FM station in Milwaukee; Dick Casper and others have moved on to other jobs. Russ Wittberger is manager of KCBQ in San Diego. Jerry Clifton left the position of national program director for Bartell to be a full-time programmer at WMJX in Miami.

Thus, radio continues to turn as fast as the disks it plays on the air.

RON JACOBS

Ron Jacobs

INTRO: This interview with Ron Jacobs, who programmed KHJ in Los Angeles during its rise to worldwide fame as "Boss Radio" and flagship of the so-called Drake Format, is a composite of two interviews, one of which was completed in 1973 after Jacobs had been programming KGB in San Diego for a year or so. The other was taped at the *Billboard* office shortly before Jacobs left KGB to return to Maui, where he had a home for years. Today he's back on the air at KKUA in Honolulu, his first radio show in more than a decade. The first Jacobs interview drew more than 100 letters and perhaps 50 phone calls, second in feedback only to that of Charlie Tuna.

Ron Jacobs worked at KHVH in 1957, his first full-time job. A year later, he became program director at KPOA, which led to the formation of KPOI where Jacobs did a morning show from 1960-62. In 1964, he organized format and staff for a station in Hong Kong that never went on the air. He rose to U.S. fame as program director at KMAK in Fresno, Calif., against Bill Drake at KYNO—a legendary rock battle. Later, Drake hired him to program KHJ in Los Angeles.

Hall: When you took over KHJ in 1965 what was the original lineup?

Jacobs: I don't know if I can exactly remember. It was Robert W. Morgan from 6-9 AM, Roger Christian from 9 until noon, Gary Mack from noon-3 PM, Don Steele 3-6 PM, Dave Diamond 6-9 PM, Sam Riddle 9-midnight, and Johnny Williams from midnight-6 AM—I think. I forget who was the first swing guy.

Hall: KHJ was a dog in the market, wasn't it?

Jacobs: Plus the fact that KHJ had gone rock, tentatively, a few years before, then headed the other way the minute the payola scandal erupted. KHJ was on Vine Street with air personalities like Wink Martindale, and had old McKensie pre-cartridge machines doing this tentative rock thing, trying to challenge KFWB, which had captured the market all to themselves for about four years. KHJ turned the other way as soon as the payola thing hit, so what we were greeted with in 1965 was: "What do these longhaired, bearded weirdo freaks think they're doing?" That was the attitude at the TV station. The big deal in the building at the time was KHJ-TV, channel 9—they were making all of the bucks with their Million Dollar Movie. They wouldn't even talk to us. We had to fight to get a parking place.

Hall: And to get past that guard in the lobby.

Jacobs: On the day I was hired, that evening Robert W. Morgan and I walked through that station like a couple of kids in a candy store, with our mouths open saying things like: "Far out! We're in Hollywood. Look over there, there's a film room! This is really the big time." A couple of months later we were more cynical about it, to put it politely. But when we started in Los Angeles, the attitude in the building was: "Who are these young weirdos?" They had been through an endless series of programming changes at the station, and your average engineer at KHJ had worked there, I would imagine, something like 20 years. And we were just the new guys passing through because somebody upstairs had another wild idea. Too, everybody was saying: "Come on, we don't need another rocker. There's already KFWB, KRLA, and KBLA." However, Los Angeles was an entirely different vibe from 1965 to 1967. 1967 was an incredible year in Los Angeles. Particularly for us at KHJ because FM had just started up really big, you know? KHJ was *the* station. In 1966, the *Los Angeles Free Press* thought that KHJ was the hippest thing going and thought that it was anti-establishment . . . thought it was terrific and wrote nice things about KHJ. There was no FM rock 'n' roll station around then. Wherever you went on La Cienega or Sunset Boulevard people were listening to KHJ.

Hall: What was the first time KHJ got some good numbers?

Jacobs: October 1965, the station was No. 1 overall in Hooper, which was important at the time. When we started, I kept a chart on my wall—Ted Atkins finally sent me my chart. I charted the Hoopers from when we started until when I left there. We started off with a two percent share in the morning and something a little better than that in the afternoon. We started doing well immediately in Hooper, but became No. 1 totally in October 1965. Everything that KROQ attempted later to do and screwed up, we did correctly in 1965.

Hall: When did you realize that KHJ had become almost a legend . . . or did you?

Jacobs: While the stuff is going on, you don't realize it . . . you're so into the thing that you don't realize there's any particular significance to it or any importance besides what occurs to you or what appears obvious, you know? The first time that I realized we were doing something that was bigger than what it appeared to be was when Ken Delvaney who was the manager of the station and I went to Denver to check out a machine that they were using at KIMN. Oddly enough, the program director there at the time was Ted Atkins. The way Atkins came on—wowie, gaga—and the fact that I drove around Denver in a rented car listening to bits and pieces on every station there of what we were doing . . . you know, that was when I realized that KHJ was having a more far-reaching effect than was obvious to me in Los Angeles.

Hall: How many promotions did you come up with while at KHJ?

Jacobs: You mean, how many was I responsible for creating? Virtually all of them. But they were usually based on a dialogue with Bill Drake, the programming consultant for the chain. I'd mention an idea and, perhaps because I'm more radical than he is, sometimes he would grunt affirmatively and sometimes he would grunt negatively, and usually the ones he agreed upon are the ones we would do. We threw out more than we did, you know? There was a time when we were coming up with a new promotion every 10 days. We tend to remember the good ones, but there were some awful stiffs among those that no one talks about anymore.

The first promotion that I ever did at KHJ was the least successful one. I just tried to accomplish too much with it; it went over everyone's head. I had thought it was terrific, but the phones didn't ring . . . no one wrote in. Drake was polite; he didn't say: "What is this guy doing to the station?"

We got into a slogan: "The contest never stops." A one-liner: "Boss Radio where the contests never stop."

After first thinking that was a wonderful concept, I realized later, "I've got to come up with another before that one ends!" So, it was like I'd still be at the typewriter with five minutes to go before a contest ran out. The kind of pressure often causes you to be productive and to be creative because you're forcing yourself to think.

Hall: What would you say is Bill Drake's forte? His attributes?

Jacobs: There are a lot of people who have theories that I don't necessarily agree with. There's one guy who keeps telling me that he thinks Drake is the greatest multiple choice guy going, that Drake has a tremendous capacity for perceiving people with talent and hiring men with ability. He hired me. He hired Robert W. Morgan. He hired Don Steele. Drake's major contribution to radio has been that he eliminated a lot of the adolescent crap that by 1965 had not only crept into but almost overran the Top 40 genre.

But there were two major things that he did: First, to *establish* that programming or a programmer could have autonomy and would not be influenced by what the sales department could expediently make available to advertisers—that the programming department could operate without the influence of the sales department or the meddling of the management in programming in a way that would be ultimately detrimental to the station. The second most important thing that Drake did was, given that autonomy, he set up a situation where the commercial load per hour, very important on a Top 40 station, would be limited, regardless of the ratings success of the station. So when KHJ began to get good ratings, rather than in the past when a station would get good ratings and management would then put on so many spots that they'd wipe out the ratings in a matter of months—they'd be carrying 18 minutes of commercials easily just from the used car lots. Well, the second most important thing that Drake did was to establish that the commercial load would not increase, but that the proper thing would be done—the rate card would be increased. The first year and a half at KHJ, it seemed that every time you turned around there was a new rate card coming out. But we never went over our spot load limits, which were 13 minutes and 40 seconds per hour.

Hall: You once told me that Bill Drake had the idea for "The History of Rock 'n' Roll" documentary but that you did most of the work.

Jacobs: We were sitting in Nickodell's where a lot of ideas would surface after a few winkyboos—which is Drake's euphemism for a good stiff belt—and Drake said something like: "We should do a history of rock 'n' roll." And that was about the extent of what he said. I went off and chewed on it and got together with Pete Johnson who was then the music critic of the *Los Angeles Times*—I think he was the last intelligent music critic on a daily newspaper, at least in Los Angeles. Pete was terrific. He immediately grasped what the show could mean. It was exciting at the time. I mean, no one had ever heard Fats Domino talking and then, *Bam*, right into, "Blueberry Hill." It was the first time anyone had used that technique. The program was sloppy and shoddy, and I have regrets that it has become as big in retrospect as it has. It went over—and got a larger response intellectually than anything we'd done at KHJ.

Drake brought the idea up, I filed it away. Then I talked to Pete about it, and we started giving it a structure. We were producing that thing for 12 hours a day for what seemed like an eternity. Actually, we worked on it from October 1968 to February 1969, and in the last stretch there, we were recording every day for as much as 12 hours a day, six and seven days a week for two months, with Pete writing the scripts and coming up with them five minutes before we were actually ready to do them. Mouzis, the engineer; Robert W. Morgan, the emcee; Pete Johnson and the girl who later became his wife, Ellen—those are the key people who worked on that program. Drake came by once with Gene Chenault and listened to an hour demo that we'd made--we had the first 12 hours done. Drake had a party at his house and had a lot of his friends over to listen to it once the documentary was on the air. That's about what he had to do with it creatively. I think he liked it.

I really objected to the use of my ideas on all of the other RKO General radio stations without any reciprocation. Not so much monetarily as the fact that there was never anything coming back from the other stations. By the time I left KHJ, there were full-time people whose job it was to xerox copies of things we had produced and send them out to the other RKO stations. When it first started, I thought: "Terrific, I'll be getting something back! And there'll be a month where I'll be able to take it easy because there'll be some terrific promotions that guy thought up in Boston or Memphis." But frankly it never happened. I felt that by 1969 I was being exploited.

Hall: Do you think that record people disliked you when you were programming KHJ in Los Angeles?

Jacobs: When I got to KHJ, it quickly became obvious to me that I had to do everything I needed to do between 8 AM and 5 PM . . . because now it was the big time and there were unions involved. And you've got to get your work done during office hours. In the old days in smaller markets if I had an idea at midnight, I'd go down to the station at 1 AM, write the thing up, grab some music, put in on cartridge, and drive home at 3 AM and hear it on the air. There was no limitation about what you could do. At KHJ, if I touch the tape recorder, the guy who lets me do it gets fined $50. I had to adjust my whole modus operandi, right? I couldn't touch the tape recorder. Operating that radio station was as if I were driving a car, you had the clutch, and somebody else had the brake. It required a different kind of concentration.

As soon as I got to Los Angeles and saw the way the record guys were coming on, I realized that if I took the time to socialize a promotion guy for two hours next door at Nickodell's and I gave equal time to the next guy, I wouldn't have time to do anything but go to lunch. It would be August before I got through with them. So I decided to be indiscriminately rude—or so they interpreted it—to everyone. A record has got it or it doesn't. Regardless of what a guy tells you about it, whether it's delivered by a chick in a harem costume, or by a guy riding an elephant, or even if it comes in through the mail slot. So why should I spend two hours in a ritual involved in the receiving of a record when I could be doing a better job for the record company by working at my programming job on the station that will be playing that record?

Hall: When did you go to KGB in San Diego?

Jacobs: In February, 1972. So, I was there 45 months.

Hall: Why, at this particular time, did you decide to leave?

Jacobs: It's no spur-of-the-moment thing. When approached by the Browns, who own the station, the original intention was to go to KGB for a year. It's only because things got really good there that I stayed longer.

Hall: Do you feel that you achieved everything you wanted to achieve with KGB?

Jacobs: More, than not. The main thing is that in the last two years—with the coming, in fact, of Jim Price to KGB as general manager—we have been able to achieve something extremely important, a good bottom line. The stations—AM and FM—have been successful at selling time. From an economic standpoint we've achieved more, I think, than we expected to. And radio is a different ball game than it was 10 years ago. Being No. 1 is great, but nowadays it's No. 1 in what? All ratings are very fragmented, and you just don't get a 60 percent share of the audience anymore, like you could in the old days in a Hooper.

Also, in the time I've been in San Diego we've improved the physical plant—rebuilt the entire two radio stations, studios, transmitters. Everything down to a new carpet on the floor. I can honestly say that the stations are better than when I got there and that's what I went to the stations for. With Jim Price as general manager, and with his understanding of programming, he has been able to sell advertising time extremely well. Why would a client want to buy time on a KCBQ, an AM in the market, when they can get time on both KGB-AM and KGB-FM at the same time? And why should anyone buy advertising time on KPRI, an FM station in San Diego, when they can buy time on both KGB-FM and KGB-AM? The two stations together are a hell of a package. Jim Price has fired up his salesmen with this concept. And, as a result, Price has broken every single sales record at the station . . . top national sales, top local sales, top total sales. The stations are fantastically successful.

Hall: When did you start to simulcast?

Jacobs: On Aug. 1, 1972.

Hall: And what was the reason for going simulcast on AM and FM? Was the signal on AM bad?

Jacobs: The AM signal of KGB is not terrific, particularly in the nighttime pattern. However, it is sufficient for the station to have been No. 1 in the past. San Diego has gone through a complete Top 40 cycle at least twice that I know about. At one time the original Bartell group had KCBQ. There were KDEO and KGB-AM. The Browns took KGB-AM over about 10 years ago. The dominant leadership rotated between the stations for some while. Whereas our AM signal at night isn't that terrific, matched up against KCBQ, our FM signal reaches into a large part of Los Angeles. The idea for the stations to simulcast belongs to Mike Brown and, I think, in the long run that's one of the most significant things we've done here. Other radio owners have been spinning off their FM stations and changing the call letters, without perhaps realizing that one station can be used to complement the other. There are distinct advantages to AM radio and distinct advantages to FM radio. And, if you have the same programming emanating from both, one is going to promote the other.

In concept, the AM station is our single and the FM station is our album—just as record companies use a single today to promote an album. If we can hang people up when they're driving in their truck on the way to Ensenada, then when they get home cause them to tune us in on their FM set, where we know people listen much longer—the span of listening on FM, according to our research, is more than two hours a day—then, the simulcast thing, in retrospect, may be the most significant thing about the KGB-AM-FM trip. Right now, I don't know of any major rocker that's simulcasting. In a few minutes, AM will join with FM and you'll have the same programming coming via two different mediums. I think that's exciting. When I got here, this station wasn't making it on AM, and the FM was in the last days of some syndicated programming. So, it seemed logical, particularly to Mike Brown, to use one station to promote the other. For years with me it's been, FM is just around the corner, you know? I thought it was a neat little thing, but there was no money in it . . . I wouldn't want to get involved. I think now that FM is certainly going to be the dominant form, if it isn't already.

Hall: In 1973, you called to tell me that the demise of Ron Jacobs in radio was premature. Why did you say that? Were people in the industry down on you . . . did you believe they thought you were a loser?

Jacobs: When we started KGB, people in the industry couldn't comprehend it, because it didn't fall within the perimeters of what's already been done on radio. They were a little hesitant to expect that it *could* make it, you know? A lot of people have the idea that there are either winners or losers. For the most part I've been lucky enough to be associated with things that have been successful. But what we did at KGB was so radical by radio standards—not radical by the overall standards of the world, but by radio standards with its limited tunnel-vision criteria—well, I guess the concept was too far-out for most people to handle. I guess it jeopardized their security, because suddenly they had to start learning something new.

Hall: In general, do you think that radio overall has made any improvement since you went to San Diego to program KGB? Because I remember that when you originally resigned as program director of KHJ in Los Angeles several years ago, it was because you had sort of grown tired of Top 40 radio?

Jacobs: I don't think KHJ improved, do you? I don't think KHJ is doing anything but riding a big roller coaster. KHJ has a hell of a lot of momentum and zero competition. With a good signal. Without Bill Drake, Robert W. Morgan, Don Steele, where would KHJ be today? The KHJ of today is based on the dues paid by us 10 years ago.

In general—regardless of my personal association with KGB—radio has tended to level off during the past couple of years. The most disturbing thing is: Where are the young guys with talent? I've had the feeling in the past year or so that if a young guy 25 years old or less came in the door of my office and pounded on my desk, I'd probably hire him. Because, where are the aggressive guys that used to be in radio? I think it's not just radio. I think it may be symptomatic of what's happening in the world today. There are too many people who just want to collect food stamps . . . or unemployment checks. It doesn't seem that people are as motivated as they used to be in the, quote, "good ol' days," you know?

To me, at my age, it's as if they are changing the rules in the middle of the game—things, to me, that were important values when I was a kid trying to make a name for myself seem to be changing. There are a lot of people who seem content to go off and be quiet and not enter the rat race. Well, I can dig that; I'm not putting it down. It's the other way around. That's one of the reasons I'm going back to Hawaii, because I happen to agree philosophically with that premise. But, if life isn't every man for himself, then a person had better make sure he has his thing together—you know, the consolidation of one's life into a meaningful reference.

Anyway, I don't think you can be a program director of a radio station full-time and do it indefinitely. It burns you out, the way a hit record burns out. I think that people who have been on the job a long time and say they don't have to get away from it occasionally are either kidding themselves or kidding the people they work for. Having been away from radio for a couple of years—involved with Watermark Inc. in Los Angeles—I went to San Diego with a fresh approach. But now, I feel, is a good opportunity to pull back and become more objective about radio. You see, when you're in the middle of a job—and responsible for a major radio station—you really can't, to use an old cliché, see the forest for the trees. I don't think radio's any worse off than anything else. But let's look at everything else. In 1975, the Cadillac looks like the 1974 Cadillac. And the 1974 Cadillac looked like the 1973 Cadillac. And the 1975 television season looked like the 1974 television season, except maybe worse. So it isn't just radio that's suffering from lack of creativity. Tell me of a guy 23 years old or younger who's really done something unique and original. Someone who has management potential, understands the business, is pragmatically involved with the operation of a radio station other than just picking the music, and can work with people. Where is such a person?

So it isn't just radio. I think we've got to adjust to the fact that things are different from the way they taught us it was going to be. And if we don't reorient ourselves to the way things *are*, we might be kidding ourselves the rest of our lives. As far as radio is concerned—to look at it analytically—what new developments have there been? I haven't heard a thing in San Diego that isn't a version of something done before—and I haven't heard one damned thing in Los Angeles radio that isn't a variation based on a variation, you know? Where are the guys from whom the creative ideas come?

Hall: When did you come up with the idea for the KGB-AM-FM format?

Jacobs: Well, the KGB-AM-GM format . . . we've refused to accept any label here. This is not an X, Y, or Z kind of station, and I don't even know if the term *format* applies to what we're doing on KGB-AM-FM. I had spent two years out of radio and when I was asked by the Browns to come down and listen to San Diego radio and write what subsequently turned out to be a very long report, I was operating under the premise that I didn't know anything. Now we're going to find out. The first thing we did was find out what radio was all about today; who're the people who listen to the radio; how long do they listen; what do they listen for; what do they want; what don't they like? What are the patterns and characteristics of the audience and audiences of the stations that are presently on the air? San Diego is a neat little microcosm—this is a town where there's a progressive AM station and a Top 40 FM station. San Diego has two automated cassette stations operating across the border from the Avenida de Television . . . Schafer stations . . . there's almost every kind of radio station imaginable. So we went out into the field and did a very comprehensive survey about what people listen to the radio . . . what their motives are . . . and from that, basically, we began to assemble a programming structure which could get all of this on the radio. To me, radio has always been a contextual thing, and the individual elements of radio don't mean anything. If you take an element out of radio and look at it under a microscope, it means nothing. Radio is an ongoing sequence of events. Radio is a series of impressions. If you took someone and played the KHJ *a capella* jingle, with blank leader tape on either side of it, alone in a room in 1966, they would have probably been disappointed and felt let down. So, radio is a context of things.

The best way to assemble things—and in what context—is what we tried to develop at KGB-AM-FM, based on the research that we'd done. The chief thing is that we were trying to program the station in terms of a week rather than a given hour repeated over and over again. Because the audience indicated through all of our research that they're not interested in listening to the radio—at least the people over the age of 16—to hear the same thing over and over again. They want more variety than repetition. And that's the chief holy war and crusade that I was on at KGB-AM-FM . . . that it isn't necessary to repeat the same thing over and over again.

Hall: But repetition was the thing that brought Top 40 radio the success it had back in the 50s.

Jacobs: Right, Claude, but one of the exciting things about being alive—or witnessing history—is that whole structures collapse or wear out or evolve into something else.

Hall: When the research for KGB-AM-FM was being done, did you do some of it yourself? Did you go into the field, too?

Jacobs: Not as much as everyone else. I was in the field long enough to know how the process worked and made sure it was a practical and applicable one. The research was done by 29 people who either worked for the station or were married to someone who worked for the station—people that we could trust.

When doing the research on the KGB-AM-FM format, everyone out in the field had a clipboard with a questionnaire which was developed in conjunction with Ken Moy, who's on the staff of San Diego State. The first thing that would be noted is where the interview took place and who did it. Then the interviewer would put down demographic information about the person . . . you know, the obvious things, their age, sex, and so on. Then on the second page, if I were interviewing you, I'd ask whether you liked the records on this list. About each, I'd ask if you liked it a little, a lot, disliked it a little, or don't care much about it either way. If you haven't heard some of these records, that's okay, too. The first one is "Bridge Over Troubled Water." Did you like that a lot or what.

Hall: I like it a lot.

Jacobs: Okay. The interviewer would make an indication there on this form. And we would go on down through the list. Then I'd show you this list of artists and ask you if all of these people came out with an album today and you could afford to buy just one, which would you buy? And this list ranges from the Osmond Brothers to Black Sabbath with people like Glenn Miller and Charley Pride mentioned.

I'd want to know when you listen to the radio during the weekdays, on weekends, and so on. After those questionnaires were finished and run through the computer, I could tell you, based on all this, what almost 4,000 people, which is half of one percent of the population of San Diego, indicated to us. Remember, the ARB survey, in comparison, is based on only 900 responses. The top line, starting at midnight and going to the next midnight, is when people listen to the radio in San Diego, and these readouts all together are like a damned textbook. On the all-night show, the listening audiences drops down to its lowest so we know that the minimum radio listening is at 3:30 in the morning. Your peak audience is right there at 7 in the morning, then it drops down. At lunchtime you can see a blip. They start pulling up again in afternoon drive . . . between 4 and 4:30 in the afternoon.

This one graph alone is interesting because it tells us what a true statistical sampling of people in San Diego do in the way of listening. But when we cross-tabulate this information, that's when it really gets exciting. By cross-tabulating, we find that on this other graph, this line here is the people who like "Bridge Over Troubled Water" a lot. The dotted line is the people who never heard "Bridge Over Troubled Water." Now this is a very simple and obvious choice. It was a popular record and the graph illustrates that. But now, let's go to selection No. 13 on the list. Here's a song where, in chief morning drive, the major segment of the audience has never heard the record. Interestingly enough, between 7:30 in the morning and 2:30 PM all of a sudden the record takes over, and there is a positive response. Between 7:30 AM and 2:30 PM the largest number of people who're aware of that record like it. No. 13 was "Blueberry Hill" by Fats Domino.

Now this is that same line about when people listen to radio, broken down by narrower age groups than anyone ever saw on an ARB. The ARB considers teens as anyone from 17 years old to born yesterday, right? We can look at these computer readouts and see where just on weekends the 10-13 audience is. Where the 14-15 audience is. You know yourself that there's a big difference between the 16-year-old and the 14-year-old. But the ARB considers all of these three groups as teens. We, however, wanted to find out exactly where they were at, and we can see which age group actually dominates radio listening on an hour-by-hour basis. Now it's no coincidence that KGB-AM-FM just came out of the Pulse and ARB both winning in every 18-34 category. Because we based those subjective music reactions against information like this. So when you say something like "format," well format compared to what we're doing at KGB-AM-FM is like something from the Stone Age.

Hall: In other words, you took the music and evaluated it rather than any format?

Jacobs: Right. I don't want to get too specific in this interview, because to me this information is invaluable. It's important that we be historic, but I don't want to make it easy for people to copy what we're doing. But look at the difference here between Saturday night and Sunday night. We found that Sunday night is really the same as a weeknight, as far as kids are concerned, because they've got to have their homework assignments in by the next day. Now look at the difference in the 14-15 age group. They are the dominant group at 10 PM on Sunday night. Whereas they're nothing on Saturday night . . . because they're probably out doing their stuff. I'd never have thought, from 10 years in Top 40 radio, that this age group is so important on Sunday night. So we program accordingly. Most program directors treat weekends separately from weekdays. But there's a difference, which you can see here on this graph.

Hall: You correlate the specific music, according to whether it's liked or not, with these charts as per target demographic audience available.

Jacobs: Right. We started with space. All we've got to deal with is 168 hours a week. Blank canvas. We had, based on our research, factual information that showed hour-by-hour what percentage of the audience was available above the age of 16. The kids have, say, the most influence around 7 PM at night where only 68.1 percent are above the age of 16. So this is one of five bits of information that was there at the time we put our 168 hours together. Now here is a graph of every hour of the day showing the dominant age group. In other words, we know that from 8 AM until 3 PM the dominant age group listening to the radio is 24-plus. And we have very specific information. I mean, we know that on Sunday from noon to 2 PM the dominant age group listening to radio, for some reason, is 10-13-year-olds. And that's the only time we see those people take over. Parallel with that, we have this information. What is the average age of the listeners by the hour? In other words, we can say with statistical authority that on a given weekday at 7 PM the . . . .

Hall: For all of radio?

Jacobs: All of the San Diego sample that we surveyed. I don't know if this would apply to Cleveland.

Hall: You had data on every station in the market, didn't you?

Jacobs: Every station. The oldest person we interviewed was over 70 or something.

Hall: It occurs to me that all of this research may have been great for starting the station's programming, but what are you going to do about the future? Don't you have to continually do this type of research?

Jacobs: We're constantly doing research out in the audience. How the hell could you program to an audience if you didn't talk to them? Find out what they like? They can tune you out in radio faster than anything. I could go to the newsstand and, if I had the money, make a conscious choice to participate in more than one thing in a magazine or several magazines. But you can only listen to one radio station at a time. If you're driving in a car you can change radio stations quicker than you can change your underwear. If listeners don't like what you're doing, bam, they'll go somewhere else. There are other radio stations available.

I could give you other examples of things that we've done in San Diego that I feel are important and which I believe will be valuable for the station for a long time to come. If the computer situation works out in San Diego, it'll be the first time a station is totally wired to a computer. I mean you can push a button and do the payroll, send out affidavits with billings about when an ad schedule ran, choose between two clients who're trying to get a particular spot in favor of the client who has bought the most time on the station over the past year, find out when you should raise the power on the transmitter because of the sunset regulations, and even be told at 4:45 AM to wake the morning man so he can get out of bed and get to the station in time to start his show. We spent hundreds of hours with a computer firm; they virtually lived at the radio station in order to learn what it is that a radio station does.

If nothing else happens with KGB, I feel that I will have achieved something because of the computer operation that was installed during my tenure as program director. Because I don't think anyone has been able to make total use of a computer before at a radio station.

Hall: For programming, too?

Jacobs: It will do *anything,* providing the input is there. Right now, the only thing preventing all of the wonderful science fiction stuff from happening in radio is the fact that we do not have the capacity, in a small physical space, to store music. On a one-inch by two-inch piece of computer tape, we can store hundreds, thousands of bits of information. But on audio tape, that's only a 15th of a second of music. Whenever we achieve solid state storage of music, so that a tiny chip might be the entire Jefferson Starship album—or perhaps, their entire catalog, so that a radio station doesn't have to have a gymnasium-sized room for its music library—then we'll be able to completely use the computer. If you were only programming the playlist of a Top 40 station, you could use the computer 100 percent now. But try programming 3,000 songs, try programming 6,000 songs, try putting them all on cartridges and programming by computer. You'd have to have people on roller skates whizzing around the room going up and down ladders, racing from Instacart unit to Instacart unit. You'd have to have a building full of Instacart units.

All of the computer technology for radio, short of music, exists now. Our computer trip in San Diego has taken hundreds of hours of thinking time and physical labor on the part of the radio station and the computer company, Martin-Wolfe.

Hall: I'm very interested in the use of the computer in programming. Are you still using several thousand song titles?

Jacobs: At least a couple of thousand. And we can print a list of those records at will.

We have a list computerized by our categories, by artist and title, if it's an album, what the name of the album was, the label, the manufacturer's number, length of song, length of intro, if the record was on the *Billboard* chart and how it went, and where to find the song in our library. This list is fantastic because you can cross-tabulate it, providing a list of the shortest to longest tunes, for instance, so that if you need to back-time a record to fill out a specific time gap, you know exactly what records will fit.

Hall: So the computer handles everything—not only business aspects, but programming aspects?

Jacobs: Sure. Normally, when you mention the word computer, people get up-tight. They think of a robot that will walk in and take over their job. The machine is only a tool for mankind ... always has been. It's the wheel helping man, not vice versa. Sooner or later, the computer will be a way of life in radio, helping the manager, the program director, the sales manager, the music director, the air personality ... not replacing them.

Hall: But what will be the role of the air personality in the computer world?

Jacobs: Communication. The computer has yet to be invented that can truly communicate with people. That's not to say that technology doesn't exist to make computers talk. In an airport, you hear a series of tape loops about arrivals and departures that come off computers. That's information, but not communicating.

Communicating has to do with emotions. Communicating is a human voice passing on to another human a feeling, such as: I love you, or, I hate you. The disk jockey's role in *1984*, in *Future Shock*, is still going to be to communicate.

I've been thinking about a network music concept since 1964. Why isn't there a rock network? Why isn't there a country music network? Why isn't there an MOR network? We've done a lot of rapping back and forth about it—Tom Rounds of Watermark, Bill Watson who's now with KMPC in Los Angeles, Jim Markham, and myself. And it could be terrific. In my fantasy, there is this idea: Wouldn't it be great for a program director and producer of radio to be sitting in a central studio telling the air personality or reporter in Iowa to hold up one second because some other personality is on the line from San Francisco, and Grace Slick has just done some wonderfully far-out thing. And information and music and talent would be stacking up on various inputs, and the program director and producer could select the very best things happening at that particular second, instead of just a news network, or a programming network.

What a wonderful idea. And it's more possible now than it was in 1964. In 1964 two things kept something like a rock network from being a reality—one of them was the high cost of land lines. But now we have the microwave system. National TV is using microwave for visuals and land lines for audio. And there's tremendous potential with microwave to hook up radio stations coast to coast. And think of the possibilities! You're sitting there—a guy who has spent $600 or more for your Sansui stereo receiver—and an air personality in San Francisco, in your left speaker or left earphone, is talking with a guy in Philadelphia in your right speaker.

Instead, what do we have? While we're sitting here, you and I, someone at some radio station is cueing up an Elton John record. Now, that's a bet you could make almost 24 hours a day and win: Someone at one of the 7,000 radio stations in the U.S.—or most of them—is cueing up an Elton John record.

Hall: How many stations do you foresee in your fantasy rock network?

Jacobs: I could spend hours just talking about that rock network concept. It is based on the fact that in towns like Fresno and San Bernardino—in almost every market in the nation—there's maybe more, but at least one station in serious ratings trouble and losing money. Fifty radio stations that are losing money can barely afford $1,000 for promotion. But the network with the same stations could afford a $50,000 promotion, right? Instead of a small station putting together a poorly structured advertisement for a local paper, how about a well-designed ad for *Sports Illustrated,* or a regional issue in any of the national publications?

Hall: You don't think the music network would violate FCC regulations?

Jacobs: Oh, I think it might put the regulations to the test, but perhaps they should be put to the test. The network regulations, to me, look like they were written in 1934 by someone who had a perception of a Nazi type propaganda takeover of the United States through the use of media. They might have been wise at the time, but who's to say they shouldn't be changed now?

The music network might be better for the public, because you would be bringing the best air personalities and the best newspeople to a greater range of audience.

And there are other things to consider. For example, what is the primary profile of the person that listens to FM rock radio? Is it the 18-34-year-old guy. Is he, more narrowly, an 18-24-year-old guy? I go to every Rams' home football game, and I look around and notice that there's as many 18-34-year-old guys there as anyone else. But whoever thought about teaming up Frank Gifford with a Robert W. Morgan on the air? There are so many diverse programming elements that could be assembled on the air, like a programming pageant. And record companies would support it. If they knew that this air personality in Dallas cueing up a record is going to be heard in 276 cities, it would save record companies an awful lot of work.

What's happening now in radio is that we have 7,000 radio stations doing what I consider a semi-rinkydink job. But wouldn't it be fantastic and fun to work on a network rock radio concept using modern technology—for the really great radio people to get together and play, which is what work should be when you're having fun, you know? I can hear this national rock radio network in my head.

When I was at KHJ, such a network would have been the only thing that would have worried me, from a competitive standpoint. If such a network came on the air and the producer could flash from station to station and air personality to air personality around the nation, listeners would flock to it. Then, you could set up a country music network, an MOR network, a soul music network—the possibilities are endless.

OUTRO: Ted Atkins was program director of KHJ in Los Angeles when the first interview with Jacobs was taped; he went from KHJ to WTAE in Pittsburgh as station manager, and he has been extremely successful.

KROQ in Los Angeles was already floundering when Jacobs was interviewed. It later went off the air for several months because of financial problems. In June 1976, it came back on the air. Bill Drake and Gene Chenault were, and still are, partners.

Jacobs tried to get a network interested in his rock network idea; it, however, was a little too radical for them. At least, at this time it is. The use of satellites may eventually achieve the same purpose.

Frank Gifford does football play-by-play announcing.

BILL DRAKE

Bill Drake, first interview

INTRO: Over the years, several interviews were done with Bill Drake; two were selected for this book. Drake, who began his radio career in Georgia as a disk jockey, had risen to become programming consultant to RKO General's radio division by the time this first interview took place. The first station that he consulted for RKO was KHJ in Los Angeles, then a dog in the market. Drake hired Ron Jacobs as program director and, with a phenomenal army of assistants such as Bill Watson, Bernie Torres, and Gary "Gary Mack" McDowell, marched to success. He was later to consult WRKO in Boston, KFRC in San Francisco, WHBQ in Memphis, CKLW in Detroit, and WOR-FM in New York—all with extreme success. He pioneered the oldies format at WOR-FM, then programmed by Sebastian Stone. Drake conceived the greatest radio documentary to date—"The History of Rock 'n' Roll." He was singularly responsible for refining Top 40 radio and for eliminating extensive clutter and tuneout factors. Though things have changed considerably in radio since this interview, the philosophies of Drake still stand undaunted, and because of its historical significance, this interview is irreplaceable.

Hall: Today, how do you reflect in programming what the masses really want to hear?

Drake: You have to go on a thing combined of singles and album cuts . . . cuts which are researched. I think the day is over when you have your lay-back lennies going, "Wow, man, here's a far out cut I found on such-and-such album with so-and-so playing flute." That's bull, you know. I think most FM progressive stations are now doing that. But progressive rock stations were suffering generally, until some got a little more objectivity into their programming. Those FM stations that are more objective are those making the strongest gains now.

Hall: You mean mainly the ABC-FM stations?

Drake: KLOS-FM, certainly. I think progressive stations before were a bunch of gobbledygook with guys getting haired to the middle of their back, and running around doing a whole number pretending to be far out. The public gets as tired of that as they do anything else. ABC has done very well with their format approach to progressive rock—better in some markets than in others. But I think on a relative basis with what they're doing and what's on other progressive rock stations, there's no comparison.

Hall: FM in general continues to grow, doesn't it?

Drake: It has become one of the most important aspects of our entire operation. We make a hell of a lot more out of the FM things than we do with all of our other activities.

Hall: The syndication programming services? How many markets are you in now? This includes the "Hit Parade '72" package as well as the "Solid Gold" package. Are you planning any more programming services? [Drake later changed the name of some of these packages.]

Drake: Yup. Going to do a country package.

Hall: Who's going to put that together for you?

Drake: Well, I want to be involved in it. I like country music—at least I would help.

Hall: You're just involved in too many other things to devote full-time to it?

Drake: Not only that, but I think anyone who does it would have to do it as a full-time occupation.

Hall: When do you speculate having that package available?

Drake: It really depends on other production schedules, because we won't have any trouble on research and putting the ingredients together. But production time will . . . well, we're building another studio. The load has been increasing so much that we're often working in shifts around the clock on our programming services.

Hall: We were talking about album cuts a minute ago and how most progressive rock stations, in your opinion, weren't really professional enough. But they did make an impact?

Drake: They did. I think they opened the way for objectivity to come into progressive rock radio. But in every instance I've seen where the subjective lay-back lennie operation is pitted against a station who researches their music, the lay-back lennie gets kicked in the head. The listener says, "Later," for those things.

Hall: The research aspect should come stronger into other formats, too, don't you think? Do you listen to the country stations in Los Angeles?

Drake: From time to time, but with so many other things that I *have* to listen to, I don't have much free time. About the closest I get to country music anymore is when I invite some friends up who I know dig country music, and we get half bombed and listen to a bunch of old country albums.

Hall: The country music syndicated programming that you're going to do, will it be done on the same order of your "Solid Gold" service?

Drake: There'll be some similarities, but what it will be basically is a fairly straight approach to playing damned good country music.

Hall: Are you going to research the music?

Drake: Yes.

Hall: But in country music it's said that up to 95 percent of the singles sales are to jukebox operators.

Drake: So, we'll research jukeboxes.

Hall: But how many of country music radio listeners actually go into bars where jukeboxes are?

Drake: Obviously, a hell of a lot of them. (Laughs.) We'll pay attention to the country music trade charts, of course, and research store sales. But it's also obvious that a large part of the people who go into bars enjoy that type of music on the jukeboxes, otherwise jukeboxes wouldn't be buying country records. Of course, bars are mood places. You might find that a certain record had 404 plays on the jukebox, and it'll turn out that was because the same guy's been drunk there for four days.

Hall: Getting back to Top 40, is it more and more of a problem to research singles?

Drake: Well . . . it is. You can tell fairly well how they're selling if you don't get too much of the hype and the freebies and that sort of thing. I think that the people we deal with are being legitimate and accurate with us.

Hall: Record company executives and promotion men?

Drake: I was referring to the record stores. I think that, so far as sales are concerned on singles, you can determine them fairly accurately. But then, you have the problem of whether that figure really means what people want to hear.

Hall: How much weight would you put on singles in programming?

Drake: That's hard to say. I'd say 50 percent of this radio business is *feeling* anyway. You have to look at the sales, determine if they're legitimate, and then determine objectively which of those records reflect the type of audience you're going after . . . your target audience in programming. It's intrigued me that you don't have record companies jumping up and down in anger because KPOL—the beautiful music station in Los Angeles—doesn't play their records, or because the record is No. 14 in Omaha, or because it isn't being played on KMPC or KOST. Somehow record people feel we in Top 40 radio are required to play a given record. But we program just like they do— KMPC, KPOL. For sound. We have to. But record promotion people say: "My God! It's No. 26 in town. It's sold 18,000 records." I say: "Fine. But how would that record sound on KOST?" Granted, the record might fit more with our sound. But people really think that the typical Top 40 station was designed to give them the kind of exposure they needed. However, the fact that George Beverly Shea's record is No. 3 in a market doesn't mean that the Top 40 there has to play it, not if that's not the type of sound you're trying to create. That sound is part of research, but research still has to be weighed from an objective view of what sound you want. It's just like programming a computer—you feed it errors and it'll throw them right back at you. But a lot of people misunderstand that any program director 'programs' his station, and a Top 40 program director has the same right to do that as a KOST or KJOI or KMPC program director.

Hall: In other words, any program director has the right to be selective?

Drake: Sure. Because that is the only way to maintain the image of a station like KMPC. Why don't MOR-prone record labels complain when KMPC puts on a ball game for four hours? Because that's robbing the record company of exposure time for their product. It gets absurd sometimes. But it somehow seems to me that, where a Top 40 station is concerned, just because a record is No. 36 in *Billboard* with a star, we don't necessarily have to play it.

Hall: The argument is not valid?

Drake: I don't think it is, because you have to try to relate programming to a market . . . to the competition, the particular direction of a radio station, and the type of audience it's trying to attract. If you're going after a mass audience, you have to design your programming to reflect that mass audience.

Hall: I've now got a loaded question for you. How do you tell a record promotion man that you're not going to play his record? What are the tactics you use?

Drake: I never tell him anything. You've got to remember that the final word on that would come from the radio station anyway. That's where the record promotion man would get his information. As consultants, we can't sit back and dictate that anyway.

Hall: But your word means a hell of a lot at the station level.

Drake: I can only say what I think. The program director then reacts. The situation gets a little weird sometimes.

Hall: Do you know that a lot of record promotion people have their jobs or that last salary raise, because they claim to know you?

Drake: That's really weird. I've been in this town seven or eight years now. I know a lot of people here. But I've also run into people I'm supposed to know that I never met in my life. I've found that some of the greatest experts on Bill Drake have never talked to him at all.

Hall: I'd like to meet an expert on Drake someday. But to get back to my loaded question, how do you tell a man you can't play his record?

Drake: I don't really come in contact with record people in talking about records. Most of the people I've known for a long time in the record business . . . I just don't get into discussions about records—it's a total drag otherwise. I like being around record people and radio people and talking about records and radio in general, but not specifically.

Hall: Do you find that a lot of record people know radio pretty well?

Drake: Not . . . not really.

Hall: Even the guys who think they do don't know it as well as a radio man knows its intricacies? What are their major misunderstandings about radio?

Drake: I couldn't say. I don't know. But as far as them having a definitive understanding of what it's all about, they don't. There's a hell of a lot more involved in a radio station. Like many people, who tend to deal only in records . . . well, records are a very important part of radio. Some records. But there are so many other important things, and sometimes they don't realize that. How could I say what they understand or don't understand? Yet, they may know a hell of a lot less than they think they do.

Hall: Getting back to general radio, as singles begin to slowly fade—which you've got to assume they're going to do over the next 5 years, or 10 years, we just don't know—what is your criteria going to be then for picking songs from albums for airplay? More of a seat-of-the-pants thing?

Drake: Picking records will be determined by what occurs . . . if singles sales actually fade. The criteria will be the same . . . and that is to find out what records please the most people. At that point, it becomes merely a matter of working out research methods. It's very difficult to speculate what research methods will be available to us 10 years from now. You'd have to be dealing with known factors in any case.

Hall: Have you begun setting up research techniques for the future?

Drake: Well, we go over albums. We survey albums. We study what success other people are having with particular LP cuts. Nobody can play them all. But when you collect all of the information that you can, you should generally have an idea of what cuts are the most successful.

Hall: Do you think it may eventually evolve down to where you test people's reactions to various cuts—similar to the behavioral psychographic studies now being conducted by Dr. Tom Turicchi in Denton, Texas?

Drake: Studies of that nature always depend on how accurate your guinea pigs are. But I'd feel a little silly in Los Angeles hooking people up to eight million wires.

Hall: In the recent changes among programming people in the RKO General stations that you consult, did everything work out pretty well so far?

Drake: Everything worked out fine except Washington. That was a big disappointment.

Hall: I hated to see the Washington failure. Another Top 40 station in the market would have been good for the record industry. That's something that the Federal Communications Commission doesn't consider in their decisions. To change the subject, did you read the Jack Anderson columns about payola?

Drake: No. I read a few of the articles written about the two columns.

Hall: Do you think it's as real as he makes out?

Drake: I don't know . . . I can't imagine that it would be, but I don't know what he said as opposed to what other people said about his columns. But I think that . . . I don't know, but I would find it hard to believe. And, just speculating that there were cases where payola was being practiced, I don't believe any station could be successful over a period of time and have payola going on. I think that people involved in payola would eliminate themselves. You can't put those kind of records on your radio station in the face of today's competition and survive.

Hall: About the merging of MOR and Top 40 . . . .

Drake: In some areas that has happened.

Hall: In some cities, the MOR stations are playing virtually the same records as the local Top 40 station, yet calling themselves an adult station.

Drake: It's very obvious what has happened to a lot of middle-of-the-road stations. In trying to project a younger demographic, they wind up playing the Osmonds, or the Partridge Family. What you see at that point is a mass exodus of listeners and the emergence of the FM sweet music station. Because a lot of the people who used to listen to MOR stations won't take the sort of thing that MOR stations are doing today.

Hall: They just leave. Do you think that if they go over to FM they ever return to AM?

Drake: Well, I don't think there's any absolute on that. I obviously believe highly in FM . . . and have since 1967 and before that, because WOR-FM, New York, was a pilot of things we wanted to do. And also the syndication later . . . that's the reason we got into so many FM stations—because we think that for music FM is like color TV compared to black and white TV, stereo compared to monaural. But I think that everyone switches back and forth from AM to FM from time to time.

Hall: Regarding MOR, do you think that if a Perry Como or an Andy Williams were out making more MOR records—artists of that type—were turning out more product, that MOR stations would have more product to put on the air and thus be more viable? It seems to me that many MOR stations are playing the soft rock material because they don't have any product unique to themselves. Lately the records being cut by the so-called MOR artists have merely been versions of recent Top 40 or rock hits.

Drake: Well, that's true, but it's not necessarily a new thing. I remember when the Fontaine Sisters were covering the Charms, and Pat Boone was covering Fats Domino.

Hall: Someone is always covering somebody else?

Drake: Sure. For example, the Gladiolas, or whoever it was, came out with "Little Darlin" and then the Diamonds did it. The Diamonds made their career from covering other stuff.

Hall: Are MOR stations making a mistake by playing rock records?

Drake: I don't know whether it's a mistake or not. I don't know what they're trying to achieve. Let's face it, some of those stations do pretty well with that policy. I'm aware of several that do damned well. It works for some and it doesn't for others. I guess the key is how they do it.

Hall: What is the strongest influence you see now in Top 40 radio?

Drake: When I first went to clusters of commercials two years ago . . . or whenever . . . in Top 40, people thought: "Well, he's done it now." But the problems were simple. As records got longer, you had to make room for them. You can't cram any more music in your radio hour than your commercial policy allows—and we already have a very good commercial policy now at our stations. Certainly a hell of a lot better than the normal. We couldn't say to the record companies that they had to create shorter records. Because, quite frankly, increasing the length of songs in many instances created whole new dimensions in music. And that's important. So in order to accommodate whatever music was valid, we did what we've always had to do: Make whatever adjustments we have to make. I think that radio stations or record companies or even individuals get screwed up sometimes because they don't want to adjust. They become rigid. Everybody becomes God. Well, that's bull.

Hall: Let's backtrack some more. Did you find Gene Chenault or did he find you? You were working for him as a program director, weren't you?

Drake: No. I was in San Francisco. After the KYA job blew up—matter of fact, one of the offers I had at the time was to come to KHJ in Los Angeles as program director . . . and I had one in Cleveland and one someplace else. But I figured, what is that? I would wind up the same way . . . with the sales department walking all over the station. All the gobbledygook. Chenault, I guess, had been trying to call me. But I don't talk to people on the phone I don't know . . . and he'd never gotten to me. Anyway, we met somewhere and he said he liked the things I'd been doing and he wanted me to do something with his station. I said I could dig it, but no station in a market that size—he owned KYNO in Fresno, Calif.—could afford to pay me what I'd have to have. He said: "Why don't we have two stations? That way, it could be done." We basically started from there.

Hall: Were there two stations at the beginning?

Drake: KYNO in Fresno and KSTN in Stockton, Calif. But he didn't own KSTN.

Hall: What were you doing in San Francisco?

Drake: Programming KYA.

Hall: Before Johnny Holliday took it?

Drake: I replaced Les Crane.

Hall: Where had you come from?

Drake: Atlanta.

Hall: You went directly into KYA? What happened?

Drake: The station was what, fifth? We took it to first.

Hall: Who were the jocks?

Drake: Tom Donahue, Bob Mitchell, Peter Tripp, Norm Davis, Bob Brannon, and me.

Hall: Then you went with Chenault. Where did you go up against Ron Jacobs?

Drake: Fresno. He was programming KMAK—the competition.

Hall: Who had the legendary treasure hunt that everyone always talks about as the promotion that killed a radio station?

Drake: We both did.

Hall: Only his treasure was never found, right?

Drake: It was . . . eventually. But I played a lot of psychological games with Ron. He thought that I had found his treasure. But the competition between the two stations then was a dog-eat-dog thing. Matter of fact, that's why Gene Chenault wanted me to come in there because Ron and Robert W. Morgan, Dave McCormick, Frank Terry, Jay Stevens, Tom Maul, and a couple of big jocks were all at KMAK . . . Robert Prescott. They were giving KYNO fits. They had a damned good radio station. I had a free hand, and we kept basically the same jocks and turned KYNO around. But it was a dog-eat-dog situation. They'd follow me down the street with car radios . . . it was unbelievable.

Hall: What were KMAK disk jockeys doing with radios in the cars following you down the street?

Drake: I don't know, man. I was married at the time—maybe they were trying to catch me shacking up with some chick, I don't know.

Hall: Is that printable?

Drake: I don't care.

Hall: They were doing everything, trying to wipe you out?

Drake: It was really funny. One night I was driving down Stills Avenue, and I kept hearing this talking on the left-hand side of me. I had the window down. What they'd done was pull right up beside me. One guy was driving, and the other was crouched down out of sight talking on the radio. I asked: "What's going on?" The guy looked up with a shocked expression on his face. Matter of fact, the first time I saw Jacobs he was following me around the Fresno County Fairgrounds. I had to ask somebody— Glenn Adams, I guess—who he was. I think that either one of the stations, KMAK or KYNO, could have beaten any station in Los Angeles at that time. Fortunately we wound up with 40s and they ended up with 20s, but it was weird—two stations with almost the whole market locked up.

Hall: When did you really get to know Jacobs?

Drake: I guess the first time I really talked to Ron was when he came back from Honolulu. KHJ was set. We were only two weeks away. Ron had been over in San Bernardino. Robert W. Morgan talked to Jacobs and got him to call me. Let's face it, Ron Jacobs is a hell of a radio man.

Hall: Did you ever think about programming KHJ yourself?

Drake: No. I didn't want to do things that way. Anyway, things worked out all right.

Hall: No. I guess you can't complain.

Drake: Being program director of KHJ was never the intent. Because first of all, my agreement with RKO was that I would give them the equivalent of one day a week for the station.

Hall: A couple of years ago at the annual convention of the National Association of Broadcasters, Gene Chenault told the managers present at a meeting that they should pay their program directors as much as they pay their sales managers. Is that typical of the stations you consult today? Are the program directors getting paid better than most?

Drake: I think so, as far as the general market is concerned. That's an RKO thing, and it's their business what they pay their people. But I know for a fact that they pay damned good bread.

Hall: The rumor was that Buzz Bennett got $50,000 at KGB. In fact, I think I heard him say that somewhere. Maybe he was talking about KCBQ.

Drake: Bull! $23,000. $25,000. Claude, there's a whole lot more to this business than pulling ratings on one or two specific instances.

Hall: Whatever happened to Bennett? What were the reasons for his success down in San Diego? Because I never did understand it. The very things he talked about in New York didn't work for WMCA when he was there. Yet he comes out to San Diego, and the very same techniques that didn't work for WMCA seemed to work for KCBQ.

Drake: Well, he was playing about 24 or 25 records down there.

Hall: The short playlist is not the whole criterion for success.

Drake: No, but that was what he was doing musically. And then he hired away a lot of our guys from KGB.

Hall: Well, I've never understood his success. Who, among all of the program directors in the nation, would you list as the top 10?

Drake: (Laughs.) What do you think I am—crazy? I'd have everybody else mad at me.

Hall: I've always thought Sebastian Stone was one of the best in the country.

Drake: I think all of our program directors are heavy.

Hall: Do you see that Top 40 radio is going to grow?

Drake: I think . . . continue to grow? Who knows? First, you have to break down what the term "Top 40" really means. That's merely a tag put on a certain kind of radio. What it is, in reality, is radio featuring the music that reflects a contemporary thing—a contemporary life-style, everything else.

Hall: In other words, Top 40 radio is not just the music?

Drake: Even the music has to reflect that life-style. All parts of your station do. I think there are a lot of rock stations in this town, in every town, and I guess they're all trying to do the same thing—but they do it in different ways and people put different tags on it. You know. But, as far as progressive? Top 40 is and has been progressive for a long time. It's been geared to evolution at all times. Actually I think that progressive radio, as it came to be known, was saved from extinction by *regressing* a little.

Hall: But you think Top 40 radio, because it is basically a reflection of life-styles, is going to be a dominant factor?

Drake: I think that anything that reflects the music that people want to hear and presents it in such a manner ... sure, I think that a radio station that does that will be around.

Hall: Have you ever thought about syndicating a soul music service?

Drake: Well, there's only so much that anyone can do. No, we haven't. [But he later did.]

Hall: So the next service will be a country music package. What are your expansion plans after that?

Drake: I can't say right now.

Hall: Your consulting activities ... are they still growing or have they more or less become stabilized?

Drake: We have purposely curtailed that.

Hall: You have enough stations then?

Drake: I don't know how many stations we have turned down ... some pretty big stations in big markets ... maybe 20 or 30 of them.

Hall: How do you feel about all of the people who've copied you?

Drake: I really couldn't say, because I don't know all of them.

Hall: Do you feel they were doing right in copying you?

Drake: I don't know. I think some people came fairly close, and some didn't come close at all. I don't know. Who knows what they think they've done?

Hall: But you've always said to me that you had "personalities" at your radio stations. Yet, the criteria of most of these copycat stations was to eliminate personalities as such completely.

Drake: Well, this is something you and I have talked about before. I think one of the greatest injustices done—not to me, but to some of the people who've worked in this organization for a long time—was what was written about them, that gave the impression everyone got. I think it was a great injustice to the disk jockeys who were on KHJ or WRKO or KFRC or anywhere else. It's strange that years later, when maybe the communications in the industry have caught up, most people say the disk jockeys who work with us are the best in the whole country. The same guys who were ridiculed for so long. When people talk about heavy jocks in radio, I would say that a large percentage of those in Top 40 radio have worked with us. It was never the idea just to have jocks who gave the time and temperature. I kept trying to tell people that but nobody would listen.

Hall: Some night I'll invite you to a party and play a tape of a parody about me and you—a college station up in Boston put it together. Listen to it and you'll cringe.

Drake: Boston must be a weird town. Last time I was in Boston I got calls despite the fact that nobody in town knew I was there ... I don't think. I got eight, nine, or ten calls, all hours of the day or night. From Boston radio students.

Hall: You had drinks one night with John Walton and Ray Potter. See, I have spies everywhere.

Drake: I was sitting in a hotel bar with Scotty Brink and they walked in. They were very pleasant guys.

Hall: They said the same thing about you. What kind of advice would you give a young program director who's trying to program a radio station for the first time?

Drake: Research your programming as well as you can. Think about it. Be as logical about it as you can. Be totally dedicated to it. Be totally diligent about it ... and from there on, it's perseverance.

Hall: How many hours a day do you work on radio? On music?

Drake: Hard to say. Sometimes it'll be 20, sometimes an hour and a half.

Hall: What do you do for play?

Drake: Oh, I have no real hobby. I'm single again, so that makes for different diversions. I like to play tennis. Tennis is about the only sport that I enjoy playing anymore.

Hall: What do you think of the record industry in general? Is music as good today as you think it should be?

Drake: Sales are the only gauge you have, I guess, as to how good the music is. Obviously the record industry isn't satisfied because they keep trying to come up with new artists, new records, this, that and the other—they're always looking to improve music, too. I think that some record companies are doing very, very well. I think that the industry in general has grown a whole lot ... and when I say *grown*, I don't mean in billings. I mean they've made an awful lot of progress in trying to be objective about what they're doing. As long as they're trying, how can you fault them? You can't. Because creativity doesn't come on command. The environment has to be developed for it, and the decisions have to be right about it. It all comes down to the marketplace. The companies that are doing well are obviously good companies because otherwise somebody would replace them.

Hall: What kind of music do you like personally?

Drake: Obviously, I like rock. And I like some of my high school favorites . . . .

Hall: You're still playing those on KHJ, aren't you?

Drake: Well, we don't play Roy Hamilton, you know. And I like country. I got a kick out of that Columbia Records thing—what was it? The 20 years package. That Jo Stafford stuff ... you forget that even existed, you know. I like everything from today right on back, really, as far as hits are concerned. I like r&b, but basically country music and ... I guess one of the reasons I like the progressive music sound—not the pseudo stuff, but the legitimate, reflective progressive music of today—is because a large part hinges on country music. A lot of people involved in progressive music are from that sort of bag and, as a result, I like it.

Hall: I was just talking with Bernie Torres, though, about the Statler Brothers who have a big record in country music called "Do You Remember These?" To me, it follows the same lines of their big hit "Flowers on the Wall." But Bernie says that the current record is too country. You like country, so how come your stations don't play more country product?

Drake: You can't, Claude. You see, nobody can set themselves up to throw out to the public this, that, and the other. I think the most important part of what we do in the broadcasting business is to try accurately to reflect what is going on around us in music. I don't feel whether it's Ted Atkins, me, or anybody else, that we have the right or prerogative to impose our tastes on anyone. I am very defensive about that type of thing, because I'm afraid that I might actually be playing a record merely because I liked it. That's why you have to be even more careful. It would be wrong. You only hold on to ratings by being objective.

Hall: About how much of your day is spent listening to new records?

Drake: It varies. Today, I guess about five hours.

Hall: That much? All new stuff, or some that's been out a while?

Drake: Both. Then you go back and listen to stuff again.

Hall: Do you find that you have to listen to some records more than once to decide?

Drake: Sure. Like, I gave Bernie a list of records, he brought them out, and there's a box in the office. Those were just the ones I specifically wanted to go over today.

Hall: Does Bernie also listen to records?

Drake: Yes.

Hall: Who else? Betty Breneman, of course.

Drake: Anne, Ted, Jan . . . the music people at each station.

Hall: And then you have to compile all of this music information. It's more of a feeling, right?

Drake: But you have to be objective . . . have to read everything that you can and get all of the research that you can, whether it be *Billboard* or the *Gavin Report* or whatever . . . and put all of that chart information together. Then that will move your own personal feelings one way or another. You have to be looking at other stuff, too. So you have to be not only listening to product, but putting together all of the information you can on records.

Hall: In regard to playing only hits regardless of what kind . . . .

Drake: Particularly on a country record? Well, there are many theories: One, that you should play hits on a Top 40 station, no matter what, and as long as you play the hits, you'll be in good shape. The other theory is that if you take a country record that may be a hit and play it, you're not very likely to pick up extra listeners since the people who really like that type of record are probably listening to a country station all of the time. So you probably aren't going to pull any of those people away from a station that plays only the music they like. Not with any particular record.

Hall: Does the same thing apply to Top 40 stations playing soul records?

Drake: It very well could be. I think it depends how far a record, whether country or soul, crosses over and becomes pop. And there's another theory that if you play a good country record—or soul record—then the listener may just get so much in the mood for that kind of music that they'll tune you out and go to a country or soul station.

Hall: Have you ever attended the annual convention of the National Association of Broadcasters?

Drake: No. Those people don't allow me around very much.

Hall: It's a pity that more general managers of radio stations don't care more about programming then they do. In the changes made at KHJ a while back . . . .

Drake: In staff?

Hall: It's a pity you couldn't keep Charlie Tuna.

Drake: Yes, it sure was—but that was his choice, not mine.

Hall: I mentioned to Tuna at the time that if I were program director, I'd want to put my strongest man into my weakest slot . . . or one that was one of the weaker slots at the time. But my psychology didn't work. I guess it was a question of ego.

Drake: Well, we tried everything. Like I told him, I can see his point. But I think any program director in his right mind . . . I mean the ideal situation would be to have Robert W. Morgan and Charlie Tuna on the same station. At that point, if you make the decision that you want them both on the air and they aren't, it has to be somebody else's decision. Tuna's good.

Hall: Morgan really wasn't able to build on WIND in Chicago; I guess he belongs more on KHJ.

Drake: I think he'd begun to make inroads in Chicago.

Hall: There are a lot of good albums out today, aren't there?

Drake: Yes. The thing is that for years, artists who had a hit single would put out 11 pieces of crap to fill out the album. Today, you take a Rod Stewart album — well, any album—there's a lot of good stuff on it. The artists are concentrating on making albums. Whereas, I felt that as far as album cuts in general . . . sure, they're fine and albums sell, but I maintain that until the market was really ready for them, they were not that valid for programming. They gave you variety. What I think the record business did was mature enough to where they started concentrating on everything in those albums—on the entire album instead of just a single.

Hall: But at any rate, you went to album cuts somewhat on your stations. Was that move based largely on the success of WOR-FM in New York and their playing of LP cuts?

Drake: To a degree, certainly. But it also reflects, I think, that good albums do have more programming validity today. They're obviously what's happening from a dollar volume type of thing. And what we were trying to do was be representative of what was going on with our target audience. That was the whole key. But another thing that we have done is do an awful lot of research on our research. Betty Breneman has gone through a whole thing with the people at the radio stations on really doing research on their research—as far as increasing the number of stores, finding out where the sales volume is—because it's surprising how often that thing changes from year to year.

Hall: In other words, you've got to change the system?

Drake: Well, the system is basically the same, but you have to make sure that what you're researching still has validity. Sometimes you'll find that you'll have a huge volume record store come in. Unless you're constantly researching the market for sources of information, you'll never put it in, because it has always been done by this, that, and the other. But the music research is supposed to come from the outlets that are truly representative of what the hell is going on in record sales. Today, however, a lot of outlets don't even sell singles . . . weird . . . they don't even stock them at all.

Hall: They don't bother anymore. It was a big story when I found out that White Front was going back to stocking singles in their West Coast Outlets. It gave record companies a chance again to sell singles. So, basically, your stations are clueing in again on what's happening in their individual markets—what new stores have opened up, and what stores they should check weekly for sales data?

Drake: Sure. That should be a constant thing anyhow. But every year or 18 months, you may have to scrutinize and check to see what could be done better in those areas, because you forget. You get into a routine or system that's valid, but if you keep yourself in that rut without looking around . . . .

Hall: You grow stagnant? We have to keep checking our system at *Billboard*, too.

Drake: I think one of the important things that *Billboard* does with their charts is listing the titles in a alphabetical order and listing the previous week's position. It's really important to watch the progress of a record. And it's important to watch your advance sheet. If I were going to offer a suggestion for improvement, I would list those new records that have gone on and the records that have dropped off the chart. That's really the only suggestion I could come up with on the chart, as far as convenience and information—because the information on the *Billboard* "Hot 100 Chart" is really incredible when you compare it with others. It's a very complete type of chart. But I'd like to see everything that went on and everything that went off. Otherwise, it takes me an hour and a half to figure that out.

Hall: Good point. Back to your own research. Have all stations now instigated research about their markets regarding research?

Drake: Sure, but it's not that big a thing for us. That is what we always try to do constantly.

Hall: In regard to playing album cuts, it would seem to me that choosing a particular cut would usually be a personal choice.

Drake: Not really. For instance . . . .

Hall: When I put my own tapes together . . . of course, I'd like to think that I've got damned good taste, but . . . .

Drake: But what we have to do is figure out . . . other research areas. You see, most of those album cuts, well, we didn't wind up with three cuts out of the Cat Stevens album a while back, at various times, or four cuts, for no other reason than the LP was still No. 7 in town—and after 20 weeks!

Hall: That "Tapestry" LP by Carole King was a big one, wasn't it?

Drake: I was looking at the chart a while ago. I don't know how many albums the record company sold.

Hall: Do you know that Al Jolson is still selling 30 to 40,000 albums a year? Of course, that's from catalog product. I guess the granddaddy of catalog product would have to be the greatest hits album of Johnny Mathis. [Later, Carole King's "Tapestry" went much further — more than 13,000,000 copies at last count.]

Drake: Yeah. Five or six years on the chart . . . .

Hall: More like 12. And probably still selling. But there is a validity for picking LP cuts?

Drake: Sure.

Hall: What do you do—go through and find the best two or three cuts?

Drake: Well, for instance, the Chicago LP—that's basically their greatest hits album, so we figured it's not worthwhile, but we put on Malo because the act was coming up at the time.

Hall: You don't remember how many cuts from the Malo album, do you?

Drake: Well, basically between one and four from any LP, depending on the LP.

Hall: Were the air personalities able to play any cut they wanted to?

Drake: Those LP cuts were basically catalog. At WOR-FM in New York we used two album lists. There was an A and a B list. One list was more or less what we called an image thing, and those cuts didn't get as much exposure as the B list. But the cuts were still slotted. It wasn't a thing of saying: "Pick out whatever," because, we all get a little weird sometimes, depending on our mood.

Hall: So, the air personalities were told to pick one from the A list and one from . . . ?

Drake: Basically. Well, out of an Elton John album, there were four or five cuts played, but only *those* cuts were played, and they were sometimes changed.

Hall: But why did you change programming somewhat at KHJ when it was already No. 1?

Drake: KHJ was doing extremely well. It was a *feeling,* more than anything else. We were just trying to reflect, more closely, what was actually going on in music.

Hall: But you changed the station when it was doing well.

Drake: But we always have. It's just that some of the changes haven't been as noticeable and as significant to the record business per se. This change to include some albums was not something we were doing for the first time. We'd been playing album cuts at WOR-FM for some time.

Hall: So, you had a testing ground?

Drake: We'd obviously tested the theory for some time. You have to have a certain amount of self-discipline with yourself, because otherwise you get some harebrained idea and do it, and all of a sudden you sure enough create a mess. Just like anything else, when you do make changes there should be a definite reason for doing it.

Hall: When you shifted toward the policy of more album cuts a while back, how did you break the news to KHJ program director Ted Atkins and the other guys about the changes you wanted to make? Was it hard to do? Because I don't think you rule with an iron hand.

Drake: It's not that at all, because first, that wouldn't be the method that we'd take. What we would do is . . . see, we discuss all of these things very thoroughly before you say: "I think we ought to do such and such." Well, we have these meetings, and every guy sits around and talks about these things. We also talk about the pluses— why this or that might be a good idea. We ask every guy to knock all of the holes in the idea that he can—let's find out where the flaws are before any idea gets on the air. Because, otherwise, we'd be all kidding ourselves about radio. Everything has to be thought out, and everything has to be an agreement. There were some good points brought up in meetings both for and against the album-play policy. As far as the system—the way to play the cuts and the scheduling of the albums and everything else— I'd say that everyone contributed to that. We've had a lot of ideas suggested in meetings—some from me and some from them—and when we actually got down to analyzing them, they were horrifying. We shouldn't have been considering those ideas in the first place. Fortunately, you sort of wipe those bad things out of your mind.

Hall: How often do you have meetings of your program directors?

Drake: We try to do that sort of thing every two to six months, depending on everybody's timing. This gives a program director a chance to sound off on his problems and get feedback from everybody else. We'll go over the music and the rotation policies.

Hall: Have you given much thought to speaking at the International Radio Programming Forum this year?

Drake: I just don't think those things are good for me.

Hall: No, it probably wouldn't do you a bit of good, but it would do other radio people a lot of good.

Drake: I don't mean that. I just don't think a speech by me would benefit anybody. Because when you get down to specifics about radio, radio is my job, and I'm not going to tell a whole bunch of people what I'm *really* doing.

Hall: But philosophy and theory would mean a lot to everyone. For example, your theories about progressive rock . . . .

Drake: Well, I don't know. I'll think about it. I've got a big project coming up which may take up all of my time. I'll know in a couple of weeks whether I'll be able to speak or not. I'm tempted, but . . . .

Hall: Do you listen to all radio in an analytical frame of mind?

Drake: I can listen to sweet music stations without getting analytical . . . and country stations.

Hall: I'd like to see the development of the progressive country format on FM radio.

Drake: Claude, you and I both know that you don't find that many FM radios in a pickup truck. Did you see *The Last Picture Show?* You ought to go see that . . . it'll really knock you out. That whole small town scene. I don't think there's any music at all but Hank Williams records in the movie, and it's all over the radio, a little country station.

Hall: What do you see is going to happen with radio?

Drake: Well, the problem with album cuts, which has been happening for some while— if you can call it a problem—is that you don't know *which* album cut. But I have found that the best album cuts usually surface. Let's face it, if a record company pulls a single out of an album, they generally have a good idea that it's a good song.

Hall: But the general trend has been a shorter playlist, and here your printed survey shows all of those albums.

Drake: But we don't play all of those albums. For example, there's a specific album that we'd be foolish to play any of the cuts, even though it's selling well in this market and we show it on our list. By the time an album gets into the stores and starts selling and we get enough reports for it to show on our album list at KHJ, we might not be playing cuts from that album anymore.

Hall: In the old days at KHJ when Ron Jacobs was programming the station and it was building, it seems to me that Ron used to get tapes of Sonny & Cher's new records out of the studio. Do the stations you consult still try to get those exclusives? Or do you feel they're necessary anymore?

Drake: Well, I think it's important to have exciting new records on the air as quickly as possible, but it's illegal to play a record before it's released. Anyway a record company can't afford to give any one station an exclusive—it's like telling all of the other stations in the market to go to hell, and that could cause a real problem for a record company. Playing exclusives indiscriminately hurts too many people. On the other hand, those days and the competition at that time, to play exclusives got a lot of bad records played.

Hall: Well, those exclusives helped make Sonny & Cher.

Drake: Bob Skaff and Charlie Green brought a dub by of that first Sonny & Cher hit, and Skaff wasn't even with Atlantic, with whom they were signed then. Green was their manager. It was as simple as that.

I'll tell you the reason we did that whole Sonny & Cher thing. I don't think I'd even met Sonny Bono at that point—or maybe I'd said hello to him in Martoni's—but first of all, we did that Sonny & Cher thing because KRLA was doing all of those Beatles things. People talk about all of the related excitement that concerts bring, which is true to a degree. But very few people realize today that the first time KHJ hit No. 1 in a rating period was when KRLA had the Beatles in town at the Bowl and had interviews and all that excitement. What we did was take the Sonny & Cher thing, that exclusive record, and create a diversion.

Hall: Your plans for the future?

Drake: Like I told you before, we turn down a lot of stations on consulting, because that's not the total answer to our business. We're getting more and more into FM. And Gene Chenault spends a lot of time looking for new properties.

Hall: Are you a partner in that, too?

Drake: It's a subsidiary of our company.

Hall: One last thing: Did you go out and dig up that buried treasure that sunk the KMAK promotion, allowing you to beat Ron Jacobs that time years ago in Fresno?

Drake: No, but he always thought I did . . . for a long enough time, anyway.

OUTRO: The names of the radio syndication programming services produced by Drake-Chenault Enterprises have changed, and new programming services have been added since this interview was conducted. After this interview, RKO General worried about potential governmental problems because of Drake's unusual strength as a consultant (and thus to avoid any and all possibilities of FCC questioning), made Drake an executive of the corporation. However, Bruce Johnson wanted a vice president of programming who was at hand; Drake wanted to program the stations from his office at his home. So, Johnson and Drake parted ways.

The station in Washington mentioned was WGMS. RKO intended to take the AM station to a rock format like KHJ, keeping the FM classical. Protest groups rose up in town; RKO was concerned about agitating the FCC and thus backed down and kept both AM and FM classical. Johnson, then president of RKO Radio, felt if there were that many people protesting, they should be willing to support classical programming; today, the former classical music loser is doing quite well financially.

In reference to Jack Anderson's column about payola, one of Anderson's so-called informants later turned out to be an executive with a small record company devoting itself to bluegrass; he couldn't have gotten his records played on a Top 40 station for any amount of money.

WOR-FM is now WXLO, billed as 99X.

Ted Atkins was then program director of KHJ in Los Angeles; at this time he's manager of WTAE in Pittsburgh.

Betty Breneman was then national music coordinator for RKO Radio; today, she operates a record tipsheet.

Robert W. Morgan is a swing disk jockey on KMPC in Los Angeles. Charlie Tuna is now morning personality of KIIS, Los Angeles.

The International Radio Programming Forum is an annual convention devoted to radio programming aspects. Bill Drake, reluctant to appear and speak, eventually moderated a session one year.

"The History of Rock 'n' Roll" is being revamped and modernized at this time. It will be put back on the market after a few years off the air.

Bill Drake, second interview

INTRO: It's been quite some time since Bill Drake was programming consultant at RKO Radio (in his last days there, he'd been made a vice president of the chain in order to give him more clout at the radio stations). As of this interview, he was concerned only with consulting KIQQ (called K-100 on the air) and his partnership in the radio syndication firm of Drake-Chenault Enterprises. This interview was conducted at his house just south of Wilshire Boulevard in Beverly Hills. He had not forgotten an interview with Ron Jacobs I'd printed two or three years earlier (shortly after the first Drake interview). Jacobs programmed KHJ for five years during the years Bill Drake consulted the entire RKO chain. As you'll note, the conversation quickly moved to Jacobs and that interview.

Hall: In this business it's hard to say who did what first. I've often wondered if Buzz Bennett invented the programming ideas he talked about . . . or got them from working for you at KGB in San Diego.

Drake: I never wanted to be first; I just wanted to be right. I've been first so many times and got my ass in a crack I can't tell you.

Hall: Bill Stewart may be the first person to play the same record 12 times in a row.

Drake: That was a McLendon trick.

Hall: Right, but he was working for Gordon McLendon or his relatives at the time.

Drake: I never wanted to hurt anybody or discredit anybody, and there's nobody I've worked with professionally for a sustained period of time who I have hurt, but sometimes some of the things that you see printed about me in major publications are just not true. Hey, I'm a person too, you know?

Hall: You and I used to fight. We had some pretty good battles.

Drake: Only because of a philosophy.

Hall: I think that we have the same basics at heart. We want to do something for this industry—make it better. Anytime you see something that I've written, and you wish to give your side of things, tell me. As for the interview I did on Ron Jacobs . . . .

Drake: Hey, listen, I love Ron. He's a great programmer. I can't say anything bad about him, but as far as "The History of Rock and Roll" documentary, here's what you do: Bill Watson, of course, is no longer with me . . . you ask Bill Watson about "The History of Rock 'n' Roll" or you ask Gary Mack about the KHJ thing and whether the staff was set, whether the format was set, whether everything was already there. I mean Gary's going to tell you the truth about that. Well, I find, like I said jokingly earlier, and it's true . . . that something that was originally "Drake's Folly" was later everybody else's success. And that is in no way taking anything away from anybody. I think that Jacobs is one of the most brilliant guys I've ever met in radio. But I think that things sometimes get taken a little out of context. I think Ron did a very good job with "The History of Rock 'n' Roll." But as Ron also noted, Pete Johnson wrote it with Ellen Pelissero. Bill Mouzis was actually, you know, putting this thing together from an engineering point. It's not something that Ron Jacobs has ever said or anything else. He let people assume whatever they wanted, and there's nothing wrong with that, I guess. But Ron didn't know about "The History of Rock 'n' Roll" for three-and-a-half to four weeks because Bill Watson and I were a little afraid to tell him. In those days, when you'd talk about experimentation or this, that, and the other—if you even wanted to change one jingle—I remember there was a huge discussion between Jacobs, Watson, and me one time for three days. It started originally at Nickodell's next to KHJ. I said I didn't like that jingle that says, "93 KHJ Plays More Music." When we originally cut the ID, it was fine. But we didn't take into consideration that every other jingle says, "93 KHJ." I said why don't we just invert the whole thing, be a little different? We just say, "More Music KHJ." Or "Music KHJ" . . . bang . . . and it won't be the same, and it won't be as long and drawn out and everything else. There was a three-day discussion about that, you know. I said, "Look believe me, I am not trying to destroy the format. It's not that I don't believe in it. For chrissake, I came *up* with it! I'm not trying to say it's all bad, but, you know." So, with "The History," Ron was not one to toy with things that were working. In retrospect, hindsight is always a great luxury. But in 1968, I think it was . . . or 1969 . . . when you're talking about doing that kind of special in the context of Top 40 radio . . . from a tightly formated station like KHJ . . . to go into a thing like "The History of Rock 'n' Roll . . . ." I mean, all of the music was different; it was a whole different thing. You're talking about taking 48 hours of your air time and changing it, you know. It would be like KFI in Los Angeles doing a weekend of Led Zepplin, as far as compatibility, almost.

So "The History of Rock 'n' Roll" originally came about. There were some people up at the Bel Air house one night, and we were all sitting around playing records and old stuff and playing trivia. I said: "It's really a thing about the music and all the things that have gone into what makes the whole thing like it is today. We sit here like this and we play trivia about records and things, and so many people don't even know that." I said: "Wouldn't it be great to use the music itself and actually tell the story? I mean actually give the entire history of rock 'n' roll . . . of how it evolved and where it came from and everything else." Everybody's half stoned, so everybody says: "Yeah, wouldn't that be great!" I kept thinking about the idea though. I knew the music itself had to be the focal point, because people may want to be educated, but primarily they want to be entertained. So entertainment had to be the key. I knew the key to it had to be the records themselves so we would use excerpts of some records, but generally throughout the whole thing those records would be played in their entirety. That was what had to be done—*not* to educate them on it.

Hall: You had to play the full record.

Drake: So Bill Watson and I sat down, and we lined all this out.

Hall: Did you actually fix the format to the hour?

Drake: Oh, yeah.

Hall: The whole works?

Drake: We had the whole concept down for it, because the main thing had to be the information and all that, and we had to have enough of the interviews and everything else. But primarily the music had to be the thing because we were a music station and people would want to hear music. That was it.

So, we worked all that out. Still, we were a little hesitant, and we talked to Ron about it on the phone. He said, hmmm, and something like: "Wouldn't that sound be fantastic." Well, we said, all right we need someone to write it, we need someone for this, that, and the other, and I said it should be written from a certain concept. The first writing attempt was sent back. I said: "This is not what we're doing. This is too detailed. It's too precise. You're getting a little too authentic." You know, it's one thing to be authentic but the entertainment has to be there, too. Remember, the primary thing is the music. But there were so many people involved.

It went on from there. Ron oversaw the thing because we were cutting it at KHJ, but I don't think Ron was involved in the writing any more than I was. I don't think Ron was involved in the splicing any more than I was, or the gathering of interviews any more than I was.

Hall: By the way, keep the master of that documentary for posterity. If we ever get a decent radio Hall of Fame together we want that in there.

Drake: I've got the script.

Hall: Let me read this: *"The History of Rock 'n' Roll" begins with Bill Drake, who conceived it, Ron Jacobs who produced it, Pete Johnson wrote it, Ellen Pelissero directed it, production coordinator was Sandra Gibson and Vicky Larsen was music coordinator. Audio supervision and production techniques, Bill Mouzis. This is Harvey Miller.* Great, great, great. Oh, by the way, I just thought of something I wanted to ask. "The History of Rock 'n' Roll"—how many stations carried it —300?

Drake: We would have to check the billings. We didn't have computers at that particular time. It's initial airing was February of '69. This was a sales promotion pamphlet from Art Astor who's back with us now. He was sales manager at KHJ then. "The History of Rock 'n' Roll" was broadcast the first time February 21-23, 1969. It delivered a solid 25 percent share of audience and KHJ estimates a 30 percent share on their rerun.

Hall: No idea how much that doggone thing . . . ?

Drake: We heard estimates anywhere from 300 to 500, but, Claude, we don't know.

Hall: Stations? Then, there's no way of telling how much money it generated?

Drake: Well, we'd have to go back and check through all the books and everything else. But, it depends on the market size so much, Claude, that you wouldn't know.

Hall: Well, then I'll guess at WLS in Chicago. Someone told me thay paid $17,000 for it.

Drake: Yeah. I forget what they paid, but I know it was for two runs.

Hall: Was that about the highest price paid for broadcasting it, do you know off-hand?

Drake: It would have been, I'm sure. Gene Chenault and I talked to Ross Taber, then head of radio for RKO, and we were always very careful about any of this because we used RKO General personnel and we used KHJ personnel. But, Drake-Chenault copyrighted the thing. It was our goody. We said to them, okay, we're going to broadcast this since we are working for you guys on all the RKO stations for nothing, obviously.

But, we own the rights to it. Since we're using your personnel on this, what do you want? What·we'll do is we'll jointly or, whatever, pay the cost of these people—you know, the Ellens and the other people who were brought in . . . Pete Johnson for writing and everything else. We figured studio time. We figured tape costs. And I forget what it cost to do. Something like $20,000 to $30,000. They took a percentage, which we got back recently in a lawsuit. But RKO got it free in all their markets for all the runs, which was fine for us because that's what we wanted in the first place. So, obviously, Chicago would be the largest market outside the RKO markets.

Hall: At the time you created "The History of Rock 'n' Roll," did you know what it was and what it was going to mean to radio?

Drake: Well, at that time I only knew what it meant to me. I didn't know what it was going to mean to Watson or what it was going to mean to Jacobs or to anybody else, but obviously I thought it was brilliant or I wouldn't have done it. You don't anticipate . . . I mean I certainly never figured that it would do what it did as far as money or anything else. But obviously I thought it was extremely good, or I wouldn't have been motivated to do it in the first place.

Hall: Now . . . "The Elvis Presley Story," radio documentary produced by Watermark, I know the first time around grossed $180,000. "The History of Rock 'n' Roll would put that to shame, wouldn't it? At the very least?

Drake: Well, I'll just say conservatively that it made a helluva lot more than that. As far as the figures, Claude, I really couldn't . . . .

Hall: I know. Nobody'd probably know.

Drake: It would take a lot of time going back to the books to figure it out. But the percentage that RKO had might be one way to check it out for you. Because every dime that came in, they got their percentage which I think was something like either 25 or a third or whatever.

Hall: That's high! Whose idea was it to keep part and negotiate for the rights?

Drake: The documentary was ours from the very beginning. Matter of fact, I think we had it copyrighted before we even talked to anybody. Gene Chenault taught me not to give away all my ideas. It was just basic. You know, I've talked to Gordon McLendon about a lot of things. His impressions regarding the misunderstandings about him . . . the myths. He had heard equal misunderstandings about me. And for us to sit down and really talk about it was weird because it was a thing of people really not knowing. I mean, he and I had been in the same business a long time, and Gordon was my idol, though I don't believe over the past 10 years I've done things as he used to do them . . . and I don't think he would do things now as he used to do them. But it was really amazing to find out the truth about some of the things he did. All of the time, the truth was really flattering to him. The same with me, sometimes.

Hall: I think he gave Top 40 the news concept . . . instant news.

Drake: Yes, but he was also totally involved in Top 40 radio. The contest circus idea was basically Gordon McLendon's idea . . . I mean, the flamboyance of contests and treasure hunts. He had picked up on what Todd Storz was doing as far as format, but he added promotion.

Hall: That stunt he once did for Jimmy Rabbitt—turning over several old cars alongside the freeway into Dallas and painting a sign on the bottoms that read: "I flipped for Rabbitt." Then having Rabbitt do his radio show from a glass booth in the middle of a drive-in theater parking lot. Great stunts, even for Rabbitt. Guess I've always had a fondness for Rabbitt, going back to those days.

Drake: I do, too, but . . . oh, I think he's great, very flamboyant. But as far as a disk jockey, he's . . . .

Hall: Hard to control?

Drake: No, it's not the thing to control him—it's the thing that he can't control himself—much less anyone else being able to control him.

Hall: I was with KMET general manager David Moorhead in Australia at the 2SM Radio Group Convention when that whole music policy problem came up. I think Moorhead wanted to keep him on the station, but wanted Rabbitt to back off playing so much country music because the ratings were poor. Rabbitt had to ease off; he refused and left the station.

Drake: My thing with Rabbitt . . . .

Hall: He didn't last very long at KHJ, as I recall.

Drake: Ted Atkins was programming KHJ at the time, and he, of course, knew Rabbitt's history, which has been his history since. Let's face it. He's been at every goddamned radio station in Los Angeles.

Hall: No. He hasn't worked at KBIG with its beautiful music format.

Drake: Atkins had talked to Rabbitt, and I talked to Atkins. I got Jimmy out, and I told him up front what my reservations were about hiring him for KHJ. I said: "Now, you understand what kind of radio station we are. I assume you know that because I've checked out what kind of personality you are. You've not been able to deal with what the station does in the past, and we may be even more like that in days to come. Let's not delude each other." I was very hesitant about hiring him after conversations with Atkins and Rabbitt. But Rabbitt assured me that there were no problems. Therefore, when somebody after three days on the air comes back and says to me: "Well, I didn't understand this," to me, that is horseshit.

Hall: Personally, I like to listen to Rabbitt. I wish there was a valid place on the air for Rabbitt, and for Tom Clay who is right now off the air in spite of being one of the best one-on-one communicators in radio.

Drake: Well, I could be the most lovable person, the biggest character in the world, but imagine what would happen if in my dealings with RKO or even Gene Chenault I flipped out and decided to take KHJ to a country music format. They'd tell me I was out of my mind. I do not deny that personalities are good, per se . . . that all kinds of radio are good. But when you have a particular approach to a format, that's the way things should be. Follow the format.

Hall: To what do you attribute your success? Were you ever a failure?

Drake: None that I accepted.

Hall: It was always someone else's fault?

Drake: It wasn't that so much . . . if you accept failures at certain points in your life, they become that. If you refuse to accept them, you stave off disaster until you're able to recoup whatever mistake you made.

     Blaming it on anybody? You can't, because that will be documented sooner or later anyhow. Maybe I've never had to deal with that many failures. We all have, in our personal lives and everything else. But I'd say that probably my strongest point is taking an overall view and getting a whole perspective on whatever's going on. I have a lot of faith in people, but I don't kid myself about them. I would never say because of my personality, "I can't get along with that asshole because he wants me to do this, that thing, or the other, when I knew up front about him. I don't call you up and say I want to do an interview because of the things that have been written about me are totally baised or untrue or are just opinions. I'm not that type of person. I don't think anyone's done a really definitive study on the specifics of a lot of very important aspects of broadcasting. I think it's very important that a lot of people understand what really did go on . . . what we did go through.

Hall: If you had it all to do over, would you have been involved in rock radio like you are?

Drake: Oh, sure.

Hall: In other words, you wouldn't change much of anything?

Drake: No, because I think everything that has happened was because of my initial involvement in music and liking it. When rock came along, I was in high school and it appealed to me. I think that everything else that has happened was a result. I really couldn't have planned it much better.

Hall: You mentioned talking with Gordon McLendon. Who are your heroes throughout radio?

Drake: Well, I think Gordon. I think a lot of the people I worked with whom I won't name. Bobby Tripp, who died, was one. Tom Donahue was another.

Hall: What did Bobby die of, do you remember?

Drake: Hodgkin's disease. But Bobby and Donahue and I were all together at KYA. I was program director there, and they were jocks. Bobby was doing noon to 4 and Tom 4 to 8 PM I think. And, eventually it was 3 to 6 PM for Bobby and then 6 to 9 PM for Donahue. There were a lot of things that came out of that, you know—Donahue's departure into what he then called underground, progressive rock. A matter of fact, I left KYA in a dispute with owner Clint Churchill over Donahue. Churchill wanted to fire Donahue, and I refused to fire him.

Hall: Why did he want to fire Donahue?

Drake: He said that he "didn't like Tom"—that Tom was this, that, and the other. I refused to fire him and said, "Well, Mr. Churchill, you can do whatever you like, but that doesn't necessarily mean I'll do anything you like. You want him fired, you fire him. But I'll guarantee you one thing; I think when the ratings come out next, his will probably be the highest on the station. I happen to personally think that he's one of the two or three best disk jockeys I've ever heard." And I said, "So, I ain't gonna fire him." And as a result, I left the station before Tom did. Tom and I used to sit and laugh about some of those old things, because it's so funny that Tom later became known as the Father of Progressive Radio and everything else.

Hall: Your philosophy of radio, has it changed any since 1965?

Drake: A lot of my thoughts would have to change about a lot of things. It would be absurd for me to sit here and say that I feel about radio—or about the sound of a radio station—the way I did in 1965 . . . for instance KHJ. Well, hell, that was over a decade ago—11 years, you know. At that time there was KFWB, KRLA, KBLA . . . and

KHJ was going to be the fourth rocker in the market. It was called Drake's Folly in those days. At this point it's called everybody else's success. But what we did then was come in with a much cleaner thing. At that point in time, we were much less obtrusive than the kind of Top 40 radio that KRLA or KFWB were doing. KHJ was much quicker. It had more music. It had fewer interruptions, and it had a lower commercial policy than the other stations did.

Hall: If you were to think about your major contribution to KHJ, which of course affected the world, what would you say was your major contribution? What did you do to shape all radio through KHJ?

Drake: (Laughs.) There are a lot of opinions about that. We just did away with a lot of bullshit, and we tried to do the research a little differently. You know when KHJ started, KRLA was *the* Beatles' station. They had the Beatles in the Hollywood Bowl for two concerts. At that time there were not only The Beatles, but the Dave Clark Five, Freddy and the Dreamers, plus you had the Stones and the legitimate things. But you had all kinds of weird stuff, too. Anything from England was put on the air, including disk jockeys, and the stations were Englishing themselves to death. We didn't do that. We played the valid Beatles. We played the valid Stones, but we weren't stampeded into a whole British syndrome like everybody else. We went a little the other way. We would play "What the World Needs Now," as done by Jackie DeShannon, just to avoid sameness . . . almost go against the grain somehow. As a matter of fact, I think the first time KHJ first hit No. 1 was during the height of the excitement about the Beatles' appearances at the Hollywood Bowl.

Hall: In those days, as a matter of pride didn't you go out and find new records occasionally, and put 'em on the air and break 'em and make 'em?

Drake: I think that anybody involved in radio who's not looking for the best records that they can put on their radio station has got to be some sort of an ass. A lot of things that happened to radio possibly caused my philosophy. I believe in research. I believe in being as accurate as you can. But one thing that I have always done differently than most people realize is that I think there's a hell of a lot more to the business than mathematics. A lot of people saw only the mathematics of my stations and left out the judgment. And that's the reason a lot of people sit back, and if a record shows up No. 12 on the chart—or if it numerically shows this, that, and the other—then it's a valid record to them and they don't know anything other than that.

Hall: Didn't you make judgments on records sometimes by the gut?

Drake: Oh, we all do. Still do. Always have. And so do other people out there.

Hall: Some of the younger program directors today don't. They don't make choices. They don't make judgments on records.

Drake: Well, I think they do—I just think they do at a later point. Because of a lot of reasons, not only because of me, but because of a station like WABC in New York and other tight listed radio stations or this, that, and the other—people forget the judgment area. The *feel* area, I think, is the key to success at any radio station. I mean, anybody can do the mathematics. If you can add and subtract and dial a phone and get record sales information from the stores and read *Billboard* and look at the *Gavin Report* and, check *Cashbox, Record World,* and *Radio & Records,* then you can get the numbers, you know. As far as where the records are on the charts you can say: "Oh, that's what I should be playing." Sometimes that's not necessarily the records you should be playing. It depends on what kind of station you are.

Hall: Like, for example, you played "The Last Train to Clarksville" and used a big promotion on that, as I recall, with the Monkees, but then you refused to play some of their other stuff later.

Drake: Well, I think playing or not playing any given record depends on what you're doing in programming at the time. We played "I'm a Believer" . . . "Day Dream Believer" . . . or something like that. But it's like anything else . . . like the original thing about the Sonny and Cher record, "I Got You, Babe." I heard that record on a dub, and I said that's a great record.

Hall: It made them.

Drake: And I said: "That is a great record!" I mean a good record for that time. It sounds a little strange now. But also it was a good thing for our programming purposes at the time. In addition to being a really good record it was the opposite of this whole English thing. This record, again, was against the grain so it served our purposes very well in two ways. They were here—they were available. As far as following the Beatles on tour—as did many radio stations—you could do the same with Sonny and Cher. And I just thought it was a good record off the dub. Talked with other people and everybody agreed.

You're always searching and listening for stuff. It's not a thing of looking around and saying, okay now, it went from 22 to 19 in Birmingham this week or it went from 22 to 12 in Buffalo so that must be a pretty good record. On the other hand, you take something like a Monkees' record. I mean, I wasn't particularly wild about "Last Train to Clarksville." But at the time we were trying to build teen listenership. The TV show with the Monkees was about to start. We felt that would be a phenomenon, no matter how short-lived. But that doesn't mean every record they put out is going to be a good record for us.

Hall: You mentioned something about the Sonny and Cher record "I Got You, Babe." You said that today the record would sound a little strange. The stations that are harping on oldies, do you think they should judge those oldies? Sometimes they play them by rote, you know.

Drake: Yeah, sometimes they just happen to be in the golden file, and there again it's the thing of the computer. It was a No. 1 record, so, you keep those No. 1 records in. It may or may not be valid, depending on circumstance. I mean if you've got an all-oldies station then that record is an obvious choice. But I think if we played it on K-100, or KLOS played it, people would say what the hell's the matter with them. Everything is based on individual judgments. But sometimes people try to pinpoint where you really are by a constant thing of saying okay, this, this, and this equals that. They only get part of the equation because of all of the individual value judgments to start with.

Hall: You think that the importance of a program director may have to do with the value of his judgments a lot of the time?

Drake: Well, of course. I mean, he's obviously using his judgment anyhow by just looking at numbers. I think that success lies somewhere in between. I think, again, there's relativity in radio. And saturation, as far as what's going on in the market at the time. If everybody is loose, and there are a lot of stations in the market that have very, very loose playlists with a lot of this artist's stuff on it, then a station coming in that eliminates that, sounds different and fresh. And the programming is against the grain. It's not the same old thing. That's good. But if radio stations all started copying that, the same theory would apply in reverse. In order to not be in the same bag, to attract listeners and be different, you do it the *other* way.

Hall: Is it more difficult to program a loose format station than one that's tight?

Drake: Well, of course it is, because then you have to *have* judgment . . . a little more so, you know. A little taste . . . a little feeling.

Hall: What will happen now with all the fragmentation that's going on in various cities, like Los Angeles, and New York, and anywhere you want to name. What's going to be the effect on radio?

Drake: There's only so much fragmentation that can happen, because radio stations that don't make it die out. As far as segmenting audience types, it's amazing the fragmentation that goes on, but yet it doesn't go on. Most people are checking things out pretty readily. Like in the ARB ratings before last, at K-100 we had a whole potfull of women, but we were not as strong in men as we wanted. So we made some adjustments musically and in tempo. We decided that we wanted to build that ages 18-to-24 male category because we were very weak in that. And, frankly, to our surprise, we showed up No. 1 in 18-to-24-year-old males. I think it was from 6 AM to 7 PM, I don't know about the night. I've got some figures on it here. But it's amazing how quickly adjustments like that will show and work, whereas before we did not have those.

Hall: In other words you can see results in one book today?

Drake: Well, you can, sure, but in a situation with market fragmentation, you've got to be absolutely insane to think that you can be all things to all people. You've got to take a . . . well, we did not play the C.W. McCall record "Convoy." It's a good record, don't doubt that, but to me playing that would be just as bizarre as KLAC playing Led Zeppelin even if the group recorded a good country tune. KLAC's audience would think: "What the hell's going on here!" Because their audience doesn't tune to KLAC for Led Zeppelin. See what I mean? You can do it in smaller markets. But when you get into Los Angeles or New York, you find a variety of stations doing particular types of things, and people looking for a station that hits where they're at. I could be wrong. I don't think so. I think in today's market you gotta be crazy to think that you can take a Helen Reddy record and a Bay City Rollers record and the C.W. McCall record and put 'em all on the same radio station and not piss everybody off, you know? I mean that's totally incompatible.

Hall: In other words, you must keep your music scheme going . . . ?

Drake: If people tune in to KLOS to hear a certain music that fits their life-style, and all of a sudden they hear an Al Martino record or some Perry Como records thrown in, I don't give a damn if it's No. 1 in the world, the audience has not tuned in to hear those records. I used to try to explain to a promotion man at Warner Brothers. One time he brought in, I think it was a Grateful Dead record and a Frank Sinatra record and some other kind of record. And he expected me to play them all. Promotion people seldom realize that the Grateful Dead fans would never have heard that Grateful Dead record because when they heard the Frank Sinatra they would tune out. And if you play the Grateful Dead record first—you know, vice versa. Today it's just more so, because a few years ago those people had to come back to your station eventually. Now, they have a possibility of finding a station that suits their taste and on a consistent basis plays what they can listen to over a sustained period of time.

Hall: In other words, you're advising a young program director to keep his music scheme in a single bag?

Drake: Well, he certainly has to have an identity as far as his station's musical image. Unless he's in a market where he can be all over the road. For instance, we can be much more varied in Fresno than we can be in Los Angeles simply because of circumstances and availability everywhere else. There are always exceptions to rules, but you have to generally try not to have music that is incompatible. You can't be all over the road with it.

Hall: How do you feel today—because this is a really tough question—how do you feel going up against a station you actually created—KHJ?

Drake: I think it's been fun. I don't think you really think of competing in terms like that. I think what you're doing at one time is totally different from another time. The main thing I find amusing is that the commercial slots, the IDs, the one-liner things and commercial things—the whole thing is exactly like it was in May of 1965.

Hall: They haven't changed one damn thing?

Drake: I find it very bizarre because the world has changed so drastically.

Hall: Would the station that you had on the air, though, be competitive today?

Drake: Hey, they're competitive today, too. There's no doubt about it, but you have to understand that Los Angeles is a unique situation as far as an AM station is concerned. Remember, KRLA faded out of the picture. KFWB went all-news. KBLA went this, that, and the other way. Well, what have you got on AM? I mean if there were another rocker on AM with a signal in Los Angeles, who knows what would happen? When you start looking around on the dial, it's almost a noncompetitive situation. But I think if competition were different, KHJ would be different.

Hall: If they had competition they'd have to be a different station?

Drake: Well, they wouldn't *have* to.

Hall: You mentioned there weren't any other rockers competing against KHJ. You ignored KRLA.

Drake: Well, I don't think you could call them a rocker.

Hall: Then I don't know what to call the station.

Drake: But with what they're doing now? I know that certainly Johnny Magnus is not a rocker type of guy. I don't know when was the last time I heard them, but you can just flip around . . . listen . . . and I don't think that's a rock situation at all.

Hall: Do you still scan the dial?

Drake: Oh, from time to time. To hear what a listener's impression might be if they were just doing it like you're doing it, you know?

Hall: What kind of advice would you give a young program director in the business today who's working his way up through the markets?

Drake: Stop trying to copy everybody else—that's the main thing. I think that obviously you must work hard, and you must do all this and all that stuff, which everybody says, I mean, that's pretty basic. But if you're doing all the other stuff right, you must not have a closed mind to your own intuition or your own inventiveness. You don't necessarily have to change a whole lot of things from the basics. Even subtle differences make differences.

Hall: To me, too many young program directors think 17 records, a shotgun jingle, a promotion, a cash call, is a radio station.

Drake: Well, with some of 'em, that's the case ... that's about it. There again it depends on the market you're in or how your station sounds relative to your competition—what they're doing *against* you. It can work.

Hall: What are other attributes of a program director, besides that willingness to work?

Drake: Well, he should know how to handle people. He's got to have judgment about what jocks should sound like. He's got to have a programming concept himself, before he can persuade somebody else to agree with it, or even carry it out. He has to be able to communicate what that concept is and the reason behind it. I think one of the most vital things is that he has to understand music. He has to really be involved in music and know the differences between one record that's good and another record that's good. He can like them both. That doesn't necessarily mean either record is good for his radio station. He could hate them both. Doesn't mean they're bad for his radio station. Judgment areas are the areas that have to be developed.

Hall: What percent of a radio station today is promotion?

Drake: Well, what kind of promotion are you talking about? Are you talking about contests?

Hall: Well, let's say on-air promotions and then we'll talk about off the air. How much of the success factor ... what percent of success do you attribute to on-the-air promotions, the contests?

Drake: You and I talked about this before. In Los Angeles, one year apart in 1965 and '66 we did a lot of on-the-air promotions at KHJ, and we did almost none at KFRC in San Francisco—both stations were successful, you know. I think that as far as today is concerned, most contests are garbage. I think that when you take our audience and KLOS's and KNX-FM's, it's obvious that most people aren't interested in contests because I know we're not running any, and I know that certainly is not KLOS's mainstay. It's not what they're all about. And you're talking about a helluva lot more people listening to those stations than any station in Los Angeles that *is* doing contests. A lot of contests that go on radio today are slapped on the air because the program director may be keeping up with what he thinks he has to do because you're supposed to do it, without really questioning whether he really should or shouldn't. It can also be a thing of his trying to convince a general manager that he ain't just sitting back and not coming up with anything.

Hall: What about off-the-air promotions?

Drake: You mean billboards, outdoor advertising? Well, I think anytime you put your call letters out anywhere that's good, whether it's the back of a bus, on a billboard, on a tee shirt or in a newspaper or in a column, you know. If, in your market, the guy at the newspaper is writing something about your station, that's great for you, man. Anyway, as far as on-air contests themselves, I just don't know how many people really believe in them or not. It's obvious the number of listeners who participate is very, very small, and the people who do, for the most part, are very, very young. Obviously you can have someone who's 65 years old. It can happen. But seldom at a rock station.

Hall: Let's get to music research. Aren't requests important? Phone requests?

Drake: Not to me.

Hall: Why? Any particular reason?

Drake: Well, because of the people you have calling over and over. In Los Angeles, we once found there were two or three people who were involved with the record who had a lot of friends calling. There were also the groups who set up fan clubs. And the general average age of your telephone dialer . . . well, who has time to sit there and dial hour after hour trying to get through to the station other than an eight, nine, 13 or 14-year-old who's not allowed to date yet. They can't go out anyway. They've got nothing else to do. So, consequently, you get a very biased viewpoint.

Hall: What weight do you place on store sales today? I'm not talking about yesterday, but I'm talking right now, today, in programming.

Drake: Well, I think that a certain amount of weight is okay. The stores don't have that accurate a thing. A lot of times they're giving you back your list from the week before. They may have a buddy who works at X label. It all has to be taken into consideration. You also have this thing of album sales versus singles sales. I understand you have a problem of freebies.

Hall: I don't know how much of that goes on today in record stores, but it used to.

Drake: I don't either, but you hear about it. I think you have to take a look at the general marketplace, but you should look at singles and albums. I think if you've got a situation concerning a Dylan single, it's thoroughly absurd to look at your store sales on the single and think, well, that's not a hit record, when maybe the album's sold a million in the market because of that or one other cut or maybe just because he's Dylan. I mean, obviously, there's not going to be many people who buy a Dylan—or a lot of other artists'—single.

Hall: What do you do then . . . make a judgment?

Drake: Well, sure you have to make a judgment.

Hall: Well how do you make a judgment about a cut on an album?

Drake: Well, there are ways to get a consensus on that. I mean you can take a look at what's happening at other stations, too, just like with singles. One of the best ways is to listen yourself. You talk to the people on the staff, but generally, if you find a lot of people agreeing about a certain thing, that concensus is pretty valid. If you've got three or four people on your staff who say this LP cut is fantastic, and you look and you see that *Billboard* says that these are the cuts and that *Gavin* says these are the cuts and *Radio & Records* says these are the cuts and you look at a KLOS here and you look at WNEW-FM in New York and you look at other stations that are playing LP cuts and they all generally agree, even if you don't, you've got to be sort of a horse's ass not to say, "Hey, I could be wrong, you know."

Hall: You do take a consensus then, on a lot of things?

Drake: You have to. You have to because, otherwise, you haven't taken a look at the entire horizon.

Hall: What are the major attributes of a disk jockey? What are the qualifications he should have?

Drake: Talent, brains, and discipline.

Hall: And yet you've had some of the most undisciplined jocks in the business.

Drake: Strangely enough, some of the jocks I've been associated with who people thought were the most undisciplined, were not. It was because of the image they presented. Some of those guys were more disciplined, more regimented—self-regimented and self-regulated—than I will ever be, and these are some of the ones who were supposed to be very, very bizarre. Because a real professional in any area *takes care of business.* You find so many people who want to come in and play the role of being a disk jockey or play the game. You can become a character or name or this, that, and the other, but many people spend so much time building a name that they forget to take care of business. Image is one thing, but taking care of business is some-think else again. You can take a guy like the late Bobby Tripp, or Don Steele, Robert W. Morgan . . . whoever else was involved, their main focus was to get things right on the radio as they saw it.

Hall: In other words, the disk jockey should . . . he can have his image, if he wants to, off the air, but on the air it's business he has to take care of.

Drake: Yes, of course. I doubt very seriously that Mary Tyler Moore is really as funny as she appears, you know? I doubt she's really exactly like that. It's like any other area of the illusion business, and that's what we're in, you know. Whether it be radio, or movies, the stage, television, or anything else, it's illusion.

Hall: Are you carefully watching the scene? What's happening today? What do you think is going to happen to radio? Are you ready, for example, for quad, the use of the computer?

Drake: Oh, absolutely. We've been using computers for years.

Hall: Well, I know you are using a computer in the playlist areas at Drake-Chenault, but . . . .

Drake: K-100, too. That's merely to keep track of things. The computer helps on things that used to take our music people weeks to go over. If it's coded, you can eliminate things and have an entire print-up in minutes. It's merely a thing of information. It's like writing things out as compared to typing. The computer does just about everything for us out at Drake-Chenault Enterprises as far as clients, shipping, billing, addressing . . . .

Hall: How many records do you think are the right length for a radio station playlist today?

Drake: Mmmm, it varies so much depending on what you're doing. You can't . . . well, it depends on what type of operation you're talking about. I think even more important is how many current records a program director plays in an hour. That determines more how your station sounds then anything else I think.

Hall: Well, how many records were on the playlist at KHJ when it was in its peak?

Drake: It varied. I would say probably around 35. There was a basic 30 plus the new stuff. Sometimes we would add extras or stuff like that.

Hall: How many were repeated?

Drake: The 30 would have been repeated fairly often. Much more so than we do to-day. I think they're still doing the same thing at KHJ today, but we don't at K-100.

Hall: Because today a radio station plays about 7 or 8, maybe 12, fairly frequently, and the rest of them get slugged in?

Drake: Well, I suppose other records are still in high rotation, maybe not as much as those 12 but still in there really heavy. The entire sound really depends on how fast your records turn around. When I hear a program director playing the No. 1 record every hour, he must be in a very fortunate situation, either with a signal that is the only one covering the whole market or his competition must be awful. Playing the same record every hour? I just don't think that's valid today . . . sorry. I think that anything less than four hours, at least for my purposes, is not good. We shoot for a minimum of four hours.

Hall: Why?

Drake: Because of the tune-in factor. You know, I think it's so absurd, if you look at it logically. Now think about this: All the research people with their computer stuff and this, that, and the other and so and so forth—they take the ARB at their station or the Pulse or whatever they go to. Basically, it's the ARB. They break out their ARB diaries, and it shows that the listening span of the average person is 62 minutes. So they figure: "Okay, people listen to the radio every 62 minutes! So, every 62 minutes you can repeat." They fail to take into consideration the most important point of the whole matter—the reason the people are listening for 62 minutes is because of how the station was programming in the first place. All these geniuses sitting down and figuring out how long their audience listens and programming that way and then reading the same thing out of that ARB ratings survey will do it again and find the same thing happening and say: "See? We were right! That's how long people listen." Isn't that dumb? That is really dumb.

Hall: Do you believe in picking every record for the disk jockey or giving them some choice of music?

Drake: I guess that depends on what disk jockey you have and how much time you have. I think the music has to be organized within categories. Even then you have to depend on the intelligence of the jock, and the format concept has to be laid out and discussed on both sides. You can't really pin down everything because of the difference in the length of records. You may have four to six open minutes in an hour, depending on the time of day, or it may be totally full, depending on whether it's a weekend or a Friday, December or January. So you don't even know how many you're going to play. You don't know what length of records you'll need.

Hall: So it's wise to give the jock some leeway so he can have a little . . . .

Drake: I think there are a lot of good jocks around. I think there have been a handful of really great ones. But I just don't think that whether it's me or you or a jock or whether it's in Los Angeles or whether it's South Dakota or some other place, that there is that much to say everytime a record is played. I don't think Bob Hope would talk after every record. I know, originally, people used to say, quote: "Drake radio— whatever that is—does this, that, and the other—the disk jockeys are nothing but automata . . . they're robots, they're not allowed to say anything. It's automated radio." Strange thing is that automated radio is not a bad term anymore. Those same people who talked that way . . . well, all of a sudden your heavy personalities in Top 40 radio, were guys like Steele, Sebastian Stone, Robert W. Morgan, and now Charlie Van Dyke. People forget how many of those people were on our radio stations. All of a sudden they're looked back on as being "personalities" whereas, then, they were being ripped to ribbons because critics said: "Well, that's nonpersonality radio." It was all horseshit then. It's horseshit now. Being a "personality" is not a thing of how long you talk, it's what you *say.* I just don't think that no matter how good a jock is on radio, well, if a disk jockey is *that* good, he ought to be on a talk station and not waste his time with all those ridiculous records.

Hall: Have you ever thought about automating K-100?

Drake: Well, you think about that, sure. But we haven't done it because of one reason. It's not because I would be afraid to do it as far as the result at all. I think it's a situation that could be done very, very well. You take computers, you take the sophisticated equipment today that can do things as well and more error-free than a lot of people can do. I mean, I'd rather have a push-button elevator, you know, than some dude sitting there getting the thing a little off-level at each floor. You think about that and sure you'd save some money by automating. But I wouldn't, really, because this station is my programming laboratory, for our Drake-Chenault radio syndication programming services.

Hall: That's a good point.

Drake: And therefore, since I am here, I want this. If I have K-100 automated, I wouldn't have that laboratory anymore. So, that's what it is to me.

Hall: How often do you think about radio? I mean just sit down and try to think of a new format or a new concept or some way of improving?

Drake: Well, sure, almost constantly. Of course, you think about it all the time.

Hall: Do you find that radio is still as much fun to play with as it used to be?

Drake: The fallacy, I think, is in people who think that, Christ, radio is this and radio is that, and they say: "It's not exciting any more." Those people aren't willing to deal with modern radio on the basis of understanding it. You don't have to come up with something totally new and different than anything that's ever been done before—a dramatic change. People who require that are feeding their own egos, and the necessity for doing that is what destroys them. They can't accept the fact that what you really should do in any situation of your life is take things that are obviously there—they're facts—and build from those. Radio to me is a business. It's my work, it's also my hobby. I happen to enjoy it. Always have. It's a lot of fun for me. I mean I really like it because I know, too, that there are a lot of things out there that haven't been done, a lot of areas that haven't been tapped, a lot of things that could be done but haven't been done yet. I don't think the improvements all have to come at one time. There are so many things that haven't been done. Any of these things can be successful, and they can work, and they can really justify your own creativity—taking something that maybe nobody else saw and doing something with it. Whether it be a concept, an idea, a format, or anything else. But it's not going to be a thing that's continually stimulating and motivating . . . that's gonna be topsy-turvy overnight. To say, "I'm bored now and there's nothing else to do," is horseshit. You hear people talking like that—like people say: "I'm going to get out of the record business because it's not exciting to me anymore." Well, it's obvious at that point that they're getting out because they only fed off the excitement, you know? They should, instead, feed the excitement, a little bit, you know. Lay their own balls out there on the line from time to time. Take a gamble with a new idea or concept *themselves.*

OUTRO: KBLA became KBBQ, a country music station; it then became KROQ under new owners who programmed rock music. KLRA eventually gave up the rock battle and was a mishmash of MOR, but currently programs oldies; license for KRLA is still in limbo and an estimated $9,000,000 has been spent in legal fees alone by the various applicants fighting for the license. A firm headed by Art Linkletter and Bob Hope seemed to be the frontrunners at press time.

CHARLIE TUNA

Charlie Tuna

INTRO: The most successful—in terms of popularity—interview that I ever did was this one with Charlie Tuna when he was phasing out of KHJ in Los Angeles. Tuna, then and now, is an extremely creative air personality who labors on his daily show, both on and off the air. Approximately 250 letters from all parts of the world praised the interview; I received about 100 phone calls commenting on the interview. To this day someone on the phone will mention it, or I may bump into a radio man in Austin, Tex., or Miami, Fla. or somewhere else who'll tell me they have a tearsheet of the interview and still reread it from time to time. On one occasion, 30 of the nation's major Top 40 program directors voted Charlie Tuna as the best Top 40 disk jockey in radio.

Hall: Do you prepare your show?

Tuna: Preparation is somewhat sporadic over a day. I pick up bits and pieces . . . I hear things. Driving around Los Angeles I look at billboards. I sit down in front of the tube at night. Everything is just a constant looking around for ideas. Then at night I'll sit down with a spiral notebook—that's why I have to attribute a great deal of my success to Larry Lujack at WLS, Chicago. I used to watch him in Boston—he'd come in and sit down with a spiral notebook. I used to wonder what he was doing, until one day I looked over his shoulder and saw he was writing all his thoughts down and I thought, "That's wild." So I knew then and there—that was the way to prepare a radio show. When I came to Los Angeles, I got a spiral notebook and said to myself: "This is the way I'm going to do it." When you get to work in the morning all of your thoughts are there, and you don't have to go searching through your mind. I also go through the *Los Angeles Times* and get ideas. There are some wild stories buried inside that thing. That's about the way I prepare my show and it's been successful so far.

Hall: Then the selection of material written in your notebook is all at random?

Tuna: It's a hit-and-miss situation, because one of my favorite actresses for looking at has always been Raquel Welch. So, I was thinking: wouldn't it be wild to get her on my radio show. One morning I walked in and set up a bit where I pretended some close friend of hers had slipped me her private phone number, and I would try to call her at home. I set up a series of phone bits, on one, I got no answer. On another, I got a busy signal. And finally, through just a priming of the pump, I'guess, her milkman's wife called me. And then her coalman called me. And I finally talked to her agent . . . and this was shortly before I left KHJ. I think I could have eventually gotten her on the show—but it never was consummated, for lack of a better word.

278

Hall: Did you prepare those phone bits?

Tuna: Well, the milkman's wife and the coalman were live. The other bits . . . I knew a couple of numbers that I'd get no answer on and one that was disconnected. I love to do phone calls on the air because the listener has a great deal of empathy for them.

Hall: One of the most interesting comments about you was from Dan Clayton, program director at WLW, Cincinnati.

Tuna: I've heard of him.

Hall: He once told me that every time he came into this market, he made it a point to listen to you. He always figured you were going to burn out at any second, and he wanted to catch it.

Tuna: When I first came here, they said: "Hey, you've got to cut down on your material, you're going to run out in six months." They've been telling me that since I started in radio. I don't see any bottom of the well. Everybody figures, just one more day for Tuna. In Wichita, Kan., there's a gentleman named Art Miles who said, "You belong in Los Angeles." I told him he was kidding because I was only 20 years old at the time. But he said to go ahead and go to Los Angeles, but be careful because most jocks burn themselves out in Los Angeles in three years. I said, okay. So everybody figures I'll burn out one of these days. But I'm only 27, and I feel I have a long way to go yet.

Hall: How long have you been in radio now?

Tuna: Since I was 16 years old. I started out in Kearney, Neb. at KGFW, 250-watts. I was a junior in high school and I'd do my morning show and dash off to high school . . . work out for football or track in the afternoon . . . and dash back to the station to do an evening show and some production. Then I'd go home and get four hours of sleep and start the whole routine over again. I'd actually started doing record hops at the age of 14.

Hall: Did you make any money at it?

Tuna: I was the first one that did in our area. $25 a week. At 14 that was a lot of money, and better than I did on my newspaper route. I went down and auditioned for the radio station in this town of 12,000, and I got the job after six months of "don't call us, we'll call you." From there, my career sort of skyrocketed, it seems. It's been over 13 years that I've been playing disk jockey.

Hall: Where did you go from there?

Tuna: To KLEO, Wichita.

Hall: You bounced right up there?

Tuna: A friend of mine who's still in Wichita—Don Williams—and . . . .

Hall: He's been in that market a good while.

Tuna: We were good friends in Kearney. I hired him to do the nighttime show there. We'd decided to go down to Elkins in Dallas and get our first class licenses, and he stopped back by KLEO and got a job. I went on to Kearney, but he kept doing numbers on me, asking them to listen to his buddy up in Wichita. Two months later, I got a job 10 PM to 1 AM there. Then I got a shot at the morning show. I was in Wichita for about a year, then went to KOMA, Oklahoma City, a 50,000 watter, which was a trip, because the Beach Boys would come in and say: "Yeah, I was lying on the beach in Hawaii listening to you on my transistor."

Hall: I heard that station while in Carlsbad, N.M., once.

Tuna: You can drive down Sunset Strip at night and listen to them right here in Los Angeles. Anchorage called one night when I was there. I started out doing the 7-midnight show, which was the glamour spot, or so I thought, because everyone could hear you all over the country. Kind of an ego trip. Eventually I got a shot at the morning show and did that. One December Lujack was driving across country, on his way to a job in Boston, and was punching around the dial and heard me from a snowdrift in Wyoming. When he got to WMEX he told them about me. WMEX called me and offered a job and I said fine. I was doing the traditional market-rise most jocks go through and that was the sixth market in the nation. I was doing afternoon drive and Bill Drake heard me and asked if I'd like to come to Los Angeles. So in the space of a little over three years, I went from Kearney, Neb. to Los Angeles, Ca.

Hall: But why do you prefer the morning slot and having to get up so damned early?

Tuna: I love it. It's always been the most attractive slot to me, simply because you have a greater rapport with your listeners. You don't have a lot of the problems on your mind that clutter you up later in the day. You're just out of bed, fresh, and optimistic. It's the most ideal spot in radio I feel. As far as money and prestige, it's the number one spot. It's the quarterback slot of any radio station. Without a good morning man, a station will never get off the ground.

Hall: Did you always feel you were going to be an air personality?

Tuna: Yeah. As a matter of fact even when I was five years old I used to sit around the house in front of a turntable and pretend I was on the radio. There was a guy on KGFW named Jack Lewis. He's dead now but he was the morning man, and I guess he's one of the reasons I always had that underlying desire to be a morning man. He used to do wild things—have a dressing race . . . talk about flying saucers— just wild. And I loved him and was very inspired by this man. Eventually I got him on my paper route when I was 11 years old.

Hall: Have you ever thought about becoming a program director?

Tuna: I think they're always getting buried under paperwork, and I've always liked the glamour end of radio. There's more money . . . and more satisfaction to it personally. If I've ever had any frustrations, radio seemed to be the answer.

Hall: Can you vent your frustrations on the air?

Tuna: I think in a subtle sort of way, you can. I've always come out of the studio at 9 AM completely purged.

Hall: It's funny—here you've been in radio since you were around 16 and it hasn't gotten boring or tiring to you.

Tuna: No. Robert W. Morgan, when he left KHJ to go to WIND in Chicago, said: "You do your spiral notebook trip, but it's going to get tiring to you one day and you're not going to want to do it anymore." I said: "I don't see that day in the future . . . I've been on the air half my life, and I don't feel any boredom." He said: "Maybe when you're 40." I told him that I'd be in radio about as long as anybody wants me.

Hall: I would hope you've been banking your salary over these years. I told Don Imus of WNBC in New York to be sure and bank his salary.

Tuna: The public is extremely fickle. If anyone ever wonders about some of the high salaries paid to air personalties sometimes it's because of the risk involved.

Hall: Gary Mack once told me that you could tell the size of the market of the air personality by the size of his U-Haul trailer.

Tuna: Gary was the one who broke me in at KHJ. He picked me up for two or three nights, and I look back on those days . . . .

Hall: Was it a lot of fun?

Tuna: Very exciting. But all of my years were exciting.

Hall: Did you ever have much to do with Bill Drake?

Tuna: Normally, no. He consulted KHJ, but his thoughts were relayed through the program director. I probably saw more of Bill the last two weeks before leaving KHJ than I did the previous four years. But I have a great deal of respect for the man.

Hall: I wonder why he'd want to cut down on the humorous bits you were doing?

Tuna: They just felt that I was sometimes overdoing it. What the scale is for overdoing it, I don't know. I always tried to keep myself in check. I would argue that they listened as radio people, but the average listener out there is listening maybe 30 minutes at a shot and he doesn't hear half the things you do. Yet I got tremendous reaction from listeners to the bits.

Hall: Robert W. Morgan fits well into the present-day KHJ approach, I think. And Walt "Baby" Love is a Drake-type jock. The only traditional personality on the station would be Don Steele, I guess.

Tuna: Steele is a personality, period. It's somewhat disillusioning to me—I had the feeling my bits were working and the impression I got from the man on the street was that they were working. I'd hang around parties in Glendale. Never went down to Martoni's which is a notorious hangout for record-radio people. Haven't been to Martoni's yet—and I don't want to because that's *playing* to the industry people, and if I start playing to the industry people, then I've lost the other eight million standing out there. So, I've always tried to direct my thoughts to the lady at the clothesline in the backyard with three kids, and a copy of *Good Housekeeping*. That's where my thoughts are all the time. I don't want to play to industry people. I realize that there are a lot of air personalities who do, because that's the only way they can keep their jobs. But I can't see it. If something I say on the air appeals to an industry person, fine, because it hit that other listener first.

Hall: If you had it all to do over . . . all the way from Kearney, Neb.

Tuna: Make sure you spell that right. I'm going back for a high school reunion in six months. And I'd hear about it if you misspelled it.

Hall: Would you have done things differently in your career?

Tuna: I've often wondered because I've thought: What a rat race it has been! But I don't think I would have. There have been a lot of heartaches . . . a lot of sad times. Because when you're going up that fast—from Kearney to Los Angeles in three years—you're going to maybe hurt some people, offend someone because you left them or another reason . . . though you may not want to hurt them. But I guess I'd do it all over again. I have to give a lot of credit to my wife, Sherry, who has raised our three kids, and kept the home fires burning. She's been with me since Kearney, so she's seen me grow up. And some of my career-building has been hell for her.

Hall: It's always bad on the wife of an air personality.

Tuna: Yeah. Especially in the beginning . . . in Wichita and Oklahoma City. Before we had any kids she would often be sleeping on the couch in the lobby of the radio station waiting for me to finish up some production chore at 2 AM in the morning. I had 18-20-hour days, and she would hardly ever see me. But she stuck with me. She's a radio wife, and she's been my greatest asset.

Hall: A wife can mean a lot to a guy's career.

Tuna: She'll either make you or destroy you. And Sherry's made me. My advice to any young guy starting out in radio is to make sure you get a woman who understands radio and loves it like you do—otherwise . . . .

Hall: Bonnie Campbell, Tom Campbell's wife, knows a hell of a lot about radio.

Tuna: My wife's the same way. She understands format ...she knows jingles, logos. She knows the records, she knows pacing. She can tell when I've screwed up on the radio. She knows about a program log.

Hall: What chore do you find most boring about radio work, keeping the log up? What's the most trivial part of being a disk jockey?

Tuna: Damned good question. I guess it's a peeve to a point—but I wish I had someone to answer the phones. We used to have them at KHJ, but in an economy move about a year and a half ago, they got cut. So I have to answer all my own phones, and when you've got eight lines going, picking music, and—that's the thing I'd like to have done for me if I ever get another radio show—someone to screen the phone calls for me. But they'd have to think like I do, because if someone calls in and says they have a mynah bird that can sing "Happy Birthday," I want them to feed it to me, to say: "Hey, we've got a ding dong on the phone." You get a lot of ding dongs on the phone in the morning—that is where I get a lot of stuff. They're lovely, lovely people, and if it wasn't for them . . . .

Hall: You'd like a producer?

Tuna: No, just a phone person. I produce myself. My Armed Forces radio show, too. So, at least I've got my fingers still in radio and I won't get too rusty.

Hall: Do you wing some of your stuff on the air?

Tuna: Yeah. My best shows are probably 50 percent prepared, 50 percent off the top of my head . . . off the wall. There have been a lot of my shows where people would comment: "You must have spent a lot of time preparing it." And quite honestly, I winged the whole thing. People have said they enjoyed me more in the last year or two—they said: "You seem to have a little more looseness." I think that, finally, there's a certain maturity involved—I'm getting my style in radio—and I'm winging more. I'm coming to the studio prepared, but it's like an outline now instead of a script. I find it works better, and it's more fun.

Hall: More fun for you, personally?

Tuna: Yes. It is because I don't even know what I'm going to do some days. Like that Raquel Welch thing I mentioned earlier—I just came in and told myself: Let's do that this morning. It sort of *happens* . . . .

Hall: It's fun to do a show like that when you're prepared?

Tuna: Yes. I like to have about half of my stuff prepared so I can have that to fall back on.

Hall: Fortunately, on a typical Drake station you always have the records to fall back on.

Tuna: Right, the format will carry you. We've often talked about it, and I guess I may have the opportunity to find out: What do you do without your security blanket—the format?

Hall: Does your ego ever let you down?

Tuna: You need a tremendous amount of confidence and self assurance in radio to be a No. 1 air personality. I found that out myself. I was somewhat ill at ease when I first came to Los Angeles, and I thought: "Well, this is the big one . . . this is make-it-or-break-it time. Because if you bomb out here, it's probably back to Wichita." And you have to have that self-confidence that you're No. 1. Otherwise you're going to be a second-rate disk jockey. You have to go into the studio with the idea that you can beat anybody anywhere, in any time slot.

Hall: When you came that first time to Los Angeles did you drive in?

Tuna: I flew in. My wife came with me. We lived in a hotel for about our first month here. It was a real drag. About the only time we got out of the hotel was to see the Santa Claus parade. We'd just had a baby. Michelle is six now. Christy is four. Danny is three. Christy was just a baby at that time. It was an unsettling time. But we both love Los Angeles, although I'm a little disappointed in radio right now in this city. Feel there's a certain sterility. There's no excitement. There's nothing happening in radio right now.

Hall: I keep feeling that something will happen before long.

Tuna: I'd like to stay in Los Angeles, although I feel I can work *any* market. I'm trying to work out an amicable parting with KHJ. Bill Drake said he wanted to leave the doors open for me. I'd like an amicable parting. I've had to stomp out of the last couple of stations, because they didn't want to release me from my contracts. When I left Oklahoma City the manager there wasn't going to let me go, but we finally parted. In Boston I had to buy my way out of that contract. The manager socked it to me. It cost me something like $2,500. It was a bitter experience to say the least. Probably one of the darkest periods in my life. But it worked out all right, because of the KHJ job.

Hall: It's true, it seems to me that one has to have a hell of a drive to become a top-rated air personality.

Tuna: You go through a lot.

Hall: You suffer so much to reach the peak.

Tuna: When I was in Oklahoma City, I was making $500 a month and all of the teen hops I could get.

Hall: That wasn't much of a life, was it?

Tuna: No. You had to work so hard. And the $500 was a raise. In Wichita, I got $425 a month. I guess things have gone up since then. $20,000 a year is scale at KHJ. The weekend man gets that.

Hall: Do you know the scale at WNBC in New York is supposed to be $65,000?

Tuna: Scale? That's not bad. I'd like to work in New York, Chicago, or Los Angeles. I'd really like to stay in Los Angeles, if I can get a KHJ release. I just really don't know what I'm going to do at this point.

Hall: What do you personally think about the move toward album cuts on the Drake stations? Was each cut picked for you?

Tuna: We worked from a list of album cuts. The misconception has been that we didn't select our own music. We worked from lists.

Hall: Blending the music yourselves?

Tuna: Yes, I think that a void has been created in radio—that there's no station today playing the hits. Radio stations are a hodgepodge of album cuts and singles. I realize that more and more; the artist is going into the studio and not thinking about creating a song but a whole album concept. The danger is . . . why should listeners listen to radio when they can get the same thing on their stereo record player at home?

Hall: You'd prefer the personality approach?

Tuna: I think a good personality can outdo a station that just plays the music. But what has happened is the growth of a computer generation in radio, and I think it's going to have some backlash to it. At many radio stations, it's like there's nobody there at the station. This may be fine for the programmers, but it's dangerous for the disk jockeys. I don't like the situation. We're bound to work ourselves right out of a job.

Hall: In other words, the air personality had better start making a comeback? There's very sophisticated equipment being used at automated radio stations today.

Tuna: Right. And there's never a mistake with a machine.

OUTRO: Larry Lujack, once a leading Top 40 disk jockey in Chicago on such stations as WLS and later WCFL, sat out a contract on WCFL after the station switched to a beautiful music format. He then returned to WLS. Dan Clayton is now general manager of WBBF in Rochester, N.Y.

Tuna changed his mind about being a program director—probably as a matter of economics—in order to earn more money. This doesn't necessarily mean that his philosophy changed.

Don Steele, after leaving KHJ in Los Angeles, found it difficult to get another job in the market and was reluctant to leave the city. At the time of this writing, he was involved in putting together a syndicated radio show. Whether it'll happen or not, who knows? He then returned to the air at KTNQ in Los Angeles.

Tuna worked at KCBQ in San Diego for a while after leaving KHJ and then worked at the ill-fated KROQ before joining KIIS as a personality, and later program director as well. He grew tired of it and cut back to do just the KIIS morning show.

BRUCE JOHNSON

Bruce Johnson

INTRO: Bruce Johnson, one of the New Breed in radio today who is bringing educational background from allied fields and applying them to radio (Johnson is a lawyer; higher degrees in psychology are also popular today among radio executives both in programming and management). Johnson rose to national fame in radio when he managed KFAC, a classical radio station in Los Angeles and not only put it in a bright financial picture, but helped reprogram the station to appeal to a wider audience with classical music. He then put KLAC in Los Angeles on the map as a country music station. From there he went to RKO Radio as president and began to put that already successful radio firm into high gear. He startled the industry when he dropped the programming consulting services of Bill Drake and replaced him with Paul Drew as vice president of programming. But, under the golden touch of Bruce Johnson and Paul Drew, RKO Radio continued to build. When Johnson left to join the Sterling Recreation Organization as chief of their radio division, it was another surprising move. But, as far as his career was concerned, it was another step upward, a step well calculated. In this interview, Bruce Johnson discusses at length financial and career planning.

Hall: What are the major attributes of a radio manager today?

Johnson: Well, maybe I can answer that better if I can just say a little bit about management style, as I practice it, and then from that maybe I can get back to answering the question. The principle that I work on is something that everybody, I guess, talks about—and a lot of books are written about—but very few people really practice it, and that is a *goal-oriented system.* By that I mean: Goals between myself and the managers are mutually decided upon. Now, the influence that I would have on this can be great, so I try to bend over backwards not to superimpose my will on their judgment. For example, when we go into budgets, I try to let them come to me first with what they think they're going to achieve in terms of revenue. I let them come to me with what they think they're going to spend in terms of expenses, and what they think they're gonna accomplish in audience ratings and all aspects of operating a radio station. Then we sit down. We have a long conversation. At that point, I get very tough and demanding on their being able to support all the things they say are going to happen. A lot of people don't like goals and budgets because they say you can't predict. But I think you can.

    I think that one of the failings that we've had in radio is it's one of those mediums where we sort of sit back and hope for the best rather than plan for the best. Normally, if you shoot for a profit margin or bottom line, you usually get there.

Sometimes you surprise yourself and go even further. So, we use a goal-setting philosophy that is mutual in its concept. Then from the goals come plans. By plans I mean specific and concrete plans as to how they're going to get to their bottom line and profit margin. If a general manager tells me he's gonna do $100,000 worth of revenue in the month of January, I want to know exactly how he's going to do it. I want to know specifically how every dollar's going to get on the station, where it's going to come from, what promotions and packages they have designed to achieve their goals, and how the goals are assigned to the sales people. I want to know all these things.

At the same time, I want them to justify each and every expense. The way we do this is with a concept called *zero-base budgeting.* This is not an original idea. What we do is take the radio station and, figuratively, clean it out. We have the four walls sitting there. And then we sit down and decide about all the functions that we need during the given year or given time period. Then we add people and services back until we have filled those functions. Now, normally when you do that the first time—if it's a radio station that has been going on for years and years and really hasn't tried to cut expenses . . . and every time a new problem has popped up, they've added another person to the staff—you blow out 15 to 20 percent of the people. There usually are a lot of people at a radio station who are just not doing anything . . . or are practicing Parkinson's Law. If you do it every year, the attrition is less, but you still find things that have crept in over the years. It isn't just people, it's services or things that a station might be using that it really doesn't need to use. So zero-based budgeting is an interesting exercise to go through. It really helps the manager know more about what's going on inside his radio station. I've used it now for the past three years. I wish I'd had it six or seven years ago, because it really does work. You really get an idea what you're doing and where you're going.

So when that's all settled—when we do the zero-based budgeting—your plans become sort of obvious to you as to how you're going to get there specifically.

After the plans are developed and we've got budgets approved, the goals are set. After that, it's a question of monitoring. And this is where you can get in trouble, I think. I got in trouble the first time that I tried it. I set the goals and I set the plans, then, they went into a drawer and I didn't look at them again. You have to study them semi-monthly as you go—you've got to pull that guy's plan out of the drawer and look at it, see if he's achieving it. The planning and goal setting becomes ineffective if he isn't following the plan or the plan is going wrong. You've got to step in quickly to get him either to follow or change the plan. Now, that seems like an awful lot of work, and often people really resist this type of thinking. Most managers resist that kind of penetration into their operation. They would rather sort of go along and hope that the round number at the end comes out all right.

I am as much upset over someone who, for example, has a plan for the month of February that says we're going to do $100,000 and we should have a five in the ARB. If, when February is finished, instead of doing $100,000 we did $180,000 I'm just as upset at that as I would be if he did $20,000 because I know he didn't have a plan, and I know that we didn't do it right somehow. I don't mind if someone goes over 20 or 30 percent, but when they're off by 40 or 50 percent or more, then I know that it was a lot of luck and not a result of the plan. It's pretty interesting to go back when an operation goes bananas in a particular month and get the guy to try to explain to you how it happened. Normally, he can't. So, every radio station gets lucky once in a while. I don't object to that. But what I'm trying to do is train the managers so that they are watching periodically what's going on, and they're following or they're changing or adjusting their plan when it looks like the plan isn't working. And that's basically it. Then at the end, what's very important, I think, are rewards.

There are all kinds of reward systems that you can use . . . money incentives or other things . . . but the important thing about rewards is that they be given immediately on the accomplishment of the goal. That sounds very simple, too, but I mean if you've announced you're going to give a general manager a bonus if he makes a profit by December 31, that's his deal. When he makes it, I always believe in being there with a check in hand the minute the clock strikes midnight. I put it in his hands so he relates the reward to the accomplishment . . . you know, the achievement.

Everyone has little spiffs for program directors and disk jockeys. They say: "Boy, if you get that thing up from a three to a five from this ARB book ratings, I'll give you X dollars or a trip to Spain or Tahiti or whatever." If you're not there the day that ratings book comes out to slap those tickets in his fist, the rewards technique simply will not be as effective the next time.

That, to me, is a very important thing. It's the hardest, most difficult problem I've had with major corporations because it takes so long to process a check or get a trade deal through, or whatever it is you're going to do for the guy. Reward must immediately follow the accomplishment of the goal that you set up. And I find that when I do this, if I set the goals with the person—we make a plan, we follow the plan, we measure its performance as we go along, and we immediately reward upon achievement—the next time we are that much more effective when we go to set up the new plan and goals.

Now, again, this all sounds very basic, and you've read it in books and everything else, but *nobody does it.* And this is interesting . . . let's say that you and I plan to take our wives to Brazil . . . to Rio . . . in two months. We would probably sit down and have a dinner and plan where we're going to go. We'd go to a travel agent and map out the trip. We'd know when we're going to get there, how we're going to fly, who is going to pick us up at the airport, and what we're going to do each day. We'd make plans to get theater and concert tickets. We'd write all the radio stations and say we're coming, and we want to see you and the record people and whatever. And we'd spend all that time on a trip that might take a couple of weeks. Yet people won't spend one single minute either planning their lives or planning their business, and that's really true. If you want to build a house, you wouldn't call up a brickyard and tell them to send a lot of bricks. You'd know how many bricks you wanted and you'd tell them to send 5,000 bricks.

People just don't plan. That's the most difficult of all the tasks that I face—getting people to plan. Sometimes you just have to take 'em by the scruff of the neck and rub their noses in it until they do it. And some people simply still won't do it, and those people simply don't last very long.

Hall: This is the modus operandi a radio firm should have at the top. Do the same things apply at the radio station level?

Johnson: Yes. They're supposed to filter down.

Hall: Manager, program director, and the entire staff?

Johnson: Right. They are all to have goals and plans and each department head of programming, sales, business, engineering—everybody—has a plan that filters up and keeps going until it gets all the way up to the top.

Hall: Have you created this type of business pyramid in Sterling Recreation Organization now? Is it in operation?

Johnson: Yes. Yes it is.

Hall: How long did it take you to set that up?

Johnson: Well . . . .

Hall: It's not something you do overnight?

Johnson: I think to convince everybody it was a good idea—it took me over 30 days. To get them to start to do it, took another 90 days, I think.

When it falls apart it's usually my fault because I'm not monitoring plans quickly enough. In the early stage, it's sometimes a little hard—I have to make myself sit down someplace for a few hours and look at their plans and monitor performance. You've also got to have information systems flowing back to you that allow you to monitor. It takes quite a while. I guess more than anything else, it takes a long time to set up the information systems—the information, the data flowing back to you from the real world. It also takes a while to get people to start telling you what's *really* happening. Most people want to tell you the nice things and the neat things that have happened, and they want to shove under the carpet all of the bad things that are going on.

That's the other difficult problem in setting up your information systems—getting people to tell you what's really going on. But after a while they get used to it, when they find out that when they call up and say, "Gee, we just blew this or that," they don't get bawled out. Once they find that out, then they're quite ready to let you know what their problems are. And the idea, of course, with their letting you know what their problems are, is that hopefully you can help them solve them. At least, two heads are better than one at trying.

So information systems are vital and they're difficult to set up—not conceptually, just difficult to get the people to start feeding you the proper information. That sometimes takes a period of head-pounding until they finally do it.

Hall: You've been responsible over the few years I've known you for helping launch some good radio station managers. I don't think that was an accident. Like Bill Ward, for example.

Johnson: Well, I think achievers *achieve,* mediocre people do *mediocre* jobs, and losers *lose.* I've never really gone wrong going out and getting a really good individual. I don't think I've picked, in the past, many people who were already on top of the heap. What I've tried to do is go out and find somebody who's coming up through the ranks who really looks like a star. Bill Ward [now general manager of KLAC in Los Angeles] was one of them. And, if I have anything I can lay credit to, it's being able to spot them . . . to know where they are. People like Pat Norman at KFRC in San Francisco, or Tim Sullivan at KHJ in Los Angeles, or Herb Salzman at WOR in New York, or Dwight Case and Paul Drew at RKO Radio headquarters in Los Angeles. I didn't exactly spot Drew, but he was nowhere near where he is today when we first found him. And Jerry Lyman at WGMS in Washington was an absolute sensation and still is . . . and I can mention a lot more. Rick Devlin at WXLO in New York. I mean really superior people who were kind of down in the lower levels of the ship. You spot them and bring them along and all of a sudden they become the superstars of the business. It's gratifying to be able to do that. But I must admit to a number of significant failures in people whom I thought were going to do well and ended up not doing it for me. In a lot of cases, I think it was my fault, not theirs. Perhaps I wasn't able to push the right button. But over the years I think I found some pretty good people.

Then it's a question of bringing them into the management role. The problem is that they either come from sales or programming, and depending on which side they come from, they don't know the other side. That's the difficulty—getting them to be sensitive to the other fellow's feelings and learning as much as they can about the other side of the coin, whether it's programming or business.

Hall: What are the major attributes now of a manager at a radio station? What should he know? What's his foundation?

Johnson: Well, and I don't want to get too broad, but I think it's important to point out—the major attribute is character, and that includes honesty and integrity. Extremely important. Second is the ability to be an SOB when a manager has to be one—not to be afraid to bring somebody up short when they've done something wrong in a nice firm way, not mean or sadistic or whatever. And third, I think, to be very innovative and creative in all areas of management—or at least be able to spot talent.

I don't use the old Supreme Court decision of obscenity: I know it when I see it.

I think that those are the three attributes I look for *first* in a radio manager. Finally it breaks down to his or her ability to keep a lot of balls in the air at one time, and to be very fair with people and very objective. And also the ability to stand being lonely.

Hall: Which is more important—is it more important to know programming or is it more important to know sales to be a manager?

Johnson: I think it's probably . . . today, a little more important to know sales than it is to know programming. I think the reason is that you are perhaps dealing 30 percent of your time with the federal government and attorneys. In your day-to-day business operations, you are dealing with contracts, sales procedures, audience fragmentation, and with dollars not increasing for radio. The marketing problem has become intense.

In the last three or four years it's crucial that you develop a very good marketing program because no longer can you get a 30 percent share of the audience and expect to get all the dollars. As you well know, in Los Angeles you come in with a seven or eight share, but there are an awful lot of other people who've got seven and six and five and whatever else. You're not . . . nobody's a must advertising buy anymore. Thus, marketing's an extremely important area. I won't say that a good programming person who really understands audience—and has empathy and ego drive and all those things—can't become a manager, because I think they can. But I think it's more difficult to spot that kind of program director, and I think a lot of people will have second thoughts about taking a chance on anyone who has not managed before.

I, for example, would make Paul Drew a manager, but I have the advantage of having worked with Paul. I know he's a hell of a good administrator, he's very well organized and he knows programming. But he's also taken the time to learn the sales end. He's one of those guys who when he was programming KHJ for us—when I was president of RKO Radio—before we made him group program director, he was always running to the sales department with ideas for them to go out and sell. And he put the ideas together, you know. If I can find that kind of a program director someplace who really understands sales and wants to understand and will learn, I'd hire him as general manager in a minute. I just haven't met too many of 'em yet, but maybe I haven't been in the right places to meet them.

Hall: How do you set up a marketing program for a radio station? Where do you start, and what do you do next?

Johnson: Well, let me see if I can . . . okay, I'll give you an experience, I guess, that I had at RKO. The first thing we do is separate the retail sales department from the agency or established account sales department. Then we sit down with all the accounts that we think are potential for that particular station. These aren't just the accounts that have been on radio for a long time, but every single account in the entire town. We use the yellow pages, the newspapers, all kinds of directories, and everything else. We add them all up, then we sit down and divide them between the two sales staffs. Next, we go back and look at all of the accounts that have run on our radio station for, say, the past two years, and we categorize those by, let's say, appliance stores, stereo stores, soft drink firms, airlines, and banks, and all the way down. Then we get sort of a grid that shows us where we've been strong; it also points out where we've been weak. In other words, where we have not gone after certain account categories. At that point, we develop a tremendous amount of support material—sales tools and ammunition—to sell those accounts that we haven't sold much of before. For example, you get to a rock station . . . in a lot of markets you find they don't have much bank advertising. Well, it's only because station account executives never really consciously mounted a campaign to get them. They've tried and they've gotten turned down. They've been told the station's audience demographics are wrong or something, so they go back to the head shops and the . . . .

Hall: Clothing stores.

Johnson: Bars and whatever . . . wherever they feel comfortable. But we found . . . for example, when Tim Sullivan took over as general manager of KHJ, I think KHJ had had three airline commercials on the air in the past two or three years, and they were quite concerned about it. Tim did the type of thing I'm talking about. He developed an awful lot of material, set up a specific program, a goal-oriented program with the sales department, especially concentrated on the national advertising reps, and I think inside of about seven months he had 14 airlines on the air. I haven't seen a monitor lately since I left, but I'm sure he's still got the same number.

Now that was considered impossible in those days, but it was a simple task of just zeroing in on it, getting enough ammunition—and there's plenty of it—and going after it and he got it. So we do that in all categories, and it's amazing how fast sales go up when that happens. The thing is to crack an account in one of those categories and once you do, motivation by example takes over, and all the other sales people run out and start closing them too. It's like nobody ran a 4-minute mile for years and years and all of a sudden Bannister broke the thing, and about 10 guys broke it the next few months. That happens a lot.

Hall: The ammunition that would develop—this would include ratings regardless of the market size. I guess you have some kind of ratings to go by.

Johnson: Right.

Hall: Letters of . . . .

Johnson: Well, success letters . . . where you're most successful is in going to the industry you're targeting. Most all industries that are worth their salt—or the ones you'll want to deal with, anyway—are going to have trade associations. They do all kinds of surveys, and they're free for the asking. In fact, there's usually a guy who is the executive director of the Hand Laundry and Dry Cleaners Association. He's dying to send you something because that's what his job is all about. In fact, he'll probably write a letter to his boss, saying that his material is well received. So you get their material, their own self-generated material from their industry, then you got into a dry cleaning shop and you show the guy this kind of information, it's pretty hard for him to dispute it—it's his own association putting it out. And the guy that taught me that a number of years ago—Kevin Sweeney—I don't know if you know Kevin, but he's a legend in the radio marketing business. He now operates a consulting firm.

Hall: Where's he located?

Johnson: He's in Encino, Ca.—Young Adult Marketing. He deals mostly with contemporary radio stations.

And then you've got the Radio Advertising Bureau which has a ton of material that nobody ever uses but should use. There also are things like target group index and there's brand rating index and there's more material than you know what to do with . . . if people just go look for it. Then you just put it together in a nice form, fairly simple, and just go out pounding on doors. Pretty soon it starts to happen.

Hall: If you don't have ratings, you can still find ways to work this whole process out?

Johnson: Very definitely. If you don't have ratings, you are almost forced to go to the retailer—where you should be going anyway, because the retailer really doesn't understand ratings. He's been buying newspapers for years and years. He understands packages and promotions.

The biggest mistake that radio people make when they go and try to sell a retailer advertising time is talking "spots" to him. They say this spot's worth $50 or whatever, and you get 24 of them. Well, he doesn't understand that. He understands a newspaper advertising salesman who comes to the door and says this ad's gonna cost you $1,020. That's it. The hardest thing we had in teaching our sales people to go sell was that you go in and say this "package" is gonna cost you $1,020. He's used to the newspaper guy coming in with a layout. You don't talk about spots. Later you get to that.

The other thing is the production which you pretty much have to do yourself because he doesn't know how to do it. The radio sales people who are most successful usually produce the spots for the client. And this has an advantage in that it helps you to control the quality of the sound on your radio station. You don't get the guy screaming and yelling and beating pots and pans or car fenders or whatever.

Hall: Does this technique of producing the spot and taking a sample out to the potential client work even in larger markets?

Johnson: Works even better in larger markets. But, boy, it was like pulling teeth to get the production department or the programming department to produce the example commercials. But, now, when their spec sells, we normally reward them for their part in achieving the sale.

Hall: That's good.

Johnson: Everybody does it in a different way, but that's one good way to do it.

Hall: Then you carry this reward system all the way down throughout the entire structure?

Johnson: Yes. The program directors, chief engineers, sales managers, salesmen, jocks, engineers—we have rewards. I like reward systems going *everywhere* so that everyone's tied into the same thing. It's unfair—as I keep telling the managers who fail to set up such a program with their department heads—for me to expect you to come up with X dollars this year if nobody else in the radio station knows that you have to do it. Everyone should have their part in the goal system—each salesman should have his or her role, and each jock should have his or her part.

Hall: Do you outline this program or do you get them to come up with their own in this particular case?

Johnson: We start right at the bottom. We ask. The way it's supposed to go—and it works this way most of the time—is, let's say, salesmen are asked to come up with their projections, account-by-account, for the year. That all comes together and the sales manager then goes back and forth with them until they decide how much they're going to do. Then it comes up to the manager's level, and he, depending on his budget requirements and the things he's got to achieve, hassles with the sales manager. At this point he's also wrestling with the program director and the chief engineer for the projects he's going to do that year. Then it comes up to the division level, and the manager and division head hassle. Somehow it all filters back down, and adjustments are made, and we all come to an agreement as to what our goals are going to be. The important thing is to get *everybody* to agree that that's the goal. If you arbitrarily give them unrealistic goals . . . if you arbitrarily tell them to do 15 percent more this year and it filters back down, nine times out of ten they won't make it. They'll just give up. And I wouldn't blame 'em.

Hall: You've had enormous success in management—specifically in group management. But let's get back to the station management level where we're talking about a typical man . . . what type of attributes would he expect out of his program director? What kind of a man would he want for a program director?

Johnson: Probably the first and foremost quality is not necessarily creativity, but honesty. I think that must be first. And I'm not talking about the question of moral turpitude as much as a guy who's honest with himself or a gal who's honest with herself. That goes back to the business of character. After that you're looking for a high degree of creativity and a high degree of ego drive—somebody who is resourceful—who can get up and go and you don't have to give a kick in the seat of the pants to get going. I think those things are the important things. But character and honesty have to come first.

Hall: How much does experience play in this?

Johnson: Well, I can't say that experience is most important all the time 'cause we have hired people who hadn't a great deal of experience over people who did. I think we're always looking for fresh, new ideas and new talent. But I guess by and large—I don't know if I'm contradicting myself—but experience has a lot to do with it. Of course, the larger the market, the more experience you're going to demand. In some of the smaller markets, you can't expect very much experience from the people you hire, of course.

Hall: What attributes would you expect out of a general sales manager at a radio station?

Johnson: Well, character and honesty first. The second would be a high degree of organization. Third, the ability to recruit and to train sales people. That's an absolute must. You've heard this story so often—and it happens with jocks or with sales managers or in any other business—often the high achiever on the individual level does not make a good manager. One of the reasons is that he can do it himself, but he can't show anybody else how to do it. So, the ability to recruit and train ... to spot good prospects, get them to come with you, and then be able to train them. And the fourth area, and I put this down the line always because I think the others are more important: If you have the first three then motivating is a fairly easy situation. Everybody tries to put motivation first and I don't think it belongs first. That comes after all the other things are done. Because you can't motivate people to do something they don't know how to do or are not capable of doing. So I look for those things first, and usually if you get the first three then the fourth comes because they've got all those things. Of course a high degree of intelligence helps, too, but I've had some guys who were not that swift who are sensational sales managers and program directors.

Hall: One of the things that intrigued me which I'm in favor of, too, was that you said a person had to program his business career and also to program his own personal life to a great extent. Let's talk now about programming your business career. I would assume you've done this; in fact, I think I've observed it. How does a person go about programming their career?

Johnson: Well, I think you have to sit down and really decide what it is you want to do first. I mean, if you had your druthers and anything was available to you, what would you want to do? Then I think you'd take the industry or the area of the industry that perhaps you wanted to either get into or become a part of or a leader in, and realistically sit down and look at how many jobs were available and where they were. Then, mix your personal desires and the availability together, and realistically try to say to yourself: "Yeah, I think I can; you know, I can do it if I get the chance."

If you want to become president of CBS and you think you can do it and you've got the ability, then that's a realistic goal. If you feel, "Well, maybe I won't do it or maybe I won't like it," then I don't think that is a very realistic goal. Really, it takes tremendous honesty to be able to sit down and do something like this.

After you set the goal, whatever it happens to be, then you make your plan and you say to yourself: "Well, if I'm going to be president of CBS, I should know—say I've been in programming—I'd better know something about the financial area of business. I had better know a little bit about accounting, I had better know something about the law, I'd better know something about engineering or at least enough to get me by. So, how do I get to know those things?" Well, if you stop to think about it, they're just ten thousand ways you can get that information. The simplest way is talking to people in the business. Second is going to work in those jobs over a period of time— which is what I did. I made sure that I worked in every single phase of the business before I got up to the point where the opportunity would come. A lot of times it is luck. But lucky people are always standing there somehow when it falls on their head, and so any degree of chance has been taken out of the situation for the most part. My own plan of action that I set forth on about 15 years ago, the first really specific one that I did was about 11 or 12 pages, and then I revised it. I would revise it every two or three years. Now I revise my plan about every three months as to where I'm going.

Hall: Is it down to fewer pages?

Johnson: Yeah, it's not so many pages now. In the broadcasting business I haven't got that many hills to conquer so it's many fewer pages now, but I'm looking at other industries as well at this point and other things to do. I don't want to stay in broadcasting always. I don't think I want to leave it, but I have other areas that I'm interested in now ... things that I want to do ... and so I just continue to revise that plan. In fact, I just finished a major portion of it last weekend. I find that when you put it in writing and you keep reviewing it, it reminds you of things you're supposed to do and you recall: "Gee, I should have called so and so and had lunch and found out about, I don't know, some subject, whatever it happened to be," or: "I should enroll in that seminar," or: "I should go to the International Radio-Programming Forum and hear so and so speak on quad." But you should write those things down. I've got to do it and now go back and check 'em off and then . . . .

Hall: That's what I do all the time.

Johnson: That avoids the worst enemy of us all, and that's procrastination. If you keep the list in your mind, it's so easy to put off, but if it's there on paper every day, and you look at it, it goads you into doing something about it.

Hall: And so you keep updating or upgrading this particular proposal, plan of action, whatever, and you carry this same thing through from the very lowest level in radio, right?

Johnson: Yes.

Hall: From being a disk jockey . . . all the way?

Johnson: That's where it should start, really.

Hall: You set goals for yourself and achieve the goals?

Johnson: Right . . . right. Sometimes you have to modify. Sometimes you get to a brick wall and rather than just continue to bang your head . . . well, there's nothing wrong if you come to a brick wall, or a place in the road where a cliff drops off, in going the other way, you know. I know a lot of people have that problem—they set something in their mind and they go off, and they come to a point where it's absolutely impossible for them to go any further, and they just keep standing there banging their head against the wall. It's happened to me a couple of times in my career. I got into career positions where I knew that the guy in front of me was never going to move, and you just have to go up and around, you know. I've never climbed over anybody's back. I guess I'm not built that way, and I wouldn't do it that way. But I guess that's one way to do it. However, I've always felt if I run into something like that I'd just turn around and take another road to get there. I'm glad that I have. Somebody said to me the other day, "You've moved around a lot," and I said, "I've moved *up* a lot." I distinguish between the two directions, you know. Sometimes you have to move around to move up.

Hall: You haven't moved around a lot.

Johnson: Maybe more than I would have liked to.

Hall: I've admired your stability. Well, maybe the airplane travel . . . in that sense.

Johnson: I really don't miss that . . . I'll tell you. Well, my dad, for example, was in the construction business for 45 years, had the same job as a general contractor and worked for himself; my wife's father was with the Civic Telephone Company for 40 years as sales manager of the Yellow Pages out here, and had the same job. Well, those two get together and look at me and say, "What the hell, can't you keep a job, what's the matter with you?" I'd say, "But Dad, look at some of the other guys in our business and you wouldn't believe some of 'em." Our business is like that, and you and I know it. You know, it's funny, I was reading a book the other day on management written by a management recruiter who was saying that today if anybody sticks in the same management spot for too long, they start to get suspicious of him. Maybe he's found his comfort zone or something. But I guess I got off the point.

Hall: No, that's fine. How do you program your personal life? Do you also set goals?

Johnson: Yes. I haven't been as good as I should have, I think, but I've paid more attention to it in the last year or so. At RKO Radio, I got on a treadmill—from a personal standpoint. I felt if I didn't get off pretty soon that I was going to fall off or something because I just had no time to myself at all. I mean, literally no time. If I wasn't traveling, I was back here, and I'd go home with two briefcases full of stuff. I'd get up early on Saturday morning and I'd probably take my wife out to dinner on Saturday night or go to a party, and I'd be back at it Sunday. I literally was working, I don't know, maybe 80 hours a week, which was foolish. A lot of people say, "Well you ought to be able to do it in a helluva lot less time than that," But I couldn't find out how to do it.

I fell off my own personal plan. I mean, my personal plan includes a good deal of reading, playing some golf, and spending time with my family. I try to program that out and set aside time for my family. Matter of fact, my family and I sit down once in a while and map out a calendar for the next three months and decide when we'll have time to be with each other. If we don't do that, than we don't get the time. Somehow there's always an excuse or something. It's amazing. The kids love it; they think it's a good idea. I have to laugh all the time because they're the ones that always break the date, see? Now I'm getting back at them. They say, "Daddy, when are you coming home." Now I am home and . . . .

Claude, I've got something here for you that I guess we can put on tape. This is about management performance. These are the value figures, indicating the degree of importance we feel for this particular period of time. We would change these values, as certain items become more important like labor relations or minority affairs or programming or ratings or sales or whatever. We assign a value to each item, but these values might change as we go along. The grade—the highest being 11, the lowest being 1—is then added in here next to the value. It's like a diving contest . . . degree of difficulty? So, for example, profit to budget is the first item here. Now the grade is 1 to 11. If this guy is on budget, he'd get an 11. And if he was half way there, he'd probably get a 5 or 6. You'd multiply that times 14 which is the value we give it. This gives it a total score. Out here is the percent of ideal, which means that if he got 11 times 14, whatever that adds up to, that would be the most he could get. We'd give him a percentage. Then we go all the way down the sheet, and we add it up at the bottom. It gives him a grade at the very end on all these things. It also tells him each category where he's weak, where he's having problems . . . and he has this in his desk.

I'll tell you, most general managers need something like this on their desk because they tend to do the type of things that are more fun to them or they're more familiar with. But this ratings critique requires them every week or every month to sit down and say: "What am I doing in community affairs, what am I doing in minority hiring, what am I doing to strengthen my signal? What am I doing, whatever?"

Hall: Your two greatest things—you put minority hiring and employment even above difficulty level?

Johnson: Yes. Now that went down as we increased our female complement . . . that went down in importance although it was always high in importance because it was one of the major problems we had at RKO. So we put heavy emphasis on that and at the end of the year, the winners, in terms of the managers we had, received a top award which we called the Superior Achiever and the next two guys down—or gals, because we had a female manager—got Achiever Awards. And those were awarded at a banquet we had at our management meeting.

Hall: Is that the one you took out an advertisement for on the front page of *Spot Radio*?

Johnson: Yes, and as a matter of fact, there are the plaques we advertised in *Time* Magazine about the Achievers.

Hall: Sensational.

Johnson: Now this year, I think they didn't have the awards banquet at the managers meeting. It's going to be in February in New York, I think. But they're continuing it, and it's amazing. It means a lot more to people than money does.

Hall: How often was this filled out?

Johnson: Monthly. And I fill it out from their own reports. I believe there were 16 quantitative categories and 5 qualitative categories. I can't remember. I kept adding things to it as we went along—so it wouldn't be so much a seat-of-the-pants thing by me. I would just look at the numbers and I could tell if they were on or off, depending on where they were . . . or the dollars or the ratings or whatever. Then in about five of the areas it was subjective judgment on my part in evaluating their monthly report to me and how they were doing. Involvement in the community is a tough thing to quantify, but I could tell from what they were doing and the questions that I asked whether or not they were doing a good job. I thought it was a very fair system. There was a little grousing once in a while, especially if someone ended up last. Somebody always had to end up last.

Hall: Did the managers set the same type of thing up within the station for the program director and the sales staff?

Johnson: Paul Drew did that at RKO Radio for the program directors. He has the same type of a thing; different categories. The program directors and managers could also do the same ratings at each station. Some did it, some didn't. But as far as I was concerned, it was voluntary. I didn't feel they had to do this if they didn't want to, and usually it was the high-achieving managers who did it. The others didn't.

Hall: Is receivables a big factor? You have a 10 weight here.

Johnson: Yes. That's a rough thing. Worse today than it was then.

Hall: It is? How does a manager solve the problems himself? Like on receivables?

Johnson: Well . . . .

Hall: Because you have a public relations factor as well as . . . .

Johnson: You do, you do. But you really have to get tough. I'm not just talking about advertising agencies. Everybody is slow to pay today. Where it used to be you'd yell and scream if anything got over 30 days, then five years ago you'd yell if it got over 60 days. Now, you'd be happy if you can get it in 90. And in other industries . . . I belong to a couple of management organizations, and we talk about problems we have. I mention that 90-day figure, and the people start dropping off chairs. They can't believe that anybody, any industry, would allow this problem to develop as far as it has, but it has. I mean, you're lucky today to get paid in 90 days, and that amounts to a terrible cash-flow problem because it means a lot of the time you're having to borrow money to stay in business. You're gonna get paid, you know you'll get paid, and the banks are willing to lend money to you, but it just adds to your cost of doing business. But we have systems set up now. We're on the phone every day, and the old adage that the squeaky wheel gets the grease is true. If you pound hard enough, you get your money.

Hall: How important is it for the manager to be out in the community? We're talking about any size market?

Johnson: Very important. Very important.

Hall: How do you rate that, see? That's difficult. How do you *know* he's out there?

Johnson: Well, he has to tell me where he's been. In the monthly report, I find out every place he's gone, the people he's seen, what he has discussed. That comes to me in his report, and now and again I'll kind of check to see what's going on, and . . . .

Hall: It's becoming increasingly important for the manager today to maintain government interface, isn't it?

Johnson: Yes. Local government . . . and I think federal, too. I think that most managers ought to visit, one time or another, the Federal Communications Commission in Washington. You know that nobody ever goes to visit them? Unless they're in trouble.

Hall: And called in on the carpet.

Johnson: I have to admit I didn't go till 1974 when we got in trouble on a violation of some rule at one of the stations. I went down to plead our case—not to the commissioners themselves but to the FCC staff. And I was, you know, surprised. I said, "Gee, I've never been here before." They said, "Nobody ever comes here unless they want to complain about something or they're in trouble." We were going to set up a situation where we would have regular visits to the FCC by our managers when they went to New York for a national sales trip. They'd zip down to Washington and go in to talk to Complaints and Compliances at the FCC or the Broadcast Bureau or the Renewals section or whatever and, you know, find out what's going on. The FCC staff are the servants of the people, although we tend to think of them as cops . . . which they also are. Most managers are just scared to death of that place. Most radio men have this idea that it's some big super building on top of a hill where people rain down lightning bolts on radio—and it is sometimes. But they're all just people like us in there. Bill Ray, of FCC's Complaints and Compliances, was with NBC, I guess, for years.

Hall: I like Bill.

Johnson: They're all just nice people. I must confess I looked upon the FCC differently before I went there, and I think there should be a lot more dialogue among the broadcasters and the commission. Maybe there'd be less misunderstanding and better rules.

Hall: Do you think that radio is now being given a fair shake in the broadcasting industry as opposed to television?

Johnson: No, I don't really think so. I just see one instance after another of our getting caught in the wake of television. I was up in Oregon the other day where they want to pass a business tax, and what they did was put businesses in different tiers. If your profits were 35 percent of revenue, you paid one tax. If they were 20 percent, you paid another tax. If they were 10 percent you paid a different tax, and 5 percent on down. They had lumped radio and television together as "broadcasting," and showed that radio and television made an average profit of 13 percent. Well, they do; but television makes 21 percent and radio makes 5. So we jumped in and we're having a very difficult time with the state government, trying to get them to discern the difference between the two classes of service. They lump it all together—broadcasting. And the same thing happens at the federal level. I just think that something really has to be done to differentiate the two services. Of course, two years ago I proposed to RAB this federation idea to kind of bring everybody together under an umbrella, to separate the National Association of Broadcasters into radio and television groups with their own boards, operating separately. That's apparently starting to happen from what I see in the trades. The two mediums are not the same. They have different problems. But people lump us together.

Hall: How does a radio station fight increasing costs?

Johnson: Well, one way, and this seems like an oversimplification, is the zero-based budgeting method that we discussed earlier. The other thing is automation of one degree or another, whether it's in traffic and billing or programming. Whoever you are, I think automation is one of the answers.

Hall: You think automation's going to be an important factor in time to come?

Johnson: I think everything will be automated eventually, to one degree or another. I don't mean that everything's going to be on reel-to-reel tape, but I think the engineering function will eventually be automated—and should be. It can be now. And then, it's a question of how *live* you want to sound. I'm sure in time, we'll find ways to make automation sound live or spontaneous.

Hall: How important is promotion on a radio station?

Johnson: Extremely important. And today, I guess, more than anything else, external promotion has become very, very important because there are just so darn many signals. There's so much competition for the ear and the eye.

Hall: What percent of your typical budget should be used for internal, and how much for external promotion?

Johnson: Well, I had a different answer at RKO Radio than I would now at Sterling, because at Sterling we have a lot of properties that are just coming up with small audiences. We're trying to grow and make them get bigger, and so our promotional budgets would be heavier externally at Sterling. At RKO, they've got huge audiences—they've got big audiences—and so the emphasis there would be, and is, on internal on-the-air type of promotions.

Hall: On-the-air promotions . . . to try to get people to stay tuned?

Johnson: Yes. But at Sterling we have a problem just getting people to find us, first of all. Then we'll worry about how long they listen. But right now we're trying to build the total audience up at those stations.

Hall: What percent of a radio station's budget should be in promotion?

Johnson: Again, I think that would have to depend upon the stage of growth you were in. I just don't know.

Hall: Can you give me examples of some budgets that you know of?

Johnson: Oh, I think some people spend as much at 5 to 7 percent or more. I'm not spending that much now, and I don't think we spent that much at RKO, as I remember. Of course, we had ... when you're talking about some of the RKO stations you're talking about such huge grosses that percentages are relative. If you're looking at a KHJ versus—well, I wouldn't want to mention the station—a small FM in town, I mean KHJ's 2 percent would be a helluva lot higher than their 15 percent; so ....

Hall: What percent of the business today comes from retail as opposed to national, I mean local as opposed to ...?

Johnson: Well, I can only speak for RKO Radio and Sterling in that respect. I guess RKO is up around 10 to 15 percent now.

Hall: Local ... or national?

Johnson: Well, 10 to 15 percent of local billing. At most stations now, it's about 70-30 local versus national and the national percentage is shrinking. It may be 75-25, I don't know. The retail end of it has been growing. I know it has at RKO and Sterling. Whether it is at the other groups, I don't know, but it's extremely important. We need more dollars. There aren't enough dollars to go around.

Hall: National dollars or local dollars?

Johnson: There aren't enough national dollars to go around. And, also there aren't enough local dollars out of the normal channels that we have experienced all these years. We need to build new advertisers. There are plenty of them out there. We just haven't tapped 'em yet, that's all.

Hall: I've heard some good views on this aspect—that radio has got to go out and create new radio advertisers.

Johnson: Must. You know, radio's billing hasn't grown all that much. I saw a commerce department study that said radio billing would triple by—what was it—1985 or something like that. But I don't know ... the way it's going now, it certainly doesn't look like it. It's gone up 5 or 6 percent a year. That's not enough.

Hall: What do you see as the future role of a manager in radio?

Johnson: I don't see his role really changing a great deal. I think that a lot of radio groups will have to give more local autonomy to the managers than they have in the past. I think we've gone away from any situation where you could kind of run things from miles away. I think you have to find really good managers and give them their heads and let them go because radio changes so fast that by the time headquarters in New York or Los Angeles or Chicago finds out about it, it's too late to do anything. You've got to give the guy or gal enough rope to make instantaneous decisions on market conditions that they think are important. I've never seen an industry like radio that can change as fast as it does—overnight. Musical tastes are changing, you know, much more rapidly than they used to. The whole "future shock" idea.

Hall: Do you see any changes in programming techniques coming down? We've become highly scientific lately and the old seat-of-the-pants programming routine doesn't work anymore.

Johnson: Oh, yeah ... I think we'll see much more in the area of research. I just don't know that attitudinal research yet is developed to the point that we can rely on it. But I see many more sophisticated attempts, anyway, to get at the root of the problem—to really find out *why* people do things.

Hall: Why they listen, why they ....

Johnson: Yeah ... whatever they do. And I would certainly like to be the guy who figures that one out. I'd be living on my yacht in the Caribbean about six weeks later if I could.

Hall: How much faith do you put in ratings today? Audience ratings?

Johnson: Oh, I put a great deal of faith in the cume. I put very little faith in the average quarterhour because the cume, of course, is the most pure part of the sample. It's merely the diaries divided into the population base; each diary then achieves a certain weight. They weight up and down a little bit, but that's the figure I watch more closely than anything else. And, of course, average quarterhour is merely extrapolated from that figure. That's where the errors really start to pop in. You see a radio station with a cume dropping and the average quarterhour blown up, you know that just around the corner it's all going to be over. We can't get agencies to buy that way. They want to know who's listening at a specific time. But, from a programming standpoint, that's the number I pay attention to. If I start to see wild fluctuations, especially if they're going in a downward or upward curve, I know something's going on . . . something's either wrong or good . . . one way or the other.

Hall: In the cume?

Johnson: In the cume.

Hall: How do you advise a program director who is . . . say he's beginning to slip at his station—what do you do? What's the first step? Other than getting a new program director?

Johnson: We usually sit down and try to analyze it; figure out what went wrong. Now, at RKO we had two sets of numbers, and I haven't done that here at SRO because I don't have enough numbers to deal with yet. But every time a rating book came out at RKO Radio we would get what we called the *real world* set of figures, which our research department did for us. These really told us everything that happened—bad or good. And then there's the other set of figures that are used for sales, which are all positive, obviously. I don't see anything wrong with that. We're an "advocacy" kind of society anyway and that's what salesmanship's all about. But we would always look at all ratings ourselves with a very critical eye. The reason we did that is . . . I'll never forget a guy who I once worked for in a major group. We were at a big management meeting and he was bewailing the fact that this station's sales had gone into the sewer. It kept going down and down and down in spite of fantastic ratings that the station was getting all the time. Well, it was one of those situations where the research department had gone into that book and found something. We had more left-handed plumbers listening between 3 and 4 PM in the afternoon, but it was a report of three or four pages of really neat things. It had given him the impression as top management guide that the station was doing very well. And it wasn't. It was doing terribly. So I've always *insisted* that I see both sides of the ratings picture. Then, when we get the *real world* figures, we sit down with the program director and we go over it—try to figure out what went wrong—and normally you can see it. Then, we try to take steps to correct it. Of course, after a while, if the program director seems incapable of turning it around or making the right decisions, then you normally go find someone else who can.

Hall: How important is education in radio today? And I'm talking about the whole aspect of it.

Johnson: I'm for a good liberal arts education for anything you do, especially radio . . . especially radio.

Hall: Just to start?

Johnson: Yes. Good liberal arts. I think the most important thing in the world is to learn how to read and write and how to add and subtract, and after that you ought to be able to do anything else that you want to do. That's where I'm so happy that I have that kind of foundation rather than a business administration type of background. I'm also happy that I went through school at a time when they taught you how to read and write.

Hall: What about continuing education after you get in radio?

Johnson: Oh, I think it's an absolute necessity. If you're going to go anywhere you've got to study—no matter how you do it—whether you read books or attend seminars. There are so many things on cassette today that you can get. I make myself do something every week—read a book or listen to a cassette thing or go to a seminar, if I can. And I join organizations that have seminars about things I want to learn. In fact, I just finished reading a book on finance and accounting that I felt I needed to know more about. So I continue to do that, and I try to get into as much formal education as I can. Of course, I've gone to undergraduate school and law school, so I'm not going to do anymore of that. I'm not going back to school, but . . . I might go take a class someplace at any time if I think I can learn something.

Hall: Anything else that might be applicable?

Johnson: The final thing, I guess—and maybe I've already covered it—is that managers should engage not only in a lot of training of themselves and self-discipline in terms of learning and acquiring new knowledge, but every manager, whether they're in radio or not, should be engaged in some sort of formal training program for his people. An ongoing thing, a structured thing that they have to, or should, attend. It should be on a regular basis at a specified hour on a specified day. We try to do that everywhere. It's just got to help you and your station. I don't see how it can possibly hurt. People normally won't do it for themselves. You try to do it for them if you can.

Hall: That's a good point. I like that.

Johnson: Finally, I guess the best teachers that you could have for this business or any other are good managers.

OUTRO: Slowly, but surely, Bruce Johnson built up the radio properties of Sterling Recreation Organization, located primarily in the Northwest, into viable entities—by upgrading facilities, profits, and staff. Then, he moved on to Starr Broadcasting to lift that firm from financial woes.

GARY OWENS

Gary Owens

INTRO: Gary Owens is, without question, consistently one of the best disk jockeys in the world and a true representative of the disk jockey as entertainer. He never does a weak show. In spite of the fact that he's involved in voicing commercials and a cartoon series, emceeing and performing on television shows, writing books, and a myriad of other activities, he never shortchanges his radio listening audience. He's constantly involved in charity work of one kind or another; his days are long. Yet, he always seems to find time to help someone out, talk to a fledgling disk jockey and give advice, or make one more phone call.

He has several times been voted best MOR air personality in the nation by his peers in radio. A disk jockey who creates most of his own humor, Owens probably earns $300,000 a year or more from his various labors on radio and television, and via commercials.

Hall: What do you feel is the main job of an air personality?

Owens: To entertain. But there are other facets that go with the entertaining. In other words, your show should be informative—the time, the temperature, which are just basics . . . the traffic report, too, if that's the style of the station. But I think the major forte of anyone on the air should be to entertain. This doesn't mean he has to tell jokes or give sillies or say aphorisms. He might entertain in a million ways; he might be the smoothest disk jockey in the world or he might be extremely knowledgeable about records. He might tell you that the artist on a given record once sold frozen gazelles door-to-door, if that's interesting to the audience. Or whether the artist grew up in the slums and became a billionaire overnight, because the audience finds that interesting, too. Therefore, the on-the-air personality should be exactly that—a personality.

Hall: Are you entertaining on the air?

Owens: I feel that I am. I try to be. I've researched enough things. I should point out that I'm basically a researcher; I own between 5,000 to 7,000 books. I have four different offices in Los Angeles that are stocked with these books. And I'm a voracious reader. Well, Sir Francis Bacon said that knowledge is power. I think that's especially true for radio: You must prepare. Of course, I had the best teachers in the world every place I worked. And I worked for umpteen different radio stations . . . only one, fortunately, in the last 13 years—KMPC. But I started as a disk jockey for Don Burden.

Don was always a taskmaster—maybe more so in those days, because he was fighting Todd Storz at the time, a very difficult battle for him, and I ended up in the middle of it. I had a great ego in those days, as everyone maybe does at one time. If you don't have a great ego when you're very young, you may not make it. I'd never been a disk jockey before. But I sauntered in from KMA in Shenandoah, Iowa. Don was manager/owner of KOIL in Omaha. I walked in there trying to get a job as a newsman because I was ticked off with small-town radio—Shenandoah was only 10,000 people. Don as the first man I'd ever met who was the manager of a Top 40 radio station. Chick Crabtree was his business partner at the time. They were doing very well but apparently someone had just left . . . I'm a little hazy about it because this was around 1957, my first job as a disk jockey. I walked in there using the deep voice of a newsman, and said: "Hello, I'm looking for employment as a newsman. I work at KMA." And he said that was fine, they could use me as a newsman, but they also needed a disk jockey and "You've been a disk jockey, haven't you?" I said: "Certainly." And I'd never played a record in my life. So, you can see that it took a lot of balls.

Today, I'd have to be more truthful than that, and say: "Well, I haven't but I'll try." Anyway, my first day on the air as a disk jockey was probably the worst day in the history of radio because I did everything wrong. The only thing that was a saver for me was that I think I was mildly humorous. I made fun of everything I did. But I think I goosed every record. We had six turntables, and we'd stand while doing the show. And we had two Magnacord recorders, so you were always running around like an octopus while on the air. That day was almost disastrous. I went home with tears in my eyes and stood there at the front of my not-too-lavish apartment at the time in Omaha, and I said: "I think I want to go back to South Dakota—not Iowa, but all the way back to Dakota—to be a newspaperman, because I don't think this is the field for me." I'd been a newspaperman for a number of years prior to that. I'd been in radio since I was 16, but it was a lot different—Top 40 radio—from the days when you'd legitimately cup your hand over your ear and say: "This is the Mutual Broadcasting System and we're broadcasting from the Creomyer Ballroom." I'd never been a Top 40 disk jockey . . . I'd never been any kind of a disk jockey. It was a very traumatic moment.

Hall: What did Burden say?

Owens: Well, Burden never spoke to me directly, putting me down, but a number of disk jockeys have told me since that he said: "My God, what a terrible disk jockey!" I saw Don in Las Vegas some years ago and we didn't talk much about my past career because I've been very fortunate over the years in having formative teachers—I never worked for a radio station where I didn't learn something. I think that what you are today is an amalgamation of your past. So there's a little bit of me that is KOIL in Omaha, there's a little bit of me that is KIMN in Denver, where I went after Omaha, and quite a bit of me is the McLendon training. I received that training from Gordon McLendon and Don Keyes, and from the great McLendon program directors in all of the markets I was in throughout the Texas triangle—WNOE in New Orleans, WIL in St. Louis, John Box, Crowell-Collier, KEWB and KFWB . . . and then, of course, KMPC in Los Angeles because it has been the only pure MOR station I've worked at. I joined KMPC in 1962. All the rest have really been rock.

Hall: What was the first station you worked on in Los Angeles?

Owens: KFWB. I came down from KEWB in San Francisco; I joined them in 1959. We changed from a classical music station, KLX to Top 40. And I came down to KFWB . . . not, surprisingly enough, to go to KFWB. They wanted Don French to be program director and me to be morning man at WMGM in New York, which Crowell-Collier was going to buy. In the meantime, a strike took place at KFWB and so Don

French and I spent most of our time in the back room at the station writing silly commercials. During the strike, the negotiations for WMGM fell through, so French and I became men within an organization, but without a station. Then, apparently the ratings were not too good early in the morning at KFWB, and they put me on the air. Fortunately, after that the ratings became very good. The station was a good experience for me because it was probably at that time the No. 1 radio station in the United States.

Hall: Was Chuck Blore then program director?

Owens: He was national program director for the chain. Jim Hawthorne was program director of the station. Both very fine people. Chuck has always been a perpetual happy face button—even before they were invented. It's always been: "Hey, gang! Let's do this!" And Hawthorne had been an idol of mine, even when I was a kid. Not that he's that much older, but he had the Hawthorne Egbert and his twanger . . . they used to do a show out of Pasadena for NBC. He was one of the persons that took Steve Allen's place at KNX-AM after Steve went into television. Bill Ballance was also a man that I admired very much, and I still do; we're very good friends.

Hall: How did you get to KMPC from there?

Owens: In a most unusual way. During the strike—I don't know if this is known or not, perhaps—but the strike was a trying time for us. I don't think anyone really wanted to be in a strike, and it was one of those situations where I was a man without a country. I was either on the side of AFTRA or management, or so the public must have thought. But that was not really true. I didn't want to be out of work. Yet, by the same token, I wanted to make money doing commercials, and I knew that if I became a strike breaker, it might be injurious to my commercials career. And I do commercials—this year already I've probably done a couple of hundred commercials. When you do those things, you must think of the future, and as long as commercials are an integral part of the union, you must have union okay to do them. I didn't want to endanger that. So, I went on strike. Which involved holding a picket sign and walking up and down in front of KFWB. During the strike, Bob Pursell sent us telegrams saying that all of us who didn't report back to work by a given date would have their contracts declared null and void.

Hall: Who was Bob Pursell?

Owens: He was manager and president of Crowell-Collier, manager of KFWB. I don't recall that anyone went back to work at that time, so our contracts were null and void, which meant that we were free to go to work anywhere else. That was the first time since I'd been in radio that I was free to go somewhere else without being at the end of a contractual period, which was the best thing that ever happened to me. I was unhappy at KFWB. But the reason I wanted to work in either New York or Los Angeles was in order to make as much money as I could in the other areas. For what I do there are really only two cities I can work in—New York or Los Angeles, because I do commercials, voice animated cartoons, and acting. Anyway, Pursell had sent his telegrams, and after the strike was terminated we went back on the air at the station. Then several months later, Hugh Heller, who was then program director of KMPC, offered me a job. To do the afternoon show. I was bugged with the morning show—I'd been getting up at 4:30 AM for so many years of my life that I felt half of my life was being missed. And that's true. You must have a strange, sado-masochistic streak in you to be a morning man because you miss out so much. If you enjoy going to bed at 8 in the evening, I guess it's all right. There are some guys who can do mornings and still stay up all night the night before. You make more money in a Top 40 station doing the morning show. This is invariably true. It is not true at a KMPC type of station where Dick Whittinghill and I basically make the same salary. We're both No. 1 in the demographics that they want us to be No. 1 in, which is the 25-49 age group. You know, that's the crappy thing: It's a b.s. syndrome that I went through in Top 40 in that they would always plug No. 1 ratings ... but they really aren't No. 1 ratings. They drove so much on being No. 1 in total audience rather than demographic audience, because the emphasis then was not on demographics. For example, KMPC has always stressed the 25-49 age listener—or maybe even older than 49, maybe going up into the 60s—because those are the people who have money to spend. KMPC is consistently one of the top two stations in the United States in terms of gross. I have no way of looking at the actual figures but I do know that KMPC grosses around $8 million a year, which is probably next to WOR in New York, which I presume is the No. 1 biller.

I find you have to ask yourself, what are you really after in radio? You have to sit and analyze: What does radio really mean? Why am I in it? What is the end result? People seldom do that because ego is involved; a lot of factors are involved. But a KMPC type of station is very good for an air personality because, first of all, they let me have pretty much free rein in what I want to do. I prepare my show. I spend a lot of time in the preparation of it. But we're reaching the audience that we want to reach.

Hall: Do you also have a choice in the records that you play?

Owens: Yes. We have a playlist as a guide. And we use *Billboard;* we have the *Billboard* Hot 100 up in our studios. And we also have a sheet called *The Pendant,* which Eric Norberg, program director Mark Blinoff, and music director Alene McKinney get together and formulate once a week. However, I use that as a guide. I program my own music—Noreen, my secretary, programs it for me. We get together—Noreen Doyle and I, who's been working for me for six years now—and she puts down my music for me. We get together once a week, we check over *Billboard,* the various charts, but there's still such a thing as personal feeling toward a record. For example, you may find an artist who has never recorded before and you believe in that artist and say: "Well, let's give him a break." You can't be totally formatted, because after all we are a personality station. There are not an awful lot of personality stations. There may be people who only listen to KMPC because they like Dick Whittinghill. They may not like his music, they may even hate his music, but they like him. They may think: "Well, here's a little double entendre I haven't heard before!" What Golden West Broadcasting has always sold is personality radio. And that's why I feel it's a good form of radio to be in.

Hall: How much time do you devote to the music you play?

Owens: As far as picking the music, I spend two or three hours a week. In total—I mean that as a tabulation of maybe the total hours I spend, because my secretary physically does it for me. I'll go over the charts, she'll make notes, and I'll say: "Well, maybe let's try the Captain and Tennille." They have a very fine record on a small label, Butterscotch Records or something like that. Wink Martindale brought it to my attention. He started playing it, and I think it's going to be a hit when a major label picks up the master to it. It has a great sound. We try to play those kinds of things.

Hall: Do you think the music is an important part of your show?

Owens: Oh, yes. I think that music is at least 60 percent of the show. The other 40 percent is everything else that I do—the sillies, the traffic, the news.

Hall: I think a lot of what you do—you may call them sillies—is in your head already.

Owens: A lot of it is ad-lib material, but ad-libbing is nothing more than an accumulation of the ideas you've had over the years. Obviously, if you're a 16 or 17-year-old jock, your ad-libability may be good, but it won't be what it will be 15 years later. The more knowledge you have, the more experience you have, the better ad-libber you're going to be. That's why Milton Berle, who has probably memorized every joke that has ever existed, has a humor memory bank . . . for example, you could say: "Give me a joke beginning with A," and somewhere in his mind is cataloged several jokes beginning with that letter.

Bizarre or absurd is what most of my humor really is. It's filled with parody or satire—the kind that pokes fun at ourselves or pompous people. You know, it's funny, but no one thinks of themselves as being pompous, and that's why everyone can enjoy humor that is satire. And that's why we got by with a lot on the *Laugh In* television show—we would insult practically everybody. But everyone would say or think: "Hey! I know a guy just like that!" And all along maybe it would be him that we were making fun of. So, I guess I do a lot of ad-libbing, to get back to that.

Hall: Do these things just come up spontaneously in your mind? Or have you thought out basically what you're going to do in a show?

Owens: I prerecord a lot of the commercials' satires. For example, maybe one on Flogger's Instant which turns out to be prune juice instead of coffee. In parody of the MGM Grand Hotel, I'll do a production thing on the Rin Tin Tin Motel which was built for $47,000 and is about 50 miles from Las Vegas—they raised it from the money for an old Dagwood and Blondie movie. Those things will be planned, naturally, since you can't do a good production spot off the top of your head. You must really write those . . . lay them out . . . decide whether to put this sound effect, that music, and so on. But still, that's what makes my show different from most other shows. I may spend as much as five hours on these things—if I get off at 6 PM, I might be there until 11 PM with my engineer, Wayne DuBois, who's been my engineer for a number of years. We'll spend hours on these production bits, working with them until we have a high quality product—the same as you would with an album. I want the same quality on one of these bits as I would in an album or in one of the commercials I do. It takes a lot of time. Most people don't realize that. They probably think air personalities just sit down in front of a mike and open their mouth. So, I'll have Kathy Gori, KMPC's all-night personality, do some of the voices with me. Joannie Gerber is probably the highest paid woman announcer for commercials in the United States. She probably makes at least $250,000 a year doing commercials. She's just brilliant, and so's Kathy. Kathy is usually around the studios in the daytime preparing to do her show. She also does a very fine silly show, and has this great sense of humor. So, I have a group of friends who do these bits with me. Sonny Melendrez is on quite a few of the spots that I use. Sonny is sort of a younger Chuck Blore in many ways; he has this great joie de vivre where everything is like *Wow!*—it's exciting. It's nice to see that, because among a group of old crusty cynics like myself who tend to wind up with an H.L. Mencken feeling about things, it's nice to see that some people are still up about the world. You know, the world isn't really all that great if you sit and analyze it. But it's our job, as entertainers, to not put things down. It's our job to make people laugh or point out the absurdities. Do you know that during the Depression there were two businesses that did not lose money—books, because people wanted to escape, and movies, for the same reason.

Hall: What percent of your salary is from your radio show?

Owens: About a third, I guess—and a third from television and a third from commercials. Sometimes, though, commercials outweigh radio and TV, if I have a good year. Sometimes, you may make $18,000 to $25,000 in a year just from one commercial if it runs for a long enough period of time. I never want to get out of that business, though, because sometimes you can make more in a three-minute commercial than you could working a year in radio in Creomyer, Neb.

Hall: But, not every air personality could do commercials like that.

Owens: That's probably true.

Hall: What's the forte that you have to have in order to do commercials?

Owens: First of all, I think you have to have an identity. Now Casey Kasen is a very good disk jockey and he does a lot of commercials. And Casey has a down-home sort of voice—that is, it's not an announcer's voice. I have an announcer's voice, but it's a put-on announcer's voice. For example, a funny thing happened the other day. I was eating over at The Shack and one of the waitresses told me about hearing someone in the restaurant that she thought was Gary Owens, and the man told her that he wasn't Gary Owens, that he was here first. Well, I came back that night to get a sandwich, and Hugh Douglas was sitting there. He was one of my idols, and he was the guy who sounded like me. He was a big announcer on such radio shows as *Suspense, Escape,* those kings of shows. And perhaps unknowingly, my voice style was that of Hugh Douglas, Marvin Miller, Paul Frees, because as a kid you have heroes. Steve Allen is certainly a hero of mine.

Steve and I were at Jonathan Winters' art show a couple of months ago. Jonathan is a marvelous painter. One of his pictures was Doris Day's dog and cat drowning in a pool, a painting that sold for about $2,500. A TV producer came over and told me that Steve and I sounded so much alike, with little word plays and so on. Steve said: "Yeah, we do, but we're both entirely different." Yet, I was influenced by Steve's word plays, by those of Robert Benchley, Ring Lardner, Frank Sullivan . . . people like that. And I think, as you grow older, the good filters to the top and the bad to the bottom. Perhaps the top is the best of what you really wanted to be as a kid.

So what gives you that special forte for commercials? Well, I think you must have a definite categorization, or be able to do a lot of different voices. Now I don't do many voices—only about five. But basically they hire me for my own voice, which is that of an authoritarian, but with kind of a put-on. They know that I'm not being too serious when I do certain things. I did a spot for the movie *The Three Musketeers,* which was sort of a satire on the old Superman opening . . . "faster than a speeding bullet." They thought I was exactly right for that spot. Once, a coffee company came to town and auditioned several hundred people for a commercial, asking each of them to "try to sound like Gary Owens." The recording engineer said: "Why don't you hire Gary Owens?" But they said no because I didn't audition. That's true, I don't audition for spots any more. Not that I wouldn't want to—I just don't have the time. You could spend a full day just auditioning for commercials. After trying all of these guys for the coffee commercials—and all of the men were fine in their own way—none of them had this exact put-on sound that I have, which is that of an old-time radio announcer with just a touch of silliness. The reason I don't audition for spots anymore is that I feel I should spend my time creating. In an article that I wrote for *Human Behavior Magazine*, I researched the abnormalities of people in the past—things you wouldn't believe. Cardinal Richelieu thought he was an animal, a horse. At times he would gallop around the courtyards of France and neigh and whinny. After each little thing I wrote, I would write another little bit like: "It's a good thing he never broke his leg while running around like that because we would have had to shoot him." Now, it's a straight, factual article. But publishing is one of the benefits, along with performing on TV and commercials, that you don't find in many other cities outside of New York, Los Angeles, or Chicago, it would appear.

These things are extenuations of everything that I wanted to do—what my life *is*, even though I'm seldom really and totally happy. You might say I'm driven—I was driven here by Arnold my chauffer—I think I am driven to the point where I want to do creative things. And when a person wants to do creative things, he should do them. For example, there'll be disk jockeys who'll read this in small towns—people who want to build their career. And my suggestion is that if they feel like writing an article, write it. Submit it to whatever publication they wish. You don't have to be in Chicago or Los Angeles to submit things. Same thing applies to newspaper articles or whatever the case may be. And if rejected, keep trying. Ray Bradbury, the science fiction author, told me that he often submitted stories 100 times—he would write an article or story for a science fiction magazine and it would end up in *Cosmopolitan*. And I think that's true of radio. Franz Kafka was a great writer of allegory, and he wrote something that I think applies very well to radio. He said: "In a fight between you and the world, bet on the world." In essence, I think he meant that you must please a lot of people. You can still have individuality, but make it palatable . . . for everyone. For instance, you can still be an individual and work within a radio format. You can't just play Count Basie all day—there's not that much demand for jazz.

Hall: But can you be creative?

Owens: Certainly. You have to give, bend a little bit. It's often a give-and-take proposition—something we may not exactly like too much—but you sometimes have to do those things. As much as I loved Top 40 radio . . . and I still love the production of a Top 40 format. I think every new disk jockey should work first in Top 40 radio . . . .

Hall: How do you advise someone building a career?

Owens: I left KFWB because all of the contracts became null and void during a strike. So when Hugh Heller, then program director of KMPC, offered me a job, I jumped at it because I wanted to go into other fields. I felt no one was hiring Top 40 disk jockeys to do commercials. When I turned on the radio, I heard voices that happened to be MOR disk jockeys and I said to myself: "My God, I'm defeating my purpose by being on a Top 40 station now that I'm in Los Angeles." I thought that I ought to take advantage of the fact I was in Los Angeles. Plus, Top 40 stations in those days were living from day to day in the ratings book—as were the disk jockies. And no two ratings books are going to show the same thing. You can't really live that way, living from ratings to ratings.

Hall: You didn't like that kind of nebulous Top 40 life?

Owens: I really didn't. I've always been an angry young man. Now I'm an angry older young man or whatever the case may be. Much of it, I think, is the drive a person has. I've always tried to get along with people, but in the last couple of years I've come to the conclusion that if you're going to get an ulcer or give an ulcer, it's far better to give one. Where I used to take a lot of crap years ago, I don't do that anymore. There are, of course, a lot of reasons. *Laugh In* was fairly good for me—that was six long years, and we had 35 million homes a week watching us. And there's a new TV series for producers Chris Beard and Allan Blye, two of the silliest people in the world. They produced the Andy Williams Show, the Sonny & Cher Show, and the new Sonny Show on the ABC-TV network. I was on the Hudson Brothers show with Ronnie Graham and Stephanie Edwards, the three of us starring with the Hudson Brothers. I guess that has benefitted me—obviously, a person who is known nationally rather than just regionally has advantages.

Hall: Did the people producing the Hudson Brothers show seek you out?

Owens: Well, I've known Chris Beard . . . he and I would do silly things in the hallway when he was one of the writers on *Laugh In*. He knew my frustrations—I ended up doing one character on the show for six straight years—the announcer person, who is a silly person, but is not really what I do.

Hall: Is that the same character you are on the air . . . do you think of yourself as that character on the air?

Owens: No. It's a funny thing. My voice is that way, the basic announcer's voice. But I don't know how I think of myself on the air. I do put myself down in instances . . . where you try to do a great thing and suddenly your pants fall down.

Hall: Do you take yourself seriously?

Owens: Never have I taken myself seriously. Sometimes people will write the wrong things into that.

Hall: What can a jock do in a smaller market to improve himself?

Owens: Prepare. Preparation is the greatest thing they can do for their radio shows. If they're doing humor, have a large gag file so they can switch the gags around to fit the occasion. Maybe we should have an 11th commandment: Thou shalt not commit banality. I think that's the killer, more than anything else in radio—banality. To be boring. That's a time waster. Too many disk jockeys come in one minute before they go on the air—and maybe even pull the records while they're on the air. They've no idea about how to place records so there's a smooth cohesive factor. I'm still a firm believer that you don't play all uppers or all downers, as far as pacing is concerned.

Secondly, there should be thought in what the disk jockey does. In every station I've been, we've come in and listened to the commercials before going on the air. Now how many men do that today where they work? You might take a line for a commercial about Ford that says: "It's the best news yet . . . " and see how many intros you can do into that commercial . . . plan something. To make your show like one giant melody being played—that's good advice.

OUTRO: Because the programming approach of the radio station has changed in the past year or so, Gary Owens no longer does his own music. Though Owens doesn't audition for commercials because of lack of time (or his unwillingness to waste it), he doesn't stint on time when it comes to doing charity work or helping people.

DWIGHT CASE

Dwight Case

INTRO: What better way to introduce Dwight Case, president of RKO Radio with headquarters in Los Angeles, than to let him tell his own story.

A Case History

I feel like I've had a classic career in radio. I started as a copywriter at KFRE in Fresno, Calif. for $175 a month. Because I was already married and had two kids, I had to work nights in the post office to make ends meet. But I believed in radio and wanted to be in the industry.

I worked and was promoted to an announcer's position, then I became a disk jockey. My first job as a program director was at KFIV in Modesto. I programmed a couple of stations, then went into sales, became a general sales manager, later a manager. Next I managed a group of stations, but even then had to work my way up from executive vice president of sales. Ultimately, I took a run at buying my own station. If you look at my call letters in the industry, it looks as if I haven't been able to keep a job.

In August 1972 I came to RKO as acting manager of KHJ and KRTH in Los Angeles and eastern regional vice president. In July 1973, I joined Bruce Johnson, then president of RKO Radio, as his executive vice president. When Johnson resigned in May 1975, I became president. I got my first job the way I constantly advise young people to do today: Keep knocking on doors until something nice finally happens to your.

Some days, I would give anything to have everyone in the same time zone. These days, I get up early and call eastern radio stations and our advertising rep company, to see if there are any problems. Some days there's no reason to call. Between 6-7:30 AM I cover those time zones in case there are any problems or anything I can help with . . . or any anger I have to emote. Then I have breakfast and go into the office on the seventh floor of 6255 Sunset Boulevard at about 8 AM. By this time I can begin phone calls to our Midwest stations in Memphis and Chicago, and perhaps the rep firm in Atlanta. I'm cycled into the rest of the world because the West Coast is alive and New York hasn't quite gone to lunch yet.

Toward the end of the day, there's thinking time, time to do dictation, and to catch up on things. After 3 PM you're not bothered by calls from the East or Midwest too often.

This schedule works out pretty well for me.

Of course, I also travel a great deal because I like to have first-hand knowledge of the people in the stations, and have personal contact with them. Sometimes an objective observer comes into a station and in a couple of hours can pick up on a morale problem. Obviously, my fulcrum is New York, because that's the location of corporate headquarters—RKO General.

This week is a good example of my traveling: Tuesday, I go to Memphis and will be there all day before flying to New York. I'll be in New York on Wednesday, Thursday, and Friday. But I'm only going to touch one station this time, so I'm bringing Erica Farber, general manager of WROR in Boston, to New York so we can go over her station's budgets. Next time I go to New York, I'll probably go to Chicago first, and maybe come out through Washington, just to spend a day so I don't forget the names of the people working for us.

Above and Beyond the P & L

You can run a company in many ways. For example, you could be totally dedicated to money management—and money management is a craft. Some people are very good at money management. You could take a group of radio stations, only deal in dollars, and allow your real responsibilities to roll off your back. It's eight-to-five you're going to be all right—if you have a good staff of lawyers to keep you out of trouble.

But with this company—I work under Frank Shakespeare and get along very well with him because I feel the same way he does—the modus operandi is that making a budget and showing a profit is *given*. You just *do* that. Okay?

But after you do that, you should perform the other things that the radio business allows you to enjoy. Obviously, the manager of a multimillion-dollar business in a market such as Los Angeles is a very important man. And because of the power of the voice of his station—regardless of the demographic area the station serves—the manager is very important politically. Thus he has more responsibility . . . he *owes* his community more simply because he's where he is and is as powerful as he is.

Unfortunately, because the radio and advertising industries are as large as they are, especially in a city the size of New York or Los Angeles, many managers get lost in their own life. You could always go to lunch or dinner with someone in the industry, and never meet a congressman or senator, or never meet the man that runs the store on the corner of Eighth and Main. And if you do meet the guy that runs the store, he automatically feels you're trying to sell him something. But that's not true. The people who run the Broadway and the May Company are very important people in our community because they have the ability to cause the community to grow and prosper.

So, the manager's job is to make the P&L. Okay? But after that what we try to infuse into our stations is personal growth of the managers and their staffs, and stronger community involvement. Knowledge of world affairs is vital today. We're sending Pat Norman, general manager of KFRC in San Francisco, and Tim Sullivan, general manager of KHJ in Los Angeles, into the Pacific basin on what I conceive to be an extended learning trip. From the East Coast we're sending Jerry Lyman of WGMS in Washington, to Europe, We're not sure where. When the time comes for each man to release himself temporarily from his station, the political climate of the time will determine the best place for him to go to learn about what's going on in the world.

These men, you see, are responsible for editorializing on their station; they're responsible for the kind of public affairs programming that goes on the air. They need to know more about the world. We intend to cycle all of our managers into foreign countries in the next two-to-four years so they'll be able to discuss things with more reflection than if they'd stayed home. Also, each of the men has the necessary funds in his budget to attend management courses at such schools as Harvard, MIT, or

Stanford. Each man will report to the others what he's learned. The man RKO sent to Israel last year—well, it was important to all of us because of the information he brought back. He saw it entirely different than the rest of us who got our information through the *Los Angeles Times, The Post,* or other newspapers. We learn from our roving instructors, but I also feel the trips are a great strengthener for them personally. You see, regardless of whether you're in Wichita Falls or New York, or you're with a rock 'n' roll station or an all-talk station, if you have a listener circulation you must talk to the people about how you feel and how you think your community should grow. I'm very concerned about the industry. Rick Devlin, manager of WXLO in New York, was sent to the National Association of Broadcasters to observe and come back and tell us about it. He is attending one of the NAB Fall Seminars, and he talks to all of the other managers by phone. So if there is an opportunity for us to put a vote in on anything, or make a suggestion, or even influence an attitude about the way we feel as a group, we can take time to do it.

One of the greatest experiences I've had in a long time was at an Alaskan broadcasting meeting recently when I sat down and talked with Abbott Washburn, a man with a phenomenal mind. Now I know that I can talk to him and get a feeling about something in Washington, if I have the need. Not meeting people like him, or not getting to know them better, or not having social contact, is a great mistake that a lot of broadcasters make. At a cocktail party many radio men run over to join someone they know instead of walking over and meeting a stranger.

If our managers got anything out of our 1976 management meeting in Apopka, Fla., they learned Dean Birch hasn't changed a bit since he left the Federal Communications Commission. But Dean Birch is one hell of a guy. He was a hell of a guy when he was there with the Commission. I called him at home one day because I had a project I thought was the greatest thing since sliced bread. Dean shot it down, and correctly so. But I got him at home, he was sitting on his patio eating breakfast one Saturday morning. He was a guy you could reach. I don't think FCC chairman Wylie is any different. I just haven't met him yet.

So, what we're trying to do is move the men into meetings—and not just in a social way, but with total absorption so they can build their own ideas, their own thrust. The way this company used to function was that the company did the interface with the FCC, not with the commission, necessarily, but with the bureauracy. Our men are now their own interface. That doesn't mean we won't help them, but it puts a Tim Sullivan or a Herb Salzman of WOR in New York into direct contact with the FCC so they can grow and learn. No longer do they just read the directives that come from my office because those directives have been filtered through our minds here. Now they have to study on their own and find out how the FCC sees it. Schools, travels, FCC interface—I think these will make our men stronger. And we'll end up with better *citizens* at each of our radio stations.

Exciting Things Happening

There are some very exciting things happening in our industry. I'm very interested in FM radio. We obviously have some of the big AM facilities around the nation, and our FM facilities are standing alone in some of the marketplaces. We'll have more standing alone later as we diversify markets. I'm very concerned about the rate structures of FM radio stations and how much they can charge for advertising time. When they oppose and have the same kind of circulation figures—if I may use a non-radio term—as an AM station in a given market, invariably they can't get the same kind of rates merely because they're an FM station.

By accident, Jack Thayer's News And Information Service at NBC may help FM tremendously, whether radio ever gets all-channel legislation or not. You see, the current pattern of the NIS stations—whether for positive, negative, or even accidental reasons—is being sold to a tremendous number of FM stations. And I happen to feel it's one of the best things that could happen. For this reason: When FM started, it was basically for the people who wanted to listen to classical music—a very esoteric bunch who were interested in squeakers and tweeters. After a while, FM moved out of classical and into the good music room of the house. FM stations still had low commercial content, as a practicality.

Then the next people to come on the scene were progressive rock people, who, very frankly, I don't consider to be very far from classical programming in nature. It's my opinion that if you took a survey at a college campus, such as the University of Southern California in Los Angeles, you'd find KFAC [the classical station] and KMET [the progressive station] have crossover listeners. And MOR happened on FM. Along with Top 40 and oldie stations. But, if you wanted news, you had to go to the AM band.

Now, with so many news stations on FM, the FM band has turned into a full-service radio band. And this makes it a more competitive band. Promotion for FM will change dramatically. Soon, it'll be the AM guys who'll be bitching for all-channel legislation instead of the FM owners. They're going to plead for all-channel radios then.

Out of his all-news network service, Jack Thayer, president of NBC Radio, might have accidentally punched the button to cause FM to become a real spectrum.

We have a lot of trouble now with FM rates, especially in market places where we have two stations. Getting an FM rate up in Los Angeles, New York, or San Francisco is different than getting an FM rate up in Detroit or Chicago. This is a Dwight Case observation and may have no foundation in fact. But my own P&L and my talks with other radio people indicate my observation isn't *all* wrong. Chicago and Detroit clients, for some strange reason, if they're not anti-FM look upon it as a different kind of way to buy. They don't look for *radio*. In New York, San Francisco, or Los Angeles, very often if you've got the numbers you get the buy. If at WXLO in New York, general manager Rick Devlin was able to beat Rick Sklar at WABC in midday ratings, Devlin would have a dynamite shot at getting the business at whatever rate is out there, as long as the buy is efficient in cost per listener. It has to be a relatively efficient buy, but the advertiser doesn't say, "This is AM," or, "This is FM." They merely see that the cost efficiency is fine and buy 99X [WXLO]. The same situation is true in Los Angeles with KLOS. If they are an efficient buy, they don't get a lot of hassle about being an FM station. The same is true in San Francisco frankly because of James Gabbert, owner of KIOI, and the success he's had with that station. He can be very proud of the work he does. I've watched his station for years.

In the major cities, FM rates aren't higher due to one reason: Lack of courage. You've got to go out and ask for $120 a spot, instead of saying: "Well, the average FM rate is $46, so if I go to $50 or $92 or $126 . . . ?" The result is that the broadcaster ends up cross-commiserating and stays far beyond AM rates.

In New York, Rick Devlin is a very courageous man. We are now moving up into the soft underbelly of the AM rates. We are up in the $80s, $90s, and $97s. We haven't crossed the $100 barrier yet, okay, but he's charging the same kind of money as many leading AM stations in the market.

In other markets, it's just a matter of saying: "I'm going to raise my rates from $45 to $92 per minute, because my cost per thousand will be $4.54 and that's better than what KFI provides at $94.50 for a minute spot and what KHJ gets at $126 per minute." It's mere courage.

You can make speeches about it, but when the sales manager at an FM station finds out you lost the Coke buy because you were $54 and you could have had it at $8, all of the courage in the world seems to subside.

In the old days when I was turning rockers around, I used to have a saying: Every time the ratings fall, raise the rate card. People became so fascinated by the concept, they'd buy. The thing is, you were negotiating from a hell of a lot better base than when you had the higher ratings. Then, when you got the ratings back, you could raise the rate card again. Again, *courage.*

Or, maybe it's a matter of insanity. I don't know. But, why not raise the rates?

There's no rationale for when you raise the rate card. There's no reason Tim Sullivan, general manager of KHJ in Los Angeles, couldn't go to $150 per minute tomorrow. Why not? I don't know why not.

The old theory was that every time you got a bad audience ratings, down came the rate card. But, no! You don't work radio that way. How come you're not more important out there in the marketplace, for example, when the audience ratings are going down? After all, the people are talking more about you, right?

But in Chicago or Detroit? I don't know. We have a station in Chicago and we're doing well. We're making our living off Michigan Avenue. But not in the shops at all. Some national business, and the trend is up. Actually, the station is not doing that badly. It's an efficient buy. But there is definitely a dichotomy between AM and FM radio in the market. You are an FM person. Same is true in Detroit; you are an FM person. In New York City, San Francisco, or Los Angeles when you say FM no one jerks their neck.

I also think FM has been hurt—and this may sound very tangential—by the VHF and UHF split in television. People think about VHF as the place where they spend the big money because it's network. We, with our FM stations, suffer from that—that feeling that UHF is a movie station or a Spanish-language station or where public-supported television goes. When, in fact, with the all-channel TV tuner, it isn't that way anymore. But the advertising buyer thinks of VHF and UHF like AM and FM. More so in the Midwest, unfortunately.

I don't see AM ending up as a talk or news band either. I think two or three things happen with an AM station that do not happen, at this time, with an FM station. For one things, the AM station has greater reach. A 5,000-watt, low-frequency AM station has greater signal range than a top class C FM station. Eventually I think that programming on AM stations will change rather drastically . . . but then, music today is forcing us into some programming changes. People accept more different kinds of music than they used to accept. And our lifestyle is changing radio. But, basically, I don't feel AM will become merely news and information stations. I don't think I'll see that in my time.

This doesn't, of course, mean that one or two more all-talk stations won't come along in any market—perhaps some kind of a Bill Ballance "Feminine Forum" format in Los Angeles. Who can say what's going to happen down the road? But, no, you won't have 32 AM stations in Los Angeles programming all-talk and all-news.

New formats? Oh, yeah. Formats are constantly arriving in radio—starting back in the early 1950s when the idea developed in radio that people wanted to hear the same record over and over. And then the computer came along. Though the computer didn't play a lot of emphasis on, say, Bill Drake, it was a *way* we were thinking at the time. The computer has had, in my mind, an enormous effect on radio. Because, though at this stage we are using the computer usually for only billing and logging, people *think* computer. Everyone tends to reason more mathematically than we used to reason.

As radio came into a strong formula approach, like Bill Drake put together for one of our stations, everyone began to think that formula was the answer. Now that the lengths of records are changing in and out, you can't even tell what's going to come out next—albums being as low-priced as they are, and the flagging sales in 45-rpm singles—all of this is having a great effect on us now in our programming at all of our stations.

Paul Drew, my vice president of programming, commented when Tom Donahue died: "There went down the drain the next great format." In his mind, when Donahue passed away as general manager of KSAN in San Francisco, there might have been another great format such as progressive rock.

Paul Drew, as program supervisor for a large organization, has no doubt that there will be something else in programming down the road. Right now, the music is forcing us into cycling our programming. We are not doing it creatively, we are cycling.

Right now we want more public affairs in prime time. This forces more creativity in programming, whatever the format. Whatever the nature, the work of becoming more integrated into the community—being, in fact, a town clarion in your maximum listening times—causes more creativity in order to keep your audience listening. I know, on our stations at least, it's going to. It's the nature of the demand that we are putting on the general managers and the program directors. It's the same creativity we expect of a program director to take 12 commercials an hour and be creative enough around that. Play "Rhinestone Cowboy" enough times to keep the young people listening and began to train for the next cycle of listeners. It *demands* that you are a creative program director. Creative programming is not limiting spots; it's weaving them in such a way as to build listeners, weaving them with all of the other programming elements to make a very entertaining radio station.

I believe that there is still a strong and very human tinge of entertainment in the radio business. Because of this, it tends to draw a very creative type of person. Television has shut off a lot of the avenues for creative people who wish to get into it. They robbed a lot of good people from radio in the early 50s. But what's happened is that television has become so expensive to produce that it chews up product and talent at astronomical rates. Just try to name all of the shows of 1972, or even two years ago; George Gobel, one season, then he's gone—and he's a fine comedian. Television generates a low-end fear in people who might want to get into it. I think we're getting a great flow of young creative brains into radio that ordinarily might have gone into television. Because we're a longer-term job situation with the talent that exists, we don't burn it up. Radio is not as expensive to produce as television, so there's a little more security in radio.

Real talent has a chance in radio, whereas television is very difficult to break into. In television, a producer is very hesitant to hire low-end talent. We're able to pay about the same kind of money, and to also give them a chance to build their careers over a longer period. Television has shut off some avenues of growth for young people.

Education Vs. Dollars

What has happened is that we're still living through a period where colleges and universities tend to turn out an extremely liberal product. Not that it's any different than when I came up through college. Students were a touch short of being red when I was in college. But two things have happened: Not only do young people have an unrealistic point of view about how much money they can make in radio once they get their degree, but also they have strange visions about how much money people in radio make. They assume that the average radio station manager, because he's been at the job 15 years, and is so damned smart, is probably making somewhere between $99,000 and $100,000 a year. Well, not true! You and I know that because we know the life-styles of many managers of radio stations. Some general managers of radio stations don't make as much as their general sales managers do . . . at a top station in a top year. But when you think you might hire a young kid out of college, you've probably missed the figure he had expected by $10,000!

If you've only missed it by three grand, you can still talk to one another. But they have the feeling the dollars in radio are a heck of a lot higher to start then they are almost anywhere—whether it's working at a store or a guy in middle management at Sears. When you mention a real salary, they think you are shucking them.

Don't Sit Quietly!

Radio is very complex, and that's one of the things I enjoy about it. It keeps you on your toes. But I don't think anymore that a broadcaster can live quietly, after reading the directives that are coming down from the Federal Communications Commission—governmental regulations are moving into the area of legislation and potential legislation. No broadcaster can sit quietly in the small towns of America and not have direction from legal counsel in Washington. Because the federal bureaucracy might be, in fact, making a lot of rules that, tacitly understood, no one need do anything about. It's for the one bad guy out of 7,000, right? Unfortunately, government is applying that rule to all and sundry. Governmental legislation is definitely moving in on us.

Do I see nationalization of radio? No. But I do see—unless the small coterie of 15-20 broadcasters who own multiple stations make inroads—the bureaucracy acting more and more on rules that have gone through while some of us haven't even read them yet, because they were passed two to five years ago.

The timing of the things that can happen and the costs of a man's business being affected by some incidental legislation, make it imperative that a broadcaster have someone who can interpret possible legislation or rulemaking and turn the gist of such into simple businessman terms.

Washington is a whole different vocabulary than radio. It's a whole different world you have to live in when you're face to face with the Federal Communications Commission. Whether, in fact, you're owner of just a single radio station or you own several. The problem develops when an owner of a radio station in Bakersfield, Calif., or Wichita Falls, Tex., is handed a piece of legislation or rulemaking which could cost him one percent of his gross. He is more than likely not as concerned about it as, say, a station owner or manager whose station is doing $5,000,000 or $10,000,000 a year.

What seems to happen in government today is that it's only people who rear up on their hind end who get noticed. And what seems to happen in government is that the only people rearing up on their hind end getting noticed are the ones who obviously have the most to gain . . . or lose.

Consequently, the government says: "Well, obviously RKO is concerned because of their billing. But we haven't heard from the little guy out in the hinterlands, so if you take a broadbase average it doesn't affect the little broadcasters that much

because he hasn't complained. So, obviously, the rulemaking is correct."
This, however, is a scary situation.

If you get right down to it, there are probably only 24 broadcasters really concerned about the bill by Senator Hugh Scott that will create a royalty payment paid by broadcasters for record artists and record companies based on airplay. But those 24 broadcasters may represent as much as 50 percent of the total revenues in radio.

But radio people in Colorado Springs, Wichita Falls, Tex.; and even in Dallas (I've talked to people down there) take the attitude that they're not going to bother ... not going to write their congressman ... not going to become involved with it ... just take whatever is handed down to them by the government. They assume that one percent is not going to hurt them too much. But it isn't only the one percent that bothers me ... it's the fact that they aren't involved with the most important fulcrum that their station operates around.

My feeling is that no matter how large or small you are in broadcasting, you should have some kind of attorney relationship in Washington, someone who would not only tell you what a rulemaking or legislation is going to do to your station, but what it's going to do to the entire industry.

With a broadcaster paying dues to the National Association of Broadcasters and the Radio Advertising Bureau, I look upon the attorney situation in Washington as something a radio man could "belong" to, much as a broadcaster pays NAB and RAB dues or dues to his Junior Chamber of Commerce. But a broadcaster desperately needs someone in Washington today who can keep you in touch with what's going on so you have the right to stand up and be counted as one of the voting group. I think that kind of relationship has to happen. If not for the personal benefit of the radio man, then for the benefit of the industry. We just can't be loners anymore.

We've got to make some kind of effort to keep the quasi-government control away that's moving in on us. And I can't do it because I'm so-called Big Business. And Hal Neal can't do it because he's Big Business.

The trouble is that the radio men in Wichita Falls think they don't matter. They probably feel it's tough enough to break even at the end of the year. And that's a short-sighted philosophy. Because later on, as radio gets more and more involved with this type of governmental interface, the small broadcaster is going to be forced to governmental interface whether he wants it or not.

In reality, the small broadcasters in Modesto, Calif., and Wichita Falls are bigger than they know.

If we just had two more guys to stand up with us and say they didn't like a particular rule or piece of legislation, it might be the tiebreaker.

Again, if we don't have a strong radio group—our own lobby as such—if the guy in Wichita Falls or Duluth is not writing, talking, seeing his congressman, then I'm not so sure but it seems as though we'll almost deserve the legislation and/or rules that might be falling on top of us.

Angrily Against Another Association

Certainly, I'm in favor of a stronger organization in radio ... as a matter of fact, almost angrily so. I have nothing against James Gabbert and the National Radio Broadcasters Association, who I feel are dynamic spark plugs. I just think there's a better way of putting together the National Association of Broadcasters so that radio gets a correct wash, rather than starting a splinter group which gives you that and a Radio Advertising Bureau, so that we're not loaded up with overbearing dues and attorneys working against each other. I would like something put together that would allow the NAB to use the solidarity it has built on the hill in Washington—the lobbying strength. I also believe and agree with John Summers of the NAB executive staff that there is often legislation in the area where the interests of radio and television are the same.

But perhaps there's a way to absorb the NRBA so that the NAB would have television down the hallway someplace and radio would have its own lobby on the hill, its own legislative bill trackers, and its own radio staff. If we combined the solidarity of the NAB with the energy of the NRBA, I think we'd have a sensational organization. Because I think radio people, in general, are energetic, straightforward, and creative.

I think you could operate all interests—ownership, management, FM, sales— under one roof and under the banner of the NAB. But I believe we need one very strong organization and we need it tomorrow.

OUTRO: Dwight Case, as of this writing, is still president of RKO Radio and still cracking—determined, aggressive, poised. He is, in effect, a very strong radio man. At a party held in Case's honor, Bruce Johnson, former president of RKO Radio, paid tribute to the man in whom he'd seen enormous talent.

Case is a pure example of a real radio man who, in spite of his dedication to his wife, children, and family unit, spares little of himself in sharing his time, his thoughts regarding his radio stations, his personnel, in the communities in which his radio stations broadcast, and towards the public in general.

There have been a few management changes since this interview, but no philosophical changes. In fact, Case later went back to college himself for a three-month course.

The News and Information Service failed—a good idea, but perhaps impractical to implement, or maybe ahead of its time.

GEORGE BURNS

George Burns

INTRO: For years, George Burns was national program director of the radio chain of Pacific and Southern. He left to form Burns Media Consultants, Los Angeles, which creates programming for TM Programming, Dallas—"Stereo Rock"—that is featured on more than three dozen radio stations coast-to-coast. Burns also creates and produces special projects; he, his wife Judy, and Sylvia Clark have created several "magazine type" albums on radio programming strictly for a select list of program directors and general managers. Burns also consults several radio stations.

Hall: It's been said that radio has stolen the youth from TV. What do you think about that, and what other evidence is there of the importance of radio in the market today?

Burns: Well, you know kids grow out of television. They start out with television, but at 12 or 13 years old they drift out of the cartoons. Radio, especially with youth, pinpoints life-style. Television can't do that. And television basically doesn't occupy people in any broad-based way until they're 25 or 26 years old. Radio is fundamentally a life-style medium. I don't see how I can underline that further. Radio attracts people by tastes. It's like a beer. You like Coors and so-and-so likes Dos Equis. You take this beer internally, and you take radio internally. We're talking about music radio. There's more to radio than music, especially on AM.

Television is an entertainment or information medium, primarily. But radio is an internal medium. People fill in the gaps in radio. They listen in the bathroom, they listen in bed, they listen while they're making love, they listen while they're cooking, they listen while they're scratching their head. And they supply a lot of the color in the medium. So radio is important in the culture as the major fantasy medium. It deals with peoples' fantasies, which is as personal and as creative as you can get.

Hall: How did radio become that way? Why did it become so big? There was a time when radio was not that all-encompassing giant that it is now.

Burns: I think that you have to realize that any medium will adapt to the circumstances. There was a time when radio was what television is. That is, people gathered around a radio set and listened to Jack Benny—I know you remember those things, I'm sure; God knows I can—radio was like a listening post that people gathered around. When television came along, radio lost that sort of listening post power, and it went down the tube for a while. The thing that saved radio—initially, I think, after the television threat—was the music. It happened to coincide relatively close to the music explosion. Music has since become the primary literature of the day. Most of us are fairly literary, sequential-oriented people. Most of us read a lot, but everyone is fast becoming a post-literate society. This doesn't mean that people are going to stop reading. But a few years ago when a John O'Hara novel came out, everyone would look forward to it. Now people await the next Rod Stewart album with the same kind of excitement. I was talking with Darryl Dragon the other day—Darryl is one of the most intelligent people I've ever met. But he is not literary. His whole life is in music. Young people's ideas, their principal conceptions of how they feel, their spiritual attitudes, and their moral and cultural attitudes are being expressed today in a non-literary way.

So, I think that had a lot to do with radio's resurgence after television. People were saying how they felt about life in music, and people were hearing about how they felt on radio. I think the record business has tried—and if I were them, I would have too—to merchandise music outside of radio, but the fact remains that radio is still the best forum for a new record or an old record.

People consume radio like drinking a beer, not like reading a book. It gets down inside you, and then your body begins to process it. We really are in a post-literate society. That's why some people can't even fill out a job application today and I think that's too bad. I'm not a post-literate person, but I've had to learn how to live that way. You realize that this has corresponded with the population explosion, which is the key factor in all of American business today—that the people who were born between 1941 and 1952 are controlling business in this country. These war babies are the principal consumers. It's a big population bubble that may not exist for many, many more years because they're taking the pill and having vasectomies and these other things. But the point is: They have their music and they have it transferred to them on radio. And so in this gigantic post-literate society, radio may not be bigger than television—because I think television's much bigger—but radio will culturally be more influential than ever.

Hall: In programming, how do you feel about other nations? How are they doing?

Burns: Well, I can't speak for all of them.

Hall: As many as you know.

Burns: I think that in regard to programming most of the world is about five or eight years behind the United States. And again that's not a value judgment. Things are *happening* in radio in this country. All of our friends in Australia, for instance, they know things are happening here. That's why they're here all the time. Doesn't mean they want to be Americans, but they want to see where the ferment is, where the turmoil is, and Lord knows this is where it is. So, I think the rest of the world is behind America. I think America is continuing to anticipate radio programming trends. For instance, in Australia and to a certain extent in England, the music and the way it's being presented is still what I would call dependent on the personality of the disk jockey, or on the personality of the station's presentation. I think we're taking our music straighter and straighter here, instead of drinking highballs, we're taking it on the rocks. In fact, we're coming closer to taking it straight up, perhaps with a beer chaser. There seems to be less and less tendency for show business in radio programming here, and more and more emphasis on the straight product. Show business is more in television.

Hall: Is this the way of the future? Is it wise?

Burns: I think it's the way of the future. But you have to understand that the excitement today is the music itself. It's the post-literate society. For instance, if a man comes on the radio and says, "Now here's a great record, ladies and gentlemen . . . and

I talked with Bobby Rydell last night, before he cut the record in a phone booth and he told me this and that and such and such." This type of thing would have been very popular when I started in radio 19 years ago—it amazes me, this would have been terribly popular. Now, people would rather hear what the singer has to say—but more specifically what the musician has to say. The lament that the announcer, or disk jockey is fading into the distance—and I don't think the disk jockey is going to fade out forever or totally—is essentially associated with the post-literate society. When a guy says: "A funny thing happened to me on the way to the studio" or "Now take my wife, please" . . . that's essentially the literate society. You start from left and you go right . . . or, if you're in Israel, you start from right and go to left and on the back page. But the direction seems to be more post-literate. In that sense I would say: Yes, it's the direction.

Hall: In other words, the music is more important than the jock these days?

Burns: I don't think there's any question of that.

Hall: It wasn't true a few years ago.

Burns: Absolutely not. In fact, when I got started in the radio business the jock was more important than the music. You could play trash on the radio and get away with it. Now you can't. There's no way. You can't buy a hit record today. The only way a record company could ever buy its way to a hit was to buy the exposure. Today you might be able to buy exposure—and I don't know any case where you can buy exposure today—but the exposure won't do a record any good if it isn't a hit. Then, people run to the store and buy the complete works of Rod Stewart or the complete works of Cat Stevens. It's a post-literate society. They're into the music because . . . .

Hall: They don't read books.

Burns: It's an interesting thing. They *do* read. Just when you think you've got it down tight, they read *Rolling Stone,* and *Rolling Stone* is a very literate magazine. If you read *Rolling Stone* carefully, you'll note that some of the best young writers in the country write for it and similar magazines. The publishing business is splitting down: specialty magazines, specialty papers, radio's the same way. Publishing is just following suit from radio. Radio showed fractionalization before the print medium. When *Life* Magazine died, people were saying: "Print is dead." Look at *Newsweek* and *Time* or *New York* Magazine and *Los Angeles* Magazine—special interest.

Hall: Radio as a medium—is it communication, entertainment service, or mostly music?

Burns: In 1967, I worked with Jack Thayer here in town at KLAC. We had a talk station. It was the first all two-way talk station. At that time it was very revolutionary, now it isn't. The medium was never done as well as the numbers of people who listen indicate, because of the demographics. There's a great tendency in this country to cater to whoever the most people are. So, when I say to you that radio is mostly music, it's because of the fact that most of the population is somewhere around 35 years old down to 18 . . . that's why. We tend to entirely ignore the interests of other people, like for instance people over 50 or people over 60 who apparently like to sit around and gossip a lot, because they're all over the talk and news stations. KFWB in this town in a ratings book has 68 percent of its audience over the age of 50. It's an all-news station. That kind of audience is not interesting to the people who sell Coca-Cola or birth control pills or bras. So radio programming tends to fasten where the dollars are. But the potential appeal of radio to old people is perhaps a lot better than television in many ways.

Incidently, when this present generation, this group we're talking about is old, there will be a lot more talk stations. It may be the future of marketing in general in our country—because after all that's where the dollar is happening. People were saying you don't trust a person over 30; now we're turning on television and seeing stories about 34-year-old divorcees. Soon we're going to hear about 45-year-old people—it's all keyed to the buck.

If you're interested in radio programming, you have to understand that ultimately a radio station's programming depends on its income. This is especially true on the stations that are owned by people who have the bucks to spend on the careers of people who are programming it. Progressive radio has never made a fraction of the money it could have if the bucks people were interested. Tom Donahue never made what Bill Drake made, nor should he have attempted to, perhaps. What I'm saying is that progressive radio was an artistic movement, whereas the Drake revolution was a money-making movement. That's all it was. I'd rather be on the money-making side personally. I'm not putting progressive down. But something *really* happens when ABC discovers it, when Metromedia discovers it, and when CBS discovers it. Once they discover it, they kill it. Not that they're bad, but once you make it you're through. You've got to be on your ass or in terrible trouble to be creative. The guy who starts something usually does a creative thing, the guy who copies it . . . .

Hall: You've got the syndicated "Stereo Rock" programming service that you produced for TM Programming and yet most of the young program directors today are into ultra-research systems: Lee Abrams, Mark Driscoll, even Buzz Bennett. But you're not doing research like that, are you?

Burns: Oh, we do a lot of national research. How can I express this? There's an old Zen story that says you need a finger to point at the moon. Don't confuse the two. The finger is not the moon. Research is a tool, an important tool. Anyone who doesn't research in this business is a fool. Nobody can fly off the seat of his pants any more . . . but, as Bill Young of KILT in Houston said, did Picasso go out with a questionnaire to ask what his next painting should be? That doesn't mean he didn't research. Does Elton John go out with a questionnaire to write a song about a hooker? What questionnaire would have told Casablanca Records to have a black singer do a 17-minute orgasm? Creativity can't be burdened too much.

My problem . . . you ask about Lee Abrams. Lee Abrams is the brightest programmer I've met in years. My fear is that unless he learns the way this world is laid out, and I think he will, he's so damned smart, he probably already has. I'm not implying that his progress is poor because it isn't poor, it's outstanding. He'll realize that you don't get ahead in this world by doing a job well. You get ahead in this world and in the radio business—there's no question about it—by getting out of that job into the next job up. That's how you get ahead . . . so you can broaden your scope. Now you may turn that into money, or you may turn it into wider creative fields or both, depending on your personality and requirements. Research in itself . . . if you become buried in figures you'll be an accountant, which is fine if you want to be an accountant. Research has been overemphasized. It's absolutely vital. But to believe in it as a career goal is foolish.

Hall: Would the great radio people of today find it hard to compete against the young programmers in their 30s?

Burns: I think anyone who is 45 today and programming a radio station is either over-qualified or on his way down. I think that certainly programming is something that belongs to people in their 30s. There are some people who are very good in their 40s, by the way. I'm just thinking of one I talked to this morning.

Hall: Charlie Parker's good . . . does a good job in Hartford.

Burns: Well, so is Scott Burton at KFMB in San Diego. Certainly 23-year-old programmers don't do very well usually. You're talking about a simple basic fact of the biological life-style, I think. Every human life has periods—you have to translate these periods into the individual human life—but I'd say that from the period of about 18 to 24, and this is true in the radio business, you are a pretty good foot soldier. From about 25 to 30, you might make a good NCO or a platoon leader. When you're about 35, you're at the peak of your physical and mental co-efficiencies, so you're probably a good battalion leader or maybe a company commander. Then you go into the area of wisdom.

The pressure of being a program director or a national program director is ideal for a person in their 30s. When a guy gets to be in his 40s, he should have most of the hard physical, emotional work delegated out, because he can't stand it physically. And where does he go . . . into the wisdom category, perhaps a teacher. I don't think that's bad. Maybe it's because I'm heading into that area, hopefully. This is as true for the ditchdigger and gardener as it is of anybody else. You've got to go through

phases in your life. Among the successful people we know, many have hit the rocks on the dangers of life, which can involve anything from ego to sexual confusion, spiritual degeneration, drugs—the dangers that are prevalent in any business. When you get over the age of 35 you're pretty well committed how you're going to handle those things. I don't think you can say that Al Casey is any more scientific than George Wilson. George Wilson has adapted very well considering he's come through the dangers of alcohol and other things none of us care to comment about. And I think he'd appreciate that.

Hall: Here's a quote: "The success of a radio station is solely dependent on the right combination of people properly playing their roles." You think of great radio stations where you've worked, I'll bet dollars to doughnuts that you remember people, not the cart machines or the transmitter.

Burns: True. There's no question about it. One of the things that amazes me about the radio business is that it has such enormous self-respect in spite of the contrary evidence. Most program people attach an importance, a social significance to their activities, which is not recognized by anyone else.

Hall: Do you find this in actors?

Burns: That is one of the tragic things about the radio business—I mean that in the classic sense. This could be part of *Antigone*—this feeling that what we're doing is of enormous significance when, in fact, the average person may be wiping their rear end in a toilet while listening to the radio.

We have the most monumental egocentricity in this business, and there is no reason for it. It isn't justified. I don't know why it is. I think it goes back to roots of Top 40 radio in that Don Burden, Todd Storz, and Gordon McLendon—the three little rich boys whose fathers' bought them radio stations—were themselves fanatical individuals. The whole business has just spewed out from this, and it's not that big a deal. On the other hand, it's a very interesting profession, and all of us are probably not eligible for gainful employment outside of it.

The only industry more screwed up is the record business. They can really win. When you win in the radio business, it's nothing. But when you win in the record business, the guy who said, "Hey, let's come in with a 17-minute orgasm," gets rich. But the guy who says, "I'll knock off this station" and comes up with this new programming idea, he worked just as hard—probably harder—and had to sustain his creative energy longer, but he may get only a five-dollar raise. Yet, people in the radio business continue to act as though the rewards were the same, and they ain't and they never were. The only people who got rich in the radio business were rich people who bought radio stations, or people who took bribes. In the record business, if you hit something the money is fabulous, it's unbelievable. But the radio business acts as though it were also that kind of business. In fact, you see record people catering to radio people and kissing their rear ends when, in fact, they are nothing in comparison. The record business is huge. I would like to see radio people understand that and learn to manipulate within that. I could give you names of five great general managers that I know right now ... that you know ... who are desperately ... they're in their 40s ... desperately trying to jock around and find someplace to take care of them when they get old, which means when they're 45.

Hall: What makes people who are in radio love it?

Burns: I think there is a driving need in these people to be creative. It isn't a big business in terms of the dollars. The fact is that the radio business has tended to attract, even in large group ownerships, a kind of independent entrepreneur—even within ABC or CBS at times—who doesn't act like an IBM salesman. The result is that on all levels of the station, even traffic and bookkeeping, it attracts people who are personalities themselves. In the last four years, I've gone into 150-200 radio stations in one form or another. Walk in the door in Topeka, Ka. In five minutes, I can tell you who's sleeping with whom, who's stealing, who hasn't slept with whom recently, how they're stealing, and where to go to the books to look. It's like a mom-and-pop grocery store, grown up a little and larger and reaching a million people.

Why do people love the business? It's a forum for fools. It's a forum for egomaniacs. Often out of 43, you'll have 28 people who are certified. Some stations I've been to are out-patient clinics. Where would you find a bookkeeper who earns $150 to $200 a week working 60 hours a week? Where would you get that? Certainly if she were working for a plumbing supplier, she'd work only 40 hours a week at most.

Hall: What is it? It must be the excitement.

Burns: There's enormous excitement in it.

Hall: Actually, there's no rational answer.

Burns: There is no rational answer, and it's because radio has been the center for dreams.

Hall: Why do people get into radio?

Burns: That's exactly why ... it's the center for dreams.

Hall: How come the same people are not trying to get into the record business?

Burns: Many of them do, and it's a much better choice. And then the radio business considers them dirt when they do that.

Hall: They have to start out as promotion men.

Burns: Well, Joe Smith is an ex-radio man. He did well. There are plenty of ex-radio people in records. The record business offers far better rewards to a person with talent. But there are a lot of people in radio who haven't got the talent to be in show business. So they go into the radio business which is like a substitute show business.

Hall: It's the only business in the world where you can start out with no training.

Burns: Yes, or education. Now you can start out with no education in the movie business or record business, but no one *pays* you. In the radio business they'll pay you $60 a week. For instance, I wanted to write the great American novel or the great American lyric poem. However I had to eat, so I went in and got a job as a writer at a radio station.

Hall: What are the major attributes of a disk jockey? What makes a good disk jockey?

Burns: The biggest thing about a disk jockey **is:** He has to master certain basic skills— he has to learn to speak clearly so people can understand him, and he has to have a good voice. The definition of that can be highly debatable: For instance, I think we're finally at the point where women can be disk jockeys. It wasn't a case of educating management—the biggest problem was *educating women listeners,* because women listeners hated women on the air in 1967. But now they're beginning to be enlightened a bit and awakened to their own consciousness, so they understand that women may have some brains. The biggest problem getting women on the air was women listeners—certainly not men. Men love women. They may hate them some other way, but they like to be with them. It was the women who had the problem. The biggest thing a disk jockey has to be able to do is to master all those skills about speaking and being brief and getting to the point and to communicate totally on a one-to-one basis without saying, "Hello, I'm on the radio."

Hall: What's the biggest hassle the program director has to face?

Burns: Keeping his job.

Hall: Ratings?

Burns: Most program directors, and I think properly so, function as part of their boss's or their manager's career. As such, if the manager is going to take responsibility for the ratings, then it's not a very creative opportunity for the program director. But he may be able to do well. Some stooges get paid very well. I've been a stooge myself a number of times and gotten paid excellent wages. If he's going to take the blame for the ratings, then he lives with the next ARB ratings book, but his boss lives with the next book, too, you have to understand that.

That situation is changing somewhat because of the decreasing importance of national advertising business on the radio station. You can be No. 1 and have no business. God knows, we've been through that. It's all billing. You know a program director could be fired because the manager's wife doesn't like him. On the other hand, he could be fired because the manager's wife *does* like him. He could be fired because the manager's in a bad mood.

Hall: He's in a more precarious position than the sales guy or the engineer?

Burns: Yes. Well, certainly more than the engineer. Engineers and bookkeepers last longer than managers. They're impervious. I've heard bookkeepers say, "Well, you'll come and you'll go, and I'll still be here." And it's true. The manager's job may be the most frightening job in radio. Don't think I don't have any sympathy for them.

Managers are like fireflies, too. The biggest hassle is for the team to stay in. If the station's owned by a local owner, the manager may be subject to the most amazing things: How he's received at the country club, whether the owner's wife likes him, any number of things. Again, it's a small egocentric business. It's like a grocery store. Sometimes, even in very large stations.

Hall: Is there more competition between medium-sized markets stations than big ones?

Burns: I think the quality of the competition is better in medium-to-small-market stations than in major markets. Major market radio is really not very interesting . . . never has been. You get a Drake in Los Angeles in 1968 and it's very, very exciting, but he was equally exciting in Fresno and San Francisco. By and large, a good radio fight in Denver is a lot more interesting than a good fight in Los Angeles.

Programming fights today are on the order of going to see a tight jean match somewhere. Unless you know the move—you know, every movement tells a story—it's like going into a hula dance. You can't really get into it unless you know that *this* flick of the wrist means *that*. I remember the old story about Jack Thayer when he was at WDGY—he was the only man ever to beat WCCO in Minneapolis, and that was in a Hooper and Christ knows what that means. But WCCO was having a contest on the radio and they said this and that and WDGY was giving the answers to WCCO's contest. It was incredible.

Hall: When was this? It's got to be in the 50s right?

Burns: When Jack went to KLAC in 1967 . . . '66 he was at WHK in Cleveland . . . I would say it was 1961, somewhere around there. Jack was the afternoon drive guy on WDGY. Herb Oscar Anderson was the morning man, and the general manager was Robert E. Eastman. I believe Steve Labunski was the sales manager. Eastman has the big rep firm now. Well, that's a long story. That's one thing you need in radio now—a radio genealogy. You need a map like the *Forsythe Saga* on the wall to keep track of these people. What they were doing there was that WCCO has a contest on the air—like the secret word this hour is "fern" and if we call you and you can give us the secret word . . . . So, WDGY was saying you don't have to listen to WCCO. Their secret word this hour is "fern." Stay with us and we'll keep you posted on what the next secret word is. They beat 'em in a one-month Hooper. But nobody will beat WCCO otherwise.

Hall: I commented on the ratings in Minneapolis once. Mark Driscoll at KTSP sent me a thing saying WCCO did drop. They dropped a point.

Burns: You asked me; is radio mostly music? The great radio stations in this country—WCCO, WSB, KFAB in Omaha, WGN, WJR, WOR—those stations don't cater to people's tastes, they cater to their *needs*.

Hall: WTIC in Hartford.

Burns: Absolutely. WTIC is a typical station for that. Those stations don't cater to people's tastes. All of our conversation today—the excitement of the radio business, the drama, the roar of the grease paint, the smell of the crowd—has no bearing on those stations at all. They all have great signals. But there are stations with great signals that don't have great ratings. They cater to people's needs on the beer level. People get up and drink them every day. They drink 'em, they taste 'em, they digest 'em, and they . . . .

Hall: What makes a good manager?

Burns: Well, again, remember the primary requirement. Can he hold his job? Very important. We've had some great managers who've squandered, wasted their talents. Can you imagine Clive Davis as a manager? What a waste of talent. John Bayliss is a great manager. When I was national program director of Pacific and Southern Broadcasting and he was the general manager of KIMN in Denver, which was one of our stations, he threatened to break my arm because I told him something he didn't want to hear. Turned out he was probably right. But the fact of the matter is: He's a great manager. A great manager is a guy who gets the job done; who makes the people in the station love being in the station; who probably exacerbates that strange neurosis that makes people think radio is more important than it is; and who loves them in a kind of paternal way—if you were running a sausage factory the same people would burn the place down. Kent Burkhart was a great manager. Thayer is a great manager, a great leader. He can take all those incredible people which you talked about and get them all pulling together on the same horse, and then turn that into billing and good bottom line figures.

Talk about the program guys getting screwed—the salesmen also get screwed—a guy gets 20 percent commission, he reaches a certain point, and they cut him to 18. He works harder and harder, and they cut him to 15. It's unbelievable what they do to the salesmen. Salesmen and disk jockeys are very similar people ... with dreams. I think they're beginning to learn now. Now they're beginning to dress the same and their hairstyles are the same, and they're beginning to smoke the same materials. They're closer in age, too. The rewarding thing for me, working in radio stations that were starting 19 years ago, was the sudden realization that salesmen and jocks were getting together and pulling on the same side. It's really true. It's changing slower in some places. We're getting rid of the 45-year-old used-car salesman, and all of a sudden the salesman is 22 and 23. I'll be very honest with you. I have gone into some of my clients and talked with 32-year-old salesmen who are a great deal more idealistic in product and more audience oriented than I am, which is a hell of a change for me because I've been trying to fight these guys off for years. The consciousness level of the sales department today is much higher.

Hall: How do you feel the quality of radio is today in programming as well as technical?

Burns: Well, technical quality is probably better than ever. You see a professionalism about production. I've always been amazed by that. I've seen radio people in small lousy markets making $65 a week go back and cut a spot over and over and over. I've also seen a bunch of bums that wouldn't do it once if they didn't have to. I've always been stunned at that, but I think the technical quality of what you hear on the air in terms of production—and now we're getting stereo and quad—is better than ever. When I got into radio we didn't have any cart machines. We either had acetates or else we had an old Magnacord and you could reach back and say, "And here's an important word from ...." We didn't have cart machines. The first cart machine I saw was in 1961 at WPRO in Providence. At WPRO, we also cut our own acetates—we cut a thing on tape and then they would press it right in the house, but at WAAB in Worcester in 1959, we would send it out to a local place to press it off the tape onto an acetate and play commercials that way.

Hall: Was it easier to play or didn't you have a tape deck?

Burns: No, we had a tape deck. It was easier to do acetates. Technically it's much better. There's less opportunity to do creative wild things like ... even here in Los

Angeles in 1967 when I worked for Thayer, we'd run four or five commercials a day for products that didn't exist, funny put-ons that we'd be doing.

Hall: Only Gary Owens gets away with that sort of thing now.

Burns: Gary Owens is like a museum piece . . .a very thriving museum piece.

Hall: He doesn't go to anybody to clear his sillies—that's why he gets away with it.

Burns: Of course. Once you've got to clear something, someone's going to modify it. Even if your boss is encouraging you, then he's going to modify it. The degree of originality is inversely proportionate to the number of people it has to go through.

Hall: Do you feel that the program director's better off than he used to be?

Burns: I think that the best time for the program director was three or four years ago, in terms of career and earnings potential. And I'm afraid that I keep sounding in these discussions as though money was everything and it certainly isn't, but money tends to be able to build creative space. It gives you the ability to maneuver and decide which direction you're going, and I think today that programming control is being concentrated in the hands of fewer and fewer "program owners." God knows, I'm one of them. I think that's probably not too good for the personal careers of a number of programming people.

Hall: How should a program director deal with a national program director or a consultant who comes in? What does it do to him?

Burns: Depends on the situation in which he is involved.

Hall: He's lucky; he survives.

Burns: In the live operations that I deal with, I view myself as strictly a short-term consultant. Most of the consultants are trying to sell year-in-and-year-out relationships. I don't think that makes a lot of sense for a lot of operations. For an automated operation, obviously. We provide a service on a weekly basis—"Stereo Rock" programming. Every week they get new tapes and things like that. That's different. If anything, I see an increase in consultants, but I think that the existing ones are the ones that are going to do it. The number of people who stay in the consulting business is infinitesimal compared to the numbers who go into it, and it's not only because of the money. The money is very good but a lot of people don't want to do that. As more and more people like Kent Burkhart, George Wilson, and Lee Abrams monopolize the business, there are going to be less and less young guys getting involved. And I think you'll see the role of the individual fellow deteriorating. I think the training grounds for programming people are deteriorating. I used to love to work with new guys. I don't work with anybody anymore. Some of the reasonably good programmers of the past who are still pretty effective—well, Ron Jacobs every couple of years decides he needs money and goes out and makes 80 grand and then goes back into his hole . . . here's a guy who could make whatever he wanted to. What is he doing fundamentally? He writes creative ideas and syndicates them. What is Bill Drake doing? What are any of us doing? We're in the business of syndicating the things we do because we can make more money than working for a radio station.

OUTRO: Kent Burkhart operates a consulting firm in partnership with Lee Abrams, based in Atlanta. At one time, Burkhart was president of Pacific and Southern Broadcasting, and Burns was his national program director. Jack Thayer is president of NBC Radio today; George Wilson is president of Bartell Broadcasters; Joe Smith is chairman of the board of Elektra Records; and Gary Owens is afternoon drive personality on KMPC, Los Angeles.

DON IMUS AND
ROBERT W. MORGAN

Don Imus and Robert W. Morgan

INTRO: This is a rather zany interview. In fact, it's difficult to tell who interviewed whom. The participants are Robert W. Morgan, morning air personality at the time on KHJ in Los Angeles; Don Imus, morning air personality at WNBC in New York; and myself, Claude Hall, radio-TV editor of *Billboard* magazine. The occasion was a damp lunch. Morgan and Imus were already in good spirits and making a day and night of it (perhaps even the entire week!). They had just been evacuated, if that word may be used, from the studios at KHJ. The manager of the station told one story; Imus and Morgan told another. Both were only part of the truth, but if you'd like to hear something extraordinary in radio, scrounge up a copy of "One Sacred Chicken to Go" by Imus in the Morning, RCA Records LSP-4819, and listen to "The Healing of Robert W. Morgan." The liner notes say that the cuts were recorded live on KHJ in Los Angeles. And it was. Earlier that day—or perhaps it was the night before—Don Imus had phoned me at home to ask me to listen. Needless to say, after the grocery store commercial—which both men swore was live and unplanned (though it sounds like a well-produced gem)—it was but a moment or two until, suddenly, the station was seguing music without either disk jockey—i.e. Imus or Morgan. It should be noted that, by lunch time when they were with me, they either had forgotten about being eliminated for the day from the airwaves—or didn't give a damn. On the liner notes of the album jacket, you'll read: "All music and material written by Don Imus, including Robert W. Morgan's ad-libs."

Morgan got back at Imus later while guesting on his show at WNBC. When Imus went to the bathroom during a record, he came back to find the record winding down, Morgan gone, and the mike gone.

WARNING: Some of the "facts" in this interview have to be taken with a grain of salt (or perhaps a whole shaker full).

Imus: You want something to eat, Claude?

Hall: Not really, just beer. And that's going to blow my diet all to hell.

Morgan: What are you on—carbodydrates or calories?

Hall: High protein.

Morgan: Then drink scotch. There's no carbohydrates in scotch.

Imus: Scotch would blow his whole image.

Hall: When did you start in radio, Robert?

Imus: When did *you* start in radio?

Hall: You want to do this interview? Then I can just sit here and drink my beer.

Morgan: Yeah. That would be heavy. An interview with Morgan by Imus.

Imus: Didn't you start in radio when you were in the army up in Oregon, performing on weekends?

Morgan: My first radio job was at KHJ. I was working for the railroad in Palmdale, Calif. Jack Thayer saw me and said, "Come here, boy. Gonna put you on da radio and make yuh a star." Right on, right on.

Imus: You worked in . . . I can't think of the name of the place, but be serious. Don't BS around.

Morgan: Wooster, Ohio.

Imus: While going to college. But it wasn't serious with you?

Morgan: No.

Imus: You never got serious until you went in the army?

Morgan: (Pause) I've never been serious in my life about *anything*.

Imus: I know . . . but for some reason you worked in radio on weekends in the army. And Pete Gross was your program director.

Morgan: No. He never was. That's his fantasy.

Imus: Did you give him the name Tony King? Why did you do that to that guy?

Morgan: Anything is better than Pete Gross.

Imus: He had that cross to bear for a long time—Tony King.

Morgan: From Studio K.

Imus: Then after you got out of the army, you did this serious radio thing? Then you really went out and got a job? I mean, you did that stuff in the army, and then . . . . Morgan, pay attention . . . you ain't had all that much press. I mean the Real Don Steele has got the stuff, man. I read Steele's article and . . . .

Hall: Did you? I've never written an article on Steele.

Imus: There are other things around besides *Billboard*, Claude, but I don't want to break you up on your first beer. Hell, anyway, Morgan, all of that stuff about how you got to Los Angeles is not important. The fact is you got to Los Angeles when you were how old?

Morgan: I don't remember.

Imus: But where did you first meet Bill Drake?

Morgan: In the Blue Fox in Tijuana.

Hall: I thought you put Ron Jacobs and Bill Drake together the first time, and thus lined up the job at KHJ for Jacobs, in effect.

Imus: That's one of the industry rumors, Morgan.

Morgan: That's not really true. Jacobs and Drake had programmed against each other in Fresno, one of the classic radio battles of all time.

Hall: Bill told me once, I think, that the air personality lineup was already set at KHJ, and then you suggested he get in touch with Ron Jacobs as possible program director for the station.

Morgan: Ron had come to town. He and I were old friends, and he was about to get a radio network together. I didn't actually call Bill Drake and say, "Hire Ron Jacobs." Ron and I talked it out, and then I drove him down to some ripoff restaurant on La Cienega in my Volkswagen and sat outside for three hours in the car parked in an emergency area because I didn't have enough gas to drive around the block. Jacobs walked in the restaurant as my friend, and came out as my boss.

Hall: Do you remember the restaurant?

Morgan: No.

Imus: Come on, Morgan. This is history.

Hall: When you guys went on the air at KHJ . . . well, let's face it, the station was a dog in the market, even though Drake must have realized the potential of the signal. But did you guys think you were going to be as big as you became?

Morgan: It was kind of hard to comprehend, I mean I don't know what was going through his mind . . . but to guys like Steele and me—the reason I mention Steele is that he and I had been friends for years and worked together, and we came down together to KHJ. It was kind of hard to conceive of going up against these guys in Los Angeles that we'd idolized for years. And it was kind of scary to come down here. If you recall, KFWB and KRLA were then rock 'n' roll. Emperor Bob Hudson had a 28 percent audience Pulse in the morning. Dave Hull in the afternoon had a 30-something.

Imus: Is it true that you met Hudson in a bar and handed him a road map of different stations in Omaha to work at?

Morgan: To finish my answer to Claude's question, we were awed about going up against the other stations in Los Angeles, but there was never any doubt. You can't have any doubt about something like that or you're never going to do it. We were Cassius Clay all the way. I sat in Martoni's a week after we broke format, and KHJ had a 1 share and Hudson had a 28 share. I had sent away for a street map of Omaha and had put asterisks where all of the radio stations were and had been carrying this map around just hoping to run into him. I gave it to him, saying: "You're going to need this in six months," and he did.

Imus: During that time, I was working at a gas station in Los Angeles and had no idea I was going to get into radio. You can't imagine the excitement, even down to the level of gas attendants, when KHJ went on the air.

Hall: Was the format perfect from day one, or did you guys continue to make adjustments to it?

Morgan: Well, from the first day it was better than the other stations, but it kept being refined. You see, we were kind of forced in . . . well, we had to break the format earlier than we wanted to. Word got out to Don French who, I think, was the program director at KFWB. I believe he's selling insurance now. He got the word that we were going to do Boss Radio, and so he started doing it on KFWB. We decided we'd better not wait any longer, and we put it on KHJ right away. So, we didn't have time to get as together as we would have liked to. So, it was an on-air experiment that got refined and refined and became the machine that it was.

Hall: Steele, Tuna, and you—all turned out to be personalities. Yet the typical concept of KHJ elsewhere around the country was that of a nonpersonality operation.

Morgan: Let's go back to what you said. Tuna and I were considered to be personalities?

Hall: Tuna, you, and Steele.

Morgan: Steele and I, yes.

Imus: Tuna ain't . . . when are you going to wise up, Claude? Morgan, who did you pattern yourself after . . . who did you think was damned good? I mean, you didn't pattern yourself after anybody, but . . . .

Morgan: Disk jockeys? My biggest influence was Don McKinnon.

Hall: He was supposed to be great.

Morgan: He was a dynamite guy. I used to get up two hours early every morning when I was in the army at Fort Ord just to listen to him.

Hall: His brother was trying to get a job a couple of years ago, but I never heard if he did or where he did.

Imus: I·remember when Don McKinnon got killed. He was on KFWB.

Morgan: I couldn't go on the air the next day. I just couldn't do it.

Hall: What made him so great?

Morgan: Talent. He was an incredible guy.

Hall: Like Peter Potter and those guys?

Morgan: There was no comparison. Totally different situations.

Imus: McKinnon was a superfast personality.

Morgan: What makes really great jocks is a unique approach. A new kind of humor or a sense of humor. Anybody can do those Don Rickles put-down lines. Anybody can do Henny Youngman or Bob Orbin stuff. But it's the guys who're really unique and have something different to offer and who are good at it—they make the all-time good jocks.

Hall: I'm curious. Did you have to get permission before putting Imus on the air on your show for an hour?

Morgan: No.

Hall: Imus, you liar. You told me you'd gotten permission from somebody.

Imus: I was just covering Morgan.

Hall: Well, the show was pretty much of a surprise to everyone I've talked to. It created talk in the industry all over this town. What about that Safeway advertisement . . .did you guys work that out in advance?

Morgan: Total ad-lib.

Hall: It was too good to be ad-lib.

Imus: Don't you think I have any talent . . . or what?

Hall: You don't want an answer, do you?

Imus: I'm the greatest in the world except for Morgan and Steele, and I'm not even sure about Steele.

Hall: Do you work out your show in advance or do you wing it?

Morgan: No, I don't work it out in advance.

Hall: The records are all pulled for you, right?

Morgan: I select them as I go.

Hall: From a list?

Morgan: This little guy comes down from Wallich's Music City, and I'm not even sure about Steele.

Hall: Did you know all of the other air personalities on KHJ when the format was first launched?

Morgan: I just knew Don Steele, as I recall, because we were working together in San Francisco.

Imus: He met Roger Christian in a restroom at the YMCA. Thought he was the attendant. He handed him a towel.

Hall: Roger's now working with Russ Barnett in a new radio consulting firm here in Los Angeles.

Morgan: Have they got any stations yet?

Hall: Already have one in South America.

Morgan (singing): Puerto Rican Solid Gold! And, from 65, this revolution!

Hall: That might be a good format. I came up with a new format the other day: A station that would play only new records.

Imus: I think my idea for a Drake-Chenault Gay Rock format, the one I mentioned in the *Vox Jox* that I wrote, would be a good format for San Francisco.

Hall: Did I scratch that out or did it go in?

Imus: I don't know. You know, I ducked Bob Hamilton's Report because he censored me.

Hall: He did?

Imus: I said: "NBC doesn't censor me."

Morgan: Do you know who Buzz Bennett really is? I mean you've never seen Bennett and Hamilton together have you?

Hall: No, come to think of it, I haven't.

Morgan: Buzz Bennett is Bob Hamilton in [censored].

Hall: Do you get many phone calls on your show? I heard you announce a telephone number for listeners to call this morning. I started to phone you myself.

Morgan: I have a girl at the station who answers the phones for me, and we blow the switchboard out about two or three times a week.

Hall: Do any of those calls actually get through to you, or does she intercept them all?

Morgan: No, she puts some through to me.

Imus (who'd been on the air for an hour with Morgan that morning on KHJ): I talked to somebody this morning who really wanted to know if he could order that Holy Land record we were doing a bit on.

Hall: Did you actually get any calls on that?

Imus: Why don't you ask something dumb, Hall?

Hall: I haven't any idea how many calls they get during a day at KHJ.

Imus: Let me see that "bible." (This was the Bible with blank pages given to everyone attending The International Radio Programming Forum that year.) I haven't seen that yet.

Morgan: Who paid for it?

Imus: RCA Records. They really did a good job on this promotion. A thousand at four bucks a piece.

Hall: Probably wiped out all of his royalties on his "12,000 Hamburgers to Go" album.

Morgan: I've got news for you. His royalties on that album were wiped out with a cheese sandwich to go.

Hall: Supposed to be the only album ever issued where the linernotes outsold the record. [Claude Hall wrote the linernotes on the LP.]

Imus: I want to show you, Claude, how I want these little ribbons in The Holy Book. Right down this page where it says: "Heaven sent, from HIM and Don Imus." Don't laugh. I didn't go to all this trouble to have you just sit there and laugh. That's the way I want it done. Morgan looked through my bible and never saw it. And I'm the kind of guy to go around and check every book.

Morgan: What's this Don Imus bit? How come it doesn't say "Imus in the Morning"?

Imus: Because I'm changing my name now that I'm going on TV. Back to your thing Morgan . . . you've got to prepare something for your show. I know you don't write stuff down—you don't have to, but I know you prepare in your head—you have to. You don't come off with all of that crap off the top of your head . . . don't tell me that.

Morgan: I don't write stuff down because, unlike you, Don, I've nobody to steal from.

Imus: Yeah? Well, I'm the one who's going on WABC-TV.

Morgan: So's Dick Cavett.

Imus: I don't have a short problem. Anyway, Bwana Johnny is going to be my announcer.

Hall: Now that you're in New York, where do you get most of your copy from, Imus?

Imus: People send me tapes of Morgan.

Hall: I was thinking that you now found it difficult to listen to KGIL.

Imus: Hey, I'd like to clear the air on those wisecracks you've made about me. I have never even *heard* Dick Whittington . . . and never stolen a thing from him. The only guy I've ever admired . . . well there's three guys I've really thought a lot of and who've influenced me—Morgan, Bob Hudson, and Gene Sheppard in that order. And to heck with Dick Whittington. I've never heard him on the air . . . and I'm serious.

Morgan: The only preparation I do is to be aware of what's going on.

Imus: Reading newspapers and magazines and things like that?

Morgan: Yeah. Watching TV and TV news.

Hall: How often do you confer with Bill Drake? Does he ever talk directly with the jocks?

Morgan: No. The only time I see Drake is socially . . . and that's rarely.

Hall: Are you ever aware that he's listening to you?

Morgan: No, because if I were aware of him listening to me . . . well, how does just one person show up in the ARB? You can't be worried about him. I never consciously *think* that I'd better watch my step because Bill Drake is listening. I know that Bill Drake wants to hear a good job done on the radio, and that's what I try to do.

Hall: I noticed that you missed one cue on a commercial.

Imus: We didn't miss any cue.

Hall: Yes, you did, you fouled it up royally.

Morgan: If I or Imus ever start worrying about what a sponsor is going to think of what we do, with their commercial, then we'll be in a lot of trouble.

Imus: You know, I did an interview. It wasn't yours, Claude, because you won't do one with me. Do you know what the whole secret is about being a success in radio or anything else? It's being able to have it in your head that you're going to go all the way. If they won't let you do what you believe is a professional thing—whatever it is—you've got to be willing to tell them to stick it. And that's what Morgan was saying, because . . . .

Morgan: Your only security in radio is your ability to perform.

Imus: I'm not trying to fool you either, but all of the guys around the country who have some general manager or some program director threatening them . . . well, they've got to be willing to say: "Look, I believe in what I'm doing and you go [censored]. And then get another job, that's all.

Hall: Morgan, did you consider going to WNBC in that afternoon slot? Because I think Imus was pitching you like hell for it.

Morgan: I have no comment on that.

Imus: Do you ever wonder, Morgan, about what you're going to do . . . like when you're 45 years old?

Morgan: No. I don't care. What I do tomorrow morning on the radio is more important to me than 15 years from now.

Imus: Do you realize, Claude, what a big influence *Vox Jox* has in radio . . . I mean all of those guys working in Kansas, in Phoenix . . . all those places?

Morgan: It does, Claude. You ought to really be careful what you put in there. Guys read that like gospel. You are the heaviest radio columnist in America.

Hall: I try to be accurate.

Imus: You know the other day Don Steele, and I, and Meathead Morgan were talking about the odds of a guy like me coming out of a gasoline station and making it in radio. Five million to one.

Hall: Well, Morgan came out of Ohio.

Morgan: Excuse me, I'm going to eat up on this tuna sandwich.

Imus: What I'm getting around to is that you can't let the guys in radio think that it's easy to do.

Hall: Well, that's why I was asking Morgan about how he works on the air. You know, talent is something that's hard to explain. Who knows what it is? I've never had any of it . . . .

Imus: Is this a 'feel sorry for Claude Hall' pitch?

Hall: . . . and I've always had to work like hell . . . but if Morgan comes up and gives the attitude that a disk jockey can make it only on his *talent* alone . . . .

Morgan: If they have it, they can. But it's really not that simple—to be successful in radio as an air personality. You asked what preparation I do before going on the air? A year-and-a-half in Fresno; three years in Monterey; six months in Ronsonville; eight months in Oakland. Hopefully, by the time you get to Los Angeles, you have your crap together and you don't have to sit and ask yourself what you're going to do in the morning. As Don said earlier, you have to push yourself to the limit. Being successful in radio is not just a matter of knowing the right guy.

Hall: You don't operate your own board at KHJ, do you?

Morgan: No.

Hall: How long has it been since you did your own board work?

Morgan: 1964.

Imus: You can't do your own board and really be a performer.

Morgan: Bull roar.

Hall: Most guys do it unconsciously . . . never think about doing it.

Morgan: You weren't a performer in Cleveland, Imus, where you did your own board?

Imus: Well, I wasn't as good as I am now.

Hall: When you were operating your own board, did you do it consciously or unconsciously?

Imus: He does everything unconsciously.

Morgan: It becomes unconscious to a degree. Like brushing your teeth. But good production is very important to a good jock, and you can't just toss it off when it's so important to you. I've been fortunate in having a good engineer. It's like a failsafe, to have a good engineer. That's what we call him—Failsafe, because he never makes a mistake.

Hall: Is he a young kid?

Morgan: No, he's about as old as Bill Ballance.

Imus: Nobody is as old as Bill Ballance.

Morgan: Did Imus win an air personality award this year?

Hall: No. He didn't enter, in order to be able to *present* the awards.

Imus: What do I have to prove?

Hall: I'll tell you how many times I "heard" him, though—about 10 times, which is sad in a way—all those people out there in the smaller markets *imitating* . . . imitating everybody else.

Imus: Imitating me? Why?

Hall: Well, they've been imitating Morgan for years.

Imus: They're not imitating me. They're actually imitating Don McKinnon.

Hall: Do you still get a kick from doing something great on the radio . . . something smooth that goes over well?

Morgan: If you ever lose that feeling, then you might as well not be on the air. I still get a great satisfaction, for example, in giving Imus his first, his second, and third chances. And this last ripoff he pulled—getting $75,000 in New York; they offered him $100,000 and he said: "No, I want to be like Morgan." He didn't know that I make that much *every* quarter.

Imus: I spent more for the cab over here than you're going to make this year, Morgan.

Morgan: This is such an insecure business, because your only security is your ability to perform. And it's not like being a doctor or an actor where you can say you make so much a year. Radio in a major market is an every month thing, because when the ratings come in—if they're not there for a couple or three months in a row—it's "see you around." And there are so many guys in a position of authority or influence in this business who have no talent. And they're using the last common denominator to cop out, and that is *the disk jockey.* If things go wrong, *boom.* "You didn't cut it, Jack." And maybe the jock was doing a great job and killing himself, but the programming stunk. But they never think that.

Hall: So, sometimes it's the program director who should be blamed?

Morgan: I would think so, in a lot of cases.

Hall: Have you ever worked for some bad program directors? How do you handle them?

Morgan: It gets to the point where you realize you have to make your own decisions—you can't trust them. And, sure, I've worked for some bad program directors.

Hall: Do you have children to worry about when you make a job decision?

Imus: Morgan adopted me. Actually, I think he did it just as a tax write-off.

Morgan: That's what happens to a lot of guys. They get married to some chick they met at a sock hop. Get a couple of kids in school and other obligations, and then, when the moment comes to tell the station to shove it, they can't do it. It's happened to so many talented guys. That was one of the things Imus has going for him—at any moment he's willing to go back to the railroad. I am too—not as quickly as he is, because I've been doing it so much longer.

Imus: See? I told you Hall was a nice guy, didn't I?

Hall: Nice guy! What are you trying to do, Imus, ruin my reputation? You know, Morgan, the intricacies of being an air personality are still somewhat of a mystery to me, because there's so much ego involved. You've got to have it when you go into the studio and face the mike . . . realize that . . . .

Morgan: You're getting paid for something that everybody does. A doctor gets paid for something that only doctors do. Everybody talks, but we get paid for talking, and that's where the ego problem comes in that a lot of jocks have—they realize they're getting paid for something as simple as talking.

Hall: But on the air you're performing. You don't ordinarily perform at a party when you're talking with someone. But on the air, you're putting it on the line.

Morgan: We literally put it on the line every day. It's live . . . and if we're sick or not feeling well or things are not right, or the music that week is kind of down, that doesn't matter. Because that's the nature of the product, and it doesn't make any difference. We're there and we have to *entertain*.

Imus: That's what I was saying earlier—radio is the last *live medium* left.

Morgan: Imus, we knew all that back when you were pumping gas. The only reason you really got into radio is that you were lousy at pumping gas.

Imus: Say one more thing to me, and I'm going to deck you ... do you understand that? I've always wanted to punch on a real big guy anyway.

Hall: Did you see *Billboard* this morning? There was a really good interview with Lee "Baby" Simms.

Imus: I don't like any interview, Claude, unless it's with *me*. Me and Bobby Fischer are where it's at in this [censored] world.

Morgan: Do you play chess, Imus?

Imus: Yeah. I do.

Morgan: We'll play some chess at my house later.

Imus: You do not want to play chess with me.

Hall: 'Cause he cheats.

Morgan: I don't want to do anything with you, but I'm stuck for a week.

Imus: What do you mean—stuck for a week?

Morgan: You're going to hang around me ... for the prestige ....

Imus: For your information, Steele likes me.

Morgan: No, he doesn't.

Imus: That's all that's important to me—the *real* Don Steele talked to me.

Morgan: Why should he like you?

Imus: He talked to me and he doesn't talk to anybody. Say, Morgan, why did you go to Chicago to WIND that time?

Morgan: For money.

Hall: I heard $80,000.

Morgan: You heard low. You know, you're confused about Chicago—you interviewed a jock from San Diego or somewhere—or that San Diego jock was confused. We went up 90 percent in our demographic target. When I went there, the audience was mostly old people. When I left, we were No. 1 in 25-34 age demographics.

Imus: But that was pregnant white people.

Morgan: No, that was everybody.

Hall: But you didn't actually enjoy working on WIND, did you?

Morgan: No.

Imus: Do you want to know something? Morgan and WIND program director Bob Moomey came to Cleveland to hear me ....

Morgan: I didn't come to Cleveland to hear you—I came to Cleveland to get out of Chicago for a weekend.

Imus: Why'd you call and say: "Please come have breakfast with me?" Claude, I'm telling you the truth and you can talk to Jack Thayer, general manager of WGAR in Cleveland, the whole idea for the format on WIND was Morgan's. I swear to God . . . no, I won't swear to God, but . . . .

Morgan: Where did you steal the *Vox Jox* column in *Billboard* from, Claude?

Hall: It has been in the book since around 1942. I didn't start it, I just made it perfect.

Imus: You [censored] creep!

Morgan: Well, it's very important because there's nothing in that [censored] piece of [censored]. And the only people who buy Bob Hamilton and Bill Gavin are people who don't know what the [censored] they're doing anyway. But it's interesting to read *Billboard* because you can find out what medium market station Charlie Tuna is working at.

Imus: I've wondered to myself if you realize how much influence you have, Claude.

Hall: I simply don't let that bother me.

Morgan: You've got to worry about it; it's a responsibility being No. 1.

Hall: Does your dad still work in the jukebox industry?

Morgan: In Gallion . . . he's going to retire this year and go down to Florida.

Imus: Big Wilson had Robert's mother on the air on WNBC in New York recently.

Morgan: You see, when I grew up in Ohio, he was our morning man—Big Wilson on KYW in Cleveland. My mother Florence is a Big Wilson freak.

Imus: We got Big Wilson to call her, and she came on the air like a pro. Just uncanny.

Morgan: You know, Claude, this is really going to be a [censored] interview.

Imus: No. Morgan, there's some good stuff here.

Hall: Let's run it for kicks . . . it might give somebody some laughs. Later, we can do one in a more serious vein.

Imus: What do you mean? This is an exciting interview.

Hall: Aw, hell, you haven't asked Morgan any decent questions yet.

Imus: What can you ask a guy like him?

Hall: You could ask him how he keeps up-to-date on the Los Angeles market.

Imus: Well, he lives there. Anyway, Steele keeps him apprised of what's going on. You know, there's a guy who's incredible—if some agent would handle him.

Morgan: He's an Elvis.

Imus: Like Mick Jagger.

Hall: Morgan, when's the first time you heard about Imus?

Morgan: When he called me from Palmdale, Calif., one day.

Imus: In fact, he put me on the air when I was in Palmdale. That was when I was running for Congress that time . . . my claim to fame for years.

Morgan: He used to send me letters for weeks. I thought it was junk mail for a long time.

Imus: You never answered any of them. How come you never were nice to me until

I became a star?

Morgan: Who's being nice to you now?

Imus: What would you do if the program director at KHJ came in and said he didn't want you to do anything more than time and temperature?

Morgan: I'd tell him to get somebody else.

Imus: See, Hall? That's where it's all at, and that's all you need to put in this article. People, you know, have the wrong idea about Drake radio. I think Drake radio has *made* more personalities than ... think of the great personalities that have come out of Drake radio or who're on Drake radio now ... Morgan, Steele, and Humble Harve, ... there are a number of guys who've been big personalities in Drake radio.

Morgan: This whole image of a Drake jock has been distorted beyond belief. There's no such thing as a hot line where Drake calls up the jocks. I don't think Drake has ever called a jock. Doesn't happen.

Hall: Paul Drew, at WIBG in Philadelphia, used to use a hot line.

Imus: The reason Paul called so much was that he was trying to find out what was going on ... like: "What's No. 1 this week?"

Hall: Paul is doing quite well as a consultant. Has at least two stations, KAKC in Tulsa and WAVZ in New Haven. You're going to make me a villain with a lot of guys because of this interview, Imus.

Morgan: All Drake did was *cull* out the [censored] things ... the things we all have a tendency to say or do ... take them out. Make radio *efficient.*

Imus: There's nothing prettier than a Drake format being run by a person such as Morgan or Steele. You have that *consistent* sound ... and there's no—or very few— mistakes. Reminds me, Claude, of a Johnny Tillotson record, "Poetry in Motion."

Morgan: Very few people realize how Imus, in his production, uses a Drake style.

Imus: If I haven't got anything to say, I give the time and say my name a lot and that's *it.* I've always wanted to work for Drake ... I'm trying to get Morgan's job. Actually, I want to do a two-man show with Morgan.

Hall: I really enjoyed that show you two guys did together.

Imus: Is it true that you *never,* usually, listen to radio, Claude?

Hall: Some disk jockeys, certainly never more than once, and not too often on time even then. Still, I think I probably listen to more radio than any man in the world. But, that's me. As for you, what do you guys plan to do the rest of the day?

Morgan: I think Imus wants to go out and beat up a couple of guys.

OUTRO: Don't think that Robert W. Morgan and I were buddy-buddies (although I think Imus was and is close to him). After he became swingman (doing weekends and vacation relief at KMPC in Los Angeles), I criticized the music policy on KMPC, and Morgan spent a whole show (filling in for Gary Owens) describing where my ancestors came from. To show the power of the word (and not what a man actually says), several friends called me to ask how much I'd paid for the free plugs.

Pulse is an audience survey.

Don French, mentioned here as program director of KFWB in Los Angeles, is programming a radio station in Alaska at this time.

Don Steele, then a disk jockey at KHJ, Los Angeles, later went on the air at KTNQ, Los Angeles.

At the time of this interview, Morgan wasn't very appreciative of Charlie Tuna. They had both fought for the morning show slot on KHJ, and Morgan got it. Actually, everyone, including the audience and their peers, thought both Tuna and Morgan were super personalities.

Don McKinnon's brother became a very good disk jockey and is doing well in the industry. Don McKinnon was considered by many to be absolutely the best disk jockey; nearly all men of the era pay tribute to him. He died in a car wreck.

Russ Barnett, mentioned here, is a teacher at the Don Martin broadcasting school in Los Angeles. He was previously program director of KMPC, Los Angeles.

Roger Christian has been working at an oldies station in Los Angeles.

The "new" records format, mentioned here, was later tried on K-106 in San Francisco. The "Gay Rock" format hasn't been tried yet, to my knowledge.

The Don Imus television show never came off.

I used to wisecrack that Imus stole his material from what Dick Whittington, then on KGIL in Los Angeles, threw in the trash.

Bill Ballance was and is one of the best disk jockeys in the business. He rose to national fame—and was much copied—with his "Feminine Forum" double entendre disk jockey approach, mostly talk. But he's a professional and by mentioning him here, Imus and Morgan are actually paying tribute to the man. The same can be said of anyone else they mentioned. Ballance, I always referred to as "you dirty old man." Actually, he looked good in person (every disk jockey has to pay attention to their personal appearance; at least, the good ones must mold an image and cater to their on-air and off-air images).

Lee "Baby" Simms was a rascal of an air personality—the kind you'd read about in the headlines—and he still is. Where many disk jockeys matured into programming, some can't and Lee Simms was one of those who are born, bred, and branded as disk jockey and nothing else. Money doesn't matter, though they like to make good salaries to support their ladies, wine, and evenings; station doesn't matter, though they often demand prerogatives and liberties in their shows that would make most modern program directors blanch; programming doesn't matter, although they squirm for the advantage to express themselves as *personalities.* Incidentally, a good one will make you; a poor one break you. Simms, after some while on KRLA in Los Angeles, later went to Cleveland to do mornings. He is one of those vines that grow back, regardless of who may trim them. After all, he is a guaranteed factor of success, within reason. He is a *personality,* in its truest sense.

Harvey "Humble Harve" Miller is currently back on the air in Los Angeles and is also hosting a syndicated weekly radio program featured on many radio stations coast to coast.

Paul Drew had failed as a programming consultant to WIBG in Philadelphia. He minimized his losses and maximized his advantages and rose to become national program director for RKO Radio and its vice president.

Johnny Tillotson is a recording artist of the pop-country genre.

Morgan ended up as vacation relief on KMPC; Imus on WNBC in New York.

GLOSSARY

Afternoon drive. Usually 3-7 PM, Monday-Friday; when people drive home from work. Important because more people listen to radio at this time.

Aircheck. Tape of a disk jockey's show, usually with the music telescoped.

Album rock. Term used to define a radio format that primarily uses album cuts, but is often as highly and tightly formatted as a Top 40 radio station.

All night jock. Usually the new member on the staff. Does the all-night show. The time period is often used as a training ground.

A & R. Artist and repertoire—term used in reference to a producer of a record.

ARB. Accepted industry term for audience ratings of Arbitron. A trip to Beltsville, Md., to study diaries from surveys is considered a must by most program directors for any market they're working in. Arbitron's ratings services has offices in New York, and data processing in Beltsville, Md.

Audience flow. Available audience at a specific time.

Beautiful music. Term used to describe format of radio stations, most of which are automated and use syndicated programming that is very lush, i.e. records by Frank Chacksfield, George Greeley, Frank Mancini, the Johnny Mann Singers, etc.

Bed. The musical instrumental introduc-tion to a vocal before the vocal begins. Any instrumental music over which words are spoken intentionally, especially jingles, commercials, etc.

Blade. A competent production person.

Bullet. A notation used on charts to indicate that a record is rapidly becoming more and more popular and that sales are exceeding other records.

Charts. A rating of current songs that is based on record sales, which reflect their popularity. Used by many programmers to help determine their playlists.

Classical. Term used to describe a radio station with a format that focuses primarily on classical records.

Clutter. Elements on the air which are not conducive to good listening, e.g. a disk jockey talking too much or not saying revelant things, too many jingles, commercials, etc.

Coffee pot or tea kettle. Small market, low-power station.

Combo. The situation at a radio station in which a disk jockey handles his own control panel because he has no engineer to handle such details for him.

Cost per thousand. What the advertiser has to pay the radio station to reach 1000 listeners. The stated rate card price per spot divided by 1000.

Country. A format that primarily plays country music records. These stations

349

usually are formatted like a Top 40 station, but perhaps with a longer playlist. A direct spinoff of this format is the progressive country or country rock format that focuses on records by such artists as Linda Ronstadt, Willie Nelson, Waylon Jennings, et al.; this format is still experimental at this time.

Cue. To audition material before you play, i.e., cue up a record. To position the needle at the beginning of the record.

Cume. Indicates cumulative audience by projecting the number of people reached over a given period of time as determined through listener surveys. This information is usually obtained through rating services and independent surveys.

Currents. Records that are currently on the trade charts.

Daypart. Programming to a specific time period with a particular kind of music.

Dead air. Nothing being broadcast—silence; not acceptable to most programmers. To a Bill Drake or Rick Sklar, it's unforgivable.

Diary. A log of radio listening habits kept over a one week rating period filled out by randomly selected radio listeners. Used by ARB rating service to determine ratings.

Disco. Radio format focusing on records for dancing—usually rock or soul music. Format is still experimental.

Drop-ins. Programming elements fed into a regular show. For example, it could be the sound of a guy munching on an apple during a commercial about the apple industry, etc.

DXing. Listening to radio stations (mostly at night).

Elevator music. Slightly derogatory term regarding beautiful music stations; a reference, of course, to Muzak operations in elevators of office buildings.

Filler. Talk or instrumental music used to fill time until a program or event begins.

Golden oldies. Hits that are at least six months old. The term was originally used for hits that sold over a million copies.

Goof record. Record that is medium-horrible. It is used to force the listener to turn to the competing station when the competitor is into news, so that the listener will turn back to your station at a later time, thus building up your average quarterhour ratings. Resorted to usually during Arbitron rating surveys.

High energy. A radio station usually rock in format that moves everything at tremendous pace. Disk jockeys usually talk fast, hard, and briefly, if at all. Music is usually speeded up. Jingles are loud and short. Promotions hard, short, and heavy.

Hot clock. The format of a station laid, in effect, over an hour clock. Used to build consistency so that the disk jockey, for example, would play an oldie, air his promotions, jingles, etc., at a given time or specific times within the hour.

Housewife time. 10 AM-2 PM. Usually the dominant available audience is the housewife.

Intro. The introductory part of a record, usually the music before the vocal starts. Also, the intro is what the disk jockey does—or says—over this instrumental part of the record.

Jazz. A format that focuses primarily, if not totally, on jazz records. This format has been dying; only a handful of stations still play only jazz, notably, KBCA in Los Angeles and KJAZ in San Francisco.

Jingles. Identification message of the call letters usually set to music, sometimes just a capella voices singing. Often referred to as IDs. Big jingles syndicators have been PAMS and TM Productions, both in Dallas. JAM Productions is also doing a lot of jingle work.

Mediastat. Radio ratings firm.

MOR. Middle-of-the-road. Term used to describe adult music programming formats. Lately, the MOR format tends to play more and more hit records, giving them the sound of the local Top 40 station which is programmed to appeal to younger people.

Morning Drive. 6-9 AM, Monday-Friday. Time period when people go to work—the largest listening audience of the day. Often the disk jockey who does this show is the highest paid on the station, many times earning more than the general manager and/or program director. John Gambling, WOR, New York, is probably the highest-paid regular air personality (meaning salary only) in the world—around $350,000 a year.

National Association of Broadcasters. Organization generally made up of managers and owners in radio and television, with headquarters in Washington.

National Radio Broadcasters Association. Splinter group of owners and managers in radio that felt NAB wasn't devoting enough attention to radio specifically.

Network feed. Programming originating from the network that is fed to affiliated stations. Usually transmitted through phone lines.

News. Format of all-news broadcast 24 hours a day. There are two different types of this format: news formatted on the concept of a Top 40 station, and news formated magazine style.

News block. An extended period of news and information that could be from 15 minutes to 3 hours.

Outro. The fading out part at the end of the record that gives a disk jockey an opportunity to come out of the music into a commercial, psa, talk, or other programming element. Also, the outro is what the disk jockey does—or says—over the fading part of the record.

Playlist. List of records played in a given week.

Pot. Abbreviation for potentiameter—volume control, either dial, knob or slide.

Programming consultant. A person who advises radio stations on programming and on other aspects of radio management, up to and including music, disk jockeys, sales, etc.

Progressive. Essentially, a less structured format that focuses mostly on album cuts by rock, blues, jazz, and progressive rock artists and groups. The album rock format is a direct spinoff of the progressive format, the difference being that in the former format the music is usually picked for the disk jockey, while in progressive radio the disk jockey is allowed to program his/her own show from approved cuts and can often build thematic music sets or build musical messages.

Promo. A promotion for the station, disk jockey, or station event.

PSAs. Public service announcements.

Pulse. Ratings service for radio, based in New York City.

Quarterhour average. An ARB term describing the average number of persons listening in any given quarter hour. Indicates length of listening time.

Rating Period. When a radio market is surveyed to determine the popularity and size of the audience for each individual station in the market. A "sweep" is when all stations in several markets are being surveyed for audience.

Recurrents. A term sometimes used to refer to records that have recently dropped off trade charts, but are still too fresh to be called oldies.

Recycling. Process of getting listeners to

turn to another station, but encouraging them to come back at a later time in the day by offering an incentive to return to your station. In other words you're recycling the same listener by using him or her twice.

Remote. A broadcast from someplace other than studio, e.g., baseball game, etc.

Rep. Sales organization that represents your station at the advertising agencies for national and regional business.

Rotation pattern. Playing of records in a given order—some more often than others.

Run a tight board. No dead air. The next element should begin immediately after the previous element is over. Usually stated in regard to a disk jockey—"He runs a tight board."

Segue. To ease smoothly from one thing to another, usually from one record to another.

Separators or a spot breaker. A sound effect, jingle, information bit (time check, temperature) which separates commercials.

Set. A two or three-record sweep between commercials or breaks.

Shift or trick. The hours a jock is on the air.

Shotgun jingles. Very brief jingles that pop out the call letters of the station, often with no more than a drum roll.

Slusher. A beautiful music format; covers old schmaltz.

Soul. Radio format that appeals mostly to a black audience; other terms that describe the same format are: R&B, black, ethnic, etc. Format primarily uses soul or r&b records and features black disk jockeys.

Source. Radio ratings service in Los Angeles; involved in very limited markets at this time. Parent firm is Dimensions Unlimited.

Special. A produced documentary or music program that is usually separate from normal radio programming—a special programming event. It could also be broadcast live from a local business site or nightclub. Greatest special in radio was the 48-hour documentary "The History of Rock 'n' Roll."

Splice. Patching tapes together—usually, cutting and putting pieces of tape together in a different order.

Step on the vocal. When the disk jockey talks as the lyric begins. Unacceptable to most programmers, considered sloppy.

SRDS. Standard Rate and Data Service. A monthly publication of rates and station description of all radio stations in U.S. and territories. Directed to the advertising medium.

Stinger. Sound or musical effect at the end of a commercial. Sometimes known as a *button.*

Sweep. Several records back-to-back without commercials or talk.

Sweep link. Jingles from one record to another. Transitional. Will help you come from fast into slow.

Syndication. Production of programming material which is sold to individual stations by independent production company. This could encompass music, jingles, news, features and be on disk or tape.

Talk back. Generally a telephone intercom connected to a remote location that allows room operator and remote operator to talk in both directions—before and after program breaks.

Talk up. The deejay talks over the bed (musical instrumental introduction). To talk up to a vocal means he times his rap to end precisely before the vocal begins.

Target demographic audience. Age and sex of listener you are trying to reach.

Teeny bop drive. 7-12 PM on a rock or Top 40 station. Usually a big listening time for young teenagers.

Top 40. Format consisting of hit singles. Highly structured. Emphasized with heavy on-air and off-air promotions. Concept originally referred to the number of records (40) that a disk jockey might play during a three-hour show. But the format itself was developed by the late Todd Storz and program director Bill Stewart. Gordon McLendon added to it. Chuck Blore added a show business aspect. Later, Bill Drake refined it. Most of modern radio springs from the early concepts of Todd Storz and Gordon McLendon, known as the fathers of Top 40 radio.

Tuneout. Any element that causes a listener to either cut the radio off or switch to another station. News is some-times considered a tuneout factor on a Top 40 station, but a tune-in factor on an MOR format station.

Two-way talk. Radio format that allows listeners to call in and talk to a host on the air.

Voiceover. Vocal announcing on a commercial.

Wild tracks. Programming elements, usually brief, that a disk jockey might use on his or her show such as the sound of the slamming of a door, different voices, other sound effects, etc. Arnie Ginsberg, Boston, used to use cowbells, etc. To a great extent wild tracks have faded from use in disk jockey work.

INDEX

Edited by Donna Wilkinson
Designed by Jay Anning
Set in 10 point Times Roman by Copy Prep Company